The Gist of **Origin**

The Gist of **Origin**
1951~1971 / an anthology
edited by Cid Corman

Grossman Publishers
A Division of The Viking Press   New York   /   1975

First published in 1975 by Grossman Publishers
625 Madison Avenue, New York, N.Y. 10022

Published simultaneously in Canada by
The Macmillan Company of Canada Limited

SBN 670-34176-2

Library of Congress Catalogue Card Number: 73-7089

Printed in U.S.A.

c℮

ACKNOWLEDGMENTS (pages
523 to 525 constitute an extension of this
copyright page)

Margaret Avison: "Natural/unnatural"
from *The Dumbfounding*. Copyright ©
1966 by Margaret Avison. Reprinted by
permission of W. W. Norton & Company,
Inc. "The Local & the Lakefront,"
"Why Not?", "Waking Up," and "The
Typographer's Ornate Symbol." Reprinted by permission of the author.
Paul Blackburn: "Peire Vidal/tant ai longamen cercat," "Peire d'Alvernhe/Chantarai
d'aquestz trobadors," "Bernart de Venta-
dorn/Can vei la lauzeta mover," "Guillem
de Peitau/Ab la dolchor del temps novel,"
"Guillem de Pietau/Compaigno, non
puosc mudar qu'eo no m'effrei," "Pus
vezem de novelh florir," "Marcabru/
Vidas," "L'iverns vai e. l temps s'aizina,"
"Pois la fuoilla revirola," "Bertran de
Born/Razo," "Eu m'escondisc, domna."
Reprinted by permission of Joan Black-
burn and George Economou.© Estate of
Paul Blackburn, 1973.
William Bronk: "My Father Photographed
with Friends," "The Extensions of Space,"
"Aspects of the World like Coral Reefs,"
"Virgin and Child," "Skunk Cabbage,"
"A Black Clay Fish," "In Navaho Country,"
"Tenochtitlan," "There Is Ignorant
Silence," Copyright 1964 by William
Bronk, "Colloquy on a Bed," "The Differ-
ence," "The Smile on the Face of a
Kouros," Copyright © 1969 by William
Bronk, "Conjectural Reading," "Of the
Natural World," "The Abnegation,"
'Writing You," "I Thought It was Harry,"
"Something like Tepees," "The Mask the
Wearer of the Mask Wears," "In Praise
of Love," "The Use-Unuse of Us," Copy-
right © 1971 by William Bronk, "Morning
Greetings Exchanged," "Beatific Ef-
figies," Copyright © 1972 by William
Bronk, "Copan: Historicity Gone," Copan:
"Unwillingness, the Unwilled," Copy-
right © 1974 by William Bronk, "The

(continued on page 523)

iv

Contents

Introduction

1

The story of *Origin* is, in many ways, that of my own development as a poet. This means, of course, no neat rising curve. Or any sort of line at all.

December 21, 1941 my first poem occurred—a quatrain—largely the overflow of adolescence and Pearl Harbor and a steady diet of Ruskin's *Modern Painters*. Nothing could have surprised me more than that very act and I am still caught in the wonder of it. The young and eager instructor in English (freshman) at Tufts College encouraged me, probably for no other reason than the passion and energy exposed in the "extra" effort amongst students of no conspicuous talents. As it happened, he was off in the Navy before the spring had ended and I have never seen or heard more of the man since. Early in my sophomore year an unexpected kidney debility took me out of the university for a year and more crucially exempted *me* from military service. Most of my time was absorbed by trying to catch up with all the reading I had never done in poetry.

I discovered, alone, Baudelaire and then Rimbaud, and all language seemed new and strange. University, when I returned to it, seemed tame and dull and I had to make a pain in the neck of myself to faculty and students to create sense there. I moved over out of history and science into the department of literature.

There was inevitably a good deal of arrogance and ambition at work, reflecting both ignorance and uncertainty, along with an overweening desire to learn everything about poetry. At Tufts, then, there was only John Holmes, a minor poet, but genuinely driven to poetry and genial. I often visited his house and felt tremendous pleasure merely in being in the atmosphere, as it seemed to me, of poetry: he had a marvelous collection of modern poetry. He also expected a maturity of me (as, later, Olson did) which I simply didn't have.

John Ciardi, not yet thirty, lived in Somerville, near Tufts, and he became a friend and valued advisor. Because of him I did graduate work at the University of Michigan. And there too had important editorial experience. Both in Medford and in Ann Arbor, though in varying ways, I came to realize that editing a small magazine or paper is best served by a single intelligence directing it, for a staff of editors means mostly compromise. But a little mag is precisely the ground where compromises need not occur, where personal prejudices may be exposed without—hopefully—undue rancor and meanness. And it is preferable, I still feel, to have many periodicals—each of them frankly biased.

The period from 1941 to 1947 was largely one of self-education, in every sense. I had been introduced by way of an offbeat theology professor at Tufts, R. E. Wolfe, to a former teacher of his, a magnificent crotchety Yankee educator, Frank A. Manny, by then well towards eighty. He had been a mate of John Dewey when the latter was starting out at the University of Chicago. Manny, with great constancy and not a little perseverance, led me out into a "world" that I hardly knew until then existed. It included thought and event in all the arts and sciences, as well as business, and it meant, more vitally, through his vast correspondence, contact with live wires, people mostly much older than myself, throughout America and with connections abroad, backwards and forwards in time. Apart from the awakening he aroused, his encouragement made me feel more called upon than ever to share whatever it was my work would bring me to.

Thus in 1947, after a long jaunt around America, I came back to Boston bursting with a desire to foment a poetic community. I had been writing without let since the beginning and was finally (by myself) discovering affinities with the Pound and Williams, Stevens and Marianne Moore mainstream. My poetry—at its strongest—was quite unlike anything of theirs, but it was their sense of poetry and language that struck me as healthiest, nearer what I myself wanted, a poetry that spoke to the ear, the heart, and the intelligence with unswerving devotion and immediacy.

Soon after my return I started a series of poetry discussion groups in Boston, using the public libraries as base—utilizing evening space (when the places were normally rather quiet). The groups were small but extremely varied, and invariably educating for me at least. They also led to enduring friendships. Through one of the groups, the West End group (the library in an immigrant slum area), contact with the very young Steve Jonas was made. (It was he, later, when I got Olson to give a reading in mid-September of 1954 at the Unitarian Church on Charles Street and he read there, magnificently, for four hours, who brought along Ed Marshall and John Wieners, who thence followed Maximus back to Black Mountain (as I learned long afterwards from Ed Marshall).

Early in 1949—not content with the group work and feeling much more potential for poetry in the area—I propositioned my friend Nat Hentoff over at WMEX, near Fenway Park, where he was a regular announcer and a most enterprising spirit where jazz and folk music were concerned, about a possible modern poetry program as a public service (that is, unsalaried, nonprofit) feature there. He thought there was a chance and offered me a half-hour spot on his very lively folk song program for two consecutive weeks. Our plan was to get the listeners behind the show by asking them to write in asking for it. The response was excellent, and within a week after the second program (reading my own, at that time feeble, poetry) Nat and I dumped on the desk of the station manager the fifty or sixty letters received and suggested a fifteen-minute weekly spot. To my astonishment he agreed.

The first program was a reading of the animal mating poems of D. H. Lawrence. I had given a few public readings by then and had become aware of how effective his poems are when vocally delivered. The second program was of Dr. Williams' poems. I had heard him read at Harvard the previous year or so and had been impressed by a number of pieces, not least by "Impromptu: Suckers," a Sacco-Vanzetti poem. I tried to emulate his success. The result was a rabid letter from a listener about my use of profanity. I got wind of the letter in a telegram, no less, from the manager, requesting me to bring in the script used. (Needless to say, the manager hadn't heard the program.) There was no script. I simply read what I liked and said as little as possible (and spontaneously, upon the advice of Marianne Moore) in order not to waste the little time available early evening on Saturday, the worst listening time in the week. Fortunately, when I saw the manager some other mail (which Nat had already told me about and marked out for me) had also come in, and one letter was a lifesaver: from a local minister applauding the program and in particular the offending poem.

The manager, not unkindly or unreasonably, asked me to bring in for the time being an outline of what I intended to read in the ensuing weeks. After a few more weeks the whole to-do had simmered down and nothing like it recurred. The program (called "This Is Poetry") ran for three years without a break (though I had a blind listener, Al Gayzagian, a Harvard student, fill in for me during July of 1950, when I was a guest at Yaddo). It included many poets in the Boston area, whether visiting or living there, reading their own work, poets like Archibald MacLeish, John Crowe Ransom, Richard Wilbur, John Ciardi, Theodore Roethke, Stephen Spender, and Richard Eberhart. Recordings were also used, so that T. S. Eliot and Charles Olson, James Joyce and others were heard. But the most crucial contacts made were of another order.

From the very first week and every week thereafter during those three years I received word from a spastic listener in Swampscott. His name was Larry Eigner. Mostly they were badly typed postcards. But their directness of response provided me a "measure" that was unwavering, loyal, remarkably accurate and helpful. That correspondence hasn't failed me yet in all the years since, nor for all the space between us.

Before the end of the first year I was fishing for younger poets in the region who might also be, though unknown, worth propagating. A friend of my younger brother, Sarah Braverman, suggested Robert Creeley. I had, in fact, seen a few poems by him in *Accent* and *Wake*, so his name was familiar. They were hardly earthshaking, but they were alive.

Bob has himself written of our connecting in a way that makes it sound as if he quite accidentally discovered my program. What happened was that I had written him of it, invited him. It was his first public reading. He was exceedingly nervous and the poems were not delivered effectively, but we hit it off very well and I felt at once that I was meeting a contemporary with whom I had more in common than with anyone else up to that time. An unbelievably intense correspondence followed for a couple of years. (The bulk of these letters is now at the University of Texas and is being prepared, I believe, by Stan Persky for publication shortly.)

The third important contact was another early listener, an invalid also, Evelyn Shoolman. She was a woman of well-to-do parentage, ten years or so my senior, intelligent and sensitive, with a keen interest in what I was doing. She it was who eventually suggested the magazine.

In 1950—or possibly even in late 1949—Creeley had decided to launch a little mag, figuring on something like thirty-two pages and a quarterly. It seemed that a former classmate of his at Harvard, Jake Leed, down in Lititz, Pennsylvania, had a small press and could do the job cheaply and even offered, Bob told me, to do it at his own expense. Bob was to be the editor. I was rather dubious of the printing arrangement, since it seemed like too much work for anyone who wasn't very experienced at it, but I was pleased by the prospect. Material was solicited. (Creeley was corresponding with Pound, then at St. Liz, but hadn't as yet been clued in to Olson, though that was soon to occur.) The mag was to be called either the *Littleton Review* or *Lititz Review*, it wasn't decided. He asked me to submit work of my own (and had a large sampling of it intended for use) and to find interesting work for him. (I had, via the radio show, organized several new groups in or near Boston—which remained active for some years—and there were some would-be poets involved.)

One of my regular listening posts and favorite hangout was Grolier Book Shop on Plympton St., run by Gordon Cairnie. I was there at least once a week from 1949 to 1954. Bob, of course, also knew the place very well. One of my acquaintances there was Samuel French Morse, a fellow then at Harvard. Sam was himself writing a conventional but well-wrought poetry, and I liked the man. He mentioned a classmate of his (from Dartmouth) who lived in upstate New York and whose work, though unknown, he felt was quite interesting (and, like his own, somewhat under the spell of Stevens), William Bronk. That was 1950. The poetry I shortly received from Bronk (who was and remains shy of sending his work around to be rejected) struck me at once as the real thing, the work of a particular, a unique poet. I showed the poems to Bob at Grolier when he came in from his Rock Pool Farm. He was equally impressed. And he intended some of it for his review.

By the time I reached Yaddo in July of 1950 (Bill and Floss Williams were there that month too—where I first met them—he working on Book IV of *Paterson*), I was aware of Olson through both Creeley and Vincent Ferrini. Ferrini (somewhat older than me) had also been on my program and we had become quite good friends. I'd visited him out in Gloucester a number of times and the shambling house on Liberty Street became a haunt and diversion as time permitted and need demanded. Peg and Vin, with meagre income for themselves and their three lovely and lively children, were the very souls of hospitality and their place was a way-station for so many. Vin had told me of this huge guy, a local mailman, unusual poet, who had filled his doorway un-expectedly one day—responding to a poem he had seen in a local journal. Charles Olson. The first Maximus poem was with Vin at the time, intended for another mag that never got off the ground.

To judge from the *Letters for Origin*, by early October of 1950 the idea of *Origin* was well afloat. Some weeks before, Creeley had aban-doned plans for his review. I was disappointed and mentioned the collapse to Miss Shoolman (by phone). She immediately came back at me saying: Why don't you edit a mag? I'm willing—she added—to provide enough capital to see you properly started—or words to that effect. For many reasons I was reluctant, but the need seemed patent. And the offer was hard to put down.

It should be stated at once that I had *no* income and none was in sight. I had chosen, after considerable thought, to live with my parents until I felt my career as a poet was firmly established—knowing that it would be impossible to pursue that career while holding down a full-time job and living on my own. My folks, fortunately, were delighted to have me around (their other two sons having gone off), though I can't say that they ever became accustomed to my way of life and especially my being, by their lights, unemployed. My income was an allowance of $5 a week from my parents. (Occasionally I received extra cash from writings or unexpected sources, but nothing notable or reliable.) If the magazine was to go on—and I had no intention of letting it lapse after a few issues—I needed some definite backing.

Miss Shoolman ended up giving me $550 during the first year—and nothing else came beyond it, as her illness claimed more and more of her resources. I went to various local printers to get estimates on a sixty-four-page staple-bound job, normal page size. One of the best local printers, an old anarchist, wanted upwards of $660 for a thousand copies (my initial run).

Money was obviously going to be a problem.

Through Miss Shoolman, whose family were major contributors to the founding of Brandeis University, a meeting with the vice-president of that then new establishment and another member of its bursary was arranged in Boston. Although they evinced interest and it was apparent some modus vivendi was possible, I sensed that my editorial capacities were doomed to be hobbled by a faculty staff and inevitably differing tastes. I had already planned to feature Olson and Creeley and Bronk, and was not prepared to brook *any* sort of compromise. Better nothing than that. For similar reasons I refused money, tacitly, from some well-to-do poets. It wasn't a question of connivance, but merely of taking the full risk.

As it turned out, the risk was graver than I thought and kept me embattled throughout. And no doubt this will remain true if another series should somehow come about. From the beginning, *Origin* had an extraordinary amount of lip-service and virtually no steady active support.

My first letter to Olson, who had come much too highly touted from Creeley, was somewhat scoffing and it led to a snappy comeback that put me, as it were, in my proper place. However, the recovery was quick and Olson came through with a fabulous list of potential subscribers and supporters. The list included, amongst his friends and acquaintances, Charlie Chaplin, a number of well-known senators and congressmen, composers, artists, dancers, and one of Hemingway's wives. I wrote to *all*. There was no secretary or assistant (until I went off to Europe in the fall of 1954) and my now former sister-in-law, Doris Greifer, generously volunteered her services and, not without difficulties, handled the business end of the first series of the mag during its final year and a half.

Response from Olson's list and others was meagre, subscriptions were scarce. Pound had said, in the words of advice he sent to Creeley and Bob thoughtfully forwarded to me: "Where the hell can you find 36 subscribers?" His volume of *Letters* had recently appeared and my younger brother bought me a copy, which I still have, dated December 20, 1950. The ideas penetrated. I went and studied every little mag I could lay my hands on. I scoured them regularly (while I was in Boston) at the Woodberry Poetry Room at Harvard, which had just shifted from Widener Library to Lamont, and was under the considerate direction of Jack Sweeney, a friend throughout the years.

The upshot was a decision to abandon regular printing for varitype and photo offset. It was still costly. The first issue (ironically the most expensive I've ever done!) took more than $400 of the approximately $650 I then had in the till. I cut the bill down a little thereafter by going from one thousand copies (more than I could circulate or store) to five hundred copies of #2. The saving was no more than $50, but it had begun to register on me that every dollar counted. By #20 of the first series there were only four hundred copies of each issue, and that was still more than I printed in subsequent series.

Almost at once the switch from standard typography to the cheaper printing style brought me a ringing denunciation and threat from Creeley. (It took me a while to recognize a growing resentment/envy on his part for what I was doing, what he himself wanted to do, though it wasn't openly admitted until I put it to him a year or so later. It had been quite predictable, no doubt, but no less disturbing for all that.) Because my relation to him had become central to me and he was felt as so much a part of what I was doing, the sudden disaffection hit me with all the more fury. On the very eve of the appearance of the first issue, I ran off to New York for a few days and wandered around the Village disconsolately, having no one with whom to share my dismay.

Those who have seen the first issue know that it is no marvel of printing, but it is a clean and still exciting issue to read. It is far from dated, or so I feel. But then I feel this to be true of the entire series.

When the first issue did at last appear, in April, 1951, I was very high and pleased just to have managed a beginning. I brought a batch of copies to Grolier and some were put on display in the window--as was done with all succeeding issues of the series. Then I hurried up to Gloucester to share my excitement with Ferrini, who had a poem in the issue and who had lent me some Olson letters to draw on. He felt the same thrill. We knew something had occurred.

Olson's response is available now to all, dated April 27, 1951, probably an immediate comeback upon the air-mailed copy:

> the fullest satisfaction i have ever had from print, lad, the fullest. And i am so damned moved by yr push, pertinence, accuracy, taste, that it is wholly inadequate to say thanks . . . and the varitype is, actually (i do believe), *better* (in the sense of the *speed* of it, is damned wonderful . . .

That set me up. I was established, at least, amongst my own, no matter what might follow. And Creeley wasn't slow in turning over and confessing the issue was handsome, he was sorry he had blown his top sight unseen, etc., etc.

The Editing

Each of the three series of *Origin* entailed its own problems and issues, but there were certain overriding considerations (obsessions?) that claimed me from the start — even when I was trying to discover what it was I was hooking or being hooked by.

Fundamental throughout has been the "pitch" I presented in my first and, almost, only publicity:

ORIGIN
is devoted to giving adequate outlet
to those new/unknown writers
who have shown maturity/insight
into their medium
to giving
the push to creative minds, to
demonstrate the going concerns, directions of contemporary
creativity.

This extended gradually to the idea of offering work by writers, no matter their age or even if long since dead, who seemed to me "alive" and inadequately, if at all, known in America. Although *Origin* did circulate elsewhere, it was by and large read by Americans and intended for their immediate attention.

I had wanted to present new voices, fresh voices, on such a scale that they could not be overlooked. (E.P. had written: "Nothing but gt/clarity can cut thru.") The writers were often repeated issue after issue, if work was available. Certainly this would earn me the reputation of organizing a school or a clique. The risk was worth taking. To judge by the attacks from those I had published upon others that I was publishing, my own taste exceeded (in range anyhow) that of any of the contributors.

In addition to having a handful of writers from the start about whom I felt strongly and who I thought warranted whatever audience I could muster for them, the idea of editing issues as tightly knit units *and* as elements in a complete series grew on me. I had taken a statement by T. S. Eliot, which had appeared in *Poetry*, as my basis for a five-year run.

He had said that any little mag with five years of regular issuance (a quarterly made most sense to me in terms of finance and physical capacity) could say all that it had to say and were best halted then. Achilles Fang, a close friend (another relation made by the radio program) at Harvard and a most helpful advisor, suggested that I not make any definitive conclusion after the five years, but leave it open to later re-emergence, allowing for a fallow period. This too I took to heart.

The title *Origin*, I might note, was related to A.F. also, for he said that it didn't really matter what it was called, for the name's meaning would only come after the magazine became a particular thing; that would give it its sense. I wanted a name of three syllables, like *Horizon*, but with the accent on the first syllable. It was a purely personal and instinctive decision. Once it was made, however, I wanted an epigraph to go with it. By then Olson had led me to Babylonian/Sumerian mythology and S. N. Kramer. From the oldest genesis myth then came the phrase:

O my son, arise from thy bed
  work
     what is wise

—which Olson threw up to me later, during one of his intermittent challenges.

Both Creeley and Olson, naturally enough, had suggestions for me of possible contributors. And I listened to them carefully, respecting their judgments but by no means deferring to them. Through them came my contacts with Paul Blackburn (who was deep into Provençal poetry via Pound), Denise Levertov (who was living in southern France, married to a former classmate of Creeley's, Mitch Goodman), Robert Duncan (whom Olson had met on the West Coast and whose work had appeared in the same issue of *Poetry* in 1950 as my own, for the first time). There were others who extended relations, even when their work was refused.

I was open to all and any. I had and retain an interest, picked up by Gael Turnbull in *Mica* and *Migrant* and by others since, in using letters—mainly as a way of bringing the writer's life and normal use of language into more specific relation to his work, and not for confessional purposes. Some stimulated more poetry, as witness Olson's use of one of his Ferrini letters (printed in the first issue) as part of *In Cold Hell, in Thicket*.

Editorials were avoided, for it seemed to me that nothing I could say would say as much as the issues themselves. And space was precious. There was nothing to summarize or extract from, there were no manifestoes. The revolt of the poet is invariably conservative at its roots, no matter what faces are used or revealed. Not politically conservative, but imaginatively conservative, with a profound regard for what is given, as earth or air, sun or moon or stars, or the dreams of man.

Thousands of unsolicited manuscripts arrived—through friends, through word of mouth, through notices in other little mags, etc. I read everything as soon as it reached me and answered, or tried to answer, within twenty-four hours of receipt—whether ill or not. And if I was unable to reach a decision and wanted to mull the work longer I wrote the author as much at once. I had undergone long months of waiting from other editors, often hearing nothing ever, and wanted no one to face that from me. Though I started with a dollar token payment, even that had to be given up for lack of funds early on, and I paid, often quite freely, in copies instead.

The only truly unsolicited writer taken on during the first series was Ted Enslin. And that accession—later reinforced by actually meeting each other in Cambridge (he was living then on Cape Cod)—was a highlight of those years. Larry Eigner, who sent me badly written quatrains during my broadcasting period, I steered to Creeley for advice. Suddenly his work changed and blossomed. Bob's powers as a poetic educator were clear—long before he found himself "professing."

During these two decades, during the editing periods and outside of them, perhaps the largest part of my effort was reserved for writers, young and old, whom I never published, but many of whom have since made names for themselves. I was often strong and tactless in my comments, but never given to rubberstamp rejections. One rejected southern lady threatened to assassinate me, and there may still be some who wish she had done so. I was capable of telling some of these poetasters to find something better to do with themselves.

When I visited the University of Wisconsin a few years ago and spoke of *not* imposing as being the best any of us could do for anyone else, Felix Pollak, remembering my rejections of his own work, privately asked me how I, as an editor, could say that. To edit is to impose. Yes. All that I could plead was both weakness and the fact that no one was obligated to send me work: the peril was implicit. But imposition is not quite the issue. I have often frankly stated that I was not at all sure of some of the work I sent back. I did find it hard to publish work about which I was not convinced, or not enough.

There were times I published writers because I sensed potential that might effectively be brought to a head by appearing in the *Origin* context. I meant the writers to read themselves in the unexpected context. This was perhaps even truer of the later series, after the earlier contributors had begun to make a dent in the larger scene.

Finances were hard. I had to swindle my younger brother out of some of his savings at one point to keep the thing going. There were some friends, but none could help much. Even varitype, I realized by the fifth issue (costs rising again), was beyond my means. I needed a cheaper printing source.

James Boyer May—who had been in touch with me for some years already from Hollywood—had just set up a rig with John Sankey, a young would-be printer-poet who had been editing printing a small mag in London called *The Window* and had used work of mine. This was the Villiers Press. As his first job I was taken on at the lowest rate. After spending $350 minimum for the offset work, I was given a printed job, cleanly, if not handsomely, done at something like $130 or so. It was the moment's salvation. Creeley was then in Mallorca. My younger brother had met him at this point and helped him on the voyage out. Bob suggested doing the eighth issue, which was to be a selected Olson volume, with a printer he had found nearby. He offered to design the issue (Ann Creeley did the cover) and manage its production for me at $90 — for five hundred copies!

That number, which is now worth more per copy than the entire original costs, sold worse, at 75¢, than any other I've ever done. I can recall meeting Dick Wilbur on Mass. Avenue along the Harvard Yard and mentioning to him that the new issue of *Origin* had just appeared. He said, simply, with a weary tone, "More Olson?" And that was the general response.

With the advent of the third year, new money from subscriptions and the smaller printing bill brought me back to Sankey's operation. Creeley was starting his Divers Press and that needed his attention, the *Black Mountain Review* was in the offing. But with #11 I was again very hard-pressed, and Bob suggested letting his friend Martin Seymour-Smith, very temporarily engaged, as it turned out, as tutor for one of Robert Graves's children, handle *Origin* printing — which could be done at $110 or so. The money was wangled out of me, quite unusually in advance, on Bob's word and Martin's even more ravishing claims. (I have never undertaken an issue without having the cash on hand to pay the printer and have never been a day late in paying. Yankee manners, perhaps.)

What ensued aged me rapidly. After a prompt initial example of a page proof, there was no further word, despite letter after letter seeking news. The issue was overdue. I wrote Ann Creeley and then Bob, who finally told me of Martin's absconding with the funds for various "reasons," but Bob, feeling responsible, took it upon himself to do the issue for me at his own expense and labor. The number did appear, replete with errors and much re-edited from what I had intended (too much material having been provided, it turned out), but I was relieved when the copies, some of them, finally began to arrive. It was a close call. From then on I stuck to Villiers in London.

The eleventh issue featured Artaud's *Theatre and the Double* in M. C. Richards' version. She had been with Olson at Black Mountain. When I had mentioned Artaud to Olson and that I was beginning to translate that essay, he told me she had done a version already and would be happy to have me look it over, make suggestions, and print it (there wasn't space to use it all). Artaud's ideas were then closer to my own sense of theatre than anything else I had found in contemporary writing and I was excited. The oral quality of his poetry also attracted me. And in Paris in 1954 and 1955 it was his work that drew most of my attention.

By the end of the first year I began to feel that my own tastes and values ought to be stretched and enlarged by having contributors I thought might profit from the experience as well take on an issue each year. I started with Paul Blackburn and he featured his friend Harold Dicker. Later Ted Enslin brought in John Hay; Denise Levertov, Ed Dorn and David Galler and Donald Finkel. Irving Layton introduced a host of new names from Canada, including Jay Macpherson and Daryl Hine, as well as French-Canadian poets. Gael Turnbull brought me Roy Fisher and Alan Brownjohn.

There was decidedly a growing list of contributors, an expanding world of poetry, coming into my ken. In the summer of 1953 I hitchhiked up to Canada to meet especially with Ray Souster in Toronto and Irving Layton in Montreal. Through Paul Blackburn I had met Louis Dudek, the other head of *Cerberus*, in New York, where he was doing graduate work at Columbia. He made my first connections north of the border. On that first trip I carried Olson's *Projective Verse* essay. In Toronto Ray introduced me, amongst other poets, to Margaret Avison, who made a strong lasting impression. She was definitely her own creature, quiet, reserved, but unmistakable. She was struck by the Olson piece and asked me to leave it with her, which I did. Unfortunately, afterwards, when she sent me some poems at my warm request, I turned them down—gently, I thought, but for reasons that shriveled her. It was some time before I could pry more work out of her and had the chance to print her *Agnes Cleves Papers*. Years later she admitted that what I said was accurate, but that she wasn't prepared for it. On the other hand, it taught me never to solicit without taking.

Ray became a lifelong friend—though only a little of his work ever appeared in *Origin*—and a valued one. No one has been as catalytic in so self-effacing a manner as he in promoting U.S.-Canadian literary relations, with the possible later exception of Warren Tallman out in Vancouver. He steered me to Layton in Montreal, quite another kettle of fish. Irving and I stayed up all night at his suburban house that first night wrangling: he telling me that Souster was a great poet and I countering by saying that Creeley was the poet of our time. We made little headway with each other, but I liked the man regardless of his obduracy, or possibly because of it. And he was ever proud of his battling propensities. Later he came round to my thinking, to some extent, and my feeling for Ray's work has likewise improved. I met others in Montreal: A. M. Klein, on the eve of the Rosenberg execution. He, as a lawyer, was certain there would be a last minute reprieve; I, as an American, was painfully dubious.

Hitchhiking back from Montreal to Boston, I stopped to visit with the Goodmans in their country place in Vermont (they had recently returned from Europe), where they told me of the political execution, which depressed us all. Then I went on to visit briefly with Bronk at his home in Hudson Falls, our first meeting and a memorable one.

As on my radio show I had made a point of transmitting all comments that came in and seemed to me of any use of the poets involved, so with the magazine I copied out comments on contributors to pass on to them. I made a conscious effort to bring many of the writers into active relation with each other—not as a school or group, but for mutual stimulation, exchange of thoughts, community of feeling. Most were at considerable distance from one another, so that direct contact was either infrequent or quite unlikely. Black Mountain later served, for a short time, as a more concentrated locale for some of them: Olson, Duncan, and Creeley, in particular. (I myself have never been there.)

In the spring of 1954 Blackburn and I were quite close (I'd visited with him several times in New York) and he was applying for a Fulbright Grant to continue his work on the troubadors in Toulouse. He was also marrying (for the first time) and was to honeymoon, whether he received the grant or not, in Mallorca that summer. He asked me for a recommendation and I, of course, supplied one—the first and only time I know of that any word of mine didn't hurt a friend's grant application (it was apparent my name carried no weight then, either pro or con, which was perhaps a good in itself). In any case, he was eminently qualified. In midsummer 1954 it occurred to me to try for a grant to Paris. There were many reasons for going abroad just then. A friend was already there and urging me to come. And other friends from Boston were waiting as well. I applied, this time asking Paul for a recommendation. However, it was Marianne Moore's support—which I have a copy of (as she saw fit to send me a carbon)—that no doubt, apart from my qualifications, did the trick. She signed herself "Acting Editor of *The Dial*, 1925-1929." (I see from the date on it the correcting fact that the applications were entered in 1953—her letter dated October 9, 1953—though they were for grants the following fall. And I do remember now that we *knew* at Paul's wedding that we were going to be meeting in France then.) Miss Moore's very brief statement ran:

> Despite a sizeable proportion of work in *Origin* that I deplore, I feel that Cid Corman justifies backing for study in France. He has courage, energy, and a straight approach to writing and to people. Moral fibre is the question in my mind. Does he really know good from bad, and good minds from bad ones? I think he does and will find a worthy way of proving it and hope you see your way to granting him a fellowship for study in France.

I must say, after her question I read with some trepidation, by no means assuming I would gain her approval.

A major cause for applying was *Origin*: I planned to use, as I did, a large proportion of the money for the mag. Of the $155 a month then allotted I religiously put aside one-third for *Origin*, one-third for a penurious artist friend I picked up with in Paris, and the rest for my own very modest living expenses.

That last summer in the States I again hiked up to Toronto and Montreal, renewed relations there, and met Gael Turnbull, Phyllis Webb, and Eli Mandel, amongst others. They had just had their earliest work published in a joint volume by Contact Press (Souster/Layton/Dudek's pioneering poetry labor of love). Gael was added to the growing number of poet friends. He was in his early twenties, already a father, and working as a doctor up in the Hudson Bay region (Iroquois Falls).

Back in Boston at summer's end, prior to heading for New York and sailing for Europe on the *Queen Mary*, I invited Olson (at Black Mountain) up to Boston for the reading mentioned earlier. He came, as it happened, on the heels of a hurricane, which very nearly canceled the very energetically publicized event. Its success was sealed—despite only forty listeners being able to come in—from the moment he opened his mouth (after having gobbled down several sandwiches at a small counter joint across the street from the church). He read from eight to twelve and only two people, elderly ladies offended by his "Thomas Granger" poem, left during that time. No one even went out to pee.

The following day Nick Dean, my photographer friend who had been a great help in setting up the reading, drove us out to Gloucester to the Ferrini place. It was destined to be a dramatic occasion, since it was the first meeting of Olson and Ferrini after appearance of the Jargon edition of Maximus 1-10. (I had already, reluctantly and regretfully, played assistant to Olson and gone, as he asked in the postcard sent me which is embedded in the poem, "to hold his hand," as it were, in delivering the volume. I had read the entire book to an audience that included Helen Stein, who also was fond of Vin. She had raged at Olson's attack and shredded him for humorlessness and callousness. But the dagger had fallen; Vin was profoundly hurt, of course. I despised myself, still do, for having been party to any of it.) I knew that a reconciliation was in the cards, but it was tense.

We arrived just after noon and Vin came to the door.

Charles crawled out, straightened up, strode to Vin, took him at once aside and in to a separate wing of the house, embracing him and asking for a drink. They joined us half an hour later in the extra-rented part of the soon-to-be-condemned house that was used as a sitting room. Larry Eigner had been alerted to Olson's coming and his father duly delivered him. Olson took a seat opposite Larry, in his wheelchair by the fireplace. Vin was seated on the rug beside Charles. The big man read a little, upon request, from his poetry and asked if there were any questions. Larry, spasmodically trying to frame words (and C.O. frankly unnerved by the task of trying to cope with the garbled sounds), came out with, finally, as repeated by someone else in the audience, "Why did you attack Vinc in your poem?"

Olson flushed and the room was exceptionally quiet as he began to work out a reply, naturally in terms of the larger thesis involved and not as a personal attack. It wasn't quite coming off. At which point, unexpectedly, his wife, Con, who had been visiting in a nearby North Shore town, entered—to his transparent relief and joy. I never saw so large a man move so fast as he eagerly embraced her, and the scene ended there.

On the very eve of my sailing, while I was in New York later that month, I received a series of letters from Bob in Mallorca: he had quarreled fiercely with Blackburn, had wanted to kill him almost, mainly due to the bride, whom Bob could not abide. He declared I would have to choose between them when I came. I answered at once that I had no intention of choosing between friends and that their hangup would have to remain their own property. Paul had relayed his version of the events also and was obviously less angry than aggrieved. And for many years thereafter, Creeley and Blackburn, who had so much in common, were, in fact, estranged.

I mention these events in some detail to give you an idea of the volatile natures of all of us involved in what the casual reader might otherwise easily imagine was a single-minded, harmonious body of dedicated writers. The dedication was there, but the harmony was often hard to catch above the din.

The difficulties, as ought to be sensed, were a part of what was happening and in strange ways enriched whatever we managed. The complications never ceased. We were full of ourselves and often it had to be roily.

Perhaps, because his *Letters for Origin* (Cape Goliard/Grossman) are so widely disseminated now, I should say something still more of my relation to Olson in the early fifties. I myself have often been taken to task for being or appearing overbearing, often—I'm sure—with good reason. But I doubt if I could compete with Olson. Yet, as the letters reveal, what was impelling the man—and myself too, I like to believe— was a sense of personal integrity and an overwhelming regard for the task of poetry. He evidently regarded me as an agent of his whom he expected to do as he suggested or implied. My capacity for playing middleman has never been very good. More to the point he was fourteen years my senior and I was, and felt myself to be, a novice. This, it might be thought, should have made me all the more humble. But it is hard to be humble when one is being constantly called upon to be so. The spirit rebels, balks. His encouragement and stimulus were valued, but he rarely, if ever, grasped where I was at. He realized that I was not where he was at. Since Creeley's and his intentions were closer, their eventual editorship of the *Black Mountain Review* was both logical and desirable, and welcome. I felt a great deal of unnecessary pressure removed.

As I have often had cause to remind others as well: it is tough to hear what someone is saying when he is shouting all the time. Olson was very much in the hortatory line of Lawrence and Pound.

Whenever it was, in the early fifties, that Olson visited our apartment on Jones Avenue in Dorchester (suburban Boston), it was an occasion—the first (as they say now) encounter. And possibly the best. He stayed all afternoon and, invited by my mother, for supper with my parents as well. He spoke to me at some length of Dover Wilson's *Shakespeare*. The heaviness of his letters was lost in the quiet and direct urgency of his ideas and feelings. *Much* gentler in cogency. And I listened. At the dinner table he lectured my folks on the art of speech—from the degradation of the gab of the Irish policeman he had locally sought directions from all the way back to the source of man's need for utterance. He was magniloquent, unforgettable. I felt as though poetry were provided suddenly its truest ground.

Later, shortly before he took leave after staying some five or six hours, my father, having been impressed by the man's ability to put away so much hard liquor, said as much. Charles pointed to his feet, there at the end of his long legs, and answered, "That's where it all goes." My father, addressing him at one point, called him "professor." Olson bristled and shot back, "Why do you call me 'professor'?" The reply unhesitatingly came back, beyond answering, "Because you look like one."

Afterwards, when he had gone, my folks remarked on his extraordinariness, my father adding that with such attitudes the man was doomed to poverty.

I spoke to Creeley not long afterwards about this moving visit. Bob had only spoken to Olson long distance so far and was somewhat diffident of actual confrontation, which occurred a few years later.

In those days Olson might telephone from Black Mountain, North Carolina, to Layton in Montreal to congratulate him on some fine poetry and Layton call me in Boston to relay his pleasure. And Miss Shoolman, once when we were together, insisted on speaking directly to Olson in Black Mountain. Frictions, indeed, and sparks.

The relations that obtain between human beings and their "world" or "worlds" are beyond all analysis, indivisible, multiple, interacting on every level, or no level. It would be a gross mistake to believe that whatever the differences—which I would honor—I have not felt an unbreakable bond with those whose labors also went into the making of *Origin*.

The Nature of the Three Series

When I felt compelled to enter a second series from Kyoto, just ten years after the first, Vin Ferrini wrote me that it was an error, that I could never repeat or compete with the first series. All I could say was the fact: I'm not trying to repeat or compete, and whatever it may be it will be as fine in its own different way.

Others maintain there is a falling-off. I have never seen it. Each series has, for me, its own distinctions. The editing, in itself, I feel grows stronger and truer all along. But no editor can publish better work than he receives or obtains.

There is no other measure, if measure it is, than what use, what delight, what education comes of the poetry provided and what poetry it excites and encourages. So that there is a continuing evaluation that cannot halt at any one critique, but keeps changing, even as meaning changes, as it is grasped, as breath is and is breath.

The second series was—I guess—inevitable. Living in Kyoto, I had been publishing a number of small books under the Origin Press imprint. This had, in fact, begun in Italy, where I did first little volumes by Gael Turnbull and William Bronk, as well as some of my own poetry. In Kyoto I did more of my own, plus Ted Enslin's first collection and Gary Snyder's, Louis Zukofsky's *"A" 1-12* and his *It Was* (prose pieces). I had become a close friend of Will Petersen, who figures in poems by Gary Snyder, Louis Zukofsky, Clayton Eshleman, Frank Samperi, myself, and others. He was and is, though he dislikes the term, an "artist," esteemed most for his lithographs, or more exactly "stone-prints." We had become almost inseparable companions, talking all night long and all day. By the time I went back to America in 1960 we had determined to revive the magazine and work it together—he and his wife, Ami, to manage it and assist in various ways. I had made an arrangement with my printer in Kyoto, with the idea of a fixed price in mind for the projected five years. (The printer, Genichido, even saw me off on the boat one rainy day in Kobe.)

The series was to center on Louis Zukofsky. I had met Louis and Celia and Paul in the summer of 1957, during their "Four Other Countries" trip, in Florence. We had become involved in a heavy correspondence. Although he had already produced a remarkable body of work, most of it was hard to come by and unknown. I wanted, at the minimum, to bring his work to the attention of his peers and other younger poets. There were others, like Snyder and Lorine Niedecker, who also warranted more ample presentation. (Niedecker and Samperi were originally brought to my attention by Louis Zukofsky.)

This time I did away with all the subscription business. I decided to give away the magazine, but in the name of "response" (responsibility). Those who wished to receive copies were to "subscribe" by responding at least once a year, and libraries would be treated as individuals. Needless to say, the libraries were scarce as a result. But let me quote the statement appended to issues in the second series, for it speaks for itself:

> *Origin* is not for sale; it can be had for love [this was written in 1960], as it happens, not for money. Not that anyone wanting to offer money to help, coming with love also, will be repulsed. But anyone who wishes to receive the magazine may have it by writing me and letting me know. But any one must write me, concernedly, for him or herself only. What sharing occurs upon receipt is one s private affair. Requests will be honored for a year…and then must be renewed. Priority will be given those who demonstrate concern for the material, which doesn't mean, of necessity, agreement with it. Libraries will also be treated as individuals. I deal only with minorities of one…"

I learned that giving things away is often more difficult than selling them. And the higher the price, the likelier to find a buyer. (But this last point is familiar to all art dealers.) The requests we received were discussed and considered on their individual merits and accepted only by accord between Will Petersen and myself. The editing was entirely mine, though I often sought Will's response. He never attempted to negate my sense of the contents, nor I his. There was always good-natured back-and-forth. He was in charge of typography and layout, though we went over everything together. I still admire and enjoy the care he put into the production. It is anything but standardized, yet is not eccentric either. Resources at the printing shop were limited, but the most was made of them. Ami Petersen took care of the mailing and records.

How was this series financed? Chiefly through selling now valuable manuscripts and letters from the earlier period. At that time a number of libraries had both interest and budgets to work with. The Olson letters were sold at this time to the University of Texas for $600, half of which I sent to Olson, who was reputed to be hard-pressed. The other half went into *Origin*. Some readings, while I was in America (1960-1962), brought more cash into the till. A key turn was the rig worked out with Dave Randall, in charge, then, of the new Lilly Library of rare books at Indiana University. He even came to Boston, when I was back there (winter of 1960-61), to examine the papers involved. (About a year later he wrote proudly of it, in a letter published in the London *Times Literary Supplement.*)

The library there—which had by then purchased a substantial body of letters (with Mary Ellen Solt assisting)—agreed to purchase all items relating to *Origin* first series that I retained, in addition to manuscripts, proofsheets, letters, etc., of the second series on an annual basis, while the work was in progress. Of course they would be a year in arrears. The payment was $500 per annum. This, at the levels then prevailing, was enough for two issues—which meant that half the basic costs could be met through that support. The rest was expected to come from continuing sale of an endless supply of letters and papers (mostly to the Humanities Research Center, under F. W. Roberts, at Texas—which thus procured a large file of my Zukofsky letters).

I mention these facts for future students of the magazine and the authors involved, as well as hopeful editors, and for the present readers who may well wonder how one as habitually penniless as I am could afford not merely to edit and publish *Origin*, but also to give it away.

The second series was subtitled "response" and, as I've said, featured Louis Zukofsky throughout. There is work of his, I believe, in each of the fourteen issues. With this series space was marshaled more effectively than before—so that there is actually more material in play. The inside front cover—which was used in a like fashion in the third series—became what I call the *tokonoma* (the altar space found in the *genkan*—entrance hall—to any Japanese home). Here I would place uncredited quotes from contemporary or ancient sources, drawing on all of world literature. Again the issues were organized as individual units and at the same time, if you will, as modules in the total architecture. Sixty-four pages has seemed to me an ideal size: neither too skimpy nor too heavy for any reader to take as a unit and at a single sitting. It compels the reader to relate the work that appears between the covers more closely and richly than would be possible with a much larger or smaller format. And those who examine the series (the second and third, in particular) will understand how much attention has been given placement in the overall design. It has meant having basic materials either in hand or known in advance, while keeping a fair amount of space open to the unexpected and last-minute items. The authors were informed of just when their work would appear. The issues of the second and third series appeared with perfect regularity (my faith in building up anticipation and maintaining it responsible here). And comments, as before, were copied and sent the authors involved.

As a banner to this series I used a sequence of three phrases (Eshleman

in his introduction to the *Caterpillar Anthology* makes reference to them)
When touring America in 1970–1971 I often explained the sense of these
phrases in introducing my own work, since they represent ideas central
to me. They were set down as replies to Eliot's three well-known phrases
(words) in *The Waste Land*, which he had drawn from the Sanskrit,
originally opening with the daddy syllable DA, as you will recall, and
he translated them as *to give, to sympathize,* and *to control.*

My sense is rather that giving is invariably an imposition—hard to
avoid, often "instinctive," but tainted by pressure from above, a hand
down. My preference (not necessarily achieved often) has always been
for the non-hierarchical, no charity, but rather an offering, as art is,
to be taken or left alone, at the discretion of the other. Unpressured
(theoretically, at least, free of fashion or snobbery) and with only the
accepted obligations of appreciation and realization, the sharing. To
offer, then.

Not to *sympathize,* for that is pity, and pity is a form of self-pity. Not
that we have any other recourse sometimes, admittedly, but not to make
a program of it. Rather to *respond,* which means to attend and answer
quietly, fully, concernedly, to the extent one can, with all the risk of
attendance, of being present at and in event.

And finally—not to *control.* Not the imposing that accounts for
practically all human misery since man began. The person who insists
he "knows better" what is good for another or others, whether under the
title of authority, expertise, or mere age. That one even "knows better"
what is good for oneself is questionable to self-probing. To allow, rather,
for one's immense and endless ignorance. In short, then, to *let be.*

Ideals, to be sure. Difficult to live, perhaps impossible to live through
into. But an attempt to be made and at least some open acknowledgment
of what might occur to the grace of all men, and all else in circumstance.

The series ended sooner than intended because of a split between
Will Petersen and myself. It had nothing to do with the work of *Origin.*
For that we shared concern and had enduring feeling. But because of
the break I felt that continuing the mag would be a possible additional
cause for resentment and I preferred, as often, silence. Which can also
be, as many know, a form of response.

Furthermore, the Lilly Library had, without warning, and inexpli-
cably, stopped sending me their annual check. They had sent me two,
I believe. It took me the better part of a year of writing letters and
asking others to help to get any reply as to what had happened. Dave
Randall wrote finally in apology, with a very small check, but said simply
that he couldn't explain. The result was, is, that Indiana University
still owes me a sizable sum of money, which I have no means of ever
recovering. The man had been kind and helpful to me and I felt beholden

to him for what I still regard as genuine concern on his part. It was "just one of those things."

Inasmuch as the magazine was not involved in money subscriptions, stoppage entailed no refunding, etc. It did feel abortive to me, stopping then, and not surprisingly there were things left hanging—though nothing that demanded immediate usage.

The third series was set in motion in the fall of 1965 (in the face of my coming marriage). As in the second series, only three hundred copies of each issue were to be printed. (I had this time firmly fixed a constant price with the printer, which was kept, unlike the second series.) John Sankey, very busy in London now, wrote when he heard of this, that I was crazy, that he was positive he could find a thousand subscribers. I begged him to do so, and if he succeeded, I would be delighted to print the extra copies. Of course, there was no more word on the subject. Even three hundred copies is a major task for one person to manage alone. (My wife's help was largely indirect, since her knowledge of English was rudimentary.)

The new series went only to subscribers on an annual basis, to eliminate unusual labor that could only have ended up costing more. $10 per year. (The first series had gone at 75¢ a copy and $5 for two years and there was no extra mailing charge, even for foreign subscriptions, which don't generally cost more anyhow.)

It was announced in a flier that "The scope of the third series (center) will be explicitly larger—so as to clarify the editor's sense of art as the central relation of all human being, the realization of man's relation to himself (his kind) and through himself to all else in circumstance. As usual, emphasis will be given the finest work available that would not otherwise be given such clear attention elsewhere at this time."

Some friends have felt that I am often too demanding of readers and of contributors: as often as not they are the same. I may as well plead guilty of the charge and be done with it. In point of fact, however, I don't *demand* anything, but those who are interested, who claim to be, are expected to be, and share my concerns—even if as "loyal adversaries." The work is offered and no one, least of all myself, can compel readership.

This series was largely (and this time without let) financed through the good offices of the Special Collections at Kent State University, run by Dean H. Keller. (The University was utterly unknown to me and most other Americans then.) They picked up the option that had been partially utilized by the Lilly Library. Now, though, I was offered $1000 a year for the same sort of materials, plus the residual items of the second series. This covered half the rising costs of production and handling each year. $500 a year, and gradually somewhat more, was elicited from Larry

McGilvery, the enterprising young book-dealer in La Jolla, California, who undertook to deal with library subscriptions for me. Libraries normally are a year behind in their payments and I needed funds at the start of each year. For his guaranteed $500 "in advance," I sent him a basic payment of twenty copies of each issue, and that number increased as the subscriptions exceeded the base of fifty. It ended at around seventy. Private subscriptions were never above fifty to seventy-five (which was not very different from the first series) at any one time and closed, with extra solicitation on my part, at less than twenty-five—so that old Ezra's question proved only too apt. At the very end of the series, through the effort (unknown to me) of Clayton Eshleman, the CCLM (Coordinating Council for Little Magazines) awarded me $2000, and this, in effect, reimbursed me for the extra costs incurred.

The third series ostensibly revolved around my own work, though the work of William Bronk is at least as conspicuous, and much of my own work was in translations of other poets. Bronk, on the other hand, unobtrusively, as the three series developed, became, as he is clearly in this collection, the thread that binds all the issues together. Against his fixedness in Hudson Falls has been my movement around the world, so that *Origin* has had both the specific gravity of the local and the scope of the larger world community. Not that Bronk's work is ever provincial, though more grounded in place than many readers realize, or that my own work ever lacks locality, but range was reached through and beyond time or space. In the open.

In the several years since the third series ended I have received many letters about *Origin*, mostly from younger poets (some of whom only know it by repute) urging me to do a fourth series. Why not? And I would, though reluctantly (for there is much work of my own that presses me for completion). There are simply things that can be done in such a magazine that no other outlet can or will do. The "speed" of transference of work to public that Olson recognized way back is crucial. There is the access for the talented young writer to a deep community, and the stimulation therefrom. There are inevitably those, living as well as dead, whose work is slow to find audience and honor, no matter how deserving.

Perhaps the reader, as he browses, or finds himself concertedly engaged, will come to share this sense. Very few will "know" all the authors here assembled. I have preferred to use work that is less familiar by those who have become better known, but I have attempted, insofar as possible, to permit accent to fall on those writers who seem to me to have been most essential to the definition of *Origin*. The editing has followed chronology to allow for some sense of the order in which the work occurred and for some idea of changing tastes and times. I have drawn only on work that seems to me to have intrinsic enduring merit and/or historical value.

If you want to read this anthology in terms of literary history, that is your prerogative. And if you read it, as I trust many will, as new work, by and large, and mustered in such a way as to be a new context, you will respond to it as new experience and in relation, necessarily, to your own body of experience. The interaction may not be progress, whatever that might be, but it should be, as it has been for me, an act of renewal, another way or ways of feeling life, feeling alive, within the obvious dying.

Word leads to word.

This book is dedicated, as it must be, to all those who contributed directly, and indirectly, to it, and to those of you who, responsive to it, contribute yet to that life of poetry which is the event of human being aware and careful of its indivisibility from whatever there is.

If this is divinity, make the most of it.

First Series (1951~1957)

CHARLES OLSON
Letter to Vincent Ferrini

tues
nov 7
50

vinc:

*...how each of us manages to make more evident his own
resistance. For that is the way a man comes to core. By way of,
the discovery of, his own resistance. (It is also, mark you, the way
a poet—at least—makes himself of USE to society.)*

*And for the poet there is no other way than by his
language—that is, no other way by which he announces, makes
evident, (a clear and present danger) his resistance. What I heard
in HOUSE (yrs) was, a man's own language. And that's how one
knows, smells, a man's resistance. (In fact, I shld imagine that,
when I also speak of PV as propellant, I think of the man as his
own muzzle—and charge. And here you were muzzle, charge,
bullet.*

*I think you must have gone slow,
in that one: I do not mean in the writing of it, perhaps, but in the
conjuring. (But then, I am much; for a man's inertias: I figure they,
like sleep, are there for a purpose (of nature's say). For example,
there is no question you are a worker, have the habits of work. So,
you do not have to worry (as so many other men do have to worry)
abt inertia as laziness. You can afford, to go slow, without, falling
down, from losing, gravity.*

*I have this hunch: that what pressures you,
are, the business of, making things under the sword of, justifying,
economically, your trade. (This is all of us, sure, but, you do have
such hostages! And one respects you, in it.)*

Only, language, is the toughest bitch of a way of expression there

is. And the Armorican is peculiarly confronted, right here. Like it
or not, we are the last first people (he sd). And that means discovery,
anew, of speech. (I would go so far as to say that a writer in Armorica,
had better, actually, not read at all, but listen: in the streets, to
people, than to read anything of the Europeans. And (it follows) of
almost all his fellow workers. For, there would have been no
excuse for my doing the PV piece, if, around us, there was anything
but too ... much anglo american verse ...

                                    We are huge, and roily.
Mixed up. Even by perpendicular penetrations, we are discontinuous.
(What I did not stress—in PV—enough, perhaps, is this business,
of, how, when traditions go, the DISCONTINOUS becomes the greener
place. (For example, all that on syntax, is due to, this: we have to
kick sentences in the face here, if we are to express the going reality
from down in you, and me, and any other man who is going for center:
which means language has to be found out, anew...

Editor's note. "PV" refers to the significant essay in Poetry (NY), Number 3, 1950, by Olson, where he discusses what he calls "Projective Verse."

The Gate & the Center

1

    What I am kicking around is this notion: that KNOWLEDGE either goes for the CENTER or it's inevitably a State Whore—which American and Western education generally is, has been, since its beginning. (I am flatly taking Socrates as the progenitor, his methodology still the RULE: "I'll stick my logic up, and classify, boy, classify you right out of existence.")
    So when I say, it's a question of re-establishing a concept of knowledge as culture rather than a question of what's wrong with the schools, I mean that already anyone who wants to begin to get straight has to, to start, a straight man has to uneducate himself first, in order to begin to pick up, to take up, to get back, in order to get on. Which is turkey-crazy, is it not. So I say, let's take the question by another handle, let's say some simple and non-aesthetic propositions: what is the story of man, the FACTS, where did he come from, when did he invent a city, what did a plateau have to do with it, or a river valley? what foods were necessary (I am thinking here of Steffanson on diets, Carl Sauer on starch crops and how, where they could be domesticated)

4

were the people on the edge of the retreating ice, marauders, or were they (as Sauer so beautifully argues) fisher-folk? and man's first food clue, that tubers which poisoned fish did not poison humans?

and are euhemerists like myself (so I am told ISHMAEL proves me) correct, that gods are men first? and how many generations does it take to turn a hero into a god? is it 3 (ex., A. Lincoln)?

1000 more such questions, put straight down the alley, without deference to arbitrary divisions of "learning" which are calculated, are purposely brought into being (Old Stink Sock on down) to CONFUSE confuse CONFOUND

Take language (& start with Fenollosa): did anyone tell you—same anyones are so stuck with variants—that all Indo-European language (ours) appears to stem from the very same ground on which the original agglutinative language was invented, Sumeria? and that our language can be seen to hold in itself now as many of those earliest elements as it does Sanskrit roots? that though some peoples stuck to the signs while others took off with the sounds, both the phonetic and ideographic is still present and available for use as impetus and explosion in our alphabetic speech? (Why Fenollosa wrote the damned best piece on language since when, is because, in setting Chinese directly over against American, he reasserted these resistant primes in our speech, put us back to the origins of their force not as history but as living oral law to be discovered in speech as directly as it is in our mouths.)

It is one of the last acts of liberation that science has to offer, that is, modern science stemming from the Arabs, that all the real boys, today, are spending their time no longer alone but in teams, because they have found out that the problem now is not what things are so much as it is what happens BETWEEN things, in other words:

COMMUNICATION (why we are at ripe, live center)—and the joker? that from Stockpile Zilard on down, what the hot lads are after (under him at Chicago, Merritt at Columbia, Theodore Vann at the Univ. of Paris, and at the Princeton Institute) is, what is it in the *human* organism, what is the wave (is it H-mu) that makes communication possible! It kills me. And I made one physicist run, when I sd, quite quietly, the only thing wrong with yr teams is, you have left out the one professional who has been busy abt this problem all the time the rest of you and yr predecessors have been fingering that powerful solid, but useless when abstraction, Nature.

Item: to answer all who say, but is a poet that important? Edith Porada, in—get this—*Corpus of Ancient Near Eastern Seals in North American Collections*, edited for the Committee of Ancient Near Eastern Seals, a project of the Iranian Institute, the Oriental Institute of the Univ. of

Chicago and the Yale Babylonian Collection, Bollingen Series XLV (I find that she says this not in the above but in *Mesopotamian Arts in Cylinder Seals of the Pierpont Morgan Libraries*, N.Y., 1947, p. 1):

> Sometimes foreign influences were introduced through trade, sometimes through contact with the many peoples who time and again invaded the rich Mesopotamian plain from the poorer and less civilized regions of the East, North, and West. Moreover, while the actual assumption of power by a foreign king in Mesopotamia was a sudden event, marking the climax of an invasion, such invasions were often preceded by the gradual infiltration of foreigners into the country as mercenaries or laborers. The new element therefore made itself felt gradually, and a sudden break in the artistic development never took place, only the disintegration of one style and the emergence of another. It may be added that artists appear to have been so highly valued that they were spared in warfare.

Well, to hell with it, only—as I sd before—the poet is the only pedagogue left, to be trusted. And I mean the tough ones, only the very best, not the bulk of them and the other educators.

Which brings us home. To Porada, & S. N. Kramer's translations of the city poems, add one L. A. Waddell. What Waddell gives me is this chronology: that, from 3378 B.C. (date man's 1st city, name and face of creator also known) in unbroken series first at Uruk, then from the sea-port Lagash out into colonies in the Indus Valley and, circa 2500, the Nile, until 1200 B.C. or thereabouts, civilization had ONE CENTER, Sumer, in all directions, that this one people held such exact and superior force that all peoples around them were sustained by it, nourished, increased, advanced, that a city was coherence which, for the first time since the ice, gave man the chance to join knowledge to culture and, with this weapon, shape dignities of economics and value sufficient to make daily life itself a dignity and a sufficiency.

(*Note*: I am the more convinced by this argument, that I have for some years, by way of Bérard, Herodotus, & Strzygowski (Frobenius au fond with his sun-moon, landfolk-seafolk premises) felt that it was just about 1200 B.C. that something broke, that a bowl went smash and that, as a consequence, this artificial business of the "East" and the "West" came into its most false being.)

2

Suddenly, by such a smallness of time, seen as back there 3378 to 2500 B.C., the nature of life then is made available, seems suddenly not at all history, seems what it was, men falling off the original impetus but still close enough to the climax of a will to cohere to know what CENTER was, and, though going down hill, still keeping the FORCE, even though the SHAPE was starting even then to lose its sharpness.

((One may see the far end of the personages, events & acts of these years in such things as the Odyssey, Herakles, Egyptian folk tales (as Maspéro gives them), Phoenician periploi, and Ionian thought. That the art of classical Egypt and Greece are also signs of this derivation is more obvious, now that Crete, Susa and even such a late thing as Dura-Europos are available. (We are only just beginning to gauge the backward of literature, breaking through the notion that Greece began it, to the writings farther back: to the Phoenicians, to the Babylonians, behind them the Akkadians, and, most powerful of all, the Sumerian poets, those first makers, better than 2000 years prior to Homer, Hesiod & Herodotus.)

When I say gauge, I am thinking that we have *no* measure of what men are capable of, taking, say, the 700 years from, say, Dante, as comparison of like time to what those men were about in the first 700 years of the Sumer thrust.

What I am trying to crack down is, heroism. There has been, of course, no reason why, since Dante, that men should not have taken heroism solely in terms of man's capacity to overthrow or dominate external reality. Yet I do not for a minute think that this way is—or will be—the gauge of a life turning on the SINGLE CENTER. But just because of our own late, & Western, impression we continue to shy, in our present disgust with such muscularity, away from all such apparent magnifications as epic and myths seem to include.

But the thing goes farther, & deeper. What has been these last 700 years, is the inevitable consequence of a contrary will to that of Sumer, a will which overcame the old will approximately 2500 B.C. and succeeded in making itself boss approximately 1200 B.C. It is the long reach of this second will of man which we have known, the dead of which we are the witnesses. And the only answer of man to the rash of multiples which that wish to disperse causeth to break out (the multiple face of it, the swarming snake-choices it breeds as multiple as hairs) was one thing only, the only thing man had to put against it: the egocentric concept, a man himself as, and only contemporary to himself, the PROOF of anything, himself responsible only to himself by the exhibition of his energy, AHAB, end.

I pick up from the Omahas, to venture to see what happens ahead if I am right that now, only, once again, and only a second time, is the FIRST WILL back in business. A boy (or a girl, if she chose, though it was not required of the girl as it was of the boy) went out at 16, 17, alone into the woods, with nothing to take care of living, for three days of hunger & watch. The one end was, to woo a dream, and that dream, once it came, was, whatever its form, to be thereafter the SIGNATURE of that individual's life. What the boy or girl was not to do, was to speak of it. But due to the other part of the ceremony, which was to wear, from then on, a fetish to stand for the dream, it became possible for the individual instantly to know others of the tribe who had a like dream and to consort with same, as they thereafter did.

I should, myself, assume that both parts of this act rested on good cause, that whatever be individuation, there are groupings of us which create kin ("hungry after my own kind"), limits—of, say, Seven Tribes of man, or whatever—which same limits become vessels of behaviour towards *use* of self, & recognition.

It is in some such frame that the old human science of archetype figure and archetype event became relevant to individual behaviour at all time forward. And it would be my guess that we have been running, know it or not, on the invention of—the verbal function is not quite right: the recognition, obedience to, and creation of—just such archetypes by the Sumerians some time before and some certain time after 3378 B.C. (the date 2500 is only the outside limit this side of the action). And that, of course, we long ago lost the POINT & PURPOSE of what we call—and thus kill—the act of myth.

I have this dream, that just as we cannot now see & say the size of these early HUMAN KINGS, we cannot, by the very lost token of their science, see what size man can be once more capable of, once the turn of the flow of his energies that I speak of as the WILL TO COHERE is admitted, and its energy taken up.

What I should like to dispose of is, that it is a dream, any more than that, what I think we shall be able soon to demonstrate, the so-called figures & stories of the old science were never men. And I venture to say that their enlarged dimensions are no where as discrepant from them as we, going by what we have been able to see of man in recent time, including ourselves, would surmise.

The proposition is a simple one (and the more easily understood now that we have been shocked at what we did not know nature's energies capable of, generally): energy is larger than man, but therefore, if he taps it as it is in himself, his uses of himself are EXTENSIBLE in human directions & degree not recently granted.

Quickly, therefore, the EXCEPTIONAL man, the "hero," loses his description as "genius"—his "birth" is mere instrumentation for application to the energy he did not create—and becomes, instead, IMAGE of possibilities implicit in the energy, given the METHODOLOGY of its use by men from the man who is capable precisely of this, and only this kind of intent & attention.

I am struck (as Waddell tells the stories of these men-who were heroes-who became gods) by the premises on which they acted, were expected to act, & were judged. And how very small, how hairlike, the difference is from the premises we have regarded, in our inherited blindness due to departure from the old science, as essential. For example, this, from a monument of Sargon of Agade, on the duties of a ruler, apparently formulated by his tutor (his "Aristotle" or "Apollonius of Tyana"), a man variously known as Annaki or Urura (Sanskrit: Aurva or Urva), date 2725 B.C.

"arms" are allowable only as PROTECTION OF THE EARTH (I judge, in distinction from the ruler's power, or even the "people's," in the sense of volk or nation). In fact the next sentence of the inscription repeats the injunction thus:

THE GUARDIANSHIP OF THE EARTH IS THE RULER'S ESPECIAL PROVINCE.

And a later priest-king (whose statue-portraits in diorite & lapis-lazuli are straight projections of Gotama Buddha's face, the man Gotama), by name GUDA, King of the port Lagash, date 2370 B.C. in reporting his accomplishments due to the restoration of the law codes of both the Founder of that City, Uruash (c.3000), and of the patron of the city, Nimirrud (Nimrod), says this:

> the maid is now the equal of her mistress,
> the master & the slave consort as friends,
> the powerful & the humble lay down, side by side.

The whole question & continuing struggle to remain civilized Sumer documented in & out: I imagine you know the subtle tale of how Gilgamesh (King 14, and founder of the sea-dynasty of Sumeria, according to Waddell's count) was sent the rude fellow Enkidu to correct him because he, even Gilgamesh, had become a burden, in his lust, to his city's people. As I read it, it is an incredibly accurate myth of what happens to the best of men when they lose touch with the primordial & phallic energies & methodologies which, said this predecessor people of ours, make it possible for man, that participant thing, to take up, straight, nature's, live nature's force.

Letter to Vincent Ferrini

tuesday may 23 L

my dear vinc:

....anyway, a guy who wrote HOUSE of ME, just has
to go on and write more of same. He's stuck with it.
He's got it—whether he chooses at given moments to
call it a curse or a bless, he's
in there

        i guess, probably, the pressures are sociological,
he wants to get to a landing where he can give
his time exclusively to his proper business

                        but on the
other hand he must know the uncertainty wavers (gutters
in the wind, in another sense than
t s)
forever wavers, the soul
(what we call guilts—or pleasures—remain, forever
ambiguities,

        the only object is
a man, carved
out of himself, so wrought he
fills his given space, makes
traceries sufficient to
other's needs

        (here is
social action, for the poet,
anyway, his
politics, his
news)

      O my friend

        in short, this is, the bird overhead is
        Anthony of

ROBERT CREELEY
Letter to Cid Corman

Tuesday (Nov. 15, 1950)

...To figure other things, for a change—things feel tight. Some
of it, the time of the year, that time when it does go flat, the look
of things, or that the sun, now slides over, to the side, never
straight up; that color, is pretty well gone, and always in the
shade, chill in the air, that things look stripped more than bare
since there's violence in it, cold; & everyone pulls in, apart, to
get thru, to get ready for: winter/ the best they can. Sunday, was
up at six to go up to Whitefield, to haul wood for a man in the
truck; being part of a swap I'd made, for an old car, we might have
running, sometime. Anyhow, sat there for a half/hr in the truck,
before he showed up, with his father-in-law, a strange old man
with a crazy face, beautiful, soft yellow mustache drooping, &
heavy pure white beard, short, where he hadn't shaved. The man/ all
gone to fat/ crippled in his legs, lurches, peevish, abt 34 or
5, lives by his wits, parasite, but covers it, with goodwill, a
stinking mellifluous: goodwill. Went over, & met in East Concord,
near there, an old Frenchman, who'd cut it, & who was to show us
where to load. All gestures, he was. Too much. Religion. He
sd: I'll cut wood, mend things, dig, farm, sing & preach—to get
by. We took one load, & found we had to get another, to take it
all. Truck down to the X, springs real low: going slow, with this
man, I was taking it for, not giving a shit, under, whether or not I
hit a bump & broke a spring. And, as it was, what with him, & the
two old men, had most of the piling to do, anyhow, & the unloading
when we got to his place. Junk everywhere, Bits of old iron,
chickens running loose—some penned, with a lone white turkey
walking up & down (not the usual, since turkeys pick up Blackhead
from chickens, which wipes them out, fast). Abt the end of it, two
mice ran out, and the old man whacks one, & grabs the other, &
then went to find the cat. Little kids following him, this high
pitched giggling, all of them, & this big white cat (the way they
look/ white/ sick, washed out, the eyes). Deer-mice: big, big
eyes they have, reddish brown bodies. The cat grabs one & the

other starts to run, when a yng chicken nailed it, & lugged it off. To tear it apart, all the others after it. Eating dinner with them: must have been 80° in the house, a woodfire, woodstove, & the three kids, ages 2 – 9, the yngest a little boy, with long yellow hair, down over his shoulders, with dragged out little ringlets on the ends of it, they were waiting to cut, i.e., waiting for the man's father to come back from California, 2 years of it, and the kid's face, broad with small eyes, under all this hair, sort of curled up, piled, on the forehead, & then the long dank stuff hanging on the sides. Dinner: talking abt one thing & another, telling them abt my place, etc. Chickens, etc. The man: that hideous interest, leans on you, wants to demonstrate its attention. His wife: real nice, thin, dress so it came to just above the knees, hung badly. The kids all staring, & the old man, tickling one or the other, now & then.

Later: went to strip down car, another, for parts for mine. Cold, fingers, stiff. Finally back here about 6.

Now, sitting here, can look out to my left, the table is so I face NW, but looking out the window, look South, over a drop/ down of the land, a river sits about a 1/8 of a mile down, tho I can't see it. The RR track to the right, where I can catch a sight of the few trains go by, down. Two or three colors: burnt out brown of the grass/ the darker of the trees, the bark, & a little dark green from the pines. The sky/ a whitish blue—at the edges: yellowish.
　　　　　　　　　　To the left, in the room, a radio, on top of which: a few plants. In front, a few pictures I'd cut out: one shows Cocteau looking up at a small statuette of St Geo/ & the Dragon, another him looking down at the star of his La Belle et le Bete (or something); three postcards shoved into the sides, under, of the thermostat; two on top: mexican market—Foch & Joffre on horses in World War I victory Parade in Paris/ Joffre asleep. One to the side: Absalom: from the Bible printed by Steffan Arndes at Lubeck in 1494 (when the Grand Banks were already a major fishing ground); to the right side: picture— Dancing Girl, wood; carved in relief for a Sparks Circus Wagon, about 1900.

But to place me, or this, what's up here, that way, doesn't make it.
　　　Take, for example: letter here yesterday, tells me:
"Cannastra has killed himself…"

Later:
        "Trouble with sex after so long—I am now a *lousy lay*
—is bothering Peter—my god what it does to me but you can't
just say I'm really good..."

The fragments. Like any man, is himself, that collector, that
center round which: such fly.

Another letter asks me if I know a missing third line in a poem
called: My Mind to Me A Kingdom Is... As it happens, as it
only once happens—I do.

With that letter—a copy of a Prague newspaper, tells me something
not what I'd heard abt the Sheffield Conference, now removed
to Warsaw.

Another: "Scared. Jesus I'm scared. Maybe the most terrifying
lines I ever read and ripped right out of context whatever it was
were in Marlowe. Mephistopheles speaking: This IS hell, nor are
you out of it. is is IS..."

Another: "From the Cold Palace: A Present

                In the hot season
                you use this fan;
                when cool autumn comes, you
                lay it aside as you laid me aside."

Each one/ somehow love/ so joined.

At center, this convulse, this pull. To make order? It isn't order
that one wants there. Thinking of Unamuno. The excursus on
Quixote. That he WAS the sane one (no matter that most usual
irony, which there, in that context, is nothing of the kind.)

Rimbaud: "J'inventai la couleur des voyelles!"

"THE PLASTIC is sound (a noun, a right noun, is worth every
                       color in the business. Actually a
                       noun carries all the color with it,
                       and rightly used, gets back, all that
                       light has done with it, yes?)

And metric, the running, piling, pushing"

                                   (olson)

At least to see—no line, no divider, that from each movement,
comes that which bears/ in. The literary/ to be a figment, of the
dullness: not of the imagination.

Klee: "He is perhaps unintentionally, a philosopher, and if he
does not, with the optimists, hold this world to be the best of all
possible worlds, nor to be so bad that it is unfit to serve as a
model, yet he says:
'In its present shape it is not the only possible world.'
Thus he surveys with penetrating eye the finished forms which
nature places before him."

THIS hammers—

                    (the precise word) you can neither stroke

it

      with yr hand/ nor shut it down under a box lid...

(I don't have what it comes from: Pound's Ta Hio/ a trans...)

Hammers: relation/ relation/ relation: CENTER.

All I cd do, is, this declaring: of what the german writes:

"aber ich mochte ein lebenszeichen von mir geben..."

to say I'm alive.

Well, lebenszeichen: fair enough, and/or:

like o)   HELLO/
                                  write when you can:
                                                     Bob

14

CHARLES OLSON

The Escaped Cock:
Notes on Lawrence and the Real

*The man sleeps, but I am awake. For it is the Lord who casts out
the heart of men in order to give men a new heart*

1

I take it that CONTEST is what puts drama (what they call story,
plot) into the thing, the writer's contesting with reality, to see it,
to SEE;

that climax is not what happens to the characters or things
(which is, even at its finest, no more than a rigged puppet demon-
strandum) but is, instead, the issue of this contest, the ISSUE of the man
who writes—"a broken stump" said my peer, "this is what a plot ought
to be."

The issue is what causes CHANGE, the struggle inside, the contest
there, *exhibited.*

At root (or stump) what *is*, is no longer THINGS but what
happens BETWEEN things, these are the terms of the reality contemporary
to us—and the terms of what we are. If form is never more than an
extension of content then the proposition reads thus: content (contest
leading to issue arriving at change equals) form.

Myself, I take it that DHL explored the problem, was, at end,
so attacking:

(1) *ETRUSCAN PLACES*—terminus of that extraordi-
nary contest, Lawrence vs place, ideal place—end to the going-around-
the-earth—to find it, finding it there, Civitavecchia; and the work of
the last fifty months of his life following thereon:

(2) *LADY CHATTERLEY'S LOVER*: the act of simplifi-
cation to get objects in to exert *other than psychological or introspective
effects*, by pulling out of the cloth ONE (red, Guatemala red, Pompeian
red, for that matter, Etruscan or Sumerian RED) THREAD; and that the
simplest if sturdiest of all sex, and itself, here, the physical or animal,
straight, here, and (only here excusable) the word orgasm as issue intended, that is, the triumph or delight of same as Mellors is capable of
its teaching.

This—the act of simplification, the same to be carefully seen as
utterly different from the *elementary* (even Stein)—he also does in
(3) *THE ESCAPED COCK*, Part I. It is not easy to put the simplification
this time except that it is a direct question, the question the Man Who
Died asks himself, on his return: is anything worth more than the most
precise sharpening of the instrument, a human, to the hearing of—the

15

hearing of *all* there is *in* — the bronze clang of a cock's crow?

(is an X-fiction worth a cock's crow?)

In other words the next step down from *Lady Chatterley's L* was to the dark or phallic god who is not phallic or penissimus alone but the dark as night the forever dark, the going-on of you-me-who-ever as conduit of that dark, the well-spring, whatever it is. The next step down (out of the light, into the painted tomb, back into the shell, the painted shell, goes) *THE ESCAPED COCK*, is THE WHOLE SENSES as simplified from (as the next step to) the FIRST SENSE, sex. (Part 2 fails miserably, apparently because, at this new stage of narrative Lawrence was not yet able to take woman down that next step towards his etruria. His "woman" here loses by goddessissing the actuality of Constance (Frieda), an actuality the Christ gains. (Always the man leads Lawrence, in?)

2

beauty, sd the Bearded Man
in inception, in continuation, and in end

The thing is — has got so (love, affection, friendship: the dying into, or whatever) — has already become the FACT is now more than, is what DHL projected in EC Part 1, is, viz:

that the thing, that what happens between, is: to hear, absolute, as it is, the SOUND, that crow ("gold," he sd, the Man) or (as another) of another his chicken fine bird he is, two ends like they say, clean straight barring Jimmy (his father, also Jimmy, the same);

and that such hearing (to find the secret of it, which means, of course, to recognize it, then to admit it, then, of all, to participate) is worth the coming back, the putting behind one, the over-looking, a Crucifixtion.

It strikes me that where even DHL went off (Part 2) was the abandoning of that possibility which even Somers (*Kangaroo*) and Mellors come to admit: that we are, all of us, now, essentially guerillas — maquis, frontier or side-street — EVEN in the intimate, EVEN WHERE those old essentials (love, etc) are, where they took root/

it can be put this way:
that it is not a question of loss or of a lack of love (of capability) but a deep and profound difference of the way this thing gets itself expressed, nowadays. Confronted by rot on all hands yet still active enough to want to go ahead — to undo that rot — those who are front dispose themselves toward the intimate just as aslant and acocked as they do toward all those other realities, external mostly, which are moving so curiously fast and treacherously before the nose that why? anywhere? let a twig break?

Love, as they have it, is as dead as peace, as war is. There is one requirement, only one requirement, anywhere (and what's so different about it, actually, from what the predecessors made so much of, with that word of theirs, that word amor plus how-they-figured-it-ought-to-behave) —the clue: open, stay OPEN, hear it, anything, really HEAR it. And you are IN.

You are all, all of you, so glib about what is human, so goddamn glib. Take a look. Just open your eyes, as he did, the Man who died:

1: the day of my interference is done
2: compulsion, no good; the recoil kills the advance
3: nothing is so marvellous as to be done alone in the phenomenal world which is raging and yet apart.

ROBERT CREELEY

Three Fate Tales

1

I put it this way. That I am, say, myself, that this, or this feel, you can't have, or from that man or this, me, you can't take it. And what I would do, with any of this, is beyond you, and mine. But for this time, yours too.

I haven't always lived here. I used to live in the city, in the middle of it, straight, tall buildings, some of it, but where I was they were cramped, squat, four stories. There was a trolley-line ran down the middle of the street. Noise. Each day the ice-man came, under the windows. I could hear him shout. I even waited for him to shout.

Thinking of that time, as it comes here, or here and now, I think of the other, somewhat different. I say time. But I say it, to mean place.

Let me put it another way. What have we got but this, which is yourself, myself. Or that word, self. You figure there's more, some way to make it more, but what you keep is the means, the ways, make them the end. And that's the end of it, of what could have been more.

But nothing more strange, taken or not, than just this, this self, which is single. And I make it such, so call it, because it is so. I only call it what it is.

One day, any day, there could be these people, or make them three people, this man and this woman and this little girl. They live in the next place to mine. I see them go down the steps, out on to the street, there, the three of them. I don't say, look for yourselves, see them, or what you may take as enough to convince you. They are there. That is the fact of it.

17

The days are long, as it happens, hot. The sun in the city is a hard thing, up, inaccessible, hangs over the hardness of the city, out of it. Hot. I hate it but that is, again, my own business.

The woman sits there by herself, in the place with just the little girl. They work out the day the best they can. Make the time pass. I know there are at least a hundred and one things anyone can do, to get through these days. Hold to, the actions, the little things done. I have my own things. I get up, eat breakfast, sit around, read, look out the window. There are these ways.

They wait, the two of them, in the place next to mine. The noises come through. The little girl has a ball. It bounces on the floor. Its noise is exact. The woman calls her for her dinner, she complains, doesn't want to come. There is some sharpness in the voices. I listen. I hear all that I want to hear of it.

Then, as it happens, there is this one day, again, one day out of the number, fifty, twenty-five.

The chair slides across the floor. I hear the girl push it. There is no other sound. Just what comes up from the street, what I have grown used to, the trolley, and the cars, the people, below me, out the window, down. This is what I am sure of, what is down there, that I can speak of without looking, seeing, any of it. It is the one pattern which cannot be broken because it is the general, the collection. The numbers.

It is still quiet. But then out, it goes by me, and down. Stops. But I can't do anything, sit only for a moment, and then, jump, and look out, see there, down, the girl and the people already around her. Nothing of the woman until her head is just opposite mine, the mouth wide, scream, and someone I see the face of below, looks up and calls to her. It's all right. She isn't hurt. A miracle.

It's all right, or right is what they have said, that it's all right, but myself, I can't find their answers or even what they answer, to say it's all right. To her, or myself, or to anyone or even looking straight down at it, after it happens, what happens?

It isn't known. I make that sense of it, that it isn't known, any of it. This woman or this girl or what has happened, and how I would have it, or my hand there. To feel. To be felt. Which they want, or I want, more than the seeing. Any day of the week this could happen, to any, this girl, to others, me, you. I can think of it that way. I am not in this, or I think that to myself. I suppose it as something, even, done with. As it turned out. Past, and even complete. I am left with it, made different, because of it. Or, am I? We are back to that.

2

I take it another way, since in this or in what is around is, perhaps, some of it, that such can come to interest, or finds, so, some place in the attention. Let me begin.

There is an old woman who lives in the country and she is very old indeed. Her husband, somewhat younger than herself, has grown tired of waiting but being an honest man, he cannot bring himself to the act of deciding just how old she should be before she is ready to die. It is to be thought that this old woman's days are inaccessible, even to herself, and though she is certainly alive, for the most part she is dead because she cannot remember anything and when she talks, her words slide into one another and the sentence breaks down before it is even half begun. It is the practice of her husband, a rather cruel one, to have the old woman do the week's shopping, so that each Saturday she arrives in the village and totters from store to store, usually led by some old friend of the family who has happened to be standing on the street corner at the time when she is let down from her husband's car. Often the job is divided, so that one begins it and then another goes on with it while a third appears at the end to guide her back to the car where her husband sits waiting. And behind them comes the clerk carrying the groceries. It is a common sight each Saturday.

This is, it can be supposed, one of the old woman's horrors, but her joy, which is equally distinct, has to do with something which for others would be even more horrible. In the cemetery where she is, once dead, to be buried, her stone is already set in place and her name with all but the final date has been carefully cut into it. She is often taken to the cemetery to see her stone, perhaps with a certain willingness on the part of her husband who may think that if she sees it often enough, this place where she is to be laid to rest, she will hurry up the process of getting there once and for all. For some years she worried about the possible annoyance her choice of a final resting place might cause another member of her family but when with reluctant decision, she made her choice known to the family, she was overjoyed to find this doubtful one quite approved.

In any event this old woman seems to be doing it all by herself, so that when it does come time to bury her, one would not be too surprised, should the knotted old hands reach up and, pushing the shovels aside, pull the dirt over all by themselves, for at least that's one way to think of it.

3

I think we deal with other wisdoms, all more real than our own, which is to say, I think we have to do with others. Sometimes, sitting in a chair by the window, I see a man go by on foot and I wonder at the precision with which each foot advances, so controlled and so sure. I would hope that if the man and I were to trade places, he might think the same of me going by but I am not at all sure that he would.

I think it is always a question of where we are and where we have come from and where we are going. I think they are important in just that order and I think there is little else to think about. Of course, we are ourselves. It would be foolish for us to believe those who tell us different. But to know exactly, to know each time and all the time, about that I am not so sure.

After all, what do we have to do with that is not ourselves? What can exist that we are not part of or that we do not in some sense make room for. This is an old story but a true one. The world is my representation. So it is, all of it. And what is more, this world belongs to us.

But the order is important, the grasp of the keys and the lay of the land, so to speak. One must know these. Like the man with the car I see each morning, racing its motor, tearing down the road over bumps and stones, what does he know about his own possession? Certainly not enough to make actual use of it, not the use of understanding. This, then, should be criticised, such misuse, and avoided at all costs.

But it is true that everything becomes our own. It's what things are for. We see them and they are ours. It's as simple as that.

The story I have to tell has to do with familiar objects in familiar relations. Unlike the others, it does not suppose a stretching of the usual context. It has to do with a usual reality.

I am in the habit of feeding our cat each night before I go to bed after I have put coal on the fires. This is my usual procedure and one I rarely vary. Both the cat and I are at home in it. When it comes time, if the cat is indoors, she will be sitting by her dish, waiting for me to put food in it. If she is outside, I have only to open the door and there she is, waiting to be let in and fed.

On the night of which I am speaking, or now at least I am speaking of it, I had let the cat out earlier and so when it came time to feed her, I went to the door and opened it but the cat was not in sight. But do not take this as something altogether unusual. I am not such an automaton that I cannot vary my movements at all. It is often the case that I am a few minutes late with the cat's food. And the cat, too, has her differences.

I opened the door but the cat was not to be seen, so I called to her, once, then twice, but she did not come.

On that night there was a full moon. It was very bright outside, almost like day but still very different. The tall pines at the edge of the field beside our house cast their long shadows and each object in the field itself that was big enough to have a shadow had its own. But though it seemed very light and the shadows black and distinct, still there were no sharp details such as are to be seen, when a bright sun is shining.

I stood for some minutes, looking out over the fields, and then, because she made a sudden, brief movement, I saw the cat not too far from where I was standing, crouched, her own shadow black and irregular on the snow. I called again to her but she gave no notice, so I walked over to where she was, thinking to pick her up and bring her into the house. When I came to her, however, I saw that she had a mouse and although it's no pleasant sight to watch a cat and a mouse together, one, in fact, which I remember always with unpleasantness, my wife and I have decided that since we have the cat in order to catch the mice which bothered us previously, we have to put up with the unpleasantness, even though it's difficult. So it was that I started to walk away from her in order to let her finish the mouse but as I did so, I was caught by the strange sight of their shadows, the mouse's, though smaller, very distinct and the cat's, like some horrible cloud trying to erase it. I stood there, absorbed, completely caught, until suddenly the mouse's shadow was gone, but no, it appeared again, coming toward me uncertainly, jerkily, until I saw that what it wanted was to hide in my own shadow, which I now saw to be there, just as their own, long and black on the snow. It came toward me, the mouse, and then just as quickly as I had seen it, I lost sight of it again. So again I started back to the house but as I did, I fell something wriggling on my sleeve and with a sudden brush of my hand, I threw it back on the snow. Only then, because the cat jumped on what I had knocked from my sleeve, did I know it was the mouse.

I don't think that story much more than unpleasant but still it has the point of all I believe. For these things, so powerful in themselves, in their own way, are there to be looked at, I expect, and with more than the eyes. It's a case of making them ours the best way we can. I can remember that as it happened, then, even as it was happening, a good many things occurred to me, each with its relation, and if these things did, as they did, lessen that first impact of horror, they also made it my own.

There are other stories, some with more purpose, and one, perhaps, bears hearing here, tacked on though it is. In any event, it's short. After that snow and before the next, I went out, as usual, to do the chores, and found one afternoon, patches of blood on the snow. And seeing them there, I guessed that the cat had cut her foot and was able find her and dress the wound before there was chance for it to become infected.

A short time after, it did snow and the patches were covered and I forgot about them. It stayed cold for a week and then it turned warm and the snow began to melt. And going out again I saw the patches of blood on the snow and without thinking twice, I went off to find the cat, supposing she had cut another foot. But finding her, I found, as well, that none of her feet were cut and then saw it was melting of the snow had caused the old patches to come back. I expect all that this might suggest is that a reality, before it becomes our own, is often tricky and can be easily mistaken.

Le Fou

For Charles

who plots, then, the lines
talking, taking, always the beat from
the breath
        (moving slowly at first
the breath
        which is slow—

I mean, graces come slowly,
it is that way.

So slowly (they are waving
we are moving
        away from   (the trees
           the usual   (go by
which is slower than this, is
        (we are moving!

goodbye

Notes for a New Prose

1

"Language is not reality but another of the instruments by which man engages reality ... "

It is, certainly, reasonable to comment that Joyce's earlier work presents no such divergence from normality as does, now, even the mention of his name. There is, to be got at, a straight line of impact, search, thru the early work, the poems, the play (which is all "idea") to the fact of

Ulysses and then, *Finnegans Wake*. It is useless to avoid it, or to mistake its point. Which must be: it is not the content which is changed. It is the extension of the content into form that has been tempered, made strong.

To go back. We had been led to believe that connotation was this: the suggestions of "meaning" beyond the supposedly exact, denotative meaning which custom of usage had put upon the phrase or word in question. Then by way of the opening created by "associational" content of phrase, gesture, practice, ways, in short, METHOD—connotation became meaning versus meaning, became the fight, for sense, in shorthand. (Some call this "symbol...") "It isn't what the words mean. It's what they mean to you ... "

Just so, with Joyce. That is, the possible suggestions (which can now be called: manifestations) of sense (which was about to become: value) became the criteria for an ultimate "sense"(tho no millenium). Because this was done with language, or, more strictly, within the words themselves, there we took our sight, a bead on: what might be up. Wrong from the start, since it was not words for the sake of words, but, for the sake of what content, possible, might shape them, into sense. Taken as such, Joyce is the craftsman, casting about for a model, for the model,— what is in the head. Not to make himself, but to make, what is in himself.

Form is the extension of content. This was the first rule.

2

"A man must create himself, if he is an artist, instrument also IN ORDER THAT *his work be not expression but illumination...* "

Possible arguments for the supposition that poetry is, now, more able than prose, or more able to make itself an extension of the present context, this life, etc., have first to do with the fact of its ability, (1) to compress, and (2) to project supposition, as fact. In prose, the lean toward a "solution" or a stasis of idea most usually marks the book as a failure; I mean, insofar as a writer of prose is willing to give space to this fixing of idea as the logical "end" of movement, etc., just so far we usually won't go along with him. And I would figure that we are right. But we deny him, even so, the way out of it, this fix, or what could get him beyond these "logics." Take the idea of a man running alongside a train, taking notes yet. He would be about it, what is now expected— while the poet, at home, can project this iron monster to any place which may please him. It is, then, that we are still confused by the idea of "reality" in prose. We do not as yet get the basic fact, that reality is just that which is believed, just as long as it is, believed. Poets are more used to this thing: reality as variants round the center, or, simply, what has been left us.

So how could a prose catch up? Difficult to make the competition actual. It isn't. Elsewhere, it had been pointed out that "poetry insists upon or suggests a quite different ' Universe ': a universe of reciprocal relations..." The swing of idea, in stasis—is still poetry. But prose is the *projection* of ideas, in time. This does not mean that the projection must be an "actual" one, date by date, etc. The word is law, is the creator, and what it can do, is what any prose can do. There is nothing more real, in essence, about a possible prose than there is about any possible poetry. The ordering of *conjecture* will remain as "real" as the ordering of fact, given the right hand.

More to the point, to note the difference, again, between poetry and prose, one of the differences, since there are others as well. Poetry, as the formulation of content, in stasis; prose, as the formulation of content, in a progression, like that of time. This is a simple way of putting it. But sufficient to show that while poetry depends on the *flux contained*, held within the form, in stasis, prose may intend such a limiting but cannot justify one. It has no beginning or end. It has only the length it happens to have. "Might be continued..." Just here is the key to its possible reach, that, in spite of itself, it has to continue, keep going—cannot stop.

So, in some sense, the usual ideas of beginning and end have put upon prose an order alien to its nature. This is not to imply a "necessary chaos." It means only that it is, by nature, against conclusions—or is (as nature is) intent only on its present. It is the breaking out, of context, of form, and down or back, always to the progression, enforced by the nature of its content, and so determined.

It has neither beginning nor end.

3

"Are we not automatic, to think, that because prose-and-the-novel did, since the 18th, & conspicuously, in the 19th, & dyingly, in the 20th, do a major job, that it need now be fruitful?"

As soon as the novel, as soon as prose, generally supposed for itself a context other than what it might, on each occasion, make, it had done itself the greatest possible disservice. And this is not to be mistaken. We can note, perhaps, that while poetry may have combined itself in several, to mean, one thing worked in the hands of several men, at certain times with success, prose has never been effectual so taken, as a job, or so treated. I can remember the notes that Kafka had written about his attempt to write a novel with Brod—or the more amusing attempts of Dylan Thomas, etc. Certainly, the novelist hates his neighbor, hates him for writing, to begin with, and hates him doubly, for writing prose. Perhaps this is a false lead. It matters little except that it can make clear the sense of the necessary singleness of the man who writes prose. And that any constriction, is too much.

The suggestion that record-making can now be taken as one of the major jobs of those that make prose is wrong only in its supposition that there exists any occupation for prose, prior to its coming. It is wrong in the same way that positing any "frame" for prose is wrong. Prose is a plausible and profitable instrument for making records. But stories? Novels? One wonders if it is to the point to set them an end before they have demonstrated their own. "As Rousset, e.g., wrote *L'Univers concentrationnaire* (not *Les Jours de notre morte*)—and, over a weekend, because he figured to die the next week of the Causes; or Martin-Chauffier, who has been a novelist, & who chose in *L'Homme et la Bête*, to tell not even what he had heard others say (the last vestige of the novelist!) but only & precisely what had happened to him; vide Joe Gould..."

Joe Gould's *History*. One wonders. Or, who put him to such work? Joe Gould.

Pointless to argue such a thing. It is not that prose cannot be put to such work, that it hasn't that capability, that it couldn't deal with that end of things. Rather, like no thing else, it must be new. And if, say, tradition concerns itself with these frames, then prose has no tradition. None whatsoever. It should demand that it has none. More than we, or they, may have spoken.

It could be, has been, the collection of ideas. And nothing better, for such documentation. But records? It was the fact of its perspective, that made what it gave, of such, reliable. That it is without, frame. What makes it reliable. That it owns to no master, that it can't. Its terminals, ends, are fictitious. Someone does. "It was the end of THAT period..." But continual, that it repeats, goes over and under, around. Has form, frame, only as it is such a going. As someone had said of Stendhal—it all fell into exact place, exact.

It stands by itself.

4

"The reason why, at this juncture of time, one fights so hard for prose, is, that it enables him to get in, to go by, that head of his, to let it play over his things, outside objects..."

To go back to Joyce. To that mistaking we have made of him; and you may document this for yourselves or look to find who has made of those books something beyond the man who may have written them. Oddly enough, the most exact criticism of these things appeared at the same time that the books themselves did. At least, that first interest prevented the fatal preoccupations with the "purpose," of Joyce, with his own use, as symbol. At least for a time.

Speaking of James, Pound had written that the logic of the pieces the former had written for the *Yellow Book* group was that need to push beyond the curve, in order to establish it. So, generally, position is established in prose; and intention. Hence, this idea of the assumed obliquity, itself a way of placing something, in the context. Is prose roundabout? It's not that question which should be asked. Any way could be the right one. What is got to, what is placed, would be the better thing to be asking, after it's done.

Again—de Gourmont's sentence, "...d'écrire franchement ce qu'ils pensent—seul plaisir d'un écrivain..." And could it be less, granting it must be more?

A new prose... Better to think of this, only, as what may now come. I think we can hang on to those who have left us something strong enough to carry over into this time. Prose cannot exist free of its ability to apply; it can't be faked. So it would be that Stendhal can still give us the sense, or one sense, of the order, the "form," not to be taken as the form of poetry, nor as we come back to it, that more basic form, of prose. There is the fact that the more correct translation of Dostoyevsky's *Notes from Underground* must be—*Notes from under the Floor*, or, *Out from the Cracks Like Any Roach.*

Perhaps it will still be necessary to point to the fact that, while poetry will be the clear, the fact of the head, prose will be the coming, and going. Around. It is there that it can hit, beyond poetry. It is not a matter of better, or worse. There is no competition. The drift, in prose, and the way, of the swing, the reach—we have the necessary evidence, or I must believe we have.

I am very old today, the sky is grey, I am not very well. Nothing can prevent madness. As an honourable man who abhors exaggeration, I do not know what to do . . .

We begin, or end, there.

WILLIAM BRONK

The Acts of the Apostles

The second time the flesh was harder to put on
and there was no womb to shape and soften it,
unless it were Joseph's tomb in the cut rock
that shaped, perhaps, but more misshaped to a kept
mask, as a wet shoe is hardened as it dries
to a foot shape and the print of a step, but not
to the moving muscle and bone that walking was.
What wonder then that Mary, who loved his life,
mistook him for the gardener, and humbled by love,
asked only where they had laid him that took him away.

The men, too, were uncertain they saw, at first.
Thomas doubted and thrust his hand in the wounds.
There must have been some subtle difference gone
from the flesh they loved, or a difference newly come
to make a change in it. Say the change was death
that had wrought hard with it; or say the fact
this flesh appeared and disappeared without
their knowing, bewildered them. They did rejoice,
but only as though their hope had stretched too far.
And Peter went back to cast his nets on the sea.

Some grief is stronger than any joy before
or after it, and life survives. It feeds
within itself on grief, not nourished then
by other food, as winter trees survive
because they do not feed. Their mouths refused
almost the taste of the brief return; grief-seared,
they could not savor it. The time did come,—
but it was afterwards, that a new joy
leafed over their grief as a tree is leafed.
It was the tree of grief that grew these leaves.

We share the movement that young birds learn
when clumsy with size, they grow to the empty air

and fall, and find the empty air sustains.
So we are lofted in our downward course by the wide
void of loss through which we fall to loss
and lose again, until we too are lost
in a heavier element, the earth or sea.
We grow in stature: grief is real and loss is
for life, as long as life. Long flight,
soar freely, spiral and glide in the empty air.

My Father Photographed with Friends

This is my father photographed with friends, when he was young;
unsettled on the steps of a wooden porch, and the one
who lived there elegant beside him. They and the others
hopefully casual in the face of the deciding camera,
the judgements of which are unfeeling, but can be swayed.
And I, as in some later picture of myself,
look for a person identified beyond doubt, and knowing that he
is none of the ones that he is not, yet still unsure,
under the features composed and trusting, who is there.
As if the decision were long and legal when handed down,
hard to be read and truly rendered in such a case.
And hard, in the face, to find our usual, pitiful ends.
God sweeten the bitter judgements of our lives. We wish so much.

ROBERT CREELEY

The Grace

From somewhere else he could hear it, but the crying at least had
stopped, and turning, he saw her at the door, shutting it quietly, and
putting a finger to her lips.

Quiet, she said, and came in, then, to sit down in the chair opposite
him, sinking down there and letting her legs go out, slack, in front of
her. Behind him he had put the candle and it burned, flickering, but a
light, and as soft as any he might hope for.

Otherwise, there was a moon, and this rose, very gently, somewhere
back of the house. The road looked a liquid, or water there, translucent.
He left it as pleasant, perhaps, but was too tired to get up and at her
suggestion, that they might walk, said, no, and slumped back.

There is no time, he said, but knew she had another sense of it. Something, he said, makes a mess of it.

She got up to light another candle and put it on the table behind him, but bitterly, he thought, and watched her sit down again.

We can hope for another place, he added. This is just for the time-being. Call it a vacation, or anything like that.

But the house, or the rooms, something bothered, and she had little peace, accepting nothing of it, and moving with a kind of rigidity through it all. Now she got up again, impatient, and lighting the stove, began to heat water for the dishes.

Can I help, he said, when she looked at him, but she turned away again, and he relaxed.

Outside it grew light, or seemed to, almost like day, but whiter, again that translucence, and he wondered if out there one might not be another thing altogether, even though it should seem otherwise. To the west some small lights, single, each a small brightness and separate from the rest. He imagined gayety, or even singing, the tables of some place packed and people altogether without malice. He thought it might be like that, and felt, too, the moon was the sign.

She had cleared the table, taking the dishes to the sink, to put them at the side, and then filled the sink with the water she had heated. Meticulous, in some sense, she washed them one by one, to put them down again, again at the side, until they were done. Then left them there, to dry by themselves.

Sitting down, she looked up at him, and waiting, she reached over to pick up her knitting, and then began, the needles very bright, and quick, in her hands.

But he had started, and spoke, now, of what he had thought himself to have forgotten, a picnic so long ago it seemed inconsequential, though he could not have said, then, why. Somewhere his grandmother had carried out the lemonade, or he remembered it, in a bright tin pitcher, to place it on the long table, under the trees.

It should be like that, he said. What do we give of that, or what do we try to. Tell me one thing we do that is as nice as that.

She hadn't answered but anyhow he assumed her attention and wanted to make it clear.

A find old lady, he said, I mean, really. She knew what work, was, though I suppose she minded, certainly. That it couldn't have been very pleasant for her.

I don't suppose it was, she said, and looked at him.

Or that other, the one that old man told us about, his mother, who died by the window there, took three drags on her pipe, and then slipped out. How about that!

She laughed, herself, and found it simpler, the time less persistent, and had gone back again, with him, and sat in the old room, as she supposed the old lady had, lifeless, and in the dark.

That was in our house, she said. In the living room, by the back window. He said she used to knit there too, in the moonlight.

One would like to go back, he had said. One would rather not move away ever, or go anywhere but where one was.

Even so, the moon rose, higher, and now came clear through the door they had left open, and came across the floor very softly, to touch the back of his chair. He grew quiet, sinking down, and pushed out his legs, reaching her, one foot against her own.

From somewhere above the boy cried, whimpering, and putting down the knitting, she got up, to cross to the stairs, and then he heard her going up, the crying continuing, and growing louder. He started to get up himself, but then sat down, annoyed, and wondered what the matter was, calling to her, to hear her answer, nothing.

Echoes, he thought. But the crying grew less, then stopped, and soon she was back, and sat down again across from him.

He was frightened, she said, and seeing him angry added, he isn't settled yet.

The anger went, and left him lost in some other thought, of the house, and where they had been, call it, in another place.

He must miss it, he said. But there it is, I mean, one moves anyhow? And stopped, to say, isn't it? Isn't that what has to happen?

I don't know, he said, insistent. I don't know why it is so much place with them. Not that I don't get it, that is, don't get what moving does to a kid, but what else? We've been here close to two months.

She let him go on, sat only there, silent, and not with any malice. Hard to believe it otherwise, or he wondered, then, if it could be otherwise. Something he thought of as impenetrable, but getting up, he asked her to come out, saying he felt like a walk now, if she still wanted to.

She followed after him, and they started off down the road, past the other houses, close, and then off through the fields, the moon there very much a whiteness and lying on the ground with grace. He said he could not really believe it. That it was, then, a world so very close to their own.

But it is here, he insisted, and took her arm to hold it. It has to be?

They went on, following the edge of the field, the ground rough and uneven under their feet. Now and again she stumbled, and he held her up, and at last they sat down there on the grass, and lay back.

Straight up, above them, the moon was beginning to slip, and sink down, but shone with a fierceness, and made them seem bluish to each other, hands looking pale and unreal.

30

She had raised herself, a little, then leaned on him, over, and her hands took his own, lightly, as she kissed him. But he had not stopped, or only for that instant, and looked up at the distance above them, saying, he didn't know, and felt the ground hard under both of them.

It's all right, she said, and moved to stroke him, hoping to help, to ease it. One knows that it will be.

He rested, and felt her fingers very careful, finding him with a certain gentleness, or that sure. He said, thanks, and laughed a little, lifting to take hold of her, but they heard the faint crying, from the house, coming after them, and got up.

She went ahead, running, and he called to her to be careful, then saw her reach the road. From somewhere another sound, a cry, rising, to die out. He tripped and fell down, sprawling, and got up again, rubbing his knee.

Coming in, he found it quiet, and she was sitting in the chair by his own. He looked toward the stairs, but she shook her head, and told him the boy was asleep, so he sat down himself, going loose, hopeless, in the chair.

What the hell does it, he said, what starts it off?

But she shrugged, and he saw she had the knitting, and watched the needles begin, easily, moving in and out.

What a night, he said. What a goddamn miserable night.

It seemed nothing and he grew restless, watching her, intent, and could say nothing, to break it. Getting up again, he asked her if she were tired, and so she put down the knitting, to follow him, blowing out the candles beside her, while he took the other from the table to carry up with them. But there was light enough, from outside, and so he blew it out, to leave it again on the table.

Upstairs, he felt the room deeper, or open, the light making a wideness, and breaking against the sides, pushing, to make a space. He could not know that she saw it, but hoped, and undressing, quietly laid his clothes on the chair, and got into bed. He looked back to see she had finished, and then felt her slide in against him, to sink back, on the bed, then turn.

A place, she said, but didn't, and put her hands on him, again gently, and he put his arms around her, still hoping. The room was very light, and the whiteness now altogether actual, seeming even a drift, of some wave, in, to make the room a space, or an intention, or where one might come to live.

Waiting, he went back against the pillow, easily, but somewhere he heard the scream, behind him, and asked if she would want him to go, quietly, and being more, he thought, that I can do something, perhaps, which she might wish me to. But she got up, and went into the other bedroom, opening the door then, so that he heard the sounds very close

31

to him, a pain there, and continuing. Quiet again, she came back, but again it started, the boy calling, and she went back.

All right, he called, asking, and she answered, soon, and he lay back, tired, and a little lost. The moon seemed to sink, a crest reached and lost, and fell down the side of the sky. He watched it, catching the edge against the window, to try to hold it, but felt it pass.

She came in, standing at the door, and waited to see if the boy would now sleep, but he didn't, calling to her, and she went back.

What's the matter, he said, but she didn't hear. What's the matter, and she answered, again, soon, and he fell back again, to wait there, the night going deep, and on, he said, it must be late.

Then she got into the bed, and lay down, coming to him, then, but nothing, he thought, and heard it, the cry, and got up himself, to run to the door, pulling at it, and yelled, what, seeing the boy sitting straight in the bed, staring, and crying, screaming, the sound driving in on him as he came.

What, he yelled, what, what, what, and got hold of the boy, by one arm, dragging him clear of the blanket, then bringing his own hand back, hard, to slap him, the head jerking back, and down. But useless, the screaming now louder, and he felt it useless, picking the boy up, to cradle him, holding him, and walking beside the bed's length, the moon still against them, a light, a light, he said, and went back to the other room to find her waiting with a candle.

ROBERT CREELEY

A Song

I had wanted a quiet testament
and I had wanted, among other things,
a song.

       That was to be
of a like monotony.

          (A grace

Simply. Very very quiet.
              A murmur of some lost
thrush, though I have never seen one.

Which was you then. Sitting
and so, at peace, so very much, now, this same quiet.

A song.

And of you, the sign now, surely, of a gross
perpetuity
          (which is not reluctant, or if it is,
it is no longer important.

A song.

Which one sings, if he sings it,
with care.

WALLACE STEVENS

Long and Sluggish Lines

It makes so little difference, at so much more
Than seventy, where one looks, one has been there before.

Wood-smoke rises through trees, is caught in an upper flow
Of air and whirled away. But it has been often so.

The trees have a look as if they bore sad names
And kept saying over and over one same, same thing.

In a kind of uproar, because an opposite, a contradiction,
Has enraged them and made them want to talk it down.

What opposite? Could it be that yellow patch, the side
Of a house, that makes one think the house is laughing;

Or these -escent,-issant pre-personae: first fly,
A comic infanta among the tragic drapings.

Babyishness of forsythia, a snatch of belief,
The spook and makings of the nude magnolia?

... Wanderer, this is the pre-history of February.
The life of the poem in the mind has not yet begun.

You were not born yet when the trees were crystal
Nor are you now, in this wakefulness inside a sleep.

WILLIAM CARLOS WILLIAMS

The Desert Music

—the dance begins: to end about a form
propped motionless—on the bridge
between Juarez and El Paso—unrecognizable

in the semi-dark

     Wait!

The others waited while you inspected it,
on the very walk itself .

    Is it alive?

       —neither a head,
legs nor arms!

   It isn't a sack of rags someone
has abandoned here . torpid against
the flange of the supporting girder . ?

     an inhuman shapelessness,
knees hugged tight up into the belly

   Egg-shaped!

     What a place to sleep!
on the International Boundary. Where else,
interjurisdictional, not to be disturbed?

How shall we get said what must be said?

Only the poem.

Only the counted poem, to an exact measure:
to imitate, not to copy nature, not
to copy nature

NOT, prostrate, to copy nature
                         but a dance! to dance
two and two with him—
                    sequestered there asleep,
                              right end up!

          A music
supersedes his composure, hallooing to us
across a great distance

                    wakens the dance
who blows upon his benumbed fingers!

                    Only the poem
only the made poem, to get said what must
be said, not to copy nature, sticks
in our throats

The law? The law gives us nothing
but a corpse, wrapped in a dirty mantle.
The law is based on murder and confinement,
long delayed.
but this, following the insensate music,
is based on the dance:

                    an agony of self realization
bound into a whole
by that which surrounds us

               I cannot escape

I cannot vomit it up

Only the poem!

Only the made poem, the verb calls it
                    into being.

               —it looks too small for a man.
A woman. Or a very shrivelled old man.
Maybe dead. They probably inspect the place
and will cart it away later

                    Heave it into the river.
A good thing.

Leaving California to return east, the fertile desert,
                    (were it to get water)
surrounded us, a music of survival, subdued, distant, half
                    heard; we were engulfed
by it as in the early evening, seeing the wind lift
                    and drive the sand, we
passed Yuma. All night long, heading for El Paso to
                    meet our friend,
we slept fitfully. Thinking of Paris, I waked to the tick
                    of the rails.   The
jagged desert

                    —to tell
what subsequently I saw and what heard

                    —to place myself (in
my nature) beside nature
                    —to imitate
nature (for to copy nature would be a
          shameful thing)
                    I lay myself down:

The Old Market's a good place to begin:
Let's cut through here—
                         techilla's only
a nickel a slug in these side streets.
Keep out though. Oh, it's all right at
this time of day but I saw H. terribly
beaten up in one of those joints. He
asked for it. I thought he was going to
be killed. I do
my drinking on the main drag

                    That's the bull-ring

Oh, said Floss, after she got used to the
change of light
                    What color! Isn't it
wonderful!
     —paper flowers (para los santos)

baked red-clay utensils, daubed
with blue, silverware,
dried peppers, onions, print goods, children's
clothing   .   the place deserted all but
for a few Indians squatted in the
booths, unnoticing (don't you think it)
as though they slept there   .

There's a second tier. Do you
want to go up?

What makes Texans so tall?
We saw a woman this morning in a mink cape
six feet if she was an inch. What a woman!

Probably a Broadway figure.

—tell you what else we saw: about a million
sparrows screaming their heads off
in the trees of that small park where
the buses stop, sanctuary,
I suppose,
from the wind driving the sand in that way
about the city   .

Texas rain they call it

—and those two alligators in the fountain

There were four

I saw only two

They were looking
right at you all the time   .

Penny please! Give me penny please, Mister,

Don't give them anything.

.   instinctively
one has already drawn one's naked
wrist away from those obscene fingers

as in the mind a vague apprehension speaks
and the music rouses

                              Let's get in here.
                    a music! cut off as
the bar door closes behind us.

                    We've got
another half hour.

                         —returned to the street,
the pressure moves from booth to booth along
the curb. Opposite, no less insistent
the better stores are wide open. Come in
and look around. You don't have to buy: hats,
riding boots, blankets

                    Look at the way,
slung from her neck with a shawl, that young
Indian woman carries her baby!
                         —a stream of Spanish,
as she brushes by, intense, wide-
eyed in eager talk with her boy husband

—three half-grown girls, one of them eating a
pomegranate. Laughing.
                         and the serious tourist,
man and wife, middle aged, middle western,
their arms loaded with loot, whispering
together—still looking for bargains

                              and the aniline
red and green candy at the little booth
tended by the old Indian woman.
              Do you suppose anyone actually
buys—and eats the stuff?

My feet are beginning to ache me.

                         We still got a few minutes.
Let's try here. They had the mayor
up last month for taking $3000 a week from
the whore houses of the city. Not much left
for the girls. There's a show on.

39

Only a few tables
occupied. A conventional orchestra — This
place livens up late — playing the usual local
jing-a-jing — — a boy and girl team, she
                    confidential with someone
off stage. Laughing: just finishing the act.

So we drink until the next turn — a strip tease.

Do you mean it? Wow! Look at her.

                    You'd have to be
pretty drunk to get any kick out of that.
She's no Mexican. Some worn out trouper from
the States. Look at those breasts

        There is a fascination
        seeing her shake
        the beaded sequins from
        a string about her hips

        She gyrates but it's
        not what you think,
        one does not laugh
        to watch her belly.

        One is moved but not
        at the dull show. The
        guitarist yawns. She
        cannot even sing. She

        has about her painted
        hardihood a screen
        of pretty doves which
        flutter their wings.

        Her cold eyes perfunct-
        orily moan but do not
        smile. Yet they bill
        and coo by grace of
        a certain candor. She

is heavy on her feet.
That's good. She
bends forward leaning
on the table of the
balding man sitting
upright, alone, as that
everything hangs forward.
   What the hell

are you grinning
to yourself about? Not
at *her*?
   The music!
I like her. She fits

the music   .

Why don't these Indians get over this nauseating prattle about
their souls and their loves and sing us something else for a
change?

This place is rank
with it. She
at least knows she's
part of another tune,

knows her customers,
has the same·
opinion of them as I
have. That gives her
one up   .   one up
following the lying
music   .

There is another music. The bright colored candy
of her nakedness lifts her unexpectedly
to partake of its tune   .

                    Andromeda of those rocks,
the virgin of her mind   .   those unearthly
greens and reds

41

                                in her mockery of virtue
she becomes unaccountably virtuous   .
                        though she in no
way pretends it   .

Let's get out of this.

                        In the street it hit
me in the face as we started to walk again. Or
am I merely playing the poet? Do I merely invent
it out of whole cloth? I thought   .

                What in the form of an old whore in
                a cheap Mexican joint in Juarez, her bare
                can waggling crazily can be
                so refreshing to me, raise to my ear
                so sweet a tune, built of such slime?

                Here we are. They'll be along any minute.
                The bar is at the right of the entrance,
                a few tables opposite which you have to pass
                to get to the dining room, beyond.

                A foursome, two oversize Americans, no
                longer young, got up as cow-boys,
                hats and all, are drunk and carrying on
                with their gals, drunk also,

                especially one inciting her man, the
                biggest, *Yip ee!* to dance in
                the narrow space, oblivious to everything
                —she is insatiable and he is trying

                stumblingly to keep up with her.
                Give it the gun, pardner! *Yip ee!* We
                pushed by them to our table, seven
                of us. Seated about the room

                were quiet family groups, some with
                children, eating. Rather a better
                class than you notice
                on the streets. So here we are. You

can see through into the kitchen
where one of the cooks, his shirt sleeves
rolled up, an apron over
the well pressed pants of a street

suit, black hair neatly parted,
a tall
good looking man, is working,
absorbed, before a chopping block

Old fashioneds all around?
                    So this is William
Carlos Williams, the poet

        Floss and I had half consumed
our quartered hearts of lettuce before
we noticed the others hadn't touched theirs
You seem quite normal. Can you tell me? Why
does one want to write poem?

                Because it's there to be written.

Oh, A matter of inspiration then?

                                Of necessity.

Oh. But what sets it off?

            I am that he whose brains
            are scattered
                aimlessly

                —and so,
the hour done, the quail eaten, we were on
our way back to El Paso.

                        Good night. Good
night and thank you   No. Thank you. We're
going to walk

—and so, on the naked wrist, we feel again
those insistent fingers

                              Penny please, mister.
Penny please. Give me penny.

                              Here! now go away.

—but the music, the music has reawakened
as we leave the busier parts of the street
and come again to the bridge in the semi-dark,
pay our fee and begin again to cross
seeing the lights along the mountain back of El
Paso and pause to watch the boys calling out
to us to throw more coins to them standing
in the shallow water   .   so that's
where the incentive lay, with the annoyance
of those surprising fingers.

                         So you're a poet?
a good thing to be got rid of—half drunk,
a free dinner under your belt, even though you
get typhoid—and to have met people you
can at least talk to   .

          relief from that changeless, endless
inescapable and insistent music   .

               What else, Latins, do you yourselves
seek but relief!   .
with the expressionless ding dong you dish up
to us of your souls and your loves, which
we swallow. Spaniards! (though these are mostly
Indians who chase the white bastards
through the streets on their Independence Day
and try to kill them)   .

                              What's that?

Oh, come on.

               But what's THAT?

                         the music! the
music! as when Casals struck
and held a deep cello tone across Franco's
lying chatter! and I am speechless   .

                                        There it sat
in the projecting angle of the bridge flange
as I stood aghast and looked at it—
in the half light: shapeless or rather returned
to its original shape, armless, legless,
headless, packed like the pit of a fruit into
that obscure corner—or
a fish to swim against the stream—or
a child in the womb prepared to imitate life,
warding its life against
a birth of awful promise. The music
guards it, a mucus, a film that surrounds it,
a benumbing ink that stains the
sea of our minds—to hold us off—shed
of a shape close as it can get to no shape,
a music! a protecting music
                                        I *am* a poet! I
am. I am. I am a poet, I reaffirmed, ashamed

Now the music volleys through as in
a lonely moment I hear it. Now it is all
about me. The dance! The verb detaches itself
seeking to become articulate

                And I could not help thinking
                of the wonders of the brain that
                hears that music and of our
                skill sometimes to record it.

ROBERT DUNCAN

The Second Night in the Week

Now I have come to Cesare's gate

And the Spirit there, tired and raging,
who walks like a beast walks
the circumference of his cage, said:
think upon the meaning of my rage.

By Whom do you swear
that you return to this place?

I have come to the Gate
tired, tired as Asia
and as rage-full, awake
as if there will now be no sleep,

sleep being a secret in this place.

O Alexander! O Conqueror of the Wastes.

Processional of the Dead

Torches, we light our own way,
nor, in passing, notice our burned bodies.

Look, look, I said,
the heart of the flame
has gone out, the wick!

Set youself on fire once more, you said,
the way is dark.

O dead, to you this flesh
is no more than wax.

No flame guides the blind
further than here.

Torches, we appear to ourselves
flames in the distance
that extinguish themselves
before we can reach them.

PAUL BLACKBURN

Canso
tant ai longamen cercat

Long I sought what I did not need, then
I unclenched my hand

and there, that sunlight lay on it,
                    how I do not know.
Lightly it came at my bidding, and
lightly I took as I desired.
                    But now
the granted and given and grown-in-use
                    I have lost by blundering
misused, have not gained it
              and my friends laugh.
                        Ah Senher, dear Castiat,
                        I die of this villainy!
                        for my deadly enemy can
                        wound me with beauty.

                    So damned little of graciousness, I
                                        dare not try
                        the Love of a Brother-In-Law—
                                    and on this largesse
                        she expects me to survive!

                    I am obviously in the wrong country:
                    But o my dears, I stand in hope
                                of such delicious recompense!
                    from pain of love such sweet deliverance
                    and end of guile—
                    and were it not so great a sin to despair
                    I would despair.

But perhaps I speak foolishly
with my famous excess of levity,
but may be pardoned for it,
      being so much the fool
that the whole world can see it,
      how I yield to her caprice
and venture any emprize
                        if she so will.
                        Still,
I am turned out. Discretion gets me nowhere.
                        And she,
in loosing holds me, body, heart and boldness.
She veers in coldness. I turn not elsewhere.
Joy she has in abundance: I starve from lack.
Her sharp beauty, whereon it is pain to look,
poisons my sight: I see her have her joke.

With soft seeming she snared my heart so fully
that even now I cannot comprehend it.

        Dear Christ! My love without frontier
still she finds fault!
and knowing well what she does seeks how
        to give me hurt.
        I find
not love in her, nor a loving heart,
nor any warm decision, nor tender gain.
        And I cry mercy
and mercy does not come. I cry mercy
and think to die of shame.

        Yet doubt is a major party to it here,
        far from my lady, where I sing alone.
        And until I have passed the Rhone
        down toward Lombardy
        I will not satisfy my heart
        how things stand there.

        Compassion is the tongue within your
        mouth
        and all there is of mercy is your eyes.
        Where I place my strongest hope and all my trust

        I acknowledge you my lady,
        and you, my lord,
        and send a heart full of warmth and love.

    Vierna, I walk bright in loving you,
lacking only sight of Castiat, my lord.

PEIRE VIDAL

WILLIAM BRONK

The Extensions of Space

1. The point must come when nothing matters more
than who. What has been heard too often; when
and where renew with shiny bangles stuff

gone dull. It is too late now for why.
The question is, "Who is it, is it you?"

2. When I came out of the house, the world, the sky,
were moving outward. There had been a big
explosion somewhere, not here, but far.
Somewhere another explosion countered. More.
The world goes whooshing. Focus is in and out.

3. What do we do about the tortoise? We thought
we had dispensed with that nonsense, and still
some elephant's back is wanted to hold, if not
the literal globe, our worlds, our artifacts,
our facts; and underneath, a tortoise,—ground.

4. Only, if we go down that far,
there is no ground for facts or tortoises:
finally, we come to where there is nothing there
to underprop our worlds; logic rides high,
a balloon, and under it, we pass and go.

5. These are grave things, gravities,
—worlds holding in suspension worlds,
and nothing under them. But also, look:
some persons bridge all across the farthest space
that we can conceive, and are solid there.

Aspects of the World Like Coral Reefs

In the spring woods, how good it is to see
again the trees, old company,
how they have withstood the winter, their girth.

By gradual actions, how the gross earth
gathers around us and grows real, is there,
as though it were really there, and is good.

Certain stars, of stupendous size, are said
to be such and such distances away,—
oh, farther than our eyes alone would ever see.

Thus magnified, the whole evidence
of our senses is belied. For it is not
possible for miles to add miles to miles

forever, not even if expressed as the speed of light.
The fault lies partly in the idea of miles.
It is absurd to describe the world in sensible terms.

How good that even so, aspects of the world
that are real, or seem to be real, should rise like reefs
whose rough agglomerate smashes the sea.

ROBERT CREELEY

The Innocence

Looking to the sea, it is a line
of unbroken mountains.

It is the sky.
It is the ground. There
we live, on it.

It is a mist
now tangent to another
quiet. Here the leaves
come, there
is the rock in evidence

or evidence.
What I come to do
is partial, partially kept.

CHARLES OLSON

A Discrete Gloss

The tide, the number 9 and creation
whatever sits outside you is
by what difference what
you also are: this church

or this slaughter house behind it, both
under palms alongside the mud-flats the sea leaves
in front of this three-time city

In what sense is
what happens before the eye
so very different from
what actually goes on within: this man
letting a fat whore hug him in the bus
as it goes counter to the eastering earth,
and I stare, until both of us turn away
as the bus stops and she goes behind it to piss

Your eye, the wanderer, sees more.
Or do you know what it focuses on, what happens
somewhere else: where, say, the sea
is more sea, and men
do not take Saturday Sunday off, arguing
they need to clean the gurry, a boat
takes that much drying, that much
sun

When the field of focus
is not as admitted as the point is,
what loss! Who loves
without an object, who dreams
without an incubus, who fears
without cause? Or dies
without all animalness, the disgorging
of breath blood bowels so tenderly
who can say the affections
are not the conquerors?

That what we do with what we are
is what ends all distraction.
As fiercely as the eye
is fierce. Or death
is fierce. Who cares
that they have taught us otherwise,
that they still noise it about
there are abstract things, human birds
with wings which only once
(in Giotto's hands) made
black and orange sense?

You who can seize
as the sun seizes. Who drinks
by a stem as brilliant as that stopless eater of flowers. Who acts
as swiftly as a plant turns light to green. Or this chameleon's throat
wops red red red and why
I do not know, but that he does, that you do
that you can take some human thigh bone you've picked up
and with a stone tool carve such likeness on it
as much conjecture as the man you draw
was Quetzalcoatl more a sea-horse than himself—
such as you makes gorging nature at her blackest root
a silly starer too.

The day of man returns in your precisions, kin
(ahau, katun), the force
of force where force forever is
and man forgets: what is the world
that he can separate himself so simply from it,
or their soul, that I can locate it, or your act
that you can say its cause?

Man is no creature of his own discourse:
here on this beach made by the tide which passed
and dragged away old guts (or the birds
had it before the fish fed) and he turned, I turned
away, where nine madereros left a politician cut and stoned for dead
(where she pissed), it can be seen
that these boats dry in colors only he
had an eye for. And it says, it says here
in the face of everything it says
this, is the more exact.

CHARLES OLSON

An Ode on Nativity

1

All cries rise, & the three of us
observe how fast Orion
marks midnight
at the climax
of the sky
    while the boat of the moon settles
as red in the southwest
as the orb of her was, for this boy, once,
the first time he saw her whole halloween face northeast
across the skating pond as he came down to the ice, December
his seventh year.
      Winter, in this zone,
is an off & on thing, where the air
is sometimes as shining as ice is
when the sky's lights... When the ducks
are the only skaters
      And a crèche
is a commerciality

  (The same year, a ball of fire
  the same place—exactly through
  the same trees
  was fire:
    the Sawyer lumber company yard
    was a moon of pain, at the end of itself,
    and the death of horses I saw burning,
    fallen through the floors
    into the buried Blackstone River the city
    had hidden under itself, had grown over

  At any time, & this time
  a city

jangles

        Man's splendor
is a question of which
birth

                II

The cries rise, & one of us
has not even eyes to see the night's sky
burning, or the hollows
made coves of mist & frost, the barns
covered over, and nothing in the night but two of us
following the blind highway to catch all glimpses
of the settling, rocking moon

                December, in this year
is a new thing, where I whisper
bye-low, and the pond
is full to its shores again, so full
I read the moon where grass would not reveal it
a month ago, and the ducks make noises
like my daughter does, stir
in the creche of things

                (His mother, 80, and we
                ate oysters after the burial: we had knelt
                with his sister, now Mary Josephine,
                in the prayery of the convent of the church
                where my mother & father had been married

                And she told us tales of my family
                I had not heard, how my grandfather
                rolled wild in the green grass
                on the banks of that same now underground river
                to cool himself from the steel mill's fires
                stripped down to his red underwear

                She was that gay, to have seen her daughter
                and that the two of us had had that car
                to take the Sisters downtown and drop them
                where they had to go

                        I had watched them
                swirl off in their black habits

before I started the car again
in the snow of that street, the same street
my father had taken me to, to buy my first cap

At any time, & now, again, in this new year
the place of your birth, even a city, rings

in & out of
tune

What shall be
my daughter's second
birth?

III

All things now rise, and the cries of men to be born
in ways afresh, aside from all old narratives, away
from intervals too wide to mark the grasses

(not those on which cattle feed, or single stars
which show the way to buy bad goods
in green & red lit stores, no symbols

the grasses in the ice, or Orion's sweep, or
the closeness of turning snows, these
can tell the tale of any one of us stormed or quieted
by our own things, what belong, tenaciously,
to our own selves

Any season, in this fresh time
is off & on to that degree that any of us miss
the vision, lose the instant and decision, the close
which can be nothing more and no thing else
than that which unborn form you are the content of, which you
alone can make to shine, throw that like light
even where the mud was and now there is a surface
ducks, at least, can walk on. And I
have company
in the night

In this year, in this time
when spirits do not walk abroad, when men alone walk

when to walk is so difficult

when the divine tempter also walks
renewing his offer—that choice

                      (to turn
from the gross fire, to hide
as that boy almost did, to bury himself
from the fearful face—twice!—that winter

to roll like a dog or his grandfather
in the snowbank on the edge of the pond's ice

to find comfort somewhere, to avoid
the burning—To go to grass
as his daughter now suckles. Some way! he cries out
not to see those horses' agonies:

         Is light, is there any light, any
         to pay the price of
         fire?

     IV

The question stays
in the city out of tune, the skies
not seen, now, again, in
a bare winter time:

        is there any birth
any other splendor than
the brilliance of the going on, the loneliness
whence all our cries arise?

LARRY EIGNER

Act

On September 20th, as I was sitting out front, they brought a cow to feed in the field opposite me. It was the first time a cow had ever been so close to home, though of course I had been as close to them or even closer on tours of farms and wasn't afraid in any case, and when they installed her they left her alone. I was taking the whole thing as a pleasant surprise because if you live long enough, and something happens for the first time in a long while, at any rate if it happens suddenly, then you are well satisfied and give yourself up to it, doing anything at all, even though you may have had quite enough of it as a child. Though I have very vivid memories of horses since for instance one used to power the milktrucks on our route, if it had been a horse I suppose I would have been glad to see it again. I heard the cow moo while it was still out of sight, as I was sitting on the far side of the piazza, but thinking I might as well I moved over by the windows and looking through the sunroom I got glimpses of the animal between the upper parts of trees, and the lower ones, coming down the road, men leading the rather downsnouted head and then sometimes the tail, or really, the hindquarters.

They must have been bringing it down from the big house opposite the head of the street, enterprise, really, establishment, with the big built-up rock garden in front and around the right-hand corner and in back to the left half-broken-down stables where they keep the town's remaining draft-animals by some arrangement, and plows, plough-horses for hire, I don't know whether one or two or more, along with some riding horse or other which I see being ridden maybe twice in a period of five years. For all I know, this was the first time they had a cow there, and there hasn't been one since then, but it must have been from there. All sorts of undertakings seem to go on from there, although actually, I suppose, there are just as many, even more, things going on at one of the many filling station garages, and though I've never really seen any signs of life there, at least in the parts of the stables behind the doorway, and have often wondered about this. But to this area, or parts of it, there is hardly a roof, and I don't know but that the building might extend all across the back of the house to the hedges on the other side. And there was for example a sleigh, the only one I have actually ever seen, which each day used to come out around six p.m. to give the children who used to coast there a ride, as I thought, anyway, just when it was time to go home and have supper in my family; and I can't tell just how many times I saw it, how many winters, before it didn't seem to be there any more—and I can't be sure it isn't there now. Why they should be keeping a cow there I didn't know, but, after all, I can use my imagination to some extent, always, and Mr. Bursett, the knowing old head of the household, might deal in cattle on occasion, in addition to the other things.

It was Sunday. Even so (and the neighborhood had very recently filled up so that the three lots opposite me were now the only ones left to grow wild most of the time), there do not seem to have been many cars, and this is understandable, as even in the afternoon, when people are not only home but visiting, the cars aren't particularly noticeable by themselves—Sunday, any holiday, still seems rather a day of rest here, because it's a tradition, even the Fourth of July, Independence Day, feels that way, and always did in the days of private and sporadic firecracker bursts. There were two men in charge of the beast, which was quiet enough, and they came not too slowly down the quiet road, with only the slight but distinctly present sound of the lining trees, and their motions. She mooed again just a little while before they made the turn to enter the field, and I could see the definite wiseacre wrinkles that appeared around the mouth and nostrils to the eyes, momentarily and in few; in that skin which appears as an ancient heritage even in calves. They were far from entering spectacularly in front of my steps, about the midpoint, but went in calmly, while it did take two men, at the left corner, which was nearest to them and the shortest way possible. Just as they did with horses when they had plowed the land a few times in Spring and as they would do, with any animal.

And after untying her rope halter they left her alone to graze. If they had been plowing, of course, both of them would have stayed with the horse, one to dig in and hold the plow down into the furrow, and one to steer the horse, by its head, and to keep it going. There was more variety and interest then, as they rested a few times, while one would go for a bottle of pop to the corner store, for instance. And I knew them from way back, in the streets, and managed sometimes to shout a few words to them, and wondered somewhat what else to say, or whether they were perfectly all right without me. But this time the cow was left alone to its own devices in its own natural element. There was no tether or fence, but she was waist-deep in her feed and that would have held her down, in any case. She had a lot of eating to do, and I suppose they knew about when to come back for her, without calculating much, either. You don't, of course, have to make an animal wildly hungry in order to eat at proper times. That is one possible paradox that man has been able to avoid.

This was a chance to have my longest "visit" with cows, and I did have quite enough of her. Although she was a good deal hidden in the growth. I could see a few of her distinctive movements as she went about her main business, mostly ruminating. She didn't raise her head any, as if to some distance or to look at the sky, hardly at all, but kept it at about its natural, apparently most enjoyable level, slightly nodding up and down; tail flicking a few times perhaps, while when she went to lean down and take a bite she moved her legs very slightly, especially the forelegs, taking very short steps, automatic, as if closing in on something quite directly, and with a little careless fling that lets a member go partly by its own weight. And I had read a paragraph or so about "mammals" with two stomachs, after many years of vaguely accepting the phrase "chewing the cud," and would have been glad to see any sign of where these bellies were, exactly, or what contours did they give, and so on—what went on. A camel with two humps is really something to watch, I'd say, while connecting-rods on the wheels of a locomotive pulling into a station are both more perplexing and varied. But in any event, anyway, I didn't want to look at a cow all day, and as I usually have in mind a number of things to do, after a while I went back to my reading.

The date may have been April or May rather than September, I don't know. Lately Spring and Fall have become associated with each other, not so much as they used to be, once, by reason of similar temperate weather or as being intermediate seasons, but because when Spring comes I think that fairly soon it will be Autumn and in great part it might well be, since they are greatly alike. I don't notice Spring any more until I am rather deeply into it, I don't sit around and wait for it to come or its later stages to develop, and I don't concern myself at all how I should make use of my summer or take advantage of it, make hay of it, as the saying goes. And so there is nevertheless some little sadness in Spring as in Fall, with all its other points, which is something, and when winter arrives I stay inside mostly and go on from there. While I don't mind the "distractions" of balmy weather, and am in fact glad of them, if the truth were known, there is still more to do inside, and more at hand.

After some pages, after a while when I looked up I found the cow facing right at me and however it was standing there motionless each time her jaws stopped working, for the few seconds before ducking in for another mouthful. I hadn't thought before about such things as what the eye-range of animals might be, whether an animal for instance can see the horizon, as a man does, whatever height he is at, or not. I don't sup-

59

pose she was looking at me, though maybe cattle do when you are close enough, as dogs do, or as deer have done, the deer from a good distance off; she might have been looking at me at that, perhaps in some such way as I was regarding her, though again I have no way of knowing how close you have to get to this species for them to see you; but cows usually seem vacant, and this one was no exception. While in a general way perhaps it does depend on size, for all I know alertness may be even more important, a cat up in a tree might be able to see farther than a bovine in a tree or on a bluff, and I would say by looking at one that a horse, which is not too much bigger, can outsee a bull.

At the same time I did imagine this cow of mine under the circumstances had about as great a field of vision as I had myself; that is, she could see as much building, houses, mine and the man's next door, as well as the road and my driveway, as I could see the pasture. I thought that although she didn't have binocular vision, so that depth didn't appear to her very well, especially when there was no light-and-shade, her field was as wide as mine, and was just as cycloramic. And while if I waved at her with my handkerchief or anything nothing would happen, no interpretation would take place, that I could see, just the same, she must have her eyes for something. And, anyway, there was her hearing, by which she could perhaps hear things I could not, of higher or lower, slower pitch, say. If I mooed at her, or squeaked, or something, that might do something, though I wouldn't do that, I wasn't in the mood or whatever.

For some reason she was still headed this way for a good while afterwards, there were still plenty of weeds and wild plants flowering in all directions, and I looked up fairly often to see her still facing me. The head is more interesting than the tail anyway. But finally I got a little restless and I turned the wheelchair around to back up a bit and view the scenery as in the window-panes, and to have it on my right, and the storm-door which had either not had the glass panels removed yet or had had them put back in place of the screen sections just the day before. The screens were on the windows and sort of roughed everything over, slightly doubling images and thus giving them a distinct haziness. My own face, which is of course the nearest and biggest thing in a mirror, is not so much ugly as hesitant and uncertain, and it is for instance very strange, amusing or disconcerting sometimes, to see the distortions performed on heads, especially faces, by a flaw, of which there are a couple in one of our living-room windows, as people pass by it, perhaps even at the other end of the room. But my face has been becoming of late a very familiar thing and usually now I finish with it automatically, about the instant I see it; while at times, quite inconsistently, I have bucked myself up by facing it.

Other things in the window, at least when the screen is on it, are turned around, blended with a sort of honeycomb as if sound waves were to become visible, which move sort of reverberatingly as you move your head, softly but you think like buzzing flies—and a little romanticized, in places astonishingly vivid and good, because changed. The cow was there, in the field, her brown self, but more slenderly and keenly bulging, the fore-shoulders, as she stood there nevertheless squarely. It made me think of watercolors, animals airily planted with their feet firmly wide, almost but not quite cartoons, which I must have seen somewhere at some time. But that was not exactly this cow and she kept about her business and did not become too finely grained.

Then I must have become interested again in the matter I was reading about. Words followed words and while sometimes I find light or heavy reading dull, a good part of the time I read out of curiosity, simply to find out what can be said, and there are also times when I'm off, and really begin to construct, trying to take everything from the beginning into account, whether the author's thinking or something different I can't exactly say, half-imagining I am really getting a deep grasp for the moment. And whatever it was, if I stopped to try, quite likely it would take a little less time to reconstruct what I did then than was consumed in doing it in those particular surroundings. But I am never lost to the world and have never been able to get very oblivious. It seems that a hair can turn me and indeed it seems a mystery, and wonderful, too, that I am not turned more often. I don't know how long it was, but pretty soon four or five small boys came down the street, all in their Sunday clothes, of course, home from their various churches, and I think it may have been rather late for them to be on their way home at that, and the sermons may have been unusually longish that day, it may have been one of the days when pulpits were exchanged this year. I don't remember as to that, because some things are done quite irregularly in this town, and anyhow, I suppose, I don't read the newspaper much, by our standards, just looking at the front page occasionally, very seldom going into the struggle with the inside sheets.

Small boys seem very well behaved nowadays, in this district, though it might be just because I don't see them all day and because I am grown up now. I sometimes wonder if playing hookey is still a legend current with children, as it was with me, or not. And on the other hand there do seem to be a couple of blooming toughs that I know of and so maybe more, even, lately moved into the side-street two lots down from me, which stretches way out back of me, recently built up with sunny and not-too-low-lying cottages. I heard the boys exclaiming a bit at the cow's being there in that field, right around the corner from them, and when I finally looked around they had just about gone past the cow-lots and were turning to their street, but then one of the boys halted completely for a while and the others were standing around. In another minute all of them went back, and produced a couple of balls from their pockets or somewhere. Some of them got into the field, where they were almost lost in the grass and weedstalks, and, shouting to think of it, began playing catch; and it so developed that almost immediately they began following the cow and tossing balls over her head. The cow did stay in one place, of course, practically, but once or twice she moved to a side and they kept tabs on her more and more closely. She would roll up her eyeballs and gaze at the thing very blankly as it sailed over, at not too great a height, then move the head a bit and face in the direction of one of the players. In a few minutes she was beginning to quicken up in this process, but the boys suddenly varied their ideas and generally started moving around in a circle, with the cow in the vicinity of the center.

It was a miniature baseball or something of the sort they were using, which could be caught with the bare hands, though. They kept this up until finally, of course, the ball hit the cow on the flank, and dropped to the ground. They reasoned that they could come back later and find it, however (for it would still be there if the cow hadn't grabbed it), and continued the game with the one remaining ball, going at it cautiously, though, and moving away from the cow, without any big ideas.

But after a while I saw one of them who was just standing at the moment doing nothing pick up a stone and throw it at the cow. It hit on the right hind leg just on the upper part where it begins to widen into the hip. The animal gave a jerk and turned around all in one heap, as it were, more quickly than I knew a cow could. But after taking a step and tilting her head in a clumsy sort of cock and staying that way, her foreleg lifted, she went to graze again. The boy had dropped out of sight in the grass. At the next opportunity he was up again and with a more purposeful but still pleasant face aimed for the buttocks and sprang forwards and sideways. And this time—the boy, with his back to me, watching with interest, I thought—the cow, mooing constantly, made for the nearest exit. At an unaccountable sort of gallop. It dashed behind the garage that is there fronting the road which is a block north from here, and went down the driveway, mooing, and up that street, of which I can't see much, but I got glimpses of it for a few seconds while it was still not too far up. Strangely enough the boys were not very fast in reacting. They sort of kept up with their game until the commotion at the end of the next street attracted them gradually, and impulsively they made up their minds to run around and see what was up.

I don't know what sort of damage there was, exactly, but whatever serious damage was caused it was freakish and not violently done. Very surprisingly they brought the cow down a couple of times more, this time, of course, standing guard over her. Though that may not be the sort of thing that happens more than once, I feel.

ROBERT CREELEY

The Crow

The crow in the cage in the dining-room
hates me because I will not feed him.

And I have left nothing behind in leaving
because I killed him.

And because I hit him over the head with a stick
there is nothing I laugh at.

Sickness is the hatred of a repentance
knowing there is nothing he wants.

DENISE LEVERTOV

Beyond the End

In "nature" there's no choice —
                    flowers
swing their heads in the wind, sun & moon
    are as they are. But we seem
almost to have it (not just
    available death)

It's energy: a spider's thread: not to
"go on living" but to quicken, to activate: extend:
    Some have it, they force it —
with work or laughter or even
    the act of buying, if that's
all they can lay hands on —

        the girls crowding the stores, where light,
        colour, solid dreams are — what gay

desire! It's their festival,
        ring game, wassail, mystery.

It has no grace like that of
the grass, the humble rhythms, the
falling & rising of leaf and star

it's barely
a constant. Like salt:
take it or leave it

The "hewers of wood" & so on; every damn
craftsman has it while he's working
        but it's not
a question of work: some
shine with it, in repose. Maybe it is
response, the will to respond—("reason
can give nothing at all/like
the response to desire") maybe
a gritting of the teeth, to go
just that much further, beyond the end,
beyond whatever ends: to begin, to be, to defy.

Kresch's Studio

Easels: a high & bare room:
some with charcoal, one with a brush,
some with loud pens in the silence,
at work. The woman
in taut repose, intent:

under violent light that pulls
the weight of breasts to answer the long
shadow of thighs,
confronts angles with receding
planes, makes play with elements.

That they work, that she will not move too soon,
opposes (as Bartok's plucked strings oppose)
the grinding, grinding, grinding of lives,
pounding constant traffic.

On paper, on canvas, stroke, stroke : a counterpoint :
an energy opposing
the squandered energy.

WILLIAM BRONK

A Vase of Various Flowers

You might say, right from the start, the sadness is what
we are after,—the flowers fading and withering soon.
At any rate, those kinds that last too long
hold freshness for themselves but not our eyes.

How many kinds of pleasure though there are
in just these yellow roses, open pink
single asters, michelmas daisies, calendulas,
verbenas : it *is* sad that they go.

Across the room from these, on another wall,
the picture of city buildings on a dark street
is not untouched by change, although it lifts
continually in the same and solider shapes.

Lovely and frail the flowers are; it is not
sadness we are after, but rather the prodigal's
ravenous spending, the cruel throwing away,
as though toward a lasting form,—as this picture, say.

The Bach Trombones at Bethlehem, Pennsylvania

They have the flamboyance of tulips or other big
blossoms,—lilacs maybe, whose massiveness,
observed close by, breaks up in complex
fretworks of joy, compounded, proud,
beautiful in its abundance, filling the air.

So, in this brassy music, massive joy
downed no more than the flowers by the sinking times,
the terrible world where hollow catastrophe
hangs wherever. The shouting brass shouts
"but nevertheless," the nevertheless of joy.

The nevertheless, the yet. The truth is all
the numbers to be added but not, in the end, their sum.
How almost like the beasts, with only barks
and cries we are, so tangent is any speech
to all we know. What opposites are true!

Her Singing

What in her singing made us hear her
was less that flowing motion singing shares
with all the graceful ways of flying birds
and more a stillness, more a hover of flight.
As trees draw outward from the rooted ground
from trunk to branch to twig to stem and leaves,
her song was as she might have drawn upon
the air a tree, and it stood still.

Her last notes turned again to meet the first,
enclosing space whose entry hearing held
since her first notes began. Whatever her words
whatever that was she sang, speaking of change,
the flight of time, of our mortality,
the flowing turmoil space in which we move,
she said the moment shaped was more than these.
Her singing took the flight and held it still.

THEODORE ENSLIN

Pasturage

One morning and another
gone!
        The upland pasture
lonely in dark cedar
or the day, for life enough is
settled there.
            The high places
can command the wake
of voyages.
        A cedar
knows where all the mornings are!

In the Rain

No, nothing happened. Pace too slow for that.
Day turned east for light.
We walked three miles to feel the rain
come through our clothes, and on the way
we talked through dense audiences
of last year's leaves.
            It was not an argument —
no sensitive importance — and nothing new.
Nothing happened: But our skins were wet.
Smooth as birch bark in the rain.

IRVING LAYTON

The Madonna of the Magnificat
for Marian Scott

I shall wander all night and not see
    as much happiness as this infant gives
to his plain sisters who are adoring him
and his mother cradling and covering
    him with her love.

She has borrowed the white moon from the sky
    to pillow his golden curls
and at her magical cry the dark roofs
the length of the street lie down
    like quiet animals.

The night will wear out and disappear
    like soiled water through the city's drains
but now it is full of noise and blessed neighbours
and all the tenement windows fly open
    like birds.

Metzinger: Girl with a Bird

Your eyes, heavy-lidded,
half-closed, make of sadness
itself a caprice, or seem to.
I have the feeling, miss,
you dream too much
of flight—on winter evenings!
Yet the mist
of those nerveless evenings
lives in your clouded eyes.

Your face
tilts towards the gay edifice
through whose casements
birds might go in and out;

and your elbow is,
to be sure,
a gesture that makes known
your will—yet hardly more;
the flexures of your breast and skirt
turn like an appetite also there.

Too small
for a swan, a raping Zeus;
the still bird, symbol
of decession and freedom,
that you fold between your full
breasts
pins you by a paradox
against the air.
There is no happiness here:

only the desire
of the impotent, the weak
who, if they wish to speak,
must first grow indignant.
It taxes my brain,
miss, to guess at the monster
or tyrant
who inhabits the shuttered building
the lines of your head and breasts
move away from with such disdain.

GAEL TURNBULL

An Irish Monk, on Lindisfarne About 650 A.D.

A hesitation of the tide
betrays this island, daily.

On Iona, at dusk
(ago, how long ago?)
often (did it happen?)
I saw the Lord walking
in the surf amidst the gulls,
calling, "Come. Have joy in Me."

Yes, with these eyes.

Now, on strange rocks
(faintly through the wall)
echoing, the same sea roars.

Detail is my toil.
In chapel, verse by verse—
in the kitchen, loaf by loaf—
with my pen, word by word—

by imitation,
illumination.

The patience of the bricklayer
is assumed in the dream of the architect.

*

On the road coming, five days travel, a Pict woman
   (big mouth and small bones) gave me shelter, and
   laughed (part scorn, part pity) at my journey.
   "What do you hope for, even if you get there, that
   you couldn't have had twice over in Ireland?"

Then I told her of the darkness amongst the barbarians,
   and of the great light in the monasteries at home,
   and she replied, "Will they thank you for that, you
   so young and naive, and why should you go, you out
   of so many?"

I said that I heard a voice calling, and she said,
   "So men dream, are unsatisfied, wear their legs out
   with walking, and you scarcely a boy out of school."

So she laughed; and I leaned my head on my hands, feeling
   the thickness of dust in each palm.

Then she told me there was not another of her race left
   in that valley, not one, nothing left. "And all in
   three generations. Once even Rome feared us. Now
   my children are mongrels. And my husband has left
   me. No matter. Or great matter. I am still a Pict."

Then she fed me, put herbs on my feet, wished me well,
   and I blessed her but she said, "Save that for
   yourself; you will need it, when your heart turns
   rancid, and your joints begin to stiffen on the
   foreign roads. Remember me, when you come, returning."

So she mocked; and sometimes, even now, ten years later,
   I hear it as I waken (receding in a dream), that
   laughter, broad, without malice.

*

Returning,
in the mind, still there,
home:
—devout green hills
—intimate peat smoke
—a cow-bell beseeching
—warm fleece in my bed
—fresh water, fresh, a brook

Here:
—rain clouds like beggars' rags
—stench of burned weed
—fret of the chain-mail sea
—hard knees on cold stone
—dry saliva, salt fish

The gulls cry:
—believe
—achieve

The bells reply:
—some
—some

At the lowest ebb
you can leave dryshod
this fitful island.

CID CORMAN

A Note on Dylan Thomas

It would not be unkind if, instead of the blatant haloings of his overamorous admirers, the equally blatant blackwashing ot so-called scrutinizers, and those one or two, like Kenneth Rexroth, who will use the man's death as lever for an attack on bourgeois society, some straight words are spoken.

Thomas often said more than he meant, but he always meant to be candid. And I can see no reason to treat him with less honesty than was his own intent. The first time I saw him and heard him read was at Harvard in March of 1950. He had been drinking, although I don't know what else any sensitive man could be expected to do, not being an academic personage, to persist in such a milieu. No other escape was permissible. His face impressed me most, though he was bulkier and less angelic than the Augustus John frontispiece led me to believe. He was under tension undoubtedly. His lips were full as his face was round, fore and aft. A certain grossness. And that was good to see in such a place. His eyes, which slanted sadly at the edges ("as though he were crying," I noted later that day), were piercing and open. He was rude to Jack Sweeney, who introduced him, but he had to say something to break into speech and that helped.

He read well. With deliberateness and practiced resonance. And sincerely, with relish for what he chose to read. The accent was not, surprisingly, Welsh so much as it was English. And he would find himself tracing the rhythms and inflections with his right hand.

When he was loudly applauded at the end, he seemed genuinely astonished, perhaps because he had forgotten they were there.

I heard him again later that spring at Brandeis (he was still being floated about the country, increasing his audience, but, I suspect, earning very little, since he always gave as many public readings as private). He was this time even more intoxicated; and I heard later that he had drunk at every bar between Boston and Waltham. He had no desire to "perform," but he was pushed onto the stage (and later directed off). I don't tell this as though I were telling some clever gossip, since, in fact, this is not news at all. But I tell it to indicate Thomas' evidently unhappy state of mind and the fact that human sympathy does not actively go very deep in such situations. I noted briefly of him then: "He has the overwhelmed look of an unnecessarily hurt child."

He was, I think that perpetual child with an ear for ditties and as though completely victimized by that moment when childhood fatefully recognizes, if it refuses to realize, that the cradle will not hold age back.

Credit for his lovely childhood expressions, of and for the life of the child, remains a critical affirmation. That was and is his kingdom.

But he could bite and bark. And at Brandeis he came up with, as nearly as I can set it down, one of several prefaces, used on the occasions of his readings. It went like this:

"A writer who stands in front of a strange audience (I don't mean you're strange, you're strangers to me) and who is willing, prepared, and even eager, please God, to read his poems, has become very nearly a man of letters. I used to think that once a writer became a man of letters if only for half an hour, he was done for; and here I am nearly a man of letters myself by this time.

"I've been all over this country, let me say that, and I feel perfectly all right. I think I must be suffering from one of the first delectable injections of insidious corruption. And being here really does suggest that I am responsible and established, that all the old doubts and worries are over, that now I need bother my head about nothing: except birth, death, sex, politics, and religion; that, shawled and wigged, sober as a judge and aloof as a bloodhound, I can summon my juvenile literary delinquents in front of me and give them a long periodic sentence. And it does invite me too to indulge in a hundred tongue-picked, chopped and chiselled, evocative shock phrases in a flamboyant rememoration of past and almost entirely fictitious peccadilloes of interest to nobody but me and my guardian angel, an unsuccessful psychiatrist in this life, who is even now lolloping above me, casebook in claw, a little seedy and down at winged heel, in the guttural consulting rooms of space.

"I'm the kind of human dredger that rakes up the wordy past of his own dead sea. Question me about my origins and I purr like a cat full of tea on the hearth. I am the kind of pig that roots for unconsidered truffles in the reeky wood of his past. But, luckily for everyone, this isn't a lecture but only a reading of poems, with sometimes a very few brief comments in between whenever they may not be necessary. There must be enough theorizing around here about poetry to last everyone his lifetime. I couldn't give a proper, I might just be able to give an improper, lecture about poetry anyway, I'll read only the poems that I like. This means, of course, that I have to read a lot of poems I don't like before I find the ones I do, but when I find the ones I do, there they are, and all I can do is to read them aloud to myself or anyone voluntarily cornered here, as you are tonight.

"I'm going to read some poems by Yeats, Hardy, Auden, and a few other British poets; then, from these, all chosen because they are direct and clear, gradually I'm going to descend into my own, and even my mother couldn't say that my poems were direct and clear. Why I should say 'even my mother' I don't know. I should say 'especially my mother.'

"I hope no one here's going to ask any questions afterwards. I don't mind answering a bit, only I can't. Even to such very simple questions, such as 'What is the relationship or the impact of a modern poet to society in this prehydrogenous age?' I can't do anything, but blush a little and stammer; only nobody would notice I was blushing. (I've just come from Florida, where I was told not to drink out of certain little water fountains, because they were for white people only. I don't know: there should be a special one for me, for purple people.) I'd like to be able to answer anybody's question fluently, but always as soon as I try to start, as soon as gauchely and inarticulately I bog, bury, and bitch myself in a sentence which can never, I know, come to an end, such as the sentence I am now bogged in, I find myself thinking of certain other subjects, all almost as interesting as the subject supposedly under discussion. You know the sort of subject that comes into one's head when one's asked these odd questions, subjects such as: 'Rilke and the Gold Standard,' or 'Charles Morgan, My Favourite Character in Fiction,' or even the very awful thing that occurs to one occasionally, 'If a Hermaphrodite Were a Schizophrene, Which Half Would You Take?' or even such esoteric subjects as 'The Influence of W. C. Fields on Virginia Woolf.' Perhaps I'd better read a poem. I can go on talking like this all the time: that's what I do..."

LARRY EIGNER
Environ s

Many shapes of wings
on the sky and the table;
and large men carefully at dusk
lengthened by lights   watering their lawns

turn, paterfamilias

   and the sweet hay as I go
   from one leg to the other
more so than I might
mingled with barber's tonic
from the morning's shops
   of papers and bright rag
          as if we could
          take time out for life

and the afternoon's seas, like yards

At some smell of smoke
I found a spray behind me
and the two on my right gone
     tending the grass, all night
   everyone beautifully
     (by themselves   the same thing

time   for the surroundings

     against the strip of hill
    ending low, as space
    on this side, hut for clouds.

ROBERT CREELEY

Review of *The Letters of Hart Crane* *

If there is a ghost, or unquiet spirit, of a man ever left to us, it may well be that Hart Crane is not dead—or not in our comfortable sense of that word. I note that Brom Weber brings this up, unintentionally, in his ridiculous preface and chronology for the book in question: "Three days later, on the 27th, he [Crane] either jumped or fell into the Caribbean Sea and was drowned. His body was not recovered" (p. xvi). Perhaps we have our own fears of the sea, and also of a man not actually "laid to rest," not finally put under as we are accustomed to do with the dead.

But lacking the body, an age of critics can still sustain its necrophilia on the body of the work itself. Hart Crane "was admittedly not a thinker..." (p. x), Weber says, ignoring, for one thing, Williams' premise that "the poet thinks with his poem, in that lies his thought, and that is the profundity..." To prepare us, Weber speaks of Crane's "acquisitive need for sympathy, pity, understanding, affection..." (p. vi), of a man "tyrannically governed by a chronic need to love and be loved..." (p. viii). One might well say the same of *any* human being.

In any case some anger can be righteous, and some usage cannot be put up with. Lacking a present means to deal with Weber, finally—the reader is advised to bypass his comments altogether. (Or better, to judge for himself the man writing "The last chapter of the Crane biography . . ." (p. x.). He is not helpful.

Crane is, however, and we have, at last, a reasonable addenda to the poetry itself which may serve as the gauge we had lacked. What was Crane's conception of poetry? "Poetry, in so far as the metaphysics of any absolute knowledge extends, is simply the concrete *evidence* of the *experience* of a recognition (*knowledge* if you like). It can give you a *ratio* of fact and experience, and in this sense it is both perception and thing perceived, according as it approaches a significant articulation or not. This is its reality, its fact, *being*" (p. 237).

More than that, what was Crane's summation of his own position— the cause back of all Weber's inanities, not to mention his biography of Crane or Waldo Frank's fantastic introduction to the *Collected Poems*. Was it absolutely this fact of "Crane's tender friendships...with boys who followed the Sea..," and "drink..." as "the Sea's coadjutor..."? So says Frank—but does it matter?

"I have a certain code of ethics. I have not as yet attempted to reduce it to any exact formula, and if I did I should probably embark

* Edited by Brom Weber; Hermitage House, N.Y., 1952.

76

on an endless tome with monthly additions and digressions every year. It seems obvious that a certain decent carriage and action is a paramount requirement in any poet, deacon or carpenter. And though I reserve myself the pleasant right to define these standards in a somewhat individual way, and to shout and complain when circumstances against me seem to warrant it, on the other hand I believe myself to be speaking honestly when I say that I have never been able to regret—for long— whatever has happened to me, more especially those decisions which at times have been permitted a free will.... And I am as completely out of sympathy with the familiar whimpering caricature of the artist and his 'divine rights' as you seem to be. I am not a Stoic, though I think I could lean more in that direction if I came to (as I may sometime) appreciate more highly the imaginative profits of such a course" (pp. 229-30).

Back of this, there are the poems, forgotten for the most part—but if this book can do anything, and one hopes at least, it may bring us back to them somewhat sobered. We know, we know, we know, etc., that *The Bridge* was a "failure"—though why, and how, we are not at all quite so sure of. Crane wrote to Allen Tate: "... I shall be humbly grateful if *The Bridge* can fulfil simply the metaphorical inference of its title.... You will admit our age (at least our predicament) to be one of transition" (p. 353). It has done that, I think.

The shorter poems, those found in *White Buildings* and *Key West*, have escaped the "failure" of *The Bridge*, but they have also been affected, i.e., they seem to be thought less "significant." And there again we have the critic's help. "One is appalled, on reading his [Crane's] explication of "At Melville's Tomb" to realize that while he could associatively justify the chain of metaphors comprising the poem, he was oblivious of the difference between a random and logical mode of association." (Which is Grover Smith, from within his own oblivion.) But the poem?

At Melville's Tomb

Often beneath the wave, wide from this ledge
The dice of drowned men's bones he saw bequeath
An embassy. Their numbers as he watched,
Beat on the dusty shore and were obscured.

And wrecks passed without sound of bells.
The calyx of death's bounty giving back

A scattered chapter, livid hieroglyph.
The portent wound in corridors of shells.

Then in the circuit calm of one vast coil,
Its lashings charmed and malice reconciled,
Frosted eyes there were that lifted altars;
And silent answers crept across the stars.

Compass, quadrant and sextant contrive
No farther tides... High in the azure steeps
Monody shall not wake the mariner.
This fabulous shadow only the sea keeps.

This is the *GREATEST* summation of Melville I have ever read.
O well....

"I don't know whether you want to hear from me or not—since
you have never written—but here's my love anyway..." He did all
any man could.

Review of D. H. Lawrence's *Studies in Classic American Literature* *

It's an odd feeling now to read a book like Cooper's *Deerslayer*.
There is hardly much left of that place, and I wonder how far one
would have to look, in the United States, to find timber still standing
in its first growth. It must have been a fantastic world. We are, of
course, the heirs to it.

So Lawrence says: "...It seems to me that the things in Cooper
that make one so savage, when one compares them with actuality, are
perhaps, when one considers them as presentations of a deep subjective
desire, real in their way, and almost prophetic." Beyond the prose,
heavy as it now seems, a man like Natty Bumppo is familiar enough:
"This is Natty, the white forerunner. A killer."

Cooper was one root, or evidence, of the "classic" American literature which Lawrence, and few others, had eyes to see. Even a present
reclamation of Hawthorne will not judge, clearly enough, that the
"prettiest of all sensations [is] the sensation of UNDERSTANDING."

> *The Scarlet Letter* gives the show away.
> You have the pure-pure young parson Dimmesdale.
> You have the beautiful Puritan Hester at his feet.
> And the first thing she does is to seduce him.

* Doubleday Anchor Books, N.Y., 1953.

And the first thing he does is to be seduced.
And the second thing they do is to hug their sin in secret,
and gloat over it, and try to understand.
　　Which is the myth of New England.
　　Deerslayer refused to be seduced by Judith Hutter. At least
the Sodom apple of sin didn't fetch him.
　　But Dimmesdale was seduced gloatingly. O, luscious Sin!
　　He was such a pure young man.
　　That he had to make a fool of purity.
　　The American psyche.

For Lawrence *The Scarlet Letter* was "...perhaps, the most colossal satire ever penned." It is not a comfortable implication for any of us, but there it is.

Not one of Lawrence's implications can give us very much peace, if that, in fact, is what we are after. The "great grey poet" (and/or Whitman) is given the roughest ride probably ever accorded him. And yet it is incredibly right, all of it. The "I AM HE THAT ACHES WITH AMOROUS LOVE..." is a bore of immense proportions—or no one ever indulged himself so emphatically at such length. But Crane's Whitman is also seen, again clearly, without innuendo or tenuousness: "Now Whitman was a great moralist. He was a great leader. He was a great changer of the blood in the veins of men." That is fact.

And Franklin: "Benjamin had no concern, really, with the immortal soul. He was too busy with social man." Crèvecoeur: "NATURE. I wish I could write it larger than that. NATURE."

> Franklin is the real practical prototype of the American. Crèvecoeur is the emotional. To the European, the American is first and foremost a dollar fiend. We tend to forget the emotional heritage of Hector St. John de Crèvecoeur. We tend to disbelieve, for example, in Woodrow Wilson's wrung heart and wet hanky. Yet surely these are real enough. Aren't they?

At a time when so much "revaluation" and "revisiting" are the practice, Lawrence can serve the very actual function of showing how it might be done. We have valued, foolishly, the perspective of time alone. And lost the very thing we claim to have gained, namely, under-standing of *any* of these men Lawrence cites for a classic American literature. For one example, Melville, God knows there has been enough talk around and about him to satisfy any of his admirers. But—how many come up with such a simple statement as this: "Melville knew. He knew his race was doomed. His white soul, doomed. His great white epoch, doomed. Himself, doomed. The idealist, doomed. The spirit, doomed."

Was it so impossible of realization about that? There is "American literature," in the coldest sense imaginable, as we now prune it, and pare it, to make an export commodity for the "foreigner." The one sense we overlook is that *we* are the foreigners, *are* the worst of foreigners, "white" foreigners. Doomed, doomed, doomed.

To have a literature Lawrence adjudged it necessary to have a soul. And so we have laughed at him—how funny. How funny is it now?

"The old American literature. Franklin, Cooper, Hawthorne & Co.? All that mass of words! all so unreal!" cries the live American.

Heaven knows what we mean by reality.

IRVING LAYTON

The Cold Green Element

At the end of the garden walk
the wind and its satellite wait for me;
their meaning I will not know
     until I go there,
but the black-hatted undertaker

who, passing, saw my heart beating in the grass,
is also going there. Hi, I tell him,
a great squall in the Pacific blew a dead poet
     out of the water,
who now hangs from the city's gates.

Crowds depart daily to see it, and return
with grimaces and incomprehension;
if its limbs twitched in the air
     they would sit at its feet
peeling their oranges.

And turning over I embrace like a lover
the trunk of a tree, one of those
for whom the lightning was too much
     and grew a brilliant
hunchback with a crown of leaves.

The ailments escaped from the labels
of medicine bottles are all fled to the wind;
I've seen myself lately in the eyes
     of old women,
spend streams mourning my manhood,

in whose old pupils the sun became
a bloodsmear on broad catalpa leaves
and hanging from ancient twigs,
     my murdered selves,
sparked the air like the muted collisions

of fruit. A black dog howls down my blood,
a black dog with yellow eyes;
he too by someone's inadvertence
    saw the bloodsmear
on the broad catalpa leaves.

But the furies clear a path for me to the worm
who sang for an hour in the throat of a robin,
and misled by the cries of young boys
    I am again
a breathless swimmer in that cold green element.

La Minerve

And if I say where my dog's vivid tongue
Clapped the frogs under their green fables,
Or the rock's coolness under my hand
Told me clearly which way the sun passed

Or if I say in a clean forest
I heard myself proclaimed a traitor
By the excellent cones for I thought
Where the good go, green as an apple

And if like our French grocer, Mailloux,
I lay these things on your white table
With a proud involuntary look,
And add a word about the first gods

I take satisfaction from your smile
And the inclination of your shoulder
Before the birds leave off their singing
And slowly the dark fills up my eyes.

But when you stand at night before me
Like the genius of this place, naked,
All my ribs most unpaganlike ache
With foolstruck Adam in his first wonder.

July 29, 1954

Letter to Cid Corman

Lac Desert, County Lab
Quebec
August 5, 1954

Dear Cid,
    ...In all these poems I've tried to express the idea "in
the image," for although as a rule I leave theorizing about
poetry to others, there are one or two work-a-day rules I try to
govern myself by when writing verse. For me, rhythm and
imagery usually tell the story; I'm not much interested in any
poet's ideas unless he can make them dance for me, that is
embody them in a rhythmic pattern of visual images, which is
only another way of saying the same thing in different words.
If I want sociology, economics, uplift, or metaphysics; or that
generalized state of despairing benevolence concerning the
prospects of the human race which seems to characterize much
of present-day poetic effort, I know my way around a library as
well as the next man. Catalogues are no mystery to me. I
regard the writing of verse as a serious craft, the most serious
there is, demanding from a man everything he's got. Moreover,
it's a craft in which good intentions count for nil. It's how
much a man has absorbed into his being that counts, how he
opens up continuously to experience, and then with talent and
luck communicates to others without fuss or fanfare or
affectation, but sincerely, honestly, simply...

Yours,
Irving

Golfers

Like Sieur Montaigne's distinction
between virtue and innocence
what gets you is their unbewilderment

They come into the picture suddenly
like unfinished houses, gapes and planed wood,
dominating a landscape

And you see at a glance
among sportsmen they are the metaphysicians,
intent, untalkative, pursuing Unity

(What finally gets you is their chastity)

And that no theory of pessimism is complete
which altogether ignores them.

Epitaph for an Ugly Servitor
to Three Queens

Providing food and comment for a mole
Who nightly nibbles at my calluses,
Death altered not a whit my destined role:
I, who served three Queens in different palaces.

A Plausible Story

After the first week in school my colleagues ceased to interest me.
Their ambitions were commonplace, their concerns trivial, their
outlook—well, I couldn't say really what it was. As high priests of
education they genuflected mystically every three months in front of
an oblong strip of blue paste-board; for the rest there was no nonsense
to them. After a time, to make them bearable, I invented for each of
them an afterschool existence in which, suburban avatars, they lived
intense, extravagant lives. Miss Raymond, maths, kept house for thirteen
black dwarfs; dainty Miss Lerose, the French instructor, was a flea-
catcher with an international reputation; and Mr. Sloper, a tall bony
man who taught chemistry to the older boys, was at work on a powder
for shrinking headmasters. When I met them hurrying along the corridors
it lifted me to know that each of them had a preposterous story to tell
me. Of course they never breathed a word to me; they were too close-
mouthed and secretive for that, or perhaps they suspected I already
knew. In any event, their secretiveness was an item in the absurd
circumstances I'd woven around their lives.

Bored, and sometimes desperate, I tried yet another expedient.
During school hours I engaged upon a long stupendous blasphemy—
I played Creator! I don't remember exactly when I first began to copy
the Omnipotent; probably at the beginning of my career as a pedagogue.
Fool-proof, this expedient was also simple. I merely imagined that
whatever happed during the hours of school happened solely by my
permission. In the courtyard, in the class-rooms, in the Headmaster's

office, my writ ran everywhere; and my rule, like that of the Creator Himself, was as sweeping as it was not-to-be-seen. No one ever arose to challenge it and no one, as far as I can recall, ever complained. My colleagues innocently did my bidding; they accepted without a murmur their prescriptive existence. They diverted though they had long ago ceased to astonish me. Unfortunately even omnipotence sometimes began to pall. By frequently amnestying my subject and re-distributing the main roles, I learned to cheat monotony of its inevitable triumph. My mood at last became serene and complacent. It had the winging pinion, the charming hauteur of the poet baylaurelled with success.

If you can imagine a bacchanalian satyr squeezed into a forty-two: fifty business suit you have a picture of Mr. Porlick. He was the school's Headmaster and one of my most remarkable creations. No other made me feel as omnipotent as he did, for he never voiced an opinion but I knew beforehand what it would be. He was balding and paunchy. On bad days I thought my colleagues had been condemned to rotate in hell around the naked infernal rotundity of Mr. Porlick's belly. He was egotistic, sentimental and good-natured. He suffered from headaches and frequent attacks of depression; this, he said, was because he was an intellectual and read too many improving books. Porlick's routine for dealing with a misbehaving boy never changed. He'd hurl himself out of the chair, lean his overfed torso to one side, and pumping his arm frantically, demonstrate to his stenographer his famous technique of puff and bluster. If the boy cried—good! Porlick, an embarrassed smile on his face, would begin to comfort him, appearing surprised and happy that anyone should have taken his words so seriously.

Another creation was Mr. Edwards. Edwards wore the same deprecatory smile which I had given him three years ago. An unfortunate rigidity in his make-up prevented my acting more generously towards him. I mean that in the matter of character parts he was stuck with the one his mediocre talents made the most suitable for him. I did the best I could, however. I saw to it that he mistook his irresolutions for the promptings of a fastidious conscience and his futile explosions for the rampings of a lion. The squint in his right eye, nevertheless, was not of my doing; nor the queer look in that orb when he removed his glass, as though astonished at its own misplacement.

I had made Edwards' afterschool endowment an exercise in wish-fulfilment. His skin was fresh and rosy; his figure athletic; his hair black and abundant; and his squint was gone. Or rather his squint was not gone. But now he dwelt in a land where a squint-eyed person had never before been seen. His defect was a defect no longer. On the contrary, it possessed all the appeal of an intriguing singularity. Women with lovely white skins, their bodies scented with subtle, oriental perfumes, pursued him everywhere. He held them at bay with brilliant epigrams which only inflamed them the more until, touched by their despairing entreaties, he removed his glass to let them catch a glimpse of his abnormal, voluptuous eye. After that they fainted at his feet, and he strode over their bodies triumphantly.

But here in school Edwards was a failure. He was loquacious and bitter. His pupils despised him; on lavatory doors they rang changes on his name. One of them had even penned an ode to him, ingenious and metrically correct—on toilet paper! They made fun of his person, imitated his gait and mannerisms, encouraged one another to new hilarious feats of mimicry. His appearance in the classroom was a signal for an artillery duel of bag-bursting, popping noises that sent him scurrying for the Headmaster. Mr. Porlick, lines of worry appearing on the fat orgulous face, averred that Edwards was "unable to keep discipline." When Edwards was gone, the Headmaster would address himself briefly to his circle:

—Dope!

And raise his voice and add:

—The Dope gave a course in Educational Psychology at the Teachers' Seminary. His students revolted. They threw him out. Ha! Ha! Some teacher of psychology! Ha! Ha! Ha!

They listened fearfully while the caves of hell seemed to the farthest phosphor-gleaming crag to fill with his laughter. When the walls had stopped echoing, they broke into self-conscious snippets of mirth to erect a wall, however fragile, between them and him. The words "unable to keep discipline" rang menacingly in their ears. They were dismayed, and in hell they shivered.

Edwards, drawing his lips back, was preparing to speak to me, when the morning bell began to ring. That was the signal. Children tumbled into the corridor, doors banged and shivered in their frames, the floor under us trembled. The noise was earsplitting. As if by command, the circling around the Headmaster's belly suddenly stopped. This was the first monitory bell. The teachers looked at one another sadly, ruminatively, without speaking. They were bracing themselves for the day's work.

Was it Edwards or another who said:

—Animals! Dirty little animals!

I'm not sure. But one of them did say:

—Animals! Dirty little animals!

I guess it was Edwards. He was the more likely to say it. He was the failure, the despised one, the sole inspirer of lavatory odes.

Edwards placed his nicotined fingers on the back of my wrist. He puckered his face, stretched his rubbery lips over his teeth, and smiled. Glaucous bubbles appeared in the corner of his mouth. He was expecting me to enter into his mood at once. When I kept silent he searched about in his mind for something more to say, perhaps a joke to cover up his indiscretion. Since I hadn't endowed him with ready wit — except in my after-school fantasy — he searched in vain. The failure made him bitter, and he fairly hissed at me:

— You don't like me much, do you?

What had made him say that? Those were not his lines. Where had he gotten them from? Who or what had put them into his head? Had he rebelled, insanely resolving in a flash of defiance to be out-of-character? Milton's opening chord, organ-booming, vibrated in my brain:

Of Man's First Disobedience, and the Fruit
Of that Forbidden Tree whose mortal taste
Brought Death . . .

Mr. Edwards, too, should not go unpunished. Heretical impromptus — in my position I could not suffer them!

To uncover the source of his black rebellion I said:

— I don't know what makes you say that.

The second bell cut short his reply. I think he was relieved, preferring to let my question hang in the air unanswered. One word leading to another I might have admitted to disliking him. Edwards was no fool and knew perfectly that once such words are spoken there is seldom a retreat from them. People acquire a vested interest in their stated prejudices, utterance robing them in the false rags of objectivity.

My next thought was a queer one. It had nothing to do with what had gone before. It was of brussels sprouts. Edwards' face was like a cooked brussels sprout, flabbily round, its palegreen steamy leaves ruffled.

Were brussels sprouts merely cabbages without ambition?

The bell's fevered crackling died away. A young straggler, panting and happy, dashed into the open classroom next to us. Taking out some foolscap and my attendance book, I folded the brown annunciatory wings of the cupboard. I curved my arm over my back and raising the coatjacket over the nape of my neck said affably to Mr. Edwards:

— Well, let's put on the harness, shall we?

He made a face and shook his head.

— We must eat, mustn't we?

And saying this, he stepped aggressively in front of me into the long wide corridor. It led to our respective classrooms and for me, alas, to Ava Rickstein.

Little Ava was my masterwork, a figure I'd raised from the depths to tease my brain with hints of man's illimitable perversity. When I came into the classroom her frail body stiffened, and I saw the beleaguered look in her wide mocking eyes. Little Ava, I'm afraid, hated me. She hated me with all the fanatical vigour of a fourteen-year-old adolescent. She was a brilliant pupil who, by irony and composure, overawed her more boisterous classmates. She read eagerly everything she could put her hands on — histories, biography, travel, fiction. Her poise was astonishing. I thrilled to see her, sitting upright in her seat, so close I might have rapped on her desk with my pointer. Like the Arch-Creator Himself I'd insured myself against the sin of pride. I too had made someone in my own image, sensitive, perverse and intractable.

For a few seconds I looked at the expectant faces.

— Take out your history books, I said when the room was quiet.

The twenty faces disappeared, reappeared. There was a clatter of books and pencils, a banging of desk seats.

The day's work was starting.

— Melvyn, what's the date for the execution of Charles I?

— 1649, Sir.

— Good. Very good, boy.

— David, what great Englishman besides Charles was called king?

— Pym, Sir. "King" Pym.

— I see you've prepared your lesson. Good.

— Alan, what was the name of the persecuting Archbishop?

Silence. A helpful whispering in the aisles.

— Well, Alan?

— I . . . I . . . Archbishop Laud, Sir!

— Did neighbour Joey help you?

— No, Sir.

Fibbing little wretch. My eyes fell on Ava.

— Ava, give the dates of the English Civil War.

She moved her knees noiselessly out of her seat and stood up erectly.

— 1642 to 1646, Sir.

As usual you are quite right, I smiled.

Her face was unanswering. I began to drum on the desk with my forefinger.

— What were the causes of that war?

— You said, Sir, it was because Charles had sold the soap monopoly to a court favourite for a sum of money he badly needed. This favourite now controlled the supply of soap in the entire kingdom. He charged whatever price he wished since as you once said, Sir, that is the raison d'être for possessing a monopoly. The court favourite raised the price of a bar of soap so high the English people didn't bathe themselves more than two or three times a year. Finally they gave up bathing altogether. And this — as you said, Sir — at last caused an awful stink in the country.

The class began to titter.

I cut short her triumph.

— Silence, I commanded.

There was silence, instantly.

I got up from my seat and sat down on the edge of the desk, facing her.

—Were you trying to be disrespectful, Miss Rickstein?

—No, Sir.

—Then why all the as-you-saids?

—Oh, I don't know, she said indifferently.

—I feel that you were trying to parody me, Miss Rickstein.

She was probably the only pupil in the class who knew the word's meaning.

—I wasn't parodying you. I only repeated what you told us the last history lesson.

—Was that all I told you?

—No Sir, You told us a great a deal more. Do you wish me to tell you the rest?

Bold little Ava, exasperating worm.

—No, Miss Rickstein. You have said enough. In heaven may you have your reward, suitably. Sit down.

—Thank you, Sir.

I returned to my seat and sat down. Looking at Ava sitting in front of me, I began for the hundredth time to compare her to her sister Evelyn. I had taught Evelyn in this same classroom three years ago. The girls were alike in almost everything but their attitude towards me. Evelyn had revered me, and hung upon my lightest word. I'd played my best roles for Evelyn. I'd been Shelley, Lincoln, Debs, Papineau, and no actor could have striven harder than I to win her silent applause. Each day I lived through a masquerade of noble roles. Occasionally I tried for new subtleties and nuances of character; her perspicacity pleased and chagrined me. No one had ever come to take her place.

I asked the class several more questions, went through the lesson for the day, and then told them to write a synopsis of the history chapter. I glanced at my wristwatch. Noon was still a long way off. I reached my hand into my briefcase for a book I had taken along to read. The time passed slowly. Ava was writing carefully into her looseleaf. Why did she hate me? I could think of no reason. Was I a stone left in her path by her older sister, a challenge which she coldly and proudly declined to accept? Was that the answer?

The class was growing restless. They had finished their task and were waiting for the next lesson, which was literature, to begin. I told them to take out their verse books.

—Who wrote "The Gift of Tritemius," I asked.

Several hands shot up in a Roman salute. I saw myself with a sunburnt furious baldhead, an apron of balcony about my waist. The voices in the room were plaintive, straining, eager.

—Me. O please, teacher, me. Me, teacher. I know the answer.

I thrust out my jaw and looked stern.

—Bramson, do you know?

—John Greenleaf Whittier, an American poet.

—Good. That's the idea.

In the third row a boy playing Sink My Battleship with his neighbour.

—Stand up, Joey.

The boy got to his feet slowly, his fearstricken face turned to his grinning classmates.

—Give me a full summary of the poem, I said.

—I don't know what you mean, the boy replied.

—By what? By summary?

—Yes, Sir. Do you mean the moral of the poem?

—No, I mean the story.

—It's about this here Abbot, the boy began painfully. A woman comes to a mon...a mon-stry and asks for help.

—Why, why does she come to him asking for help, I prodded. He had come to an abrupt stop.

—Because her son's a slave...a galley slave with the Moors.

—That's better, I said. Now tell us why he's a galley slave.

The boy inclined his ear blotterlike to soak up the whispered noises about him. He shifted his weight from leg to leg and began ritually to scratch his head and elbow. The faces upraised to him were as blank as his own. No one was waving his hand wanting to answer. He took courage.

—It don't say in the poem why, Sir, he blurted.

—True, Joey, I said with a laugh. It doesn't. But haven't you an imagination? Couldn't you think up a likely story to explain how the son came to be a galley slave? Or am I asking too much of you?

Joey grimaced to show that he thought I was. I had manifestly been unfair. I sensed that the mood of the class supported him and did not press it further.

—Go on, I said kindly.

—Well, this here Abbot offers the beggar woman his prayers, but she says what are you mocking me for? I need money to ransom out my son.

—What does ransom mean, Joey?

—It...it means...

Hands began to wave in front of me, plantlike.

—Please, Sir, I know.

—Please, please, Sir. O-oh I know, Sir.

—You never ask me, Sir.

—Quiet, class, I made myself heard. Let Joey answer if he can. If he can't, I shall ask someone else. Well, Joey, do you know?

—I...I know it. But I can't say it in words.

Ava's eyes were on me, self-assured, ironical. I was impatient to have the story finished.

—You tell the class, I said to her, what ransom means.

She rose to her feet silently.

—Ransom means to redeem, she said slowly. To redeem from captivity or bondage, or the like, by paying a price.

—That's right out of the dictionary, I laughed.

—That's where I got it from, she said coolly. May I sit down now, Sir?

—No, I said, finish our little story for us. Sit down, Joey. You have acquitted yourself handsomely.

The boy made an ugly face and sat down noisily.

—Go on, Ava, I said softly.

—The woman persuaded the Abbot to give her the two silver candlesticks which were on the altar. His hands trembled as he gave them to her.

—Why, Ava, why did the Abbot's hands tremble? I interrupted.

—He wasn't sure he was doing the right thing.

—And was he doing the right thing, I asked.

—Yes. That same day when the Abbot arose from his evening prayers he saw the chapel lit up with golden candlesticks. It proves that God loves mercy more than sacrificial gifts.

—Excellent, Ava, I said hypocritically. How Evelyn had ridiculed Whittier's banal homiletic three years ago! Ava was disappointingly conventional.

—Now, class, I said, after telling Ava to take her seat, I want you to use your imaginations. That is, if you have any. We have seen that the hand of the Abbot shook as he gave the silver candlesticks away. Was it because he was worried and afraid? Or was it for another reason? Supposing his hands trembled because the woman was his wife, long believed to be dead. Supposing the son in the Moor's galley was his. Supposing...

I raised my voice slightly.

—Tell me, children, I said, a plausible story.

But at that point someone knocked at the door. I went to open it, knowing beforehand it would be Mr. Edwards. His words also did not surprise me.

Remember, I was omnipotent.

—I want you to do something for me, he began nervously.

—Sure, I said, feigning ignorance. What is it?

He closed the door and led me towards the staircase.

—You're the only one that can help me, he began again. You've heard of the Teachers' Seminary?

—Yes, I nodded.

Edwards did not look at me.

—Porlick is gone, he said after a time. He's gone for his cigars and won't be back for the rest of the morning. We all know how well you keep discipline in your classes. I've got a free period. I thought if you observe me giving a lesson, you...

I waited for him to finish the sentence.

—You might give me a few pointers, he brought out in a low voice, his face reddening.

—Say no more I said.

Poor Edwards. How ashamed and dilapidated he looked. How different from his afterschool self!

I told him we had been doing "The Gift of Tritemius" before he knocked at the door. Did he know the poem? Yes, he knew it; and fortunately he knew the children also, having been their class teacher the year before. He would simply continue with the lesson, since if there was one subject more than another which he liked teaching it was English Literature. As we entered the classroom the children looked at us wonderingly and asked each other what was up. I explained to them humorously that they had so tired me out with their puerilities this morning I had asked Mr. Edwards to relieve me. There was a groan when I finished. I silenced it by staring hard at an inoffensive boy in the far corner of the room, an effective method I'd discovered for ending a disturbance in the class. When I turned my head, I saw Edwards' white face, and his hand was shaking.

Edwards remained standing. He looked nervous but resolute. I tiptoed to the back of the room where out of sight of the children I could observe the lesson. There was a chair near the cupboard. I sat down on it and felt as a dramatist might at the premiere showing of his play. The curtain was about to go up on the first scene.

Well, there could be no two thoughts about it. Edwards wasn't Nature's gift to the profession. His voice was not right, he spoke too often, and he lacked the sense of drama that makes the really good teacher. His movements were awkward and unconvincing. He couldn't find the words that would take him right to the hearts of the children, and so remained a gesticulating, slightly absurd stranger to them all the time he was talking to them. When he saw they were growing restless, he attempted to hold their attention by a sprightliness he did not feel; that was perhaps the most pitiful thing of all. It was a heart-breaking spectacle to watch. He picked up the verse book from the desk and began to turn the pages unsurely.

—Stephen, can you tell me who the Abbot was, he asked in a defeated voice.

Stephen was the class jokester. He was a short, swarthy-looking boy, with an irritating smirk on his face. A day seldom passed without my reprimanding him.

—He plays shortstop for the New York Giants, he said in a loud unabashed voice.

His impudent answer was the wanting spark. There was an explosion in the room.

—Naw, he's the prime minister of this country.

—Yer crazy, he's the minister for defense.

—Wanna bet?

—Yeh, wanna bet?

—Ah, yer crazy!

I sprang to my feet but the uproar subsided as suddenly and as quickly as it had arisen.

Edwards held his temper. He waited till perfect quiet had been restored to the class. When he had everyone's attention again he began to harangue them on the importance of literature. He spoke softly and persuasively. He almost surprised me. His performance for the past thirty-five minutes had been anything but inspiriting. Now he began by telling them that literature was one of the humanities. Did the children know where the word came from? It came from the Latin *humanitas*. It was a beautiful word. It signified all that pertained to a human being. Literature helped you become more truly human. It did this by enlarging your imagination and your sympathy for your fellow-men. He was a human being, and they were human beings. Through sympathy and imagination they could understand and talk to one another. Without these human qualities the world would be a poor place indeed. If they wished to grow into real men and women they must take their literature lessons seriously. Their teachers were here to help them.

Edwards had spoken almost eloquently. I could only suppose that something deep, something that never came to the surface, had stirred in him. While he was speaking I had gotten up and walked over quietly to the side of the room and leaned my back against the edge of the low windowsill. I could see Ava's fascinating profile. What was she thinking about? Many times I had said the same things about literature, glowing words intended for her sensitive ears alone. The other children I knew were unconvinced. They were barbarians. They had attended to Edwards because it amused them to see a grown-up so earnest about words, about what to them meant merely a number of pages of homework.

When Mr. Edwards stopped speaking, he seemed pleased with himself. There was a flattering stillness in the room. Even Stephen was attending. The autumn sun spilled like a light sauterne over the yellow desks and collected into irregular patches on the floor. There was a friendly, industrious atmosphere in the room. Mr. Edwards' eyes sought my face. He smiled at the class and for the first time that morning he seemed to be at ease.

—Now, Ava, I heard him say comfortably, what have you gotten from a study of the English gems? Your teachers tell me you're an omniverous reader. What do you say literature does and is?

Ava did not leave her seat.

—I think it's bunk, she said decisively.

The class roared and several children started a violent handslapping on their desks. Mr. Edwards, a green look returning to his face, bent his shoulders helplessly and waited. He was after all used to that sort of thing. He had deliberately called upon little Ava, thinking she would help him to intensify the warm mood he had by his little speech produced in the classroom. With one ill-tempered sentence she had swept it all away.

The tumult quieted down quickly because the children were eager to hear what Edwards' answer would be. I sensed their excitement. Edwards shook his head at Ava sorrowfully.

—Miss Rickstein, he said at last, have you a reason for saying what you just did? I feel you must have.

Ava looked wretched. I now saw something which a few hours ago I would have declared to be impossible. The girl's lips were trembling and her black eyes, their mocking beleaguered look gone, were slowly filling with tears. Her famous composure was beginning to crumble. Yet her voice was steady.

—It makes people think too much of themselves. It makes them selfish and egotistic. I like honest, unaffected people. Not a brilliant show-off with no heart in her.

I hadn't missed a word of what she said. I, the omnipotent, was at last beginning to understand.

—That's quite an indictment, Miss Rickstein, Edwards said rather sharply, wishing to seize the helm again. And how do you know all this?

Ava had half-turned towards me. She seemed to be pleading with me. Her face was intense.

—O don't ask me, she cried. I know, I just know! They're snobs. They're insincere. They think they know everything because they know what a metaphor is...

Mr. Edwards, who had been pacing back and forth while the girl was speaking, halted. His patience was used up.

—You're talking foolish, he said, interrupting her. I am very disappointed. No one, I should tell you, ever heard your sister...

But Ava was no longer listening to him. She had buried her small proud head in her arms and was sobbing quietly. Her classmates were bewildered, and were watching her in deep silence. They were no more astonished than I was. Little lady-like Ava crying! I glanced up from her heaving back to Mr. Edwards' face. He was not very far from tears himself. What had he done? What had he said? In heaven's name, what was the matter with the girl? He looked at her helplessly, at one moment putting out his hand as if to remonstrate with her, the next moment drawing it irresolutely back. Poor Edwards, squirming and flailing about on the implacable hook of his own incompetency. I could not bear to see his deep misery and humiliation and began to walk to the back of the room. I heard the door open and then shut with a loud noise. When I turned around Mr. Edwards was not to be seen anywhere. He had fled. Ava was still crying. I made no attempt to comfort her.

—Put your books away, class, I said from the back of the room.

But no one stirred.

DENISE LEVERTOV

In Obedience

"The dread word has been spoken.
I expect, like myself, you have known it
all along. He does not guess it, I think,
and yet..." And yet he knows it. "We live
from day to day, not
dipping too far
below the surface, and therefore
quite happily.
        You, too,
be happy, dear children"... So be it:
bow the head for once. Shall it be
in the red
almost-invisible spiders circling
a hot stone I shall take pleasure today?
The veery
        hidden, his song
          rippling downward, inward, over & over,
almost-visible spiral?

95

More:
let there be more joy! —if that
is what you would have. I dance
now that work's over & the house quiet:
alone among fireflies on the
dark lawn, humming and leaping.
"After all, life
is a journey to this goal
from the outset." And Mr. Despondency's daughter
Muchafraid, went through the water singing?
                    I dance
for joy, only for joy
while you lie dying, into whose eyes
I looked seldom enough, all the years,
seldom with candid love. Let my dance
be mourning then,
now that I love you too late.

LARRY EIGNER

Clearings

As history lays in the mind
        sudden houses of this landscape
I have watched going line by line
        blocking the rest of it
which over years I have seen
        but again it's as if time were no object
        raised while the eye travels

and who can say how a tree grew with
the sky in back of it, the
visible ocean doesn't exist
                really outlined in the night only
        the leaves crossing the sight lost
as faint elves in the known world

Or I am behind trees, wasn't I
always like this where
except for some nakedness of winter

or fall, the regular changes come off
as I had remembered
the trees still standing paused, turned black

and my road's houses, absolute hills are banked

all present greenery, turning aside
　　wind displaces my sight

CHARLES OLSON

Love

(down,
to my soul:

　　　　　　assume your nature as yourself,
　　　　　　for the love of God

　　　　　　　　　not even good enough

Stories
　　only
　　　　the possibility
　　　　　　of discrete
　　　　　　　　men

There is no intelligence
the equal of
the situation

There are only
　　　　two ways:
　　　　create the situation
　　　　　　　　(and this is love)
　　　　or avoid it
　　　　　　This also can be
Love.

The Motion

the motion
not verbal
        the newt
        less active
                than I: the fire pink
                not me
                        (the words
                        not me

not my nature
I
        Not even honor
        anything
                but that my freshness
                not be opened
                        (as my mail must not be,
                              before I do.

No doctrine
        even that the flower flames
                        if I don't. No capture
if the captive,
        even the instant,
                is not I.

Thus thou.

The Pavement

the pavement

I take so long

to go along by
        the walk

        from the house

        to the store
                I can't jump over

The obduracy

of spirit, the doubt

of person, the locus

only the place

I was not conceived in

       Only where I was named

       because I was known

       for the first time

              to be there. And I

              unknown

And

who am I

       any more than

            who knows

the lines

       I break my father's spine,
                the cracks

I break my mother's back

       are so wide,

            they are not so easily

Used.

ROBERT DUNCAN

Love Poem

Because I have been in the service of Love, I love thee.
This is a light or a shadow or darkness of sleep
as it transforms everything. This is a showing of colors
that informs beloved objects or makes radiant,

moves I mean to suggest
how in these days I have sensed thy presence,
unannounced and mysterious—there have been
joyous revelations—reflections?
as if clouds were passing in a windy weather,
happy turnings about. This was
her face radiant and, yes, transformed;
this was the loveliness of the hour
created by a joy or the joy
created by a loveliness. Or his head
bent almost as if yearning but not yearning.
There is no yearning,
no burning in thy transient passing
that casts the light of love carelessly.

Then I have my eternal devotion.
Then I have my meaningless freedom.
Then I have my surcease from my history.

Careless, useless, transient
intimations of the pure service of Love.

Friedl

The tough blue of the ideal—an idea I mean,
an ideology of images. Azure of Mallarmé
between and our daily blues.
The far away is near as an innerness
is far away or long ago or not reachd.
Not to be reachd. Yet. This is a spring of blue temper,
the twang of the everlasting water.
r-r-r-r-r that is a metal in language.
The afterwards. Full bodied image
as a carnal sentence afterwards
in its blue reverie. It does not disappear.

Then picture her as she was and will be,
a dolour that incarnates itself—
the fleshy scattering, a full abandon
in flowering; always
as if aroused so in the midst of slumber.

Picture the heat of the blood
as it suffuses the flesh—before awakening—
a ripeness always
rising below its own surface.

If we see her in her dreams,
she is like a rose submerged in its own heaviness,
she is a body drowned in its own deep.
And imagine the impenetrable heaviness
as the blue we imagine. See

all this real heaviness wavers,
does not awaken, but persists,
as rises, blue from our blue mind.

Songs for the Jews from Their Book of Splendours

I

Well of the Hebrews, well of days.
—I am that Well, we picture her as saying,
that comes once more among the jews
I am that beneficent Moon of the rising waters
rising once more to greet you. Do you know me?

You have so long despised me, the World,
but ease, ease—the ecstasies of my order
are simple as walking, I am that
deep talking well of easiness, respite
of the weary. O weary in your world contempt,
O contemptible jews, the world
is this well of my waters.
—I am that Well, again I return to you.

The pollutions of history are over.
Cease jews, cease ancient troublers.
The pollutions of history are over.

The left side of justice is mute.
The right side of mercy is mute.
It is in the disorder of speaking

that is easy, that respite comes,
the Moon, well of waters.

The Zohar tells us: Verily, altho Sarah died,
her image did not depart from the house.

II

O when the serpent jews!
—cunning Isaac and Jacob in his cunning—
skin-shedders, whisperers,
whisperd to the people in the garden
and twisted their story into our story,
persistent truths of the desert.

Did the Moon shudder?
worshippd and reviled by them
among her children? in her fullness
revealing all that goes on in the desert places,
the cold light shuddering and still?
the angelic whispering in history?

As the Zohar tells us: In the same way Jacob sent word to Esau, saying
"I have sojournd with Laban and stayd until now" as much as to say:
"I have stayd with him twenty years, and have brought with me a deadly
snake who slays people with his bite."

A Dream of the End of the World

We came down to Darling Lake where the deceivers were. What
did we care there? All of the deceptions were pleasurable. Darling
Lake is for summer visitors.

Now let me introduce both of us to you. We are winter inhabitants
and will pass willingly away with the holidays. The holidays are days
for our passing away.

The mayor at Darling Lake greeted us as gladness. This is because
all were visitors and everyone of winter in a crowd of summer is a
lively reminder.

Wherever we were we decided we were there. If we were not
starting, we were not easily startled. A Dream of the End of the World.
If you look no further you can look all about you:

At the lovely about to be cremated mountains, at the cool about to be steaming streams, look at the green growing trees that are about to be witherd. This end of the world is a burning scene that being seen no further is a mountain resort.

At night along the shores of the lake in the continual little waves lapping there were loons singing. Their singing was calling. A calling too in calling became a calling to us. Of lonely pleasures.

Now let me tell you what we were doing. We were both writing deceptive poems as resorts for deceivers. These were kindly deceptions that deceived ourselves for we were our own best friends.

I wrote a poem calld *A Dream of the End of the World*

We came down to Dar Ling Lake. Careful Americans
among these Chinese walls and summers.
Counting the holy days as they were passing
we counted the beats our hearts were not missing.
All the landscape seemd or was burning.
This we calld the End of the World, and returning
wherever we were we decided we were there.

He wrote a poem calld *In Love with a Lake* or *Looking Around Us.*

and delighted the visitors.

103

PAUL BLACKBURN

Sirventes

Chantarai d'aquestz trobadors

My tune is of troubadours who sing variously:
and the worst believes he chaunts nobly.
I wish they would go somewhere else.
Two hundred shepherds
trying to pipe
and not a damn one knows whether the tune
rises or descends.

> Peire Rogier sins at this horribly.
> To deliver my first indictment, he
> sings too openly of love,
> tho in church is worth more than a hymn book
> for besides he can carry a candlestick with
> a large burning candle.

And the second, Girault de Bornelh, a wine skin
dried in the sun:
his song scratchy & thin like a water carrier's.
Too bad he has no mirror
to inspire his remaining cansos.

Bernart de Ventadorn is the third
and a hand shorter than Bornelh.
He had a good servant in his father,
and his mother
still collects faggots to heat
the castle oven.

> The fourth is from Briva, a Limousin,
> and more beggarly a jongleur there is not
> from here to Benevento.
> His chant is so like a sick pilgrim I once heard
> that pity nearly overtakes me.

Guillem de Ribas, No. 5,
not content with being a thorough-going villain,
   must sing verse hoarsely:
such grum sounds a crow would not admit to.
   And his eyes resemble two aspirin.[1]

And the sixth, Grimoartz Gausmars,
a knight on the road as a *joglar*.
The lord makes a poor trade who grants that one
   bright green clothing.
He would have himself rigged so uniquely
a hundred others would take to the road.

   Peire Bermon abased himself when
   the Comte of Toulouse gave him what
   he could not graciously ignore
      wherefore
   he was noble to him who despoiled him:
   he missed a good chance not cutting off
      what the man carries hanging.

Number Eight, Bernart de Saissac, rises
no higher in the profession
than to go about asking donations.
I prize him something less than a garlic[2]
since he begged from Bertrans de Cardalhac
   a sweaty old cloak.

And the ninth is en Raimbautz
who makes his *trobar*[3] too proud.
   Him I consider a cipher.
   Thus we appraise these pipers
who go about asking alms.

   Ebles de Sagna, the tenth, o,
   love never came gently to him
   so he sings as if with a toothache:
      a pustular, petulant lawyer.
   They say that for two *deniers*
   he will hire himself out in one place, sell
   advice *par excellence* in another.

[1]Literally, a silver statuette: I think the feel of dullness is translated.
[2]The lowest common denomination in barter.
[3]The art of composition, lit., "to find," i.e., to find the rime-words.

105

The eleventh is Guossalbo Roitz
who fills his *trobar* with conceit.
In him chivalry has ended its life.
He has never yet struck a fair blow.
While in flight one night he invented
      a fierce reputation.

The twelfth is an ancient Lombard [4]
who shouts that his neighbors are cowards.
Meanwhile he shivers in terror.
But he makes bold songs with bastard words
      neither provençal not lombard. [5]
They call him a charming fellow.

     Peire d'Alvernhe has a fine voice
     that can sing both high and low.
     His song is known for its sweetness:
     besides he is master of all, provided
        he makes his words clear,
        for scarcely any man understands them. [6]

THIS VERSE HAS BEEN MADE TO BAGPIPES
AT PUIVERT, LAUGHING AND JOKING.

                      PEIRE D'ALVERNHE

Canso

Can vei la lauzeta mover

When I see the lark stir his wings for joy
           against the sunlight,
    forgetting himself,
        letting himself
            fall
for the sweetness that goes into his heart,
        h a i e !
so great an envy swarms on me

[4]Bertran de Born, that old war-horse. EP has given him publicity.
[5]In the text, *marabotz*, and used as an adj. A *marabotin* was an ancient Spanish coin, also the metal used in the coin, probably with the connotation of "alloy." From the Arabic *marâbitî*.
[6]Reference to his own reputation as an exponent of the *trobar clus*, or the obscure mode. He is clear enough in this piece.

to see him rejoicing,
I wonder that my heart melts not from desiring.

Hell I, who thought I knew so much of love
                    know so little:
and cannot keep from loving her whose favors
                    I shall not have. And she
has all my heart and all myself and
                    all herself and all the world, has
robbed my heart from me and left me
                    naught but my desire
                    and a desiring heart.

        It having been granted me,
                    permission,
        having been allowed my moment to look
                    into her eyes,
        since I saw reflected in those eyes
                    my image, / that
        image has held the power, not myself!
        Since that mirage, my glass, influx of breath
                    ravages my innards:
        Narcissus at the spring, I kill
                    this human self.

Really, tho, without hope, over the ladies;
never again trust myself to them.
                    I used to defend them
                    but now
I'm clearing out, leaving town, quit.
Not one of them helps me against her
who destroys and confounds me,
fear and disbelieve all of them,
                    all the same cut.

And in this, my lady appears very much a woman
for which I reproach her:
she thinks one should not want what is forbidden him.

            It happens. And here
I have fallen in bad grace,

I have acted like the fool on the bridge.
I don't know why it happens to me
unless, perhaps, I climb too hard
                        against the mountain.

The chance for grace has been lost, I shall not taste it,
for she who has most of it, has none for me, and
                        where seek it else?
It is bitter for me to look on her, who
lets this thirsty wretch die
who will have no water without her
                        and she without pity.

But I have no right, and no pity or prayer
                        can avail me with my lady:
                        since my love does not please her,
I shall do what I can: speak no more to her,
leave her, give myself up,
answer her like a corpse,
        go away.
She wishes me miserable exile, and
        I know not where.

                        Tristans, you have no more of me.
                        My miseries and I leave you for
                                the unknown destiny.
                        I am calling quits
                        with you and with my songs;
                        I take myself off to hide
                        from all love
                        from all joy.

                        BERNART DE VENTADORN

Ab la dolchor del temps novel

In the new season
when the woods burgeon
and birds
sing out the first stave of new song,

time then that a man take the softest joy of her
who is most to his liking.

But from where my joy springs
no message comes :
the heart will not sleep or laugh, nor dare I go out
till I know the truth, if she will have me or not.

Our love goes weak
like the top branches creak
on the hawthorn at night,
stiff from the ice
or shaking from rain. And tomorrow
the sun
spreads its living warmth through the branches and through
the green leaves on the tree.

Remembering the softness of that morning we
put away anger,
when she gave her love, her ring,   as sign,
remembering the softness,
I pray to God I live to put my hands
under her cloak, remembering that.

And I

care not for the talk
that aims to part
my lady from me;
for I know how talk runs rife and gossip spreads
from empty rancid mouths that, soured
make mock of love.
No matter. We are the ones, we have
some bread, a knife.

GUILLEM DE PEITAU

109

LARRY EIGNER

I Have Felt It

I have felt it as they've said
there is nothing to say

there is everything to speak of
 but the words are words

When you speak that is a sound
what have you done, when you have spoken

 of nothing
 or something I will remember

After trying my animal noise
I break out with a man's cry

HENRI MICHAUX

I Row

I have curst your head your stomach your life
I have curst the road your way goes
The things that your hand grasps
I have curst the interior of your dreams

I put a pool in your eye that sees no more
An insect in your ear that hears no more
A sponge in your brain that knows no more

I made the soul cold in your body again
I froze you deep in your life

The air that you breathe chokes you
The air that you breathe of the air of a cave
Is an air that has already been expired been

rejected by hyenas
The excrement of this air none now can breathe
Your skin is all humid
Your skin sweats the sweat of a great fear
Your armpits emit from after an odor of the crypt

Animals stop upon your way
Dogs, at night, howl, their heads lifted toward your house
You cannot escape
You havent the strength of an ant at the end of your foot
Your fatigue plants lead in your body
Your fatigue is a long caravan
Your fatigue goes on to the country of Nan
Your fatigue is inexpressible

Your mouth bites you
Your nails scratch you
Your wife isnt yours now
Nor is your brother now
The sole of his foot is bitten by a furious serpent

They have slobbered over your offspring
They have slobbered over the laughter of your young daughter
They have passed in slobbering before the face of your abode

The world escapes you

I row
I row

I row against your life
I row
I multiply to become innumerable rowers
To row more forcefully against you

You fall in the swell
You are breathless
You are tired before the very least exertion

I row
I row
I row

You go, intoxicated, attached to the tail of a mule
Intoxication like an enormous parasol that hides the sky
And assembles the flies
The reeling intoxication of the semi-circular canals
A beginning badly attended by hemiplegia
Intoxication no longer leaves you
Sleeps on your left
Sleeps on your right
Sleeps on the stony ground of your way

I row
I row
I row against your days

In the house of sufferance you enter

I row
I row
On a black band your actions are inscribed
On the great white eye of a blind horse your future rolls

I ROW

PAUL CARROLL

Las Tentaciones de San Antonio

If one has to be a saint,
this landscape's as pleasant as any
      to do the job in:
            winds tangle
            in the wheat,
razorback, drowzily at Antony's feet
        slops up the harvest sun; let
the gentle rain from heaven fall,
          he's got a canopy
          of good Dutch thatch. Lacking

a bit of balance perhaps, since
the monk's indifference
and the mocking rage in the profile

peering from the pool
                    are the only human signs:

two creatures waddle from the field
lugging a fishing-pole; one, the bottom of a bear,
              wears a spiked bright helmet,
                         flat-footed lion for companion.
                         Being human, I suspect,
always was embarrassing. To the right,
              with a show of commotion
a Viking shield, bodies of beetles propelling behind it,
                         quarrels
                         impotently with the air.

And so it goes. Even
the man in the water is no reflection:
since emotion's a sour taste on the tongue,
              his mockery, or rage, splutter for nothing
                         in the sick peace of the pool.

Where's all the nuisance that used to liven
up the old days? For God's sake!
              scraps against Grace
                         and a flesh and bone demon
                         worth risking heaven for!
Burning, that willowy Copt
turned
              in dance-twists
the very color of your bronze desire;
                         and, Antony, the slave-boy's face
                         —sad eyes had hot secrets.

Then thinking once
of taxes and inheritance
—300 acres of Nile bottomland—
              mind filled
                         with a dust cloud.

Later, business and lust and such
switched to a more important thing:
              grotesques, always
                         screwing up your meditation
                         with sullen nagging.

Si consistant adversum
        you'd delight to bellow
flat on your back from a blow.
                "Nothing much
                to worry about these days:

but, fitfully, almost in a dream,
I sometimes wonder what the world seemed
when God the Father took some pleasure in
        killing
          quarreling over, bossing, making lonely, loving

            what once He believed to be men."

CID CORMAN

Wallace Stevens

It is at this moment that a friend has called and told me that the man is dead. And it catches me. I want to set down some words about him. Best perhaps from some notes I wrote shortly after hearing him give a reading of his poems on May Day three years ago at Harvard.

I wrote then:

"About 250-300 people in the New Lecture Hall. Dick Wilbur introduced him . . . wouldve preferred less studied comments, but it was good to have had the old respected master introduced by a young poet. As Wilbur finished and went to sit down (after customary applause) Stevens stopped him, to ask him to raise the microphone to accommodate his height.

"Stevens has stockiness, leaning toward paunchiness these days, proportionate to his more than six foot frame. His rather loose-skinned face was round and ruddy. His hair thin (seeming almost Harvardian crewcut) and white. His hands were trembling as he began, but steadied as he went. He stood rather straight, just bent at the neck. He said nothing as introduction, but started immediately with 'A Pastoral Nun.'

"His voice was soft, self-spoken, aimed at the listener who would listen, as meditative and thoughtful as his lines. It was enough to drive many of those present into the shelter of the outofdoors. It was a hard voice to catch. Exterior sounds, sirens, barks, cries, blotted his voice and the words of it. But neither that outside world nor the world outside the sense of minds who would hear him discomposed him. (Afterwards, however, aside, he spoke apologetically in behalf of a bad throat.) He coughed and cleared his throat a number of times, at the beginning and as he went.

"At first I couldnt hear and the impatient noises of others didnt help, but gradually my ears focused and everything began to come through, and with a splendid clarity. He read 'Credences of Summer,' which opened to me suddenly at 'The rock cannot be broken. It is the truth,' and I was then perfectly caught up.

"He switched to the *Auroras of Autumn* collection and read first 'Large Red Man Reading,' 'This Solitude of Cataracts' (both quietly persuasive), 'In the Element of Antagonisms (the force of 'excessive' coming excellently clear, the genius for the word, instinctively, imaginatively), 'Puella Parvula.'

"Then he read from poems in manuscript. These were the best. The writing, like 'A Poem in the Mountains,' 'To an Old Philosopher in Rome,' and the exquisite closing piece, 'The Final Soliloquy of the Inner Paramour' (or some such), these came through with all the vividness of metaphor 'transceived' through the most refined, but not rarified, sensitivity, a mind perfect to poetry, claiming the whole involved imagination as the complement and compliment to life.

"The dignity of his attitude, his courage to keep from any god but his imagination's fullest, his clearest clarion to be his life at its livingest prowess, his mind's and matter's ('we know what we *are*'), these truest deepest-tried promptings and reflections, all these gave a substance and a beauty I hadnt heard before at Harvard by any poet. He had neither the power nor the desire to project anything but the entirety of what he was, is. There was nothing faked, nothing flourished. There was his poetry and it had his eloquence (which never suffered itself to be merely rhetoric) and a richness of depth that makes so many other poets appear as petty and ridiculous as barkers selling chewing-gum.

"I felt the reading as one with a quiet emotional pitch. The almost inaudible voice certainly suffered an audience, but it never wavered from itself. It delivered its language with the weight of a mind pondering itself and its ponderings and not from a too-immaculate distance. It gave his life as a poet lucidly: the fine voice too much itself and at its own volume to be accepted by its audience and yet calmly certain of its values, humble without meekness, certain without arrogance, intelligent without preening, clear without emptiness. and poetic in the degree of poetry's most precise imaginings. It had waited to be heard and it could wait."

Paris, August 4th, 1955

DENISE LEVERTOV

An Innocent (I)

The cat has his sport
and the mouse suffers
but the cat
            is innocent
having no image of pain in him

an angel
dancing with his prey—

Carries it, frees it, leaps again
with joy upon his darling plaything

      —a dance, a prayer!
How cruel the cat is to our guilty eyes!

An Innocent (II)
1st version

At 9 on Hudson St., by 10
    through rotten mounds of foodscraps
in Chelsea, and on, north, with
perhaps some glove (or what?) to show for his pains.

Pink face, curved nose, white mustache,
white hair curling
over his collar; an army greatcoat. A blue sack
      or sometimes a white sack stencilled
      with faded dollar-signs.

It's not his thoroughness and speed
distinguish him so much as the invention
he wears, intimate as a hearing aid: an aid
    to delicate poking:
    a hook
    attached to his arm, projecting
    beyond the hand.

One, hearing of
this prince of scavengers, cried out
      in horror at that bad dream of a hook
      (methodical defilement coyly reduced)
and I too recoiled then; but later

thought my disgust false:
for I'd seen on the old man's face
only the calm intense look of a craftsman:
Innocent!

He accepts what we reject, endlessly stuffing
his floursack, silent
    (no one speaks to him)
      from can to can—an endless
city of refuse. And makes
some kind of life from it. His face
                rebukes us.

An Innocent (II)
2nd version

Pink faced, white haired, aquiline old man
endlessly stuffing your floursack—with what?
—Scraps from an endless
city of refuse—
        Silent, all day from can to can
picking garbage with an ingenious hook—

It's the hook we most recoil from—
in false disgust—
      Calm, intense—
        the face of a craftsman—innocent!

PAUL BLACKBURN

Compaigno, non puosc mudar qu'eo no m'effrei

I have heard the talk
I now have proof before me, and
        friend,   I am all precaution;
for a certain lady makes complaint to me
      of her custodians.

She says she will not be tethered by right or law,
that they keep her corked up, in captivity,
      close to the three of them;
and if one gives slack rein a little, the others
      will tighten the cinches.

And that there is no point of agreement among them:
>   one, a charming companion,
gives voice like a push-cart vendor.
Set together they conduct a fracas louder than
>   all the king's heelots.

And I tell you jail-keepers

>   I warn you—
and it would be the greatest folly to disbelieve me—
that you will be hard put to it to find a sentry who
will not sleep for a crucial   half-hour
>   now & again.

For I know of no woman who grows more incensed at delay,
>   if one accept not her offer of favor, or
put her off out of decency,
sans any recourse or contrivance.

If you lay not in select grocery for her larder, she
>   will eat what's at hand.
If she cannot have the war-horse, then
>   she'll buy the trotter.
>   And,
there is no one of you can dissuade me from her.
>   Strong wine, say, is prohibited one
>   for reasons of health.
>   Die of thirst then?
No. I think, then, one would drink water.
>   Anyone will drink water
>   rather than die of thirst.

GUILLEM DE PEITAU

Pus vezem de novelh florir

When we see again the spring blossoming of the world, orchards
and meadows growing green one more time,
brooks and springs clear-running, fresh-running winds,
then ought each living man to take full measure of
>   what gives him pleasure.

I should say nothing but good of Love:
but now? when I have neither gift nor salary
of him? All
right,
I lift a bit more than I agree to. But
how easily
and what great joy
he gives to those who support his arrangements.

Always, I take it,
never can I take
pleasure of those I love;
yet neither do I miss by slow application.
Yet, when to my knowledge you make it
with several other men in a row, my
heart says to me:
"It is nothing."

Through such reasonings
I have less of that
fine knowledge than the others,
and I want whatever it is I cannot have.

But if I can last out the proverb that says so, then most certainly
"To good heart shall be added good courage, in him
who is sufficiently patient."
Which is ghastly.

Indeed,
there will be no man entirely faithful toward Love
if he have not surrendered his balls,
and is not equally pleasant to strangers
and neighbors of her
whom he would love.
As for those who live under the same roof with her, he
must be
minutely
attentive to the movements,
even to the vagaries of
their bowels. Yet

he ought to wear openly his devotion to the people
of her whom he wishes to love;

and it helps
if he know how
to make his conduct attractive,
and if in court
he manage to not
make speeches like a farmer.

Concerning this *vers*, I tell you, it's
worth the most to him who best
understands and rejoices in it.
All the words are ordered equally to the same measure,
and the tune, for I praise it myself, is a fine, brave tune.

At Narbonne (but I do not go there), my *vers*
should be openly put to him;
and I want this praise to act as my surety.

My old Bagpipe, though I do not go,
my *vers* should be publicly sung to him,
and this praise serve as my guarantor.

IRVING LAYTON

The Way of the World

It has taken me long, Lygdamus,
    to learn that humans, barring
a few saints, are degenerate
    or senseless.

The senseless ones are never by design
    evil; but get in your way
like the ugly stumps of trees; order
    bad taste or out of boredom
start long wars
        where one's counted on
to dredge up manliness, fortitude, and valor
    for their stupefactions.

But wicked are the clever ones.
    Cultured and adept
they will seduce a friend's dear one
with praises of her husband
        on their lips.

As for the wife
    a little alcohol parts her thighs.
Do not blame her: her husband's name
on the seducer's lips
    makes her the eagerer to satisfy,
teaches her she lies with her very spouse.
And that way is best; no pricks of inwit,
    but the novelty's stab of pleasure is there .

Therefore give me only lovers.
    Come, my latest one, sloe-eyed,
your firm breasts whirling like astonished globes
    before my eyes cross-eyed with lust;
though my legs are bandy
        the heart's stout
and this provocative member smooth and unwrinkled.

Till the morning parts us, I'll lie beside you
    your nipple at my tired mouth
and one hand of mine
                on your black curling fleece.

GAEL TURNBULL

Homage to Jean Follain

I think you must have written them on postcards, your
    poems, like something one sends home while visiting
    abroad;

or like woodcuts that one finds in an old book in the
    attic and stares at on a rainy day, forgetting supper,
    forgetting to switch on the light;

but not antique, though out of time, each fixed in its
    moment, like sycamore seeds spiralling down that
    never seem to reach the grass.

What became of the freak, the girl with animal fur,
    when the fair moved on to the next village?

and the old souse, when he got home from the wineshop,
    did he beat his wife or did she beat him? did his
    daughter run away?

and that horseman coming home from a thirty years war,
    did the dogs know him? why should that one bird
    cry to announce him from so far?

and the police, toiling day and night to manacle the
    world, did they finish the last link, or did their
    ink dry up? did their slide-rules crumble?

But you don't tell us, and perhaps you don't really
    know, as you drink autumn wine in the evening,
    leaning over the battlements of an imaginary tower,
    watching the unwearied insects hovering in the
    immaculate air.

Flight of the Roller-Coaster

Once more around should do it, the man confided . . . .

And sure enough, when the roller-coaster reached the peak
Of the giant curve above me, screech of its wheels
Almost drowned out by the shriller cries of the riders—

Instead of the dip and plunge with its landslide of screams
It rose in the air like a movieland magic carpet, some
                    wonderful bird,

And without fuss or fanfare swooped slowly across the
                    amusement park,
Over Spook's Castle, ice-cream booths, shooting gallery;
                    and losing no height

Made the last yards above the beach, where the cucumber-cool
Brakeman in the last seat saluted
A lady about to change from her bathing-suit.

Then, as many witnesses duly reported, headed leisurely
                    out over the water,
Disappearing mysteriously all too soon behind a low-flying
                    flight of clouds.

The Toy Ladder

You bought the bird a toy ladder
For him to play with in his cage. And are annoyed now
When he ignores it completely.
                    The reason's easy:
Even a bird such as ours, not too clever,
Knows there's little point in climbing a ladder
Which doesn't lead to something or somewhere.

PAUL BLACKBURN

Vidas

1

Marcabru was left outside of a rich man's door, and no one ever knew who he was or where he was from. Sir Aldric Anvillars raised him. Afterwards, he stuck for a long time with a troubadour called Cercamon, who started him composing. And he had at that time the name *Panperdut,** but was afterward called Marcabrun.

In those days, no one called them *cansos*, but everything that was sung was called *vers*.

He was much renowed and listened to throughout the world and feared for his language, for he made many malicious songs. In the end, the castellans of Guyenne murdered him, for that he had uttered a very great evil against them.

II

Marcabru was from Gascoigne, son of a poor woman who carried the name Marcabruna, so that he says in his singing:

> Marcabru, son of lady Brun,
> was begot in such a moon
> that he knows how love crumbles
>   falls in ruins
>   —listen,—
> for never he loved anyone
> or had the love of woman.

He was one of the first troubadours that anyone remembers. He made vicious *sirventes* and spoke badly of women and of love.

MARCABRU (C. 1130)

---

*Literally, Bread-lost. His social criticism was sufficiently barbed that he lost his patronage (his bread) at rather frequent intervals.

L verns vai e.l temps s'aizina

Winter goes and weather betters,
  hedgerows green, hawthorns flower,
for which sensible reason the birds rejoice
      Ai!
  Even man grows gay wth love,
each drawing towards his private choice,
      O yes,
  pursuing his heart's pleasure.

The cold and drizzle clink against
the gentle season to arrest it.
From the hedges and from thickets
I hear the lancing song contest it
      Ai!
I set my name on the tourney-list
will sing of Love and how it goes,
      O yes.
if I want to, *and* how it grows.

  Letching love starts, then it clutches,
  then cheats with a greedy dire will.
  Had just once, a cunt's softness
  starts the damned traitorous fire,
      Ai!
  No one who falls into that blaze,
if he really mean it, or just to try it
      O yes!
  will come out with his hair o'fridays.

  Fine Love carries a medicine
  purposed to heal his companion.
  Lechery binds & cramps his well
  then puts him in a kind of hell
      Ai!
So long as some hard money's around, hey,
it'll put on the semblance of love like crazy
      O yes,
  and when the dough runs out will say
      the road, son, the road.

Luring, enticing, with sweet bait
to get the poor gull in the trap
until they have him head and shoulders,
signal yes while saying no
        Ai!
I prefer as lover a man who's dark,
or light-skinned, or nicely tanned,
I'll make it with you—no I won't
        O yes,
crazy for a skinny behind!

The lady doesn't know Love's face
when she loves a servant of the house:
and if he covers her at her will
it's the mongrel with the greyhound bitch
        Ai!
from whence are born these rich alloys
who give neither feasts nor silver
        O yes,
and it's Marcabrus who says so.

The guardian gets into the back
and hurries to blow up the fire a bit
then drinks the smoke from the waterbutt
of milady Goodandexcited.
        Ai!
I know how well he rests when he lies down
and gets the grain out of the sack
        O yes,
and perpetuates his master's name.

Who has good Love as a neighbor
and lives on the allowance he gets,
good name and spunk and integrity
incline to him without complaint
        Ai!
He who acts as he talks, straight,
will not have the same laments as
Sir Eglain, that balancing grain-sack.

For myself, I hold no more
with sir Eble's theory of *trobar*

that's made a pile of foolish decisions
and upholds them all against all reason
                Ai!
    I say and've said, and will again
    they feed us only rationalisation
    when love cries to be differentiated
    from lechery. Plain, it's plain
            O yes,
    he who bitches against fine Love
    's a botch. Let him complain.

Pois la fuoilla revirola

    When the leaf spins,
                    its staying power
        gone,
            twists off
                falls
                    spinning
    down through the branches from the top limbs whence
            the wind has torn it,
    I watch.
    It is a sign.
        The icy storm that's brewing's better
        than grumbling and meandering summer
        congesting us with hates and whoring.

    Peace. The nuthatch and nightingale
                    turn their songs to silence.
    The same with oriole and jay; winter
                        has its will.
    For a season anyway,
    into the gutter goes the pride
    of the blackguarding bob-tailed riff-raff, who
            in summer are not afraid to make
            a show of teeth.

    Toads who toady up and snakes that sneak
    are to be expected and should frighten no one;
    horse-flies, blow-flies, they, we know
                    live on carrion.

All of them now cold,
toads, snakes, flies, scarabs, hornets, all,
I cannot hear their buzz nor, happily, smell
                              their stink.
We drink old Winter who's delivered us,
          our smiles and wine.

But take that fellow there, say, his
                    beak filed with an adz,
he doesn't lose his place in the foyer,
but he carries a pic and a little mace
which two, together, can cause some hurt.
And from being in bed too much with his mistress
          his cock hurts
It's more than his master can say.

He takes an armful of honey, morning and night,
can even get it in between the bands of a corset.
He knows how to wiggle his ass. The vavassour,
          he does his day's work at night:
              it gets him a son.
Whence, instead of a vassal's vassal, he becomes
              the lord's lord.

As that little stork slumps, rises and sinks again,
mounting and bending down, the world's in the vortex,
                    whirling. I'm indifferent, me.
                    There are eyes that will not see
that will not recognize spoilage, even
now when the service of love is given
              over to harlotry.

Marcabru? you'll hardly find him
sniffing in a corner: he knows the score.
His lady's of the good school where
          Joy is master.
And when the license is given outright
he always extends himself a mite
          more than he has to.

I pray to God he do not take
Guissart to his celestial kingdom, for
the battle-axe he uses here works
              better

in this best of all sensual worlds,
and he has left an inheritor.
And I'll never again have faith in a son
       if this one
doesn't resemble his father.

But to return to these birds,
despaired of reaching the clouds,
and being by nature fools, they
              bow
for all (and more than) they're worth.
And whether or not it's said amiss,
barons who sell out for cash
have hearts below their umbilicus.

         He has a heart a cut below his navel,
         a baron who dirties himself for cash.

Razo

    Bertran de Born was the lover of madomna Maent de Montanhac,
the wife of a Talairan who was brother to that Talairan who was count
in Perigord, and who was such a lady as I have described to you in the
razo to the *sirventes* of the "borrowed lady." And as I have told you,
she parted from him and gave him his discharge. She accused him
because of Guischarda, the wife of Comborn's viscount, who was a
worthy lady from Bourgogne, sister of lord Guischart of Beaujeu. She
was a lovely and well-instructed lady, accomplished with all her beauties.
Indeed, he praised her strongly, did en Bertrans, in recounting and singing of her before he had seen her, and was her friend for the good reports
that he had heard of her. And it was sung out before she had come to be
married to the viscount of Comborn, the happiness Bertran had of her
coming. And he made these *coblas* which go:

    Ah, Limousin, open courteous land,
    I know what honors will increase you soon,
    for joy and valor, pleasure and gaiety,
    courtesy and solace and love's service
    comes to you now: first of all there's body.
    She'd best guard him well, who has a lover,
    put him out to pasture.
    A woman should be, as this one is, built.

Recompense & gifts, dress & largesse
nourish love as water does a fish,
so valor and good manners, arms, prowess,
courts & wars, tourney-grounds decked out.
Those who have courage and those who pretend it
had better show it now—and no pretense,
for they have sent Guischards to us here.

And because of the lady Guischarda, madomna Maenz separated
herself from him, because she believed that he wished her better than
he did herself, and that she was making love to him. And because of this
separation he made the *donna soissebuda*, the borrowed lady, and the
sirventes which goes:

Eu m'escondisc, domna

Lady, I clear myself toward you,
        guiltless
of what they have said to you of me.
    And I pray you mercy
    that no man may mess
        with
or confuse your fine body, loyal,
        without artifice,
frank, humble, commanding and full
of pleasure, toward me, lady,
and by recounting lies put quarrel between us.

I hope I lose my sparrow-hawk at first cast.
May lanners come and kill her on my fist
      carry her off picked,
      may I see her plucked
if I do not love you firm & with more longing
than having of desire for any other, even
              if she accord me her love
              and keep me in bed.

To make the exculpation to you stronger, I'll
      call the worst luck down upon myself.
If ever, even in thought, I've failed you,
when I shall be in bedroom or in orchard

alone with a woman, may I be put
out of condition in such wise that
I cannot get it even half-way up.

When I sit down at a gambling board
    I hope I never win a denier.
May I never set my marker on a good play
and may I throw snake-eyes forever,
if I've ever even *asked* another lady
                other than you
whom I desire, and prize, and love.

May I my own castle be part-owner of—
Let there be four inheritors
                dividing the tower,
without any of us ever being able to agree.
Rather, I wish myself the dire necessity of
a cross-bowman, a doctor at all times, mercenaries,
a body-guard and someone to watch the gate besides,
        if ever I had heart
        to love another woman.

May you quit me for another lover, and I
never know to whom to turn for help:
let wind drop when I put out to sea, let
porters beat me up & kick my butt
in the king's court itself, the dead-center of.
Let me the first to flee when the battle locks & clashes
        if he told the truth, the one
        who fed you this balderdash.

        By damn!

With my buckler on my back and my hood on crooked,
let me ride in bad weather on a horse a bitch to handle,
with the reins too short and the damned stirrups dragging,
long stirrups on a small horse that likes to trot in mud,
to an inn which will be cold, and where my very entrance
will irritate the innkeeper: if he didn't lie,
        the SOB who handed you this rubbish!

        Say I have a fine duck-hawk:
        lively, newly-moulted, trained

steady on the take and
ready to the hand,
one who can overtake
       any bird,
swans as well as cranes,
herons white or black,
will I then want another?
a badly-moulted chicken-hunter?
       fidgety & fat
who cannot even fly?
       Lady,
is it reasonable?
As for you envious liars
and sneaky slanderers,
now you've got me out of
favour with my lady,
I'd be damned glad if you left me to myself.

WILLIAM BRONK

The Arts and Death: A Fugue for Sidney Cox

I think always how we always miss it. Not
anything is ever entirely true.

Death dominates my mind. I
do not stop thinking how time will stop.
How time has stopped, does stop. Those dead —
their done time. Time does us in.

Mark how we make music, images,
how we term words, name names,
how, having named, assume the named begins
here, stops there, add this attribute,
subtract this other: here the mold begins
to harden. This toy soldier has
edges, can be painted, picked up,
moved from place to place, used to mean
one or many. Within the game we play,
we understand. See his leaden gun
or saber, how deadly for aid or for
destruction as we aim him, and he is bold,

a game soldier. We play games
however serious we aim to be.
A true aim, a toy soldier, I think
always, how we always miss the aim.

Ponder the vast debris of the dead, the great
uncounted numbers, the long, the endless list
of only their names, if anyone knew their names.
Joined to the dead already, to those known
who have died already, are we not also joined
to many we would have known in their time —
to one in Ilium, say, who thought of the dead?
In the world's long continuum, it is not
the names of the dead, but the dead themselves who are like
names, like terms, toy soldiers, words.

I think always how we always miss it; how the dead
have not been final, and life has always required
to be stated again, which is not ever stated.
It is not art's statements only, not
what we try to say by music, not the way
this picture sculptures sight itself
to see this picture — not by art alone
the aim is missed, and even least of all
by art (which tries a whole world at once,
a composition). No, it is in our terms,
the terms themselves, which break apart, divide,
discriminate, set chasms in that wide,
unbroken experience of the senses which
goes on and on, that radiation inward and out,
that consciousness which we divide, compare,
compose, make things and persons of, make forms,
make I and you. World, world, I am scared
and waver in awe before the wilderness
of raw consciousness, because it is all
dark and formlessness: and it is real
this passion that we feel for forms. But the forms
are never real. Are not really there. Are not.

I think always how we always miss the real.

There still are wars though all the soldiers fall.

We live in a world we never understand.

Our lives end nothing. Oh there is never an end.

My Young Nephew Sends Me His Picture for a Present

You have had even to tip back
your head a little, lest there spill out
that wild glee you can barely hold until
the shutter clicks. Up-tilted, your face
is as though a bow, and the tense string
pulled back and back, your glee—oh back
so far, millenia make you a kid in the Land
Between the Two Rivers, or even earlier
in such a time as when, as now for you,
there was no other world but that world.
But we remember, are reminded, all
the Gods, the costumes, all the building styles,
ah, all those worlds since then: the lost
arrows from that bow, the clutter of time,
the dull debris. Dust from these ruins dirties us.
What, searching there, will anybody find
could have drawn its makers on, or even then,
could have been called worth it once they reached it? Our
young glee drove us, heedless, and we went,
heedless, and dropped down where the force was spent.

ROBERT CREELEY

A Marriage

The first retainer
he gave to her
was a golden
wedding ring.

The second—late at night
he woke up,

135

leaned over on an elbow,
and kissed her.

The third and the last—
he died with
and gave up loving
and lived with her.

CHARLES OLSON

A Tentative Translation of a
Newly Discovered "Homeric" Hymn

(for Jane Harrison, if she were alive)

Hail and beware the dead who will talk life until you are blue
in the face. And you will not understand what is wrong,
they will not be blue, they will have tears in their eyes,
they will seem to you so much more full of life
than the rest of us, and they will ask so much, not of you no
but of life, they will cry, isn't it this way, if it isn't
I don't care for it, and you will feel the blackmail, you will not
know
what to answer, it will all have become one mass.

Hail and beware them, for they come from where you have not
been,
they come from where you cannot have come, they come into life
by a different gate. They come from a place which is not easily
known,
it is known only to those who have died. They carry seeds
you must not touch, you must not touch the pot they taste of,
no one must touch the pot, no one must, in their season.

Hail and beware them, in their season. Take care. Prepare
to receive them, they carry what the living cannot do without,
but take the proper precautions, do the prescribed things, let
down the thread from the right shoulder. And from the
forehead.
And listen to what they say, listen to the talk, hear
every word of it—they are drunk from the pot, they speak
like no living man may speak, they have the seeds in their
mouth—
listen, and beware

136

Hail them solely that they have the seeds in their mouth, they
are drunk, you cannot do without a drunkenness, seeds can't,
they must be soaked in the contents of the pot, they must be all
          one mass.

But you who live cannot know what else the seeds must be. Hail
and beware the earth, where the dead come from. Life
is not of the earth. The dead are of the earth. Hail and beware
the earth, where the pot is buried.

Greet the dead in the dead man's time. He is drunk of the pot.
He speaks like spring does. He will deceive you. You are meant
to be deceived. You must observe the drunkenness. You are
          not to
drink. But you must hear, and see. You must beware.

Hail them, and fall off. Fall off! The drink is not yours,
it is not yours! You do not come
from the same place, you do not suffer as the dead do,
they do not suffer, they need, because they have drunk of the pot,
they need. Do not drink of the pot, do not touch it. Do not
          touch
them.
          Beware the dead. And hail them. They teach you
                    drunkenness.
You have your own place to drink. Hail and beware them,
          when they come.

WILLIAM BRONK

"In Our Image, after Our Likeness"

In what image? Michelangelo
of course, his Adam, one thinks of that, of all
that flesh, serene, symmetrical, fresh
from the hand of God without intervention; one hears
the body's innocent, pleasant harmonies.
There is this to be said for it, that everywhere
his image is always in our presence: one sees
such figures, part by part, at least, and in need
of composition, but still they are always there.

Is this what was meant, this image? This, man?
The greedy mind that eats all kinds
of phantasies refuses this one. No,
go hungry, rather. We go hungry. Man,
your image eludes the flesh as though the flesh
were a bad camera, or a slick craftsman with a quick,
dashing facility and a sure eye
for the grotesque, but little depth and out
of fashion soon, regrettably, because
the perfection and morality of the flesh can move us so.

The moral and perfect, however, are not the point.
The intrinsic image of man is what we hope
to find, and while we hope are afraid to find.
One would as soon confront God as man.

At Tikal

Mountains they knew, and jungle, the sun, the stars—
these seemed to be there. But even after they slashed
the jungle and burned it and planted the comforting corn,
they were discontent. They wanted the shape of things.
They imagined a world and it was as if it were there

—a world with stars in their places and rain that came
when they called. It closed them in. Stone by stone,
as they built this city, these temples, they built this world.
They believed it. This was the world, and they,
of course, were the people. Now trees make up
assemblies and crowd in the wide plazas. Trees
climb the stupendous steps and rubble them.
In the jungle, the temples are little mountains again.

It is always hard like this, not having a world,
to imagine one, to go to the far edge
apart and imagine, to wall whether in
or out, to build a kind of cage for the sake
of feeling the bars around us, to give shape to a world.
And oh, it is always a world and not the world.

LARRY EIGNER

A Gone

The world under the sky
clouds
all winter and summer

         a snow
descends and occupies the ground
          filled
stars,
      air
with abstracted wings

on crystalline lines
        and time
        between the stars
        a broken hinge, by
        the garage

  a flagpole   mainstreet
    five cats yoked

      the world

cant hold, really
too many absolutes

but I am shattered
and another time lost

while the sea
        slams
    the wind
or lags
            an old woman's shoe
            flapping
                on the beach
and the awning was still there

DENISE LEVERTOV

Tomatlan (Variations)

I

The sea quiet, shadow-colored and
without shadows.
From which shall rise
the sea wind, moving
swiftly towards the
steep jungles. The sea wind
the awakener.

II

The sea wind is
a panther moving
swiftly towards the
mountain jungles.
Its silky fur
brushes me.

III

The green palmettos of the
blue jungle

shake their
green breasts, their stiff
green hair—
the wind, the sea wind is come
and touches them
lightly, and strokes them, and
screws them,
until they
are blue flames, green
smoke, and
screws them again.

IV

At the touch
of the sea wind
      the palms
shake their green breasts, their

      rustling fingers—
flames of desire and pleasure.
The sea wind that

      moves like a panther
blows the spray inland.
      Voluptuous

and simple—the world is
larger than one had thought.
It is a

new peace
shades the mind here
with jungle shadows
      frayed by the
sea wind.

Village Gossip after the Long Winter

"All down up there!" and the ghost
of some abandoned farm gave up
to thaw and loneliness. Next year the raspberries
around the beams and maimed boards.
Then, rum cherries that long ago shut in the dooryard view.
Birch, maple and hemlock in that order.
All down up there.

A Sunday Interval

Vague, as in these mountain rains the next hill,
the seamed face colored as rotting straw,
or the flange of smoke, his generations
of kitchen fires, he goes leisurely
to free a cow wedged between a rock
and the fence.
                    At a neighbor's word.

A Theory of Time

Ditch water flow is time on time reduced.
It is the leisure of oiled water
in a few reeds as I envy leisure,
as I emulate it lying on yellow sand.
The only quick thing worth the name—
that muskrat—scared—now that I show my face.

The Song of One Lost

To talk of death and dead,
this father dying or this son,
this god, this emptiness, this echo into
thinnest mountain air.

Second Series (1961~1964)

THEODORE ENSLIN

March—Temple, Maine

March 3. So I made it here today. After a winter's indecision as to *when*, I've come in on snowshoes. Bright sunshine and a northwest breeze slightly stirring the few beech leaves that hang in the high trees all winter. Cold, and no fooling about that: Ten below, and the breath congeals there. But the tone is right—set by Elliott Whitney, standing on the street corner in Farmington, a little drunk, huddled in a torn mackinaw. He yells, "Jesus Christ, Mr. Man!" and that's my welcome home. Or up here on the tote road, where I get my last friendly ride, and then go into the unplowed snow—nearly six feet of it. Finally the farm—high on the mountain—and I wonder, as I always do when I first make it, why did Old Staples build his house here, when there was so much land, flat land between the hills, and rich—the intervale? A man of vision. Not much time for thinking. I break through the mound of snow in front of the stoop, and go into a dark house. Snow over all the downstairs windows. I push it away from the south side of the house first. Light fluff, and it goes easily, even with such depth. That's first, and then with the light inside, I realize how friendly this is. An old, battered farmhouse, still in disrepair, but I'm welcome here, and with a fire from the dry birch I left last time, it's complete. Alone, but certainly not lonely. A few more minutes to warm up, and then I'm off down my trail once more to bring in the rest of the supplies—too heavy for the first trip over such unsure footing as trailbreaking gives a man. By now it's time for a supper of very simple food—cheese, eggs and tea. The silence out there, broken by an occasional yap from a fox, a far off owl, and a restless puff of breeze over the beech ridge. I fall asleep with a book in my hand, drowsy from the exertion of walking in the cold, and the present close warmth. Later, I wake up to see a faint glow from the embers in the cookstove against the dark window panes.

March 4. A light snow this morning, with the clouds below and around me. The hills hold them, and a few drifting across the valleys, seem to point to a great storm in the making. Actually nothing but a flurry this morning, and the sun breaks through. My trail is softened by a fresh inch. I look at my sadly depleted woodpile. When I was here last, I had a friend with me who talks a good wilderness man, but shrinks when confronted with the necessity of becoming one. He insisted on keeping roaring fires all night, both for warmth, and I have a suspicion to frighten off some unknown dangers in the darkness. Well I can file my axe, and tighten my bucksaw, go out into the blowdowns where the birch lies across the snow. Perhaps take a shovel to dig out the butts. A whole day spent at this. The rhythm of the sawstroke in time with that of the blood pulse—my only time.

March 5. A real storm today, all day. The snow comes straight down—no wind—no sound—and intense cold—well below zero. I keep at my woodpile, dragging down tops of trees that were cut last summer. Finally, I decide to rebreak my buried trail. Each time over it makes it an easier path, and I'll have to go for supplies tomorrow. I make my routine today, deciding on two trips to the village each week, for food and mail. Daily, there's to be an hour or so on the woodpile, two or three hours in the middle of the day, for lunch, rest and reading walking until dark, supper and chores, and then more reading in the silence that is so complete, that I often hear my own blood pounding.

March 6. I woke up early this morning—still very dark—and glanced at the thermometer inside the kitchen: 52. I planned to get up shortly and went to sleep again. The second time I came to with a start—fully awake. Something unusual had happened. In another moment I realized what it was. The inaccurate clock by which I divide my day roughly had stopped. Why? It was wound last night. Then it came to me. It's very cold in here. The oil in the clock wheels must have congealed. Frost from my breath on the blanket. The fire is out, and the thermometer reads 16. Bright sun streaming through the window. Fortunate that I left the snow piled against the north side of the house, it's blowing hard that way. I look at the outside thermometer: 24 below. I waste no time in building up the fire. Then the trip to town, wrapped in furcoat and hat, but sweating from the exertion of walking in the light powder that drifts in spouts and whirls across my trail. Good to talk with people in the store. Slim who takes his usual leisure in putting up my order. (He was shaving in the postoffice when I came in.) Old Mark Mosher, and Villjo, the Finnish woodsman. I pick up conversations where we left them three month ago. Kindness and slow speech, and that's enough to warm me on the way back, into the eyes of the wind, with my grainsack-load.

March 9. The day I cut birch, and caught my axe on an overhanging branch. Deflected, the blunt side struck me on the forehead. Mumbling some sort of gratitude that I was using a single, rather than a double blade, I threw myself into the snow, and beyond a little dizziness, and hammer-ringing in my head, that was better than a whole hospital. In ten minutes, with nothing but a stiff bruise for my carelessness, I was cutting again.

March 11. I've poked at the snow heap on the north side of the roof. It has bothered me: Lying at night, and listening to the shift and creak of the rafters. Ten feet piled up on a hollow shell, even a strong shell, isn't safe. So today, I got to work on it, walking across the level, which is up to the eaves, and inching my way up, carefully prying the hard windpack away with a flattened coal shovel without tearing into the roofing paper. About three feet from the ridge it became so icy that I had no footing, but at least it seemed safer, and this afternoon, walking up the high pasture beyond the brook, I heard an unusual rumble. Looking back, I saw the black line of the ridge, bare in the afternoon sun.

March 12. The deer must be more curious as to my habits than I am as to theirs. Tracks in this great depth. A small doe must have looked in at me during the night. That's my closest encounter with other life, unless I count the couple who skiied in to see me the other day. She, being Finnish, objected to the heat of my fire, and sat in the north bedroom. She asked for a glass of water, which froze before she had finished it. The deer are wiser.

March 15. Water. It is my one real problem. The well is frozen under so great a depth of snow that I've used the snow in place of it. Slow to melt, and it yields about one bucket to eight. All right for washing, but I go to blow holes in the back stream to drink. There are always tracks there—porcupines that I never see.

March 16. Slim offers me a glass of cider when I go in for supplies today. Very good, and I take another tumbler. He winks, and suggests a third, "to get me up the mountain." So I take a third, and a half of a fourth. Cold, pure light today, and frost spangles in the air—. By the time I reach Woods Hill, I hear bells. All the churches in New England couldn't make that sound. Good cider.

March 22. Thunder clouds, and a thunder storm, but all snow, and lightning wilder than any summer's. Booming off the hills. Ambush of the north spring.

March 26. Last night. My last night here. The aurora in colors, and the sound that is rare, even here, rattle and shimmer that puts heat into the listener, standing in his cold boots.

This morning's a colder one than that other one, when I came in. Oppressive to breathe deeply, and that's a warning to take. Frozen lungs are easy. In Temple Town everyone is up, walking around in as much excitement as if it were "fair time." A house burned during the night. No water, the stream is frozen to the bottom, so they opened the door and "let her go." Slim, calling the owner (on vacation.) "Albert! Had a good vacation? Good enough, I'm going to spoil it right now. You've lost everything you had in town. Yuh, burned flat, No, no need to hurry back, nothing to come back to. Hope you had good insurance."

Landscape with Figures

A sharp smoke drifts,
clears the eaves
barely
        skims the cold ground
thins;
        mingles its smell
with grass and leaves.
Gone.

Late for a spring song
early for winter
to set
except in shadows holding the light frost.

A brooding time
hangs.
The birds
        swing close
to the house.
        A bare branch
nests them.

A man walks through
and whistles
a love song
if it's that
        for him.

The smoke drifts down.
I see
  no more.

LOUIS ZUKOFSKY

from Bottom: on Shakespeare

Magnanimity is by nature difficult when the intellective artist loves his own handiwork more than it would love him if it visibly came to life. For then to be magnanimous would be to enjoy forever, like God, the single and simple pleasure of his own intellect.

> . . .like an artist; for he can see what is fitting, and spend great sums with taste. . .Greatness of soul. . .related to great objects. . .what sort?. . .it matters little whether we look at the quality itself or the person who shows it. . .Great honors accorded by persons of worth afford him moderate pleasure, thinking he is coming by his own or even less, for no honor is worthy of perfection. . .to whom even honor is a slight thing. . .does not run into danger for trifles, and is no lover of danger, because there are few things he values. . .faces danger in a great cause. . . since he knows that there are conditions on which life is not worth having. . .the sort of man to confer benefits, but ashamed to receive them. . .who will possess beautiful and profitless things, rather than such as bring a return, for so he is free.

> Aristotle, *Ethics*, IV, 2, 3

But magnanimity is most difficult for the divided poet, who desires a single and simple pleasure like that of the eyes and is also the entalphic poet, philosopher, and philosopher of history, who attempts to order into universals its growing and decaying singulars. Then no words to him can ever literally look and be sure like the eyes. He does not *see*, but like Aristotle *observes*—wonders, searches incidentally until he relates the causes that are necessarily thinkable—talks rigorously for the sake of correct demonstration—or reason: sight is a function of (numerically) irrational biological power of the human animal, which begins as body, finds a voice that involves or generates intellect, which recalls a type head atop the most primitive human animal that from memorial time generated intellect, that is, the most *knowable* good or end of all self-rarifying human bodies.

Freud's diagnosis of history unconsciously (?) follows the pattern of Aristotle, the son of Nicomachus the doctor—a pattern apart from the

Greek logical phase of its expression much older than Aristotle:

Among the precepts of Mosaic religion is one that has more significance than is at first obvious. It is the prohibition against making an image of God, which means the compulsion to worship an invisible God. I surmise that in this point Moses surpassed the Aton religion in strictness. Perhaps he meant to be consistent; his God was to have neither name nor a countenance. The prohibition was perhaps a fresh precaution against magic malpractices. If this prohibition was accepted, however, it was bound to exercise a profound influence. For it signified subordinating sense perception to an abstract idea; it was a triumph of spirituality over the senses; more precisely, an instinctual renunciation accompanied by its psychologically necessary consequences.

To make more credible what at first glance does not appear convincing we must call to mind other processes of similar character in the development of human culture. The earliest among them, and perhaps the most important, we can discern only in dim outline in the obscurity of primeval times. Its surprising effects make it necessary to conclude that it happened. In our children, in adult neurotics, as well as in primitive people, we find the mental phenomenon which I have called the belief in the "omnipotence of thoughts." We judge it to be an over-estimation of the influence which our mental faculties — the intellectual ones in this case — can exert on the outer world by changing it. All magic, the predecessor of science, is basically founded on these premises. All magic of words belongs here, as does the conviction of the power connected with the knowledge and the pronouncing of a name. We surmise that "omnipotence of thoughts" was the expression of the pride mankind took in the development of language, which had brought in its train such an extraordinary increase in the intellectual faculties. There opened then the new realm of spirituality where conceptions, memories, and deductions became of decisive importance, in contrast to the lower psychical activity which concerned itself with the immediate perceptions of the sense organs. It was certainly one of the most important stages on the way to becoming human.

Another process of later time confronts us in a more tangible form. Under the influence of external conditions—which we need not follow up here and which in part are also not sufficiently known—it happened that the matriarchal structure of society was replaced by a patriarchal one. This naturally brought with it a revolution in the existing state of of the law. An echo of this revolution can still be heard, I think, in the *Oresteia* of Aeschylus. This turning from the mother to the father, however, signifies above all a victory of spirituality over the senses — that is to say, a step forward in culture, since maternity is proved by the senses whereas paternity is based on a deduction and a premise. This declaration in favour of the thought-process, thereby raising it above sense perception, was proved to be a step charged with serious consequences.

Some time between the two cases I have mentioned, another event took place which shows a closer relationship to the ones we have investigated in the history of religion, Man found that he was faced with the acceptance of "spiritual" forces—that is to say, such forces as cannot be apprehended by the senses, particularly not by sight, and yet having undoubted, even extremely strong effects. If we may trust to language, it was the movement of the air that provided the image of spirituality, since the spirit borrows its name from the breath of wind (*animus, spiritus,* Hebrew *ruach* = smoke). The idea of the soul was thus born as the spiritual principle in the individual. Observation found the breath of air again in the human breath, which ceases with death; even today we talk of a dying man breathing his last. Now the realm of spirits had opened for man, and he was ready to endow everything in nature with the soul he had discovered in himself. The whole world became animated, and science, coming so much later, had enough to do in disestablishing the former state of affairs and has not yet finished this task.

Moses and Monotheism, Part III, ii, 4

Freud is modest enough about the historicity of his analysis. Its importance as "truth" shows in his words "serious consequences." Tranio warns against them:

> *Mi perdonato,* gentle master mine,
> I am in all affected as yourself;
> Glad that you thus continue your resolve
> To suck the sweets of sweet philosophy.
> Only, good master, while we do admire
> This virtue and this moral discipline,
> Let's be no Stoics nor no stocks, I pray,
> Or so devote to Aristotle's checks
> As Ovid be an outcast quite abjur'd.
> Balk logic with acquaintance that you have,
> And practice rhetoric in your common talk.
> Music and poesy use to quicken you.
> The mathematics and the metaphysics,
> Fall to them as you find your stomach serves you;
> No profit grows where is no pleasure ta'en.
> In brief, sir, study what you most affect.

The Taming of the Shrew, I, i, 25

Richard of Bordeaux weeps over the "serious consequences," hammering out in the confines of a ward room the male and female principle of their breeding. His conceit of the soul fathering a world of thought recalls Aristotle's suggestive metaphysical humor as to the profligacy of the male impregnating many females being analogous to "those first principles" (*Metaphysics,* I, 6); and anticipates Freud's

151

interlinear deflection (that of the practicing doctor) from the victory of
male spirit to the sense of maternity.

> I have been studying how I may compare
> This prison where I live unto the world;
> And for because the world is populous
> And here is not a creature but myself,
> I cannot do it; yet I'll hammer it out.
> My brain I'll prove the female to my soul,
> My soul the father; and these two beget
> A generation of still-breeding thoughts,
> And these same thoughts people this little world,
> In humours like the people of this world.
> For no thought is contented. The better sort,
> As thoughts of things divine, are intermix'd
> With scruples and do set the word itself
> Against the word:
>
>   . . . But whate'er I be,
> Nor I nor any man that but man is
> With nothing shall be pleas'd, till he be eas'd
> With being nothing.
>
> *Richard II*, V, v, 1-14, 38

He hears music —*"the shadowed and hieroglyphical image of the world"*
(Sir Thomas Browne). Birds, snakes, a dark man, stars, Memnon harp-
like in the first rays of morning sun were the presences in hieroglyphics,
not shadows, musical shadows.

> Music do I hear?   [*Music.*
> Ha, ha! keep time! How sour sweet music is,
> When time is broke and no proportion kept!
> So is it in the music of men's lives.
> And here have I the daintiness of ear
> To check time broke in a disordered string;
> But for the concord of my state and time
> Had not an ear to hear my true time broke.
> I wasted time, and now doth Time waste me;
> For now hath Time made me his numb'ring clock,
> My thoughts are minutes; and with sighs they jar
> Their watches on unto mine eyes, the outward watch,
> Where to my finger, like a dial's point,
> Is pointing still, in cleansing them from tears.
>
>   • •
>
> This music mads me: let it sound no more;
> For though it have holp mad men to their wits,
> In me it seems it will make wise men mad.

Yet blessing on his heart that gives it to me!
For 'tis a sign of love; and love to Richard
Is a strange brooch in this all-hating world.

Richard II, V, v, 41-54, 61

A sign of love—if not the eyed objects of hieroglyphics—but of all abstract thought music is still "simple" tho incapable of being eyed. It is not divided as heard "Everybody knows what melody is," said the Philosopher, and let it go at that (unless his explanation was lost and there was more said).

Finally, the implicit intention of Richard's speech is revealed. It is the recurring interest of all of Shakespeare's works. Ranging and circling abstractly from an ironic "victory" of the spirit to the audible necessary confidence that runs on of "music do I hear," and last to what should be the certain good of staying eyes of the visible groom —but who solidifies Richard's abstract tears, as tragedy must have it, into the surest tragic presence of betraying horse.

... Bolingbroke rode on roan Barbary,
That horse that thou so often hast bestrid,
That horse that I so carefully have dress'd!

Richard II, V, v, 78

And Richard II is ready for the axe of Exton.

Rode he on Barbary? Tell me, gentle friend,
How went he under him?

So proud that Bolingbroke was on his back!
That jade hath eat bread from my royal hand;
This hand hath made him proud with clapping him.
Would he not stumble?

Forgiveness, horse! why do I rail on thee,
Since thou, created to be aw'd by man,
Wast born to bear? I was not made a horse;
And yet I bear a burden like an ass...

Richard II, V, v, 81ff.

These other lines of Shakespeare work the same way: the incest of Antiochus guessed only in circling thought is an argument in space— harping on the goodness of eyes, altho human eyes and, it follows, human love must be least there.

Sharp physic is the last; but, O you powers
That give heaven countless eyes to view men's acts,
Why cloud they not their sights perpetually
If this be true which makes me pale to read it?

Fair glass of light, I lov'd you, and could still,
Were not this glorious casket stor'd with ill.

Pericles, I, i, 72

Aristotle argued:

> . . . it is a mistake to say that the soul (life) is a spatial magnitude.
> It is evident that Plato means the soul of the whole to be like the
> sort of whole which is called mind—not like the sensitive or desidera-
> tive soul, for the movements of neither of these are circular.

De Anima, I, 3

"If the circular movement is eternal, there must be something which
mind is always thinking—what *can* this be?" Aristotle goes on, "For
all practical purposes of thinking have limits," etc.

(The method of factorization developed by Schrödinger can be
used for the solution of eigenvalue problems *upon which artificial
boundary conditions are imposed.* The italics are not in this contemporary mathematical text, which also says, "Such boundary conditions
effect the appearance of an infinite number of parameters—the
eigenvalues or characteristic values—in these solutions. The usual
boundary conditions applied to a differential equation only impose a
finite number of solutions.")

The theme of revealed physical incest in *Pericles* suggests the self-
sown division of logic giving away its "secret" unconscionable marriage
of talk and physical sense that is profligate in every human effort and
its offshoot of humane effort. The humane efforts obscured by talk that
longs for explained or single or simple nature are the subjects of history
as "studied."

Longing is *not* knowing; it is, "simply" speaking, *not* surely seeing.
Longing for "simple" action, which may perhaps elicit knowing from
seeing, Achilles and Ulysses "know" so to speak, but are incomplete.
They read and speak a text that might well be or is a version of
Aristotle's:

> *Achilles,* What are you reading?
> *Ulysses.*   A strange fellow here
> Writes me: "That man, how dearly ever parted,
> How much in having, or without or in,
> Cannot make boast to have that which he hath,
> Nor feels not what he owes, but by reflection;
> As when his virtues shining upon others
> Heat them and they retort that heat again
> To the first giver."
> *Achilles.*   This is not strange, Ulysses.
> The beauty that is borne here in the face

The bearer knows not, but commends itself
To others' eyes; nor doth the eye itself,
That most pure spirit of sense, behold itself,
Not going from itself; but eye to eye oppos'd
Salutes each other with each other's form;
For speculation turns not to itself,
Till it hath travel'd and is married there
Where it may see itself. This is not strange at all.
    Ulysses. I do not strain at the position—
It is familiar,—but at the author's drift;
Who, in his circumstance, expressly proves
That no man is the lord of anything,
(Though in and of him there is much consisting,)
Till he communicate his parts to others.

Troilus and Cressida, III, iii, 94

The life-long flight of *Pericles'* hero from the incest of Antiochus
fluoresces with a metaphysics of cognition that is very old and very new.
Symbolic logic owes more than an ambiguous concern with eyes to
Aristotle, and (working literally backwards, as Aristotle did) its dis-
agreements to Plato. Like Wittgenstein's logic it owes all of the abstract
quarrelsomeness of metaphysics to Aristotle, to Plato who prompted
Aristotle's contention, to Spinoza who berated yet reestablished them
both, and perhaps innocently—for what philosopher will believe it—
to Shakespeare, whose Tranio warned against Aristotle. "Simple" lovers
like Shakespeare's Pericles and Wittgenstein somehow pair off. Fortune
sees to it that the sight of the beloved is *their world*. Its uncluttered
certainty that shows itself is the thing they love most. Tho they reason
"better," they accept the sense of sight sooner than the other senses
and the reason, because love depends most on sight for its being and its
origin (Aristotle, *Ethics*, IX, 12). Pericles says of his visible day's happiness

'Tis more by fortune, lady, than my merit

Pericles, II, iii, 12

The more reasoned assurance of happiness is rather that of Pericles
father-*in-law*:

Call it by what you will, the day is yours
And here, I hope, is none that envies it.
In framing an artist, Art hath thus decreed
To make some good, but others to exceed;
And you are her labour'd scholar.

Pericles, II, iii, 13

Art with a capital A implies at best a lack of envy of eye-construing
genius. The laws of Art like love may originate singular art (lower case),

but may not be imagined *seeing* or showing up like each singular work of art. The relations of Art and singular art—inseparably conceived as an end process of nature, and so married to worrying metaphysics—are always "secretly" (tho it is no secret) incestuous. Dogberry says:

> To be a well-favoured man is the gift of fortune,
> but to write and read comes by nature.
>
> *Much Ado about Nothing*, III, iii, 14

As Dogberry usually means the reverse of what he says, his words resolve (in Shakespeare's sense *dissolve*) into a definition of nature as the father-*in-law* of inquiry, rather than as the eye-construed gift of the well-favored. But the colloquial sense of Dogberry's thought is "enormously complicated." As may be noted here, it does away with Dogberry, if the focus is on the thought rather than the speaker. In that case his words may even suggest the "critical points" of physics and mathematics at which qualities or properties suffer finite change. For example, in mathematics, a parabola is a critical curve thru which a conic passes from an ellipse into an hyperbola; in physics, there exists liquid crystal with properties of crystalline solids, not shown by ordinary liquids.

There is no simple pleasure, as of the eye, in tracing what may be read as an insistent desire to be seen as it hides in Shakespeare's writing, to Aristotle's looking glass and gloss: an overworked liquid gloss that often irradiates disarming sureties of *this* man and *this* animal in the glass. Plato, whom Aristotle charged with making mathematics identical with philosophy for modern thinkers, should to a degree have reduced Aristotle's displeasure by letting Socrates say (good dramatist that Plato was, probably not with a slip of mind on his part): *"The mind becomes critical when the bodily eye fails"* (*The Symposium*).

Plato could not have meant by *critical, nicely judicious,* instead of *attended with risk*—like Pericles thinking of Antiochus' incest? *Pericles* suggested by (?) *periclitate = attended with risk* (1623); "They would periclitate their lives"—1657. In any case—the risk of mind!—Aristotle may be imagined reading Socrates' sympathetic sentence from *The Symposium* with reassured pleasure and some embarrassment; and like the loyal pupil he was in actuality revising his estimate of the *Timaeus*. For being moved to look into it again he could see that there was no argument.

> *Timaeus.* As for that, Socrates... We, who are now to discourse of the universe and its generation—or it may be its *ungenerate existence* [n.b.! two words Aristotle could have used for lucidity in explaining *final cause*, etc., but did not]—unless we are utterly beside ourselves, cannot but invoke gods and goddesses with a prayer that our utterance

may be wellpleasing to them as well as consistent with itself. So much, then, for the gods' part in our prayer...

If . . . we find ourselves in many points unable to make our discourse of the generation of Gods and the universe in every way consistent and exact, you must not be surprised...We must be well content if we can provide an account not less likely than another's; we must remember that I who speak, and you who are my audience, are but men and should be satisfied to ask for no more than the likely story.

Socrates. Well said, Timaeus; such terms ought to be satisfactory to us. We *are* excellently satisfied with your prelude, now proceed to give us the melody itself.

Timaeus. Then let us say why becoming and the universe were framed by him who framed them. He was good, and none that is good is ever subject to any motion of grudging. Being without grudging, then, he desired all things to become as like as might be to himself. This, teach the wise, is the true source of becoming and of the world, and most right it is to listen to their teaching . . . so he took in hand all that was visible—he found it not at rest, but in discordant and disorderly motion— and brought it from disorder to order, since he judged this every way better than that... So he considered and discovered that, whole for whole, of things visible nothing without understanding would ever be more beauteous than with understanding, and further that understanding cannot arise anywhere without soul. Moved by this consideration, he framed understanding within soul and soul within body, and so made the fabric of the universe... This, then, is how according to the likely account, we must say that this our world, a creature with life, soul, and understanding, has...come to be... Being bodily that which has come to be must be visible and tangible.

Timaeus, 27, 29-31, trans. by A. E. Taylor

To the simple reader of Shakespeare the liquid crystal of his lines' self-argument—its musical and verbal liquefactions dissolving finely as it were anterior crystalline, visible properties, which confused even Aristotle in similar self-argument when he showed that the end of eyes was to think—remains unseen after three centuries. Liquid crystal is only as it must be, an incalculable pleasure of optics. Graced as the simple reader is as a biological organism not to have stopped *breathing* the Philosopher's definition of *simple*, he senses it because it is part of him, without having to "observe" its intellective contentions in Shakespeare, let alone Aristotle.

The thinking of the simple objects of thought is found in those cases where falsehood is impossible: where the alternative of true or false applies, there we always find a putting together of objects of thought in a quasi-unity.

...the word *simple* has two senses...(a) not capable of being divided or (b) not actually divided...

157

To perceive is like bare asserting or knowing... The process is like that
in which the air modifies the pupil in this or that way and the pupil
transmits the modification to some third thing (and similarly in hearing)
while the ultimate point of arrival is one, a single mean, with different
manners of being... E.g., perceiving by sense that the beacon is fire,
it recognizes in virtue of the general faculty of sense that it signifies an
enemy, because it sees it moving . . . sometimes by thoughts . . . just as if
it were seeing . . . pronounces the object pleasant or painful . . . avoids or
pursues; and so generally in cases of action....
The so-called abstract objects the mind thinks just as, if one had thought
of the snub-nosed not as snub-nosed but as hollow, one would have
thought of an actuality without the flesh in which it is embodied: it is
thus the mind when it is thinking the objects of Mathematics thinks as
separate, elements which do not exist separate.

De Anima, III, 6, 7

Aristotle's distinctions between *simple* and *divided*, *perception* and
abstraction are simple enough to any reader of Shakespeare who has
lived the definition of a point or a line in plane geometry. Nevertheless,
having breathed in a culture that has been unified by mathematics—the
Greek of which meant a disposition to learn—and having read as much
Freud as is here on a previous page, which mentions "adult neurotics,"
the case of Shakespeare may become uncommonly involved even to the
simple reader.

To go back to Aristotle: in distinguishing between *what is* and *what
for*, he said, *flesh, bone, man* are defined like *snub-nosed* not like
curved; which follows, from the principle that *Man is begotten by man
and the sun as well* (*Physics*, II, 2). What Freud further suggests to the
simple reader is that nose considered as mathematical curve gravitates
to already generated complications that inevitably show evidence of
having limited or *snubbed* it. He is told: if his as-if awake, "simple"
nature has a nose—to him naively enough *in mind* or *on his mind*—that
the *nose* as part of him sets up an omnipotent word that flies away from
nose and forms a hollow. To prove it, let his as-if "simple" nature
dream and a hollow without an omnipotent word is his nose and thought.
All that his waking *singular* nature that history has so complicated and
divided can then do for man, formerly begotten by man and the sun,
is to let nose curve verbally or symbolically more or less as it breathes
already dreaming to be stayed in a generic hollow for all human motors,
which "instinctually" desire an ungenerate dead center.

Historical offspring of Aristotle's principle of generation—man and
the sun—Freud in his *singular* way says what has already been said:
except that he *divides*, so to speak, Aristotle's *nature* by a "new" set
of terms—perhaps not too "new" at that. Spinoza also more filially

158

involved in the *Nicomachean Ethics* than he imagined had already said:

>...when we say that anyone suspends his judgment, we say nothing
else than that he sees that he does not perceive the thing adequately.
Therefore a suspension of judgment is in truth a perception and not
free will. To make this more clear, let us conceive a boy imagining a
horse and perceiving nothing else. Inasmuch as this imagination involves
the existence of the horse...and the boy does not perceive anything
that could take away from the horse its existence, he will necessarily
regard the horse as present, nor will he have any doubts of its existence,
although he may not be certain of it. We have daily experience of this
in dreams, and I do not think there is anyone who thinks that while he
sleeps he has the free power of suspending his judgment concerning
what he dreams, and of bringing it to pass that he should not dream
what he dreams he sees; and yet it happens in dreams also that we can
suspend our judgments, namely, when we dream that we dream.
Further, I grant that no one is deceived in so far as he perceives, that
is, I grant that the imaginations of the mind considered in themselves
involve no error . . . but I deny that a man affirms nothing in so far
as he perceives. For what else is it to perceive a winged horse than to
affirm wings on a horse? For if the mind perceives nothing else save a
winged horse, it will regard it as present to itself; nor will it have any
reason for doubting its existence, nor any faculty of dissenting, unless
the imagination of a winged horse be joined to an idea which removes
existence from the horse or unless he perceives that the idea of a winged
horse is inadequate, and then he will necessarily deny the existence of
the horse or necessarily doubt it.
>
> *Ethics*, Part II, Prop. XLIX, Note

Spinoza conceded, saying *"the same thing as the ancients said*, that
true science proceeds from cause to effect, save that they never, as far
as I know, conceive what we have here, namely that the soul acts
according to certain laws and resembles a spiritual automaton" (*de
intellectus emendatione*, 85). Spinoza's summation of what the ancients
said covers Aristotle but for the Greek's singular way of *seeing*. With
something like the flair of the poets in the *Anthology* he saw nature
as a flower that might come to think and like it.

Two Letters to Cid Corman

Aug 13/60

Dear Cid,

...*"A"'s* references—as you say, the context must "explain" 'em or reveal them. They are usually *constructs*, telescoping of several actual references, even if as in this section I say I'm talking or P's talking or whoever. It's "autobiography" I suppose as in any good novel or Weston's "photograph." And anyone who goes off on exact "identification" I needn't tell you is not reading or hearing. The "memos" for me as I read myself are something else again—I trust as I once told you that they somehow continue to exist in the "noise" as all life probably does that has lived....

Louis

Aug 25/60

Dear Cid,

...I've written a good bit of 13-iii now, & itching as I'm to show you spots I better go on instead before packing for Old Lyme, less than a week now; in my mind it is the *sarabande*, what you have are the *allemande & courante* (no reason for these on-my-minds in any strict musical sense, just telling you some of my sentiments nobody else's business); and after that/the *sarabande/a gigue* and *chaconne.* Anyway what interests me most on top of it as I am—too damn close for a guy who can't avoid "ideas" tho these interest him least—is not the ideas but the way the recurrences & reflections (your shadows) come up welling tho I don't *consciously* try anything like plotting 'em, of all the other movements of "A." I realize they're there, the connections, only after I reread the ms. to assure myself I can take (stand) it—e.g. Heraclitus by the shtove & p. 184 in the book. That I "know" is to the good—as for what else in the way of *content* ten years have accumulated the sooner I get that out of the way & buried in the music of the *whole thing* the better. Then I can wait unless something unexpected happens a long time before I feel movement 14 is necessary. The other thing that pleases me as I reread i. and ii. of 13 is that for example when I reword the "economics" of "A"-9 in 13 it's so much shorter (p. 8 of the ms.). Why am I bothering you—just to say it's a hard life and I hope both of us come out of it liking it I suppose.. And that a Z-sky can sneeze back at a Korzybski for all that..."

All our love,
Louis

GARY SNYDER

Bubbs Creek Haircut

for Locke McCorkle

High ceilingd and the double mirrors, the
      calendar a splendid alpine scene—scab barber—
in stained white barber gown, alone, sat down, old man
A summer fog gray San Francisco day
I walked right in. on Howard street
               haircut a dollar twenty-five.
Just clip it close as it will go.
     "now why you want your hair cut back like that."
—well I'm going to the Sierras for a while
Bubbs Creek and on across to upper Kern.
              he wriggled clippers,
"Well I been up there, I built the cabin
    up at Cedar Grove. In nineteen five."
             old haircut smell

Next door, Goodwill.
         where I came out.
A search for sweater, and a stroll
        in the board & concrete room of
        unfixed junk downstair—
All emblems of the past—too close—
    heaped up in chilly dust and bare bulb glare
Of tables, wheelchairs, battered trunks & wheels
& pots that boiled up coffee nineteen ten, *things*
Swimming on their own & finally freed
         from human need. Or?
    waiting a final flicker of desire
To tote them out once more. Some freakish use.
The Master of the limbo drag-leggd watches
            making prices
    to the people seldom buy
The sag-assd rocker has to make it now. Alone.

A few weeks later drove with Locke
down San Joaquin, us barefoot in the heat
stopping for beer & melon on the way
   the Giant Orange,
rubber shreds of cast truck retreads on the pebble
shoulders, highway ninety-nine.
   Sierras marked by cumulus
  in the east.
car coughing in the groves, six thousand feet;
down to Kings River Canyon; camped at Cedar
      Grove.
   hard granite canyon walls that
   leave no scree

Once tried a haircut at the Barber College too—
Sat half an hour before they told me
   white men use the other side.
Goodwill, St. Vincent de Paul,
   Salvation Army, up the coast
For mackinaws and boots and heavy socks
   —Seattle has the best for logger gear·
Once found a pair of good tricouni
   at the under-the-public-market store,
   Mark Tobey's scene,
    torn down I hear—
& Filson jacket with a birdblood stain.

A. G. & me got winter clothes for almost nothing
   at Lake Union, telling the old gal
   we was on our way
To work the winter out up in B. C.
     hitch-hiking home the
Green hat got a ride (of that more later)

 hiking up Bubbs creek saw the trail crew tent
 in a scraggly grove of creekside lodgepole pine
   talked to the guy, he says
 "If you see McCool on the other trailcrew over there
 tell him Moorehead says to go to hell."
 late snow that summer. Crossing the scarred bare
   shed of Forester Pass
  the winding rock-braced switchbacks
 dive in snowbanks, we climb on where

pack trains have to dig or wait.
a half iced-over lake, twelve thousand feet
its sterile boulder bank
but filled with leaping trout:
reflections wobble in the
mingling circles always spreading out
the crazy web of wavelets makes sense
seen from high above.
the realm of fallen rock.
a deva world of sorts—it's high
it is a view that few men see, a point
bare sunlight
on the spaces
empty sky
moulding to fit the shape of what ice left
of fire-thrust, or of tilted, twisted, faulted
cast-out from this lava belly globe.

The boulder in my minds eye is a chair.
... why was the man drag legg'd ?
King of Hell
or is it a paradise of sorts, thus freed
From acting out the function some
creator/carpenter
Thrust on a thing to think he made, himself,
an object always "chair"
Sinister ritual histories.
is the Mountain God a gimp?
"le Roi Boeuf" and the ritual limp?
Good   Will?

Daughter of mountains, stoopd
moon breast Parvati
mountain thunder speaks
hair tingling static as the lightning lashes
is neither word of love or wisdom;
though this be danger: hence thee fear.
Some flowing girl
whose slippery dance
entrances Shiva
—the valley spirit/ Anahita,
Sarasvati,
dark and female gate of all the world

water that cuts back quartzflake sand
                    Soft is the dance that melts the
mat-haired mountain sitter
                    to leap in fire
& make of sand a tree
          of tree a board, of board (ideas!)
          somebody's rocking chair.
a room of empty sun of peaks and ridges
          beautiful spirits,
                              rocking lotus throne:
a universe of junk, all left alone.

The hat I always take on mountains:
When we came back down through Oregon
                              (three years before)
At nightfall in the Siskiyou few cars pass
A big truck stopped a hundred yards above
          "Siskiyou Stoneware" on the side
The driver said
He recognized my old green hat.
I'd had a ride
          with him two years before
A whole state north
          when hitching down to Portland
                              from Warm Springs.
Allen in the rear on straw
    forgot salami   and we went on south
all night—in many cars—to Berkeley in the dawn.

       upper Kern River country now after nine days walk
       it finally rain.
             we ran on that other trail crew
       setting up new camp in the drizzly pine
     cussing & slapping bugs, 4 days from road,
       we saw McCool, & he said tell that Moorehead
              KISS MY ASS
       we squatted smoking by the fire.
             "I'll never get a green hat now"
       the foreman says   fifty mosquitoes sitting on the brim
                           they must like green.
       & two more days of thundershower and cold
              (on Whitney hair on end

hail stinging barelegs in the blast of wind
but yodel off the summit echoes clean)

all this came after:
Purity of the mountains and goodwills.
The diamond drill of racing icemelt waters
                and bumming trucks & watching
Buildings raze
                the garbage acres burning at the Bay
                the girl who was the skid-row
Cripple's daughter —

                out of the memory of smoking pine
The lotion and the spittoon glitter rises
Chair turns and in the double mirror waver
The old man cranks me down and cracks a chuckle

                "your Bubbs Creek haircut, boy."
                                        20. IV. 60

DENISE LEVERTOV

Clouds

The clouds as I see them, rising
urgently, roseate, the
mounting of somber power

surging in evening haste over
roofs and hermetic
grim walls —
                Last night
as if death had lit a pale light
in your flesh, your flesh
was cold to my touch, or not cold
but cool, cooling, as if the last traces
of warmth were still fading in you.
My thigh burned in cold fear where
yours touched it.

But I forced to mind my vision of a sky
close and enclosed, unlike the space in which these
                                        clouds move —

a sky of gray mist it appeared—
and how looking intently at it we saw
its gray was not gray but a milky white
in which radiant traces of opal greens,
fiery blues, gleamed, faded, gleamed again,
and how only then, seeing the color in the gray,
a field sprang into sight, extending
between where we stood and the horizon,

a field of freshest deep spiring grass
starred with dandelions,
green and gold
gold and green alternating in closewoven
chords, madrigal field.

Is death's chill that visited our bed
other than what it seemed, is it
a gray to be watched keenly?

Wiping my glasses and leaning westward,
clearing my mind of the day's mist and leaning
into myself to see
the colors of truth

I watch the clouds as I see them
in pomp advancing, pursuing
the fallen sun.

The World Outside

I

On the kitchen wall a flash
of shadow:
            swift pilgrimage
of pigeons, a spiral
celebration of air, of sky-deserts.
And on tenement windows
a blaze
            of lustered watermelon:
stain of the sun
westering somewhere back of Hoboken.

II

The goatherd upstairs! Music
from his sweet flute
roves from summer to summer
in the dusty air of airshafts
and among the flakes
of soot that float
in a daze from chimney
to chimney — notes
remote, cool, speaking of slender
shadows under olive-leaves. A silence.

III

Groans, sighs, in profusion,
with coughing, muttering, orchestrate
solitary grief. The crash of glass, a low voice
repeating over and over, "No.
                No. I want my key. No you did not.
                No."
— a commonplace.
                And in counterpoint, from other windows,
the effort to be merry — ay, maracas!
— sibilant, intricate — the voices wailing pleasure,
arriving perhaps at joy, late, after sets
have been switched off, and silences
are dark windows?

ROBERTO SANESI

La Cosa

Alive at daybreak — in insects' cries — the painful
                silence of sounds.
And in his figure flung into space, a body
capable of measures yet unknown, man meets
                the grace of things,
and space closes to open again.
                                In the garden I observe
a red dog browsing daisies, a sod, a seesaw
                tilting

167

among the leaves, Ishmael hastening to the sea, and
               the revelation
no more is in the light breaking, in the iris beguiling
               and propitious
to tired eyes, but in the darkness from which the thing
               emerges, an absence
of limits and weight.
                       Every figure's an empty sound,
               Ishmael,
a red dog dashing toward the sea with white petals
               quiet
upon its tongue, and the seesaw motionless
               in daylight.

LORINE NIEDECKER

I

Hear
where her snow-grave is
the *You*
    ah you
of mourning doves.

II

Springtime's wide
water —
    yield
but the field
will return.

III

How white the gulls
in grey weather
    Soon April
    the little
yellows.

IV

My friend tree
I sawed you down
but I must attend
an older friend
the sun.

V

New-sawed
clean-smelling house
sweet cedar pink
    flesh tint
I love you.

The Element Mother

I

She's Dead

The branches' snow is like the cotton fluff
she wore in her aching ears. In this deaf huff
after storm shall we speak of love?—

as my absent father's distrait wife
she worked for us—knew us by sight.

We know her now by the way the snow
protects the plants before they go.

II

The Graves

You were my mother, thorn apple bush,
armed against life's raw push.
But you my father catalpa tree
stood serene as now—he refused to see
that the other woman, the hummer he shaded
    hotly cared

for his purse petals falling—
                    his mind in the air.

                    III

                    Kepler

Comets you say shoot from nothing?
In heaven's name what other
than matter can be matter's mother.

You Are My Friend

You are my friend—
you bring me peaches
and the high bush cranberry
            you carry
my fishpole

you water my worms
you patch my boot
with your mending kit
            nothing in it
but my hand

LOUIS ZUKOFSKY

from Bottom: on Shakespeare

As for the anticipatory Freudian flight of divided soul (or life)
in Shakespeare's words that argue for sight only to distil themselves
into music, which suggests to itself being stilled in silence, all their dreams
are as involuntary and as divided as Richard's perception of his horse
Barbary. And when the words reason they are as adequate to waking
life as the winged horse of Spinoza that succeeded Barbary in the
growing and decaying singulars (as opposed to universals) in the history
of philosophy and the history of history. But even the simplest reader
knows that it is immaterial to Shakespeare's words (as it was to
Wittgenstein) whether what they *think* has been *thought* before—or for

that matter whether the thought they think is likely to be so "common," as Hamlet says, as to be thought again.

What is of interest in Shakespeare is the consistent longing for eyes in the words as they argue not to be divided from eyes. Not all singulars think *that*.

Since the words argue because nature made them disputatious, the necessary proportion they evolve

love:reason :: eyes:mind

means only that love and the eyes are one if reason and the mind are one. The proportion dissolves into colloquial abstract thought like "*the readiness is all*," since reason has been implicitly made to equal looking. Reasoned that way the so many unreasoning tears which obscure the reiterated case of eyes in Shakespeare's lines dissolve, but the eyes also disappear in the reason:

> For though some nature bids us all lament
> Yet nature's tears are reason's merriment.
>
> *Romeo and Juliet*, IV, v, 82

Eyes may be inferred from the word *tears*, but it is not explicit that reason's merriment physically *sees*. Logically considered that is the obscured intent of the lines, since logic always asserts identity or says something like the theological carol: "One is one and all alone." To avoid circuity is to say instead: "*No tongue! all eyes! be silent*." But no artist in words dares act the six words of this command, unless he desires not to exist.

Aside from the concern with eyes making the *Works*, this singular historical intent of Shakespeare's words remains of interest when compared with those of similar intent, not because all see the "same" thought, but because their similar qualities are like shades of one color that must be ordered if history (like poetry in Aristotle's definition) may be said to yield any generic philosophical or universal considerations at all.

> Love's reason's without reason. The bier at door
> And a demand who is't shall die, I'd say
> My father, not this youth.
>
> *Cymbeline*, IV, ii, 22

The doubts occasioned by Shakespeare's love's mind's or reason's identity with eyes are sustained by Wittgenstein, who often hits the nail on the head into the lid of the bier at door of old logic that fathered him and Shakespeare.

> 2.224 It cannot be discovered from the picture alone whether it is true or false.

4.1272 It is as senseless to say "there is only 1" as it would be to say "2 plus 2 is at 3 o'clock equal to 4."

4.461 The proposition shows what it says, the tautology has no truth-conditions, for it is unconditionally true; and the contradiction is on no condition true. Tautology and contradiction are without sense.
(Like the point from which two arrows go out in opposite directions.) (I know nothing about the weather, when I know it rains or does not rain.)

4.4611 Tautology and contradiction are, however, not nonsensical [i.e. *silly*, not to be confused with *non-sense* or "without sense" as used in 4.461]; they are part of the symbolism, in the same way that "0" is part of the symbolism of arithmetic.

4.463 Tautology leaves to reality the whole infinite logical space; contradiction fills the whole logical space and leaves no point to reality. Neither of them, therefore can in any way determine reality.

4.464 The truth of tautology is certain, of propositions possible, of contradiction impossible. (Certain, possible, impossible: here we have an indication of that gradation we need in the theory of probability.)

5.511 How can the all-embracing logic which mirrors the world use such special catches and manipulations? Only because all these are connected into an infinitely fine network to the great mirror.

5.5303 Roughly speaking: to say of *two* things that they are identical is nonsense, and to say of one thing that it is identical with itself is to say—nothing.

Tractatus

Spinoza "demonstrated" very much like Shakespeare's "Yet nature's tears are reason's merriment"—perhaps with less passivity to words, but with no less implication of *eyes* that are lost but desired in reason:

There cannot be too much merriment, but it is always good... Merriment, which we said to be good, can be more easily conceived than observed...
Ethics, Part IV, Prop. XLII, XLIV, Note

Referring to Wittgenstein, 4.464—Spinoza's first sentence in the foregoing quotation is in part *contradiction* (i.e. dealing with the impossible), in part *certain* (i.e. presenting a tautology or the catch of an identity, cf. Wittgenstein 5.511 and 5.5303—for *merriment* conceived as *good* is *not observed* but *conceived* as Spinoza says, and therefore does not determine reality but leaves to reality "the whole infinite logical space," in Wittgenstein's sense.)

Reason controls Spinoza's propositions so that, as in Shakespeare, their implicity tautological, certain physical eyes disappear; and, in place of eyes, reality shows up abstractly in his verbal symbolism as duration —

> indefinite continuation of existing . . . indefinite because it can in no wise be determined by means of the nature itself of an existing thing nor by an effecting cause, which necessarily imposes existence on a thing but cannot take it away.
>
> *Ethics*, Part II, Def. V

Reason says:

> That which is common to all (all bodies agree in certain respects), and that which is equally in a part and in the whole, do not constitute the essence of an individual thing.
> Those things which are common to all, and which are equally in a part and in the whole, can only be conceived as adequate . . . (i.e. certain ideas or notions are granted common to all men…adequately or distinctly perceived by all.
>
> *Ethics*, Part II, Prop. XXXVII, XXXVIII

The logic of reason offers *propositions* — i.e. possibilities that may be argued, but which nevertheless *show* themselves like the final assertion in what follows:

> To make use of things and take delight in them as much as possible . . . is the part of a wise man . . . to take pleasure with perfumes, with the beauty of growing plants, dress, music, sports, and theatres, and other places of this kind which man may use without any hurt to his fellows. For the human body is composed of many parts of different nature which continuously stand in need of new and varied nourishment, so that the body as a whole may be equally apt for performing those things which can follow from its nature, and consequently so that the mind also may be equally apt for understanding many things at the same time . . . if there be any other, this manner of life is the best . . . nor is there any need . . . to be more clear or more detailed on this subject.
>
> *Ethics*, Part IV, Prop. XLV, Note 2

The word *body* is used in this proposition as tho it would anticipate Wittgenstein's warning in *Philosophical Investigations* that "A smiling mouth does not smile except in a face." Two centuries before Wittgenstein the *singular* bodies of history have, in Spinoza's *Ethics*, all but disappeared in the smile of reason. Sense (the *universal* term for *singular* feeling), essence (the *universal* for singular *being*), and nonsense (i.e. non-sense, the *universal* for universal being unconcerned with singular *feeling*) have always made up the arguments of logic and metaphysics. When Shakespeare argues his interest is largely sense, tho essence always encroaches.

173

When Spinoza argues his interest is largely essence, tho (as in Aristotle) sense is hardly ever forgotten:

> ...let none be surprised that I, before having proved that there are bodies and other necessary things, speak of the imagination, of the body and its composition. For as I have said, I may take it as I will, provided I know it is something vague, etc.
> But we have shown that a true idea is simple or composed of simple ideas, and that it shows how and why anything is or is made, and that its objective effects proceed in harmony with the formality (i.e. the expressed form) of its objects: which is the same thing as the ancients said [etc., as quoted before].
>
> *de intellectus emendatione*, 84, 85

> ... words are a part of the imagination, that is, according as they are composed in vague order in the memory owing to a condition of the body, we can feign many conceptions, therefore it must not be doubted but that words, just as imagination, can be the cause of many great errors unless we take the greatest precautions with them.... they are arranged to suit the speaker's pleasure and the comprehension of the vulgar, so that they are only the signs of things according as they are in the imagination, but not according as they are in the understanding; which is clearly apparent from the fact that on all those which are in the intellect and not in the imagination, negative names are often bestowed, such as incorporeal, infinite, etc.; and also many things which are really affirmative are expressed negatively, and contrariwise, as uncreated, independent, infinite, immortal, etc., because their contraries are much more easily imagined, and therefore occurred first to men and usurped positive names. We affirm and deny many things because the nature of words allows us to affirm and deny, but not the nature of things; and therefore when this is not known we can easily take the false for the true.
> Let us avoid, moreover, another great cause which prevents the understanding from reflecting on itself. It is that as we do not make a distinction between imagination and understanding, we think that those things which we easily imagine are clearer to us, and that which we imagine we think we understand. So that those things which should be put last we put first, and thus the true order of progress is perverted and nothing may legitimately be concluded.
>
> *de intellectus emendatione*, 88-90

> For I do not understand by ideas, images which are formed at the back of the eye and, if you will, in the center of the brain, but conceptions of thought.
>
> *Ethics*, Part II, Prop. XLVIII, Note

> They do not know what a body is, or what can be deduced from mere contemplation...and with respect to those things, which we desire with such affection that nothing can obliterate them from the mind we are by

no means free...surely human affairs would be far happier if the power in men to be silent were the same as that to speak. But...men govern nothing with more difficulty than their tongues, and can moderate their desires more easily than their words...these decrees of the mind arise in the mind from the same necessity as the ideas of things actually existing. Those, therefore, who believe that they speak, are silent, or do anything from the free decision of the mind, dream with their eyes open.

Ethics, Part III, Prop. II, Note

In neither Shakespeare nor Spinoza does awareness of nonsense (non-sense) prevail—late logic and science had just begun—tho the burden of the *Tractatus* is anticipated in both:

No tongue! all eyes! be silent.

...surely human affairs would be far happier if the power in men to be silent...etc.

Those, therefore, who believe that they speak, are silent, or do anything from the free decision of the mind, dream with their eyes open.

Perhaps the chronological sequence implied in the comparison that has been made here between Shakespeare, Spinoza, and Wittgenstein suggests a convenient generic principle of "looking" at history—and that when all is said, in accordance with this principle, the thinking has spirited away the *singulars*. Perhaps as much philosophy of history may be inferred—for example, as to a kinship between historic characters —from a comparison of the second best bed that Shakespeare left to Ann Hathaway and the bed that Benedict Spinoza kept for himself after suing his covetous sister for their parents' estate, only to return all of it to her except the one bed.

The burden of the *Tractatus*:

5.551   Our fundamental principle is that every question which can be decided at all by logic can be decided off-hand. (And if we get into a situation where we need to answer such a problem by looking at the world, this shows that we are on a fundamentally wrong track).

That is: logic may perhaps be an adequate, tho not especially necessary literature (like all literature? as Shakespeare's theme—Love sees—begs the question as it leads "off-hand" to *words, words, words* and so many sub-propositions of Wittgenstein.)

5.552   The "experience" which we need to understand logic is not that such and such is the case, but that something *is*; but that is *no* experience.

Logic *precedes* every experience—that something is *so*. It is before the *How*, not before the *What*.

5.5521   And if this were not the case, how could we apply logic? We could say: if there were a logic, even if there were no world, how then could there be a logic, since there is a world?

5.5541   How could we decide a priori whether, for example, I can get into a situation in which I need to symbolize with a sign of a 27-termed relation?

5.5542   May we then ask this at all? Can we set out a sign form and not know whether anything can correspond to it?
Has the question sense: What must there *be* in order that anything can be the case?

5.556   ... Only that which we ourselves construct can we foresee.

5.5561   Empirical reality is limited by the totality of objects. The boundary appears again in the totality of elementary propositions.
The hierarchies are and must be independent of reality.

5.5563   All propositions of our colloquial language are actually, just as they are, logically completely in order. That simple thing which we ought to give here is not a model of the truth but the complete truth itself.
(Our problems are not abstract but perhaps the most concrete that there are.)

5.5571   If I cannot give elementary propositions a priori then it must lead to obvious nonsense to try to give them.

5.6   *The limits of my language* mean the limits of my world.

5.61   We cannot therefore say in logic: This and this there is in the world, that there is not.
We cannot think, that we cannot think.
i.e., we cannot therefore *say* what we cannot think.

6.1   The propositions of logic are tautologies.

6.11   The propositions of logic therefore say nothing.
(They are analytical propositions.)

6.111   Theories which make a proposition of logic appear substantial are always false.

6.123   It is clear that the laws of logic cannot themselves obey further logical laws.

6.1231   The mark of logical propositions is not their general validity.
To be general is only to be accidentally valid for all things.

6.124   ...In logic the nature of the essentially necessary signs itself, asserts. That is to say, if we know the logical syntax of any sign language, then all the propositions of logic are already given.

6.125   It is possible, also with the old conception of logic, to give at the outset a description of all "true" logical propositions.

6.1251 Hence there can *never* be surprises in logic.

6.13 Logic is not a theory but a reflexion of the world.
Logic is transcendental.

6.2 Mathematics is a logical method.

6.231 It is a property of affirmation that it can be conceived as double denial.

6.3 Logical research means the investigation of *all regularity*. And outside logic all is accident.

Cf. Aristotle, *Physics*, II, 6: "'incidentally'...nothing which is incidental is prior to what is *per se*, it is clear that no incidental cause can be prior to a cause *per se*. Spontaneity and chance, therefore, are posterior to intelligence and nature. . . . For instance, taking a walk is for the sake of evacuation of the bowels; if this does not follow after walking, we say that we have walked 'in vain' and that the walking was 'vain'. This implies that what is naturally the means to an end is 'in vain', when it does not affect the end towards which it was the natural means—for it would be absurd for a man to say that he had bathed in vain because the sun was not eclipsed, since the one was not done with a view to the other. Thus the spontaneous is even according to its derivation the case in which the thing itself happens in vain."

(Also Agassiz, *Letter to A. Sedgwick on Fixity of Species:* "The differences between animals do not constitute a material change, analogous to a series of physical phenomena, bound together by the same law, but present themselves rather as *the phases* of a thought, formulated according to a definite aim.")

6.3431 Through their whole logical apparatus the physical laws still speak of the objects of the world.

(As *The Republic*, Book X, speaks of the whorl of the spindle of Necessity "like the whorl on earth.")

6.37 A necessity for one thing to happen because another has happened does not exist. There is only *logical* necessity.

6.371 At the basis of the whole modern view of the world lies the illusion that the so-called laws of nature are the explanations of natural phenomena.

6.372 So people stop short at natural laws as at something unassailable, as did the ancients at God and Fate.
And they both are right and wrong. But the ancients were clearer, in so far as they recognized one clear terminus, whereas the modern system makes it appear as though *everything* were explained.

6.373 The world is independent of my will.

6.375   As there is only a logical necessity, so there is also a logical impossibility.

6.3751   For two colors, e.g., to be at one place in a visual field is impossible, logically impossible for it is excluded by the logical structure of color.

6.421   It is clear ethics cannot be expressed. Ethics are transcendental.
         (Ethics and aesthetics are one.)

6.423   Of the will as the subject of the ethical we cannot speak. And the will as a phenomenon is only of interest to psychology.

6.43   If good or bad willing changes the world, it can only change the limits of the world, not the facts; not the things that can be expressed in language. In brief, the world must thereby become quite another. It must so to speak wax or wane as a whole.
         The world of the happy is quite another than that of the unhappy.

6.431   As in death, too, the world does not change, but ceases.

6.4311   Death is not an event of life. Death is not lived through. If by eternity is understood not endless temporal duration but timelessness, then he lives eternally who lives in the present.
         Our life is endless in the way that our visual field is without limit.

6.4312   Is a riddle solved by the fact that I survive forever? Is this eternal life not as enigmatic as our present one?
         The solution of the riddle of life in space and time lies *outside* space and time.
         (It is not problems of natural science which have to be solved.)

Shakespeare's theme—which *knows*, that is, cannot will but asserts its logic—*makes distance seen*, and *not space* (where a point is a place for an argument); and love between the remote hearts of the turtle and his queen *extends a wonder*.

Analects

He said: Those who know aren't up to those who love; nor those who love, to those who delight in.

I do not see love of looking into the mind and acting on what one sees there to match love of someone having beauty. (In this sense, Ezra Pound knows as his translation sees, tho he says, "I do not in the least understand the text of this chapter. Only guess at it I can make is:")

He said: As a mountain (grave-mound) is not made perfect by one basket of earth, yet has position, I take position. If you dump one basket of earth on a level plain it is a start (toward the heap?) I make that start.

The flowers of the prunus japonica deflect and turn, do I not think of you dwelling afar?
He said: It is not the thought, how can there be distance in that?

.*Analects*, Six, XVIII; Nine, XVII, XVIII, XXX

6.4321   The facts all belong to the task [cf. *thought*, Aristotle] and not to its performance [cf. *"indefinite continuation of existing*," Spinoza].

6.44   Not how the world is, is the mystical, but that it is (cf. *"the simple unmoved, moving certain nature*," Aristotle).

6.45   The contemplation of the world sub specie aeterni is its contemplation as a limited whole.
The feeling of the world as a limited whole is the mystical feeling.

6.5   For an answer which cannot be expressed the question too cannot be expressed.
The *riddle* does not exist.
If the question can be put at all, then it *can* also be answered.

6.51   Skepticism is *not* irrefutable, but palpably senseless, if it would doubt where a question cannot be asked.
For doubt can only exist where there is a question; a question only where there is an answer, and this only where something *can* be *said*.

6.52   We feel that even if *all possible* scientific questions be answered, the problems of life have still not been touched at all. Of course there is then no question left, and just this is the answer.

6.521   The solution of the problem of life is seen in the vanishing of this problem.
(Is not this the reason why men to whom after long doubting the sense of life became clear, could not then say wherein this sense consisted?)

6.522   There is indeed the inexpressible. This *shows* itself; it is the mystical.

6.53   The right method of philosophy would be this. To say nothing except what can be said, i.e. the propositions of natural science, i.e. something that has nothing to do with philosophy: and then always, when someone else wished to say something metaphysical to demonstrate to him that he had given no meaning to certain signs in his propositions. This would be unsatisfying to the other—he would not have the feeling that we were teaching him philosophy, but it would be the only strictly correct method.

6.54   My propositions are elucidatory in this way: he who

understands me finally recognizes them as senseless, when he has climbed out through them, on them, over them, (He must so to speak throw away the ladder, after he has climbed up on it.) He must surmount these propositions; then he sees the world rightly.

7.   Woven man nicht sprechen kann, darüber muss man schweigen.

"Looking" away from Wittgenstein's seventh and final proposition and back a page to the negative assertion that "the riddle does not exist," has a way of generating an earlier phase of their implicit theme— Shakespeare's theme that " *Love sees, No tongue! All eyes!*," which threads the "compounding" eye-thought of its culture to a later. Together, Wittgenstein and Shakespeare look back with longing almost two thousand years to "simple" (single) nature. Shakespeare's many words enforce themselves on a reading of Wittgenstein, like Titania's moon that

> ...looks with a wat'ry eye;
> And when she weeps, weeps every little flower,
> Lamenting some enforcèd chastity.
>
> A *Midsummer Night's Dream*, III, i, 205

Enforced means here *compelled, involuntary*, and not *violated* as the glossary profanes. For Titania, like Wittgenstein, chides:

> Tie up my lover's tongue, bring him silently.

The meaning of *enforced* is then as Bassanio uses it, after having for a crewelled Venetian attained the patience of Bottom. (It is to be remembered that the weaver asks the acquaintance of Mustardseed precisely because her kindred had made his eyes water e'er now. So in his dream of love he reasons that the eyes see her not as a substance that makes them water, but as a necessary embodiment of singular nature.) In the same light, Bassanio sees the wrongs of nature as the involuntary, friendless arguments that blind his own eyes as seen in the eyes by which he swears.

> Portia, forgive me this enforced wrong;
> And in the hearing of these many friends
> I swear to thee, even by thine own fair eyes,
> Wherein I see myself—

And Portia reassures them.

> *Portia.*   Mark you but that!
> In both my eyes he doubly sees himself

In each eye, one. Swear by your double self,
And there's an oath of credit.

The Merchant of Venice, V, i, 240

Shakespeare's *Works* enforce such credit of a double self as they
constantly brighten in the "simple" event. They conceive the "compounded" to return time after time, page after page of the total natural
activity of the words to judge its thought by the "simple": "*All eyes!*"

In Dutch New York, in the seventeenth century, there was a fruit
called *forerunner*, a simple fruit it would seem by the sound, but today
unidentified or masked by another name, a changeling sound, wavering
in its discourse like Shakespeare's two uses of it: thought that recalls
its blood; and blood faithful to run ahead; but at the fixed core of both
meanings the generative fruit shines, *looking* as it were without thought.

Arthur, that great forerunner of the blood
Richard,

King John, II, i, 2

Forerun fair Love, strewing her way with flowers.

Love's Labor Lost, IV, iii, 380

So Aristotle thought in universals with the same particular universality
of some such constancy: "Man is begotten by man and by the sun as
well" (*Physics*, II, 2). So, while turning on the "*eyes of man*," Timon
cries, "*O blessed breeding sun!*" and "*Earth, yield me roots!*" And to
Alcibiades,

I do wish thou wert a dog,
That I might love thee something.

Timon of Athens, IV, iii, 50, 1, 23, 54

Lucretius has hardly been thought of as source for Shakespeare. There is

ita Ver et Venus et Veneris praenuntius ante

On come Spring and Venus and Venus' forerunner...strewing the
path ahead.

The simple "her unselfish ways...the neat body...habit alone can
win love" (*De Rerum Natura*, IV) have not much to do with the blows of
the atoms—the lag and prophecy of Lucretius' art which attempts to
prove the unseen atoms so often by seen things.

There is little about atoms in Shakespeare. Two sleights performed
with *atomies* guilelessly suggest the Lucretian source while they rate
the impalpable "compounded" even (i.e. thought) by their sensuous
stand in the "simple" look.

Rosalind... How looked he? Wherein went he? What makes he here?
Did he ask for me? Where remains he? How parted he with thee? And
when shalt thou see him again? Answer me in one word.

181

Celia. You must borrow me Gargantua's mouth first. 'Tis a word too great for any mouth of this age's sighs. To say ay or no to these particulars is more than to answer in a catechism.

Rosalind. But doth he know that I am in this forest and in man's apparel? Looks he as freshly as he did the day he wrestled?

Celia. It is as easy to count *atomies* as to resolve the propositions of a lover. But take a taste of my finding him, and relish it with good observance. I found him under a tree, like a dropped acorn.

Rosalind. It may well be called Jove's tree, when it drops forth such fruit.

As You Like It, III, ii, 232

Prophetically, *resolve* in Shakespeare sometimes means *dissolve*—like Hamlet's "resolve into a dew." The world, as one likes it or not in any language, is a world. Rosalind who answers her own questions, by saying *"ay"* to its particular fruits might, instead of relishing *"good observance,"* have resolved her propositions like Wittgenstein. Historically speaking it may be said that he aerified the sensible inclinations of this colloquy of Rosalind and Celia for its logical and mathematical aspects.

2.172　The picture...cannot represent its form of representation; it shows it forth.

2.181　If the form of representation is the logical form, then the picture is called a logical picture.

2.225　There is no picture which is a priori true.

3.　　　The logical picture of the facts is the thought.

3.01　The totality of true thoughts is a picture of the world.

3.03　We cannot think anything unlogical, for otherwise we should have to think unlogically.

3.031　It used to be said that God could create everything, except what was contrary to the laws of logic. The truth is, we cannot *say* of an "unlogical" world how it would look.

3.032　To present in language anything which "contradicts" logic is as impossible as in geometry to...give the coordinates of a point which does not exist.

3.04　An a priori true thought would be one whose possibility guaranteed its truth.

3.05　We could only know a priori that a thought is true if its truth was to be recognized from the thought itself (without an object of comparison).

3.1　　In the proposition the thought is expressed perceptibly through the senses.

3.11　We use the sensibly perceptible sign (sound or written sign, etc.) of the proposition as a projection of the possible state of affairs.

> The method of projection is the thinking of the sense of
> of the proposition.
>
> *Tractatus*

To comment: Wittgenstein's "*What is thinkable is also possible*" is implied in this sequence of propositions expressing "*a possible state of affairs*" as history:—in primitive time man looks around and into himself—his body and his cave to be decorated—then looks out and wonders how he first looked around and into himself; having reached fabling time he looks out by these means, above, underneath earth, its heard life that once made him speak now rarifying his picturing sounds of earth into song like those of an Odyssey; in late time he conceives past a vanishing point, nowhere or everywhere projecting "objects" in signs and indices which may again let him look around, into, out, up, down for an underpinning of earth (like Prospero, looking into himself but mostly forgetting Caliban, or Pericles *listening* to "the music of the spheres" *before seeing* his wife and daughter to whom he is reunited).

Corollary: Shakespeare's *Works* as they conceive history regret a great loss of physical looking. They recall with the abstracted "look" of a late time. The intellective propositions of their actions anticipate the present day's vanishing point, but unlike the present's propositions still sing an earthy underpinning.

It follows that Shakespeare's *Works* say: seeing should be the object of speech (which in fabling time resolves into song), rather than that speech (which in late time often resolves into an unsingable "music of the spheres") should be the object of seeing.

To pick up Shakespeare's other use of *atomies*. The names of his characters are perhaps more emblematic than is generally supposed. *Phebe* suggests Diana, but also Apollo, the sun, generating the visible world. And her eyes so delicately made to see the same world, which the sun pervades, shut on *atomies*, those tiny visible and invisible particles that hurt them as they exert their sense. Moreover, eyes that so effect love's reason without reason cannot harm men, as can the other organs of sense that are predatory—and by this fault untruthful, like her lover s rumoring ear that involuntarily incites her railing tongue:

> *Phebe.* Thou tell'st me there is murder in mine eye:
> 'Tis pretty, sure, and very probable
> That eyes, that are the frail'st and softest things,
> Who shut their gates on *atomies*,
> Should be called tyrants, butchers, murderers!
> Now I do frown on thee with all my heart;
> ...O, for shame, for shame,

Lie not, to say mine eyes are murderers!
Now show the wound mine eye hath made in thee.
Scratch thee but with a pin, and there remains
Some scar of it; lean upon a rush,
The cicatrice and capable impressure
Thy palm some moment keeps; but now mine eyes
Which I have darted at thee, hurt thee not,
Nor, I am sure, there is no force in eyes
That can do hurt.

As You Like It, III, v, 10

Phebe as generative force can no more help arguing the goodness of eyes than Lucretius, who generates a world of atoms, can help proving his reason, by dedicating it to the visible goodness of generative, bodily Venus. For all the intrusions of the blows of the atomic idols that strike the eyes in *De Rerum Natura*, the warning against false inference from their action is as in Shakespeare: nor can the eyes *know*, i.e. conceive, the nature of things. The eyes are not a wit deceived. The eyes see — literally *see*. Don't blame the eyes for this fault of the mind, that of conceiving the nature of things.(*De Rerum Natura*, IV, 65).

The tragedy of the poetry in both Shakespeare and Lucretius is that, while reason is proved by the eyes, not only what the eyes of the poetry see but its music must suffer its reason. Conception as Hamlet says, is not always a blessing, and as the rest of his text to Polonius suggests the pale cast of punning thought makes lewd the walking breeding daughter in the sun.

Looking has its own logic, but (it may be inferred from Wittgenstein's *looking* logic) he who *looks* is still the philosophical *I*, the metaphysical subject, the limit — not a part of the world. To say the eye sees the whole or the wholeness of what it sees means only that the philosophical *I* has reached the inexpressible, and this can only "show" itself; it is the mystical. As for true conceptions they are, as Spinoza said, "of thought," until words disguise and imperil or feign them. Their wholeness also is inexpressible; it exists. But language, too, like the feigning of imagination has its own wholeness. "That which expresses *itself* in language, we cannot express by language. The propositions *show* the logical form of reality" (*Tractatus*, 4.121). With respect then to the wholeness reached by eyes, or thought, or words: just as we cannot think that we cannot think and cannot therefore *say* what we cannot think, the eye cannot look so that it cannot look. The wholeness it sees in looking is its inexpressible ethics. Its rightness should suggest no metaphysical questions. Since nothing can be said — it *shows* itself. The result is that the philosopher is left with Aristotle's original question in natural science. After all this disquisition, it may be reworded as: just when does the one who sees

184

come to think, or if the other way round is the case, just when does the one who thinks know he saw or sees.

Apparently a child looks before he learns to speak, then sings while his intellect operates, but who really knows the stages of this growth. And if the life of a child may be said to parallel that of human culture the complications of this question for the philosophy of history are endless.

Anyone may read Shakespeare and as a consequence find it hard not to plot a graph of culture, or to express a possible state of affairs inferred from the *Works* as history. A human animal can talk with his fellows. The capacity of speaking to others is logic. He should therefore be all the more aware that the points of his projected line of philosophical and historical thought are already given to the philosophical *I*. His field of discourse offers surely as many ready complications as a tree or a child growing from day to day presumably before his eyes. "From nothing *in the field of sight* can it be concluded that it is seen from an eye." But like his fellows he "sees" the child playing near the tree and it does not contradict that he feels, as at least one other logical being feels, "the more an image is associated with many other things, the more often it flourishes...the more causes there are by which it can be excited." The association and the excitement are their own reward. One, after all, loves the child, the tree, or loves another's words, or life, as one colloquially speaking "has" religion, piety, or honesty.

> ...whatever we desire and do of which we are the cause, in so far as we have the idea of God or in so far as we know God, I refer to Religion. The desire...of doing good...engendered in us by reason of the fact that we live according to the precepts of reason, I call Piety...the desire wherewith a man who lives according to the instruction of reason is so held that he wishes to unite others to him in friendship, I call Honesty, and that honesty which men who live under the guidance of reason praise...
>
> *Ethics*, Part IV, Prop. XXXVII, Note 1

A dozen years before Wittgenstein, and writing after (or perhaps via) Spinoza and Boole, Charles Sanders Peirce thinks the "same" or "similar" thought:

> If a Pragmaticist is asked what he means by "God," he can only say that just as long acquaintance with a man of great character may deeply influence one's whole manner of conduct, so that a glance at his portrait may make a difference...just as long study of the works of Aristotle may make him an acquaintance, so if contemplation and study of the physico-psychical universe can imbue a man with principles of conduct analogous to the influence of a great man's works or conversation, then that analogue of a mind—for it is impossible to say that *any* human

attribute is *literally* applicable—is what he means by "God."

Collected Papers, Vol. VI, 502 (1906)

From a perception of Shakespeare's words that, as this reading says, involves "*The little O, the earth*" and heaven's "*sights*," as the words "*mingle eyes with one that ties his points*" (*Antony and Cleopatra*, V, ii, 81; *Pericles*, I, i, 75; *Antony and Cleopatra*, III, xiii, 156), no further instruction of reason or mind need be expected than that *eyes* are understood to be so often *there* in the *Works* it appears they wish to unite others to them in friendship. For if one does not perceive Shakespeare's words thinking this same thought, their substance may rather be said to hide what this reading "sees" as an argument of his words between themselves, so that when most expressive they may be differently "new to thee," that is, new to every new reader, as the world "that has such people in't" is for Miranda.

Nevertheless, in logic what is given cannot be taken away. Who tries to tie Shakespeare's reiterations on *eyes* as *points* (be they the Shakespeare scholar's own *laces*) to history, philosophizes by logical necessity. A reader is one or another, or one maybe who refuses to see any historical connections at all. His logic is already ethical, tongue tied to his facts (whether they are moved by eyes, the laws of thought, or language, or "simple" speech) as shared with his fellows in their mutual time—and this is their common task for good or bad: unless his "physico-psychical" leanings differ so much from theirs he might just as well act apart, and his performing is endured as "common" to their task only in his persistent absence. If he is so made as to take this latter course and still thinks of uniting others in friendship, which he must feel as his whole world's limit, so it shows up only in an inexpressible mysticism of "look, don't think," he ought literally to tie up his lover's tongue, as Titania ties up Bottom's. Then honest men who live under the guidance of reason may, for all their effort to speak with their fellows, not grudge praising his silence.

As human animal who must speak he may likely forget the reward of such praise, to find himself explaining a "precise" metaphysics and a preference for eyes in Shakespeare, or hammering them, like Richard of Bordeaux, into a ring of history, as these notes have done. Then, if he is not to betray all human eyes that ever lived and will live, his spoken or written excuse must be as Wittgenstein urges: that he at least tries to imagine the propositional sign as made up of spatial objects (such as tables, chairs, books) instead of the written signs he uses. From a red speck he will have evoked a logical "color space." It will be hard then for most people to remember at the same time that the red warmed, and that the logical "color space" is as natural science says another phase of it in the same place. For that is excluded by the logical structure of color, as Wittgenstein reasons tho he would just as soon feel it as warming him. Who ties the points of his metaphysics so as to abstract color space from red speck may very likely excuse his abstraction in still another way, saying that his words are part of the symbolism, in the same way that "0" is part of the symbolism of arithmetic.

He may also solace himself for having ostensibly caused eyes to vanish from his logical world by saying that they are still there as in Shakespeare's headiest words, which never for a moment entirely lack some subtilization of "looking." He may say that such transformations are not miracles, and do not presume anterior miracles, and note that natural science says, they are processes that have sequence. Or he may even question whether eyes are preferable to reason—tho skepticism palpably makes no sense, if he continues to be affected by the seniority of eyes as the life of *his* Shakespeare. His thought or another's may be "both right and wrong" (as one infers) at the same time: anyone can either be the case or not the case, and everything else in Shakespeare remain the same.

And that will be precisely the value of reading Shakespeare—or for that matter anyone who is worth reading—that is, the feeling that his writing as a whole world *is*, compelling any logic or philosophy of history not to confuse an expression of *how it is* with *that world is*. The thought that *it is* has, of course, no value, is rather of a region where thought is free and music is for nothing—or as eyes see and go out. The value of the thought *how it is* is that it is against confusing expression.

In this sense the preference for eyes he finds in Shakespeare may caution him not to plot his graph of culture too hurriedly as he thinks about the implications of the preference imputed to Shakespeare. The constant of Shakespeare's expression—whether the words say *"All eyes!"* or *"I want no eyes; I stumbled when I saw"*—or what any reader sees, hears, or thinks into them—is (for the purpose of asserting the sense of positive and negative and propositions) its inexpressible *trust of expression*, the incentive and end of which is to unite others to it in friendship. Otherwise there never is any *need* for expression. Granted no need—friendship removed at a great distance ceases, as Aristotle says. Then it happens that the "friends" who existed are, at extreme remove, as they may be but always the same, in universal silence. A graph of culture always approaches this sameness. Limited to plot regularity while it keeps time for historic singulars, it fixes these in proportions that show their inexpressible trust of expression only with respect to the sameness in them. Instead of asserting like Timaeus only the likely story of the wholeness of a world *as it is*, the graph of culture despite its apparently unphysiological structure also affects that *being bodily, that which comes to be must be visible*. Its linear presence exists, and anyone's "no" may lead him to another graph if he wishes. Like Timaeus it speaks of the mystical. And as it does, its peculiar inexpressible certainty of trust on graph paper exceeds whatever insight it has into *how the world is*, drawing to itself Timaeus' moving thought that *understanding cannot arise anywhere without life*—either lawfully "simple" or, as the quotes mean, judiciously divided. To be a graph so involved is only to concede that Juliet's "mask of night" is always not quite superimposed upon a face—which leads to no clean graph of culture in any event. Order may prove useful in lighting up monstrosities; but the blind, said the Philosopher, may reason about colors.

The pause which Shakespeare's inexpressible trust of expression should give any graph is that, distilled from human desire to unite others to it in friendship, it should, like the preference of Shakespeare's words for eyes, constantly dispose of questions by keeping them "simple." Graphs are always compounding events, whereas there is enough complication for them in the fact that the human creature cannot suppose simplicity in the nature of the so-called simple event, but solely in the mode of its expression.

To unite each one's different world to other worlds friends ask "how it is," so as to point a limit to expression—purifying it by intimacy as well as wholeness, suggesting as it were "the image of a voice" tho it is impossible to show it. They consort for the most part with the singulars and the accidents. To proceed by the slope of a line or in a hollow without ticking is not to proceed at all when the end is friendship. Achilles' "speculation turns not to itself…is married there…where it may see itself"; and Ulysses does "not strain at the position—It is familiar." Concepts of change of "physico-psychical" state furthered by the new science like Vico's—concepts of time, lag, speed, etc—are right for the insight and wrong or inexpressible for the case. How many difficulties, all caused by the "variables" of time and change of state, are suggested to informed friends by saying that *Troilus and Cressida* is Shakespeare's *Iliad*, and *Pericles* his *Odyssey*. Or by saying that Bach's dates (1685-1750) and Vico's (1668-1744) agree as music-perceived-as-history. And by these other examples:

A song yet unheard is countlessly interpreted.

If only they could make silent vacuum cleaners so the objects being cleaned could be seen from noise.

The concept of phase is a property of expert language, like Homer's use of ἴδεν and ἔγνω—he *saw* cities and *knew* minds: that's Aristotle's tradition.

Golding (1565) translated Ovid and retained the miracle of fable in the rare and rarefying song:

                    ...(the crooked banks much wondering
                              at the thing)
                I have compelled streams to run clean back
                          ward to their spring.

                    ....cum volui, ripis mirantibus amnes
                in fontes rediere suos

                                        Metamorphoses, VII, 199-200

A brainier Shakespeare, only 46 years later, like Biron, failing,
tired horse, his rider—shadowing forth "magical" renunciation of Prospero—can only decorate a subject:

                Ye elves...[etc.]
                And ye that on the sands with printless foot
                Do chase the ebbing Neptune, and do fly him
                When he comes back

                                        The Tempest, V, i, 33–36

The verses creep. The chant wears thin as the whim. *Printless* is non-
sense: fable worn thin by brain. And the historical significance, when
Metamorphoses XV, 62 on Pythagoras is older?

                ...licet caeli regione remotos,
                mente deos adiit et, quae natura negabat
                visibus humanis, oculis et pectoris hausit

He, though the gods were far away in the heavenly regions, still
approached them with his thought, and what Nature denied to his
mortal vision he feasted on with his mind's eye.

Non-sense is at least as old as "yes" and "no" in the oldest *language*.

In fable inanimate things pass into a voice, stir like creatures said to
speak. In animated cartoon a voice passes into inanimate electronics of
sound track and picture and ideally unchanged comes out speaking; it
is only incidental if sometimes the inanimate things, which are made to
speak, are said to speak.

This fragment of a clause—tho he is only creature with a mind wishing for a constant eye.

A history of history loves by necessity.

Beloved, sees as he grasps?

Assuming someone's potential, the arts operate with a *what for* in
mind. But how decide between Mozart, "in opera poetry must be the
obedient daughter of music," and Cloten, "A wonderful sweet air with
admirable rich words to it...If this penetrate, I will consider the music
the better; if it do not it is a noise in her ears, which horsehairs...can
never amend." If horsehair is solid state, then a sweet air should be

more "solid" than rich words? How unite or dissolve both?

After all the quotations from Spinoza, does it make a difference, or light up his picture, to say: the perceptible sense shows in his logic, 55 years after the Folio—without a question of song, except as a theme pursues sequence; he "demonstrated" geometrically but asserted dramatically: "the eyes of the mind by which it sees things and observes them are proofs." Meaning: proofs are *not* the object of the eyes of the mind. "The object of the idea constituting the human mind is the body, or a certain mode of extension actually existing and nothing else" (*Ethics*, Part II, Prop. XIII). "a certain mode"—Olearius to Bach: "In dem Choral viele wunderliche Variationes gemachet, viele fremde Thöne mit eingemischet. If you desire to introduce a theme against the melody, you must go on with it and not immediately fly off to another. And in no circumstances must you introduce a *tonus contrarius*." And in Spinoza the medieval persisted beneath the geometry?

Music frozen in a double negative—sung and gone?

> Thenceforth all worlds desire will in thee dye,
> And all earthes glorie on which men do gaze,
> Seeme durt and drosse in thy pure sighted eye,
> Compar'd to that celestial beauties blaze...
>
> With those sweete pleasures being so possest,
> Thy straying thoughts henceforth for euer rest.
>
> Spenser, *Heavenly Love,*
> *Heavenly Beautic*

The eye even in these lines contends its right, and *Fowre Hymnes* are not Shakespeare's mark.

But like the hazel, gentle eye he was said to have—and with no *straying thoughts* wanting to rest forever—not to wish to draw an end to thinking but merely to show its limits. Perhaps not to tie the points of a graph of culture at all, and so there are no points. Intimacy is not solved, nor does it solve anything, speaking as must happen, trusting to see an alphabet of subjects.

190

MARGARET AVISON

The Local & the Lakefront

The crankle can occur
in stunted trees:
a shaping line, when rain blackens the
bark, in early
spring, in Scarborough
(Toronto, East).

At Sunnyside
(Toronto lakefront, west,
        with a bricked sooted railwaystation and
                a blueglass busstation)
the sunset
blurges through rain and all
man tinfoil, man sheetlead
shines, angled all awry,
a hoaxing hallelujah.

Wharves
spidered in mist
I, stevedore of the spirit,
slog day and night, picketing
those barges and brazen freighters with their
Subud, Sumerian ramsgate, entrails and altars.

Grievance — grievance —
Committeeman, come where I pace
and learn my rain-besotted, rancorous
grievance.
Who that must die but man
can burn a bush to make a bar of soap?
Who twists a draughtsman's line
perversely, out of
a stunted tree,
or makes of the late sun an as-if-Gabriel
to trump

another day, another borough?
Someone not at home. Exporters. Glutting us
with Danish spoons
and aum.

On the flossed beaches here
we're still curling our waves.
Weather is tough.
Things happen only to trees and the
rivering grasses.
A person is an alien.

Committeeman:
there are no ships or cargoes *there*.
Believe me. Look. Admit it.
Then we start clean:
    nothing earned; a nowhere to exchange
        among us few
           carefully.

Why Not?

Maybe not any longer
should the meek lover
at slack rein amble through the afternoon
snow-whinged, or sunflower-randy
with a black heart of seeds to take
mumbling home at the
cellardoor of day
past fading rooster-crates, past
CEMENT suddenly.

(why not cement?)

Waking Up

Monkey colour, morning smokes from
the pond. Looped and festooned
with fawn heraldic rags

trees wait. Seawall of day
deafens the turmoil the true seafarer,
the Wanderer, fronts. High grass
rides crest: a spill
of grains casts stone-age shadows on the bluffs.
Selvedge of water mirrors
the always first light.
Like soil no inchworm's excremental course
has rendered friable,
today, mute quantum
of all past pitted against sun,
weighs, a heft of awareness, on
tallow, brawn, auricle,
iris. Till monkey
grinder habit turning his organ
grinds out curbs, scurrying,
dust,
day.

The Typographer's Ornate Symbol
at the End of a Chapter or a Story

This is another time.
Somebody turned a leaf in a book.
A reader.
To him I am smaller than the
wrinkle on his thumb-knuckle
which also he
need never see
and nonetheless
has.
It is not pity about me for all that.

My plain daylight
is a plainness
of particular beauty.

This is another time.
The lilac lobs, not
pretty, left alone,
alive,

in the clumsy flume
of patch-bricked wind.

The same day the chestnuts lit their
fadey chandeliers
and bees put on their
shrunk wool swimming suits,
the pump-hose poured a˙
river of quick-setting cement over
two men in an earthwork: a
foreman; an
engineer.

The clock-face has its glass
against the whinstone
sky.
This is another time.

If the reader stirs and fetches a
sigh, turning his page,
my sigh is as the
wild barley's,
a small stir from
a cool place.
Some asking of brazen questions has
had its season.
This is not autumn,
not one of the Four.
This is another time.

The book and that
blunt reader . . . the turning of a page . . .
maybe the whole *bibliothèque* vanished there, a
language lost.

It is not pity about me for all that.

Natural / unnatural

Evening tilt makes a
pencil-box of our

street.
The lake, in largeness, grapey blueness
casts back the biscuit-coloured pencil-box, boxes, toys, the
steeple-people, all of it, in one of those
little mirrory shrugs.

The north-east sky too
grows fusillage cool.

On the horizon
ghosts of peeled parsnips point their
noseless faces up,
out; ghost-bodies pile up on each other, all prone, all
pointless, blanking, refusing.

Even the west, beyond the tinged rooftops
smells of cobalt;

> "no—the
> charring of a peeled stick in a bonfire
> is the smell: newness,
> October crackling . . . "

large pink children have, all the same, sniffed
the ice in
that quirk of sunset
but refuse
fear.

There is still a lingering
sand-edge of sound
darkness explores.

Hope says it is there listening, all over,
into a voice-sound, a
voice-making, of silence.

"Hope is a dark place
that does not refuse
fear?"

Yes, but,
yes,

hope, yes,   but

O God, the natural night is pressure on my ribs.
Despair: to draw that in—
deflate the skin-pouch, crunch out the
structure of
mortality
in one luxurious deep-breathed zero—dreamed already—a corruption.

I fear that.

I refuse.

GARY SNYDER

Night Highway Ninety-Nine

from *Mountains and Rivers without End*

*. . . only the very poor, or eccentric, can surround themselves with shapes
of elegance (soon to be demolished) in which they are forced by poverty
to move with leisurely grace. We remain alert so as not to get run down,
but it turns out you only have to hop a few feet, to one side, and the
whole huge machinery rolls by, not seeing you at all.*

—*Lew Welch*

I

We're on our way
            man
        out of town
    go hitching down
    that highway ninety-nine

Too cold and rainy to go out on the Sound
Sitting in Ferndale drinking coffee
Baxter in black, been to a funeral
Raymond in Bellingham—Helena Hotel—
Can't go to Mexico with that weak heart
Well you boys can go south. I stay here.
Fix up a shack—get a part-time job—
            (he disappeared later
            maybe found in the river)

In Ferndale & Bellingham
Went out on trailcrews
Glacier and Marblemount
There we part.

     tiny men with moustaches
     driving ox-teams
     deep in the cedar groves.
     wet brush, tin pants, snoose

Split-shake roof barns
  over berryfields
    white birch chickencoop

Put up in Dick Meigs cabin
    out behind the house—
Coffeecan, PA tin, rags, dirty cups,
Kindling fell behind the stove
      miceshit
  old magazines,

     winter's coming in the mountains
     shut down the show
     the punks go back to school
     & the rest hit the road

  strawberries picked, shakeblanks split
  fires all out and the packstrings brought
  down to the valleys
      set to graze

Gray wharves and hacksaw gothic homes
Shingle mills and stump farms
      overgrown.

   II

Fifty drunk Indians   *Mt. Vernon*
Sleep in the bus station

Strawberry pickers speaking Kwakiutl
            turn at Burlingame for Skagit
                    & Ross Dam

    under appletrees by river
    banks of junkd cars

        B.C. drivers give hitch-hikers rides

"The sheriff's posse stood in double rows   *Everett*
    flogged the naked Wobblies down
    with stalks of Devil's Club
    & run them out of town"

While shingle-weavers lost their fingers
    in the tricky feed and take
        of double saws.

Dried, shrimp   *Seattle*
        smoked,   salmon
    —before the war old indian came
& sold us hard-smoked Chinook
From his truck-bed model T
            Lake City,

    waste of trees & topsoil, beast, herb,
    edible roots, Indian field-farms & white men
    dances   washed, leached, burnt out
    Minds blunt, ug! talk twisted

    A night of the long poem
    and the mined guitar...
    "Forming the new society
    within the shell of the old"
        mess of tincan camps and littered roads

The Highway passes straight through
            every town

At Matsons washing blujeans
              hills and saltwater
                        ack, the woodsmoke in my brain

High Olympics—can't go there again

              East Marginal Way the hitch-hike zone
              Boeing down across Duwamish slough
& angle out
              & on.

Night rain wet concrete headlights
                        blind   *Tacoma*

        Salt air/   Bulk cargo/   Steam cycle

                        AIR REDUCTION

eating peanuts I don't give a damn
if anybody ever stops   I'll walk
to San Francisco   what the hell

                        "that's where your going?
                        "why you got that pack?

Well man I just don't feel right
Without something on my back

              & this character in milkman overalls
              "I have to come out here
              every once in a while, there's a guy
              blows me here"

                        way out of town.

Stayed in Olympia with Dick Meigs
        —this was a different year & he had moved—
        sleep on a cot in the back yard
        half the night watch falling stars

199

These guys got babies now
            drink beer, come back from wars
        "I'd like to save up all my money
        get a big new car, go down to Reno
        & latch onto one of those rich girls—
        I'd fix their little ass"—nineteen yr old
        N. Dakota boy fixing to get married next month
To Centralia in a purple ford.

            carstruck dead doe
            by the Skookumchuck river

Fat man in a Chevrolet
            wants to go back to L. A.
            "too damnd poor now"
Airbrakes on the log trucks hiss and whine
Stand in the dark by the stoplight.
            big fat cars tool by

Drink coffee, drink more coffee
                        brush teeth back of Shell
        hot shoes
            stay on the rightside of that
                yellow line

Marys Corner, turn for Mt. Rainier
        —once caught a ride at night for Portland here
Five Mexicans, ask me "chip in on the gas"
        I never was more broke & down.
        got fired that day by the USA
        (the District Ranger up at Packwood
        thought the wobblies had been dead for
                        forty years
        but the FBI smelled treason
                —my red beard)

    That Waco Texas boy
        took A. G. & me through miles of snow
        had a chest of logger gear
        at the home of an Indian girl
        in Kelso, hadn't seen since Fifty-four

Toledo, Castle Rock, free way
        four lane
    no stoplights & no crossings, only cars
      & people walking, old hitch-hikers
   break the law. How do I know.
         the state cop
          told me so.

Come a dozen times into
                Portland
    on the bum or
        hasty lover
     late   at   night

III

Portland

dust kicking up behind the trucks—night rides—
who waits in the coffee stop
           night highway 99

    Sokei-an met an old man on the banks of the
    Columbia river growing potatoes & living all alone,
    Sokei-an asked him the reason why he lived there,
    he said

    Boy, no one ever asked me the reason why.
    I like to be alone.
    I am an old man.
    I have forgotten how to speak human words.

All night freezing
   in the back of a truck
  dawn at Smith river
    battering on in loggers pickups
            prunes for lunch
The next night, Siuslaw.

Portland sawdust   down town
Buttermilk corner, all you want for a nickel

                (now a dime)
                        —Sujata gave Gautama
                                    buttermilk,
                (No doubt! says Sokei-an, that's all it was
                            plain buttermilk.)

            rim of mountains. pulp bark chewd snag
                            papermill
            tugboom in the river
            —used to lean on bridgerails
            dreaming up eruptions and quakes—

Slept under Juniper in the Siskiyou (Yreka)
    a sleeping bag, a foot of snow
    black rolled umbrella
    ice slick asphalt

Caught a ride the only car come by
    at seven in the morning
    chewing froze salami

Riding with a passed-out LA whore
    glove compartment full of booze,
    the driver a rider, nobody cowboy,
    sometime hood,
Like me picked up to drive,
    & drive the blues away.
            we drank to Portland
                    & we treated that girl good.

I split my last two bucks with him in town
    went out to Carol & Billy's in the woods.

    —foggy morning in Newport
    housetrailers
        under the fir.

An old book on Japan at the Goodwill
    unfurld umbrella in the sailing snow
    sat back in black wood
                barber college
            chair, a shave

On Second Street in Portland
        what elegance. What a life.

    bust my belly with a quart of
            buttermilk
    & five dry heels of French bread
    from the market cheap
            clean shaved, dry feet,

We're on our way
        man
        out of town
Go hitching down that
        highway ninety-nine.

                    IV

Oil-pump broken, motor burning out   *Salem*

Ex-logger selling skidder cable
    wants to get to San Francisco,
    fed and drunk   *Eugene*

Guy just back from Alaska—don't like
    the States, there's too much law   *Sutherlin*

A woman with a kid & two bales of hay.   *Roseburg*

Sawmill worker, young guy thinking of
    going to Eureka for redwood logging
    later in the year   *Dillard*

Two Assembly of God Pentecostal boys in
    a Holy Roller High School. One had
        spoken in
            tongues.   *Canyonville*

LASME Los-Angeles—Seattle Motor Express

    place on highway 20: LITTLE ELK
            badger & badger

203

South of Yoncalla burn the engine
                run out of oil

Yaquina fishdocks
                candlefish & perch
                slant-faced woman fishing
                tuna stacked like cordwood
                the once-glimpsed-into door
                                company freezer shed

                a sick old seagull settles
                down to die.
                the ordinary, casual, ruffle of the
                                tail & wings.
(Six great highways; so far only one)

                freshwater creeks on the beach sand
                        at Kalaloch I caught a bag of water
                at Agate Beach
                        made a diversion with my toe

Jumpoff Joe Creek &
        a man carrying nothing, walking sort of
        stiff-legged along, blue jeans & denim jacket,
        wrinkled face, just north of
        Louse Creek

                —Abandon really means it
                —the network womb stretched loose all
                                                things slip
                                through

Dreaming on a bench under newspapers
I woke covered over with Rhododendron blooms
Alone in a State Park in Oregon.

V

"I had a girl in Oakland who worked
for a doctor, she was a nurse, she let him
eat her. She died of tuberculosis
& I drove back that night   *Grants Pass*
                    to Portland
non stop, crying all the way."
    "I picked up a young mother with two
    children once, their house had just
                    burned down"
"I picked up an Italian tree-surgeon
in Port Angeles once, he had all his
saws and tools all screwed & bolted on
    a beat up bike"

Oxyoke, Wolf Creek,

A guy coming off a five-day binge, to   *Phoenix*

An ex-bartender from Lebanon, to   *Redding*

Man & wife on a drinking spree, to   *Anderson*

Snow on the pines & firs around Lake Shasta
        —Chinese scene of winter hills & trees
        us "little travellers" in the bitter cold

            six-lane highway slash & DC twelves
            bridge building   squat earth-movers
        —yellow bugs

            I speak for hawks.

The road that's followed goes forever;
In half a minute crossed and left behind.

Out of the snow and into red-dirt plains

205

blossoming plums

Each time you go that road it gets more straight
  curves across the mountains lost in fill
    towns you had to slow down all four lane
      Azalea, Myrtle Creek
      WATCH OUT FOR DEER

At Project City Indian hitcher
Standing under single tarpole lamp
    nobody stopped
        Ginsberg & I walked
        four miles & camped by an oak fire
        left by the road crew

Going to San Francisco
Yeah San Francisco
Yeah we came from Seattle
Even farther north
Yeah we been working in the mountains
    in the Spring
    in the Autumn
        always go this highway ninety-nine—

    "I was working in a mill three weeks there
      then it burned down & the guy didn't even
      pay us off—but I can do anything—
      I'll go to San Francisco—tend bar"

Standing in the night.
In the world-end winds
By the overpass bridge

    Junction US 40 and Highway Ninety-nine

    Trucks, trucks,   roll by
    Kicking up dust—dead flowers—

Sixteen speeds forward
Windows open
Stopped at the edge of Willows for a bite

        grass shoots on the edge of
        drained rice plains

            —cheap olives—

Where are the Sierras.

        level, dry,
Highway turns west

        miles gone, speed
                still
        pass through lower hills
        heat dying
        toward Vallejo
      gray on the salt baywater
      brown grass ridges
        blue mesquite

One leggd Heron in the tideflats

        State of Cars.

Sailor getting back to ship
        —I'm sick of car exhaust

        City
     gleaming far away

   we make it into town tonight
   get clean & drink some wine—

    SAN FRANCISCO

```
           NO
           body
       gives a shit
           man
       who you are or
        whats your car
       there IS no
                   ninety-nine
```

PHILIP WHALEN

Address to a Younger Generation

I'm concerned about you
Where's your hands? For that matter
Where were you yesterday? Your
Memory lost as well
If I reached inside your chest & pulled out the amulet
        Its words

                I
            DESERVE
              ALL
            DELIGHT
There you'd stand, a pile of golem dust

I don't condemn you nor delight
You must know it thoroughly, where & why it is
Its worth, its character
Sunlight through a prism: We see six colors,
There they are

Lacking hands, I see you've ingeniously stuck
        your toe in your mouth
More fun than listening to me & there
        it will remain until I say
            ICECREAM
& your belly remembers & your mouth
Icecream isn't toes
You maybe don't need a memory to cry
Misery is your chief delight

I know the minute you find your hands again
You'll attack me with whatever you can
Meat-axe, screwdriver, the stove
I haven't taught you any better, you've got
No memory, & I see now your ears have fallen off
How can you know I'm the icecream man?
I must be fast on my feet & try
To find out where you left your mind & talk to it
I can't run forever
One day you'll catch me, handed
& I'm done.

LOUIS ZUKOFSKY

"A"-13

IV

Too heavy
for
my
breast pocket—

small as it
is
in
my wallet

the size of
a
vis-
iting card

but holding
no
such
thing, no need

to tell her
who
has
found the scrip

my resourc-
es
for
my son who

has looked in-
to
it
—wha-at—you

will find—by
your
own
eyes, by strength

plainly spoke-
n
yet
pardon me

whose chase is
this
world
and we in

herds the game,
when
I
spur my horse

content and
an-
ger
in me have

but one face
to
the
music his

own hoofs made
lived
in
her eye love

and beyond
love
or
reason, wit

or safety —
five
owned
snapshots my

father, moth-
er,
two
the fiddler's

at nine and
a
half
my young wife

in peacock
feath-
ered
hat the year

he was born
(vi-
o-
lin label)

"Jakobus
Stain-
er
in Absam

prope Oe-
ni-
pon-
tam 16-

56"
if
I
lose my ad-

dress, a phone
my
broth-
er's latest,

all written
mi-
nus-
cule on odd

scrap paper
no
room
it goes down

carefully
hy-
phen-
ated each

syllable
pours
in
the measure

maze I planned
song
long
since and that

would not be
hur-
ried
life into

dust (who can-
not
feel
nor see the

rain being
in't
knows
neither wet

nor dry)—a
blank
check
not for much—

two dollars
held
to
the spine of

my wallet
by
a
rubber band—

next to some
breath
cop-
ied clear and

such green lines
rush
on
root *Go, fresh*

horses the
bar-
ber's
last haircut

Thoth the price
went
up,
seraphs light

cherubs high
seas
smoke
streak Chinese

whips stage sym-
bols
for
horses, on

this bed face
a
sleep
Hop o' my

Thumb lady-
bug
wake
the things left

mastery—
by
my
short life my

body to
this
thanks
tender her—

it *lets*
offerers—
tandaradei

'THE
TOO PAUL
HIS CAT'

ROBERT KELLY

Hui-neng Chops Bamboo

To know it is to know everything
bamboo itself is used to make

especially that four-holed flute
with a note like wind under water

few Westerners can play

•

Of the strokes that make up the picture
many, as if casually, combine
to shape the radical *chin*, "axe."

•

Such a small hatchet,
so few bamboo!
                    How will we
ever fill up a picture with that?

•

He crouches in the grass. That
stupid grin. The razor in his
fist. He pounces on bamboo.

•

We have our own mountains.
I lived a summer on one and never
chopped wood.
                    There was a
lake and I chose to drink
hair-flavored water from my hat.

•

To walk one hour in those
mountains was enough

and filled my dreams with
dark trees. I could not grasp

the shape of a single tree or
what it had to do with darkness

or itself. Many trees and black
sky. A tree is never alive.

Dreaming of branched lifeless things
with sap inside them I got up

from my particular sleep. Six o'
clock. 1 went out and turned my

flashlight on eight deer under
appletrees, obviously eating apples.

•

The chips fly! That
old man can really chop
bamboo!

•

Some trees have leaves.
Some trees have butterflies

Hui-neng's bamboo is
marked "bamboo."

From any two, not one, isolated passages the full
meaning of the picture is
conveyed. What's the rest for?

The radical "axe," the character "bamboo"

That is a picture of
Hui-neng chopping bamboo.

•

After you move the blade it
starts to move by itself.

It is like riding home
fast asleep and getting there

and knowing about it only when
the others get off and leave you alone.

•

Fit the pieces together

It is not a puzzle it is
necessity
            as bamboo leaf
fits and is severed from bamboo

The Boar

stayed where he was
led. The others
larked over to the
trough & fed.

The one they were after had
blue eyes we
couldnt see under his
notched ears,

so I went over the fence
& saw him looking
at nothing, sharply,
across the field.

He had a strong white
back, even shone a
little in the sun
all round him

& on the blue steel gun
that made the dull
flat sound into
his head

he toppled over from
& lay dead & bleeding.
The feeding pigs ate
what they were fed.

1.

A pig stood in the mud,
a pig lay in the mud.
This was the animal I
was most myself in,
watching it ready to
die. Its eyes were the
color of my eyes, I had
bristles on my chin, not
many, didnt shave yet.

It knew enough to
keep its mouth shut. Would
they have killed him if
he talked? They would, & I
said nothing too, the pink
fat pig would taste too good
for them to leave it alone.

2.

I wish it had been otherwise. What kind of
country am I living in, who were those two
men, one of them the sheriff of the town, &
why did they have to kill the pig?
They had him flayed, scalded in the caldron
an hour after he was shot. The butcher came down
in time for supper, cut him up & salted the pork.

These ex-
periments in time & truth, I was thirteen &
had to see it happen. These are the things we
have to learn, not when it happened

or how the pig fell over, but that it does,
& keeps on happening, across me & my own
doings, my age, & hatred of that sheriff with
a silver star on his plaid shirt, a
Dutchman who hadnt caught a criminal in years,
were none to catch, kept his revolver
clean & oiled, ready for any animal, for the
deer they kept in chickenwire cages down the road.

3.

It was plain that pig had
nothing on his mind. For
Christ's sake didnt he
know what was happening
to him when one held him
by the flanks? No, nor the other
making click click, spin
spin noises, clearing his throat.

LOÙIS AND CELIA ZUKOFSKY

IV   Phasellus ille

Facile as can be the boat you see, my guests, says—
it was the fastest of a navy for its run,
nothing quite like it floating which had been a tree
that it could not outstrip, either its oars plying,
or—if the course sped—soaring, no slack of canvas.
To it the coast of menacing Adriatic
will not say no, nor islands of the Cyclades
and noble Rhodes, nor the horrible Thracian
Propontis, nor the truculent gulf of Pontus,
by which this that had yet to be a boat was then
a tree combed with leaves: for on Cytorus' summit
it swayed often to the sibilant talk of leaves.
Pontic Amastris and Cytorus where the box tree
grows, this you have witnessed and can witness yet,
my sailboat says; ultimately my origin
goes back to you, it says—it stood on your summit,
that those were your waters which first imbrued its oars,

and from there thru uncontrollable fretting seas
it sailed its lord, whether the winds hailed to larboard
or starboard, or as if to trumpet Jupiter
lit instantly astern to fill the favored sheets;
not a soul bespoke vows to the shore gods for her
when she came out in that furthest sea, nor all her
way here as she hastened to this unshadowed lake.
As said, this was *prior to:* and laid up in store
ages quietly and dedicates itself to you,
Gemini Castor and his twin-starred Castor.

XI Furi et Aureli, comites Catulli

Furius, Aurelius: comites—Catullus.
If he penetrate most remote India,
lit as with the long resonant coast East's wave
            thundering under—
if in Hyrcania, mull of Arabia,
say the Sacae, arrow ferocious Parthians,
why even the seven gamming mouth, colored
            ichor of Nilus—
even that Transalpine graded tour magni-
fying visions of our Caesar's monuments,
Gallic Rhine, and the horrible ultimate
            mask of the Britons—
on hand, men, come whatever gods ferret and
want of us, you who're always prompt to feel with
me, take a little note now to my darling,
            no kind word dictates.
May she live, and avail herself, in the moist
clasp of one concourse of three hundred lechers,
loving no man's ever, and doomed to drain all
            men who must rupture:
no, let her not look back at me as she used to,
at her love whose fault was to die as at some
meadow's rim, the blossom under the passing
            cut of the share's thrust.

CATULLUS

220

Virgin and Child with Music and Numbers

Who knows better than you know,
Lady, the circumstances of this event
—meanness, the overhanging terror, and the need
for flight soon—hardly reflect the pledge
the angel gave you, the songs you exchanged in joy
with Elizabeth, your cousin? That was then,
or that was for later, another time. Now—.

Still, the singing was and is. Song
whether or not we sing. The song is sung.
Are we cozened? The song we hear is like
those numbers we cannot factor, whose overplus,
an indeterminate fraction, seems more than the part
we factor out. Lady, if our despair
is to be unable to factor ourselves in song
or factor the world there, what should our joy
be, other than that same integer that sings
and mocks at satisfaction? We are not
fulfilled. We cannot hope to be. No,
we are held, somewhere in the void of whole despair,
enraptured; and only there does the world endure.

Lady, sing to this Baby, even so.

Skunk Cabbage

Because it is soon, it has a private and quiet
spring. Before the birds come, before
another leaf or flower, it flowers; and bees
come there and enter and leave, thick
with pollen. Foetid, even in the thin chill
of a wintry spring, it stinks of livingness,
rawness. Its color also is of skin
rubbed raw by wind, by cold, by sun,
and the flesh showing through. It is the flesh
responding to warmth, to sun, to the first spring.
It looks like tenderness, the way it curves
upward, and beaks over to cover within.

A Black Clay Fish from Oaxaca

First though, look at this mask. It came from the same
city, or near there. Dug from a grave.
The original was gold as this would seem
to be, but isn't. This is silver gilt.
But feel the weight of it and see how rich
the decorations are: the ear-plugs,
the nose-pendant, the fringe around the head.
It is a mask of Spring. The heaviness
of the huge, thick-lidded eyes is brought about
by what hangs over them; this represents
a sheet of human skin. The power of the thing
is in that inward smoldering, all overlaid.
Here is the fine fish. Isn't he fat!
Such sleek blackness; and happy, they say, as a trout.

In Navaho Country

To live in a hogan under a hovering sky
is to live in a universe hogan-shaped
or having hogans in it to give it shape,
earth-covered hovels, holes having a wall
to heave the back of the heart against, or hide
the head—to black the heavens overhead,
a block and a shapening in the windy vast:
this could be said of other houses too.

How it is possible for this to be so
is that the universe as known-unknown
has no discernible shape and not much
in it. We give it the limits and shape we need
it to have. What we want is a here with meaning more
than a vague void moving with weightless balls
or the distant view of a glitter of gritty dust.
We housel the universe to have it here.

We do wrong: using houses or whole
blocks of houses or other devious
enclosed volumes, ingenious inventions of space
to have us here has limits. We deceive
ourselves, but not for long. We only avoid

the empty vastness, leaving it there, unfilled,
unknown, unlimited. Where is here
when nowhere in a place of no discernible shape?

Tenochtitlan

I did not go to Coatlicue today,
to her of the writhing skirt of serpents, skulls
suspended at her neck, clawed Mother of the Gods.

Not that it mattered: if we have learned at all,
we have learned not to deny the terrible ones
their due. They have it. We are theirs to keep.

But we also learn—not knowing is it fear
or defiance teaching us—not to think
of everything always, sometimes not to think.

Xilonen, Goddess of the Young Corn, of green
and growing, grant us the solace of sweet ears
soft in the mouth; accept our truant love.

We drink to you, Xilonen, we are drunk
with deep pleasures and a deep need, drunk
with gentleness and the pleasure of gentle needs.

There Is Ignorant Silence in the Center of Things

What am I saying? What have I got to say?
As though I knew. But I don't. I look around
almost in a sort of despair for anything
I know. For anything. Some mislaid bit.
I must have had it somewhere, somewhere here.
Nothing. There is silence here. Were there people, once?
They must have all gone off. No, there are still
people, still a few. But the sound is off.
If we could talk, could hear each other speak,
could we piece something,
                    could we learn and teach, could we know?

Hopeless. Off in the distance, busyness.
Something building or coming down. Cries.
Clamor. Fuss at the edges. What? Here,
at the center—it is the center?—only the sound
of silence, that mocking sound. Awful. Once,
before this, I stood in an actual ruin, a street
no longer a street, in a town no longer a town,
and felt the central, strong suck of it, not
understanding what I felt: the heart of things.
This nothing.   This full silence.   To not know.

ROBERT KELLY

The Exchanges

I

where the spirit feeds
    under the great trees, their
    leaves falling in sunlight
    red now yellow now
        black pitch of the pine tree
& give it a name
& call it her &
        offer to become one with it in the moss
    between tree roots
          hollow of the trunk   ,   cave
       feeding backward into mountain
    veins of copper . flowing down too
everything outside

        relaxed, feeling nothing
     watching it go on inside you
lie down with her under the oak tree & be still

       or on the bed, window open
    sealight rippling on the ceiling
               take her
      the ease, quiet at dark
         shapes moving on the walls
   king & queen in the grotto

       swordsmen in the meadow

an hour of quiet . burnt sun
        purple crow against the sky
very high . he covers her in
        darkness . the knight asleep
in sunlight . the wine dries in the cup
the cold wind blows over us
        go down to the cenote
    singing
        the sacrifice . the victim gilded
            banners flapping at his shoulders
        purple & red & white . his
eyes & the pool's rippling

                        a vulture's face a priest
    . pressed to the heart
death without surprise . into the water

                        the god present

        falls
through the voices of music
        through the vowels of water in his sleep
fall
        through the sound of cave & tree & sky
                into one action
        of sound . of voices that will keep music
                        hold measure
                into nightfall & the empty streets
    trees at the pool's edge
        animals drinking the water
& not know their names
but hear their voices breathing into water
            into the gold room
        where rhythm has no center
                        everything
outside

        I have walked through the door
    I have come into the gold room
            there is no silence here
        I have given nothing away
my hands are full from the instant I am born
            to the bottom of your sleep
        drawn down by music

225

into man
     am not hungry & will eat

II

Clarified into present

standing now in the stare of the vulture Jesus
watching the wings spread the animal body writhe
leading to an immediate world
is Vision to be compromised in the glitter of steel
arched back of wildcat   tin leaves of the gumtree?

how sure you are of the residents of darkness come to life
how certain that when the rim of the circle breaks open
a form of life articulate, comprehensible will stand forth
               or that the world formed
the invisible instruments of control & banishment
are a crust only to a sweet fruit only
not the gibbering piety of the remorseless dead

gently
you have gone into her body
a knife skillful in severing   wandering up & down her
to find life? to mutilate, to be
in the first stagger of deathliness alive & singing
saying: animal of the quiet dark
animal now to burrow softly down
scour around inside her, follow those
lines of motion & supply till you come to heart
walk up & down & swallow it, looking the other way,
to find life? to discover in the consumed
whatever principle it is that brings you here
hungry & horny?

                    •

            •   •

there is in language a temperament of fear
to answer the animal is to talk about syllables
pure as a lake in Siberia
salty & rush-ridden   centuries from the sea

to which a river flows backwards   Christmas night
or gull's hornpipe lowly to the cross   in deep snow
when they hanged the first king: whose strangled throat
made consonants
            in the forests vowels
invented with the caprice of the unicorn,
goat-eyed red-bottomed mandrills at horizons,
perpetual song of lemurs: ururur, syllables,
Aurora bloody-fisted from the lake,
erect

the Madman's Vision a vision into
image or into form?

Adam's allergy to the first bite retched into speech?

                    •

            •   •

To protect you from the secret, she said,
that vowels & consonants fuck each other into speech.
which you could not bear
for not knowing the efficient question
Oeheim, waz wirret dir?
what is this here? wherefore this crummy pageantry
opening into present?

            for I would mount the cart & go
questioning the sea-girt eyes of Athene, to whom in
Troy's treasure house the great horned silver phallus stood
angular as futhorc, branched out into ocean:
whom only I would honor with my sharp teeth & slow-
moving gentle mammalian mind   understanding her rightly
a hero with drawn sword
(hinne-ni the sword of immediate presence
every rune chiseled neatly in, legible, compelling,
a message of swordmaster to armorer: let
edge be bright here, not for the cutting but
for the honor of it
            which I would draw
            with me into Babylon
            my cutthroat word

catchpenny empire
on all fours:) imagined

which is the present position of poetry
the animal rooting under the tree, black sow
at winter solstice, at 6 o'clock, evening
out of the snow: so far down, the
gods of fertile fields & hidden springs
the water rushing out of the ground into

her body foreshortened & consumed
distorted into my mouth, her blood my swollen tongue
her cunt my oxcart, groan of the ritual pretense

unanswerable animal.
year moving in rigid circles round
your flexible refusals. alone
there is only one continent of metaphor.
one rhythm you invite us to be native in,
move upriver away from the seashaped ode,
lyric dappled like pomegranate,
snapshots of the momentary real

                    .

          .   .

close to eggyolk, fertile or
sterile in one white albumen gesture
distinguish only by the tender vein
the streak of blood:

> to light in perfect fulness; so that a
> continuous rhythmic procession of phenomena
> passes by, and never is there a form
> left fragmentary or half-illuminated,
> never a lacuna, never a gap, never a glimpse
> of unplumbed depths
>
> (Auerbach on Homer)

unplumbed?
men must have looked the first time fire,
each time man covered girl in darkness
his open eyes focused in the dark

                    unspeaking mouth of the vulture

to make those things appear that he has closely hidden
in the smell & shadow of his wings

to have a mouth

protect us in the paradox? is it what
we see when we look in the fire
what we see in the dark
moving to the immediate rhythm of the visible
moving to the hidden rhythm of the real

IAN HAMILTON FINLAY

Poet

At night, when I cannot sleep,
I count the islands
And I sigh when I come to Rousay
—My dear black sheep.

Night in Rousay

Snug in their night the Headlands coorie down
And dream the moon a cuithe.   The Shallows dream
Atlantics, and the Stacks, safe in their nets,
Dream dawn again, the lazy yellow sun.
The Daisies dream of stars, the Bulls of cows
With cream upon their lashes, and the Cows
Of peedie calves to keep..... Sleep, in its ignorance,
Swings in, swings in—an island night-time deep.

The Pond of Oo Farm (Rousay)

———————————————

——————

———————

The little pond of Oo
Is flat
As that.

v   v   v   v   v
v   v
v   v

With yellow ducks of Oo
Upon it
Too.

O   O   O   O   O
o'   o'
o'   o'

And cows that low, also.
And coos
That loo.

End of a Holiday

My father climbs the stairs
Above my head
And then I hear him climb
Into his bed.

Sheep bleat—the sun's last sparks
Float through the wood
Like bubbles in last week's
Old lemonade.

I wait, and then I ask
Is he all right
Up in the dark without
A proper light.

He pulls the heavy clothes
Up to his chin.
I'm fine, he says, I'm perfect.
—Goodnight, son.

LOUIS AND CELIA ZUKOFSKY

XXXI Paene insularum, Sirmio

Peninsular arm, Sirmio, insular arm, welling eye, kiss come to what in liquid won't stagnate,

mark of the vast fare and tugging that Neptune is,
how I'm to live into your light I've come to see;
it strikes past credence: Thynia and Bithynian
plains lie back of us, and I am safe here with you.
O what most solves us but that the blessed cure is—
comes when the mind's onus, repugnance, peregrin
labors, festerings vanish, no lair or nostrum—
desire we must acquiesce to, of our own bed?
O that's what in sum makes our labors most tempting.
Salve! o Venus-tied Sirmio, I choir your good,
good that the waters choir—Lydia's lake won't die:
redoubt, laugh! what what's homey crackling every room.

XXXVII Salax taberna

Salt hacks, tavern boys, what skews, can't you burn alleys
on to your ninth pole from the Pile Hats Brothers Pillar!
So you'll put it as men you're first and last whoppers,
souls liquoring, cuddling what's puled in little arms,
conn future bawdry, put it "other caterers irk us"?
Incontinent air, wood, seated asses, sulk a
century, two centuries, and what assurance
I can't run thru two hundred rumps, my assessors?
I'd quip at that: name tagged to his whopper on the
front of the tavern, scorpion wee boys, *inscribed!*
My little one, ah me, she sins to forget me,
and that much love a quantum of bitter nothing,
procuress after magnificent belligerence,
conceded—this thick. Hangs bony but is thick with
all men—a mite loves, acquits her indignities—
all pusillanimous moochers of cemeteries:
to that prat of all men the one pileated
coney, cool lousy Celtiberian filly,
Egnatius, opaque whim of bone and faked beard, and
bared dentures rinsed with a wash of Spanish urine.

CATULLUS

232

ROCCO SCOTELLARO
Suonano mattutino

The procession has started
already at night.
I see the file of mowers
touching the star
the one left
at the top of the tortuous street.
In my long pit of a byway
the shoes of the mules on the cobbles
sound matutinal.

Monelli

The rows of cranes
that light up our sky with shrieks
no longer are seen.

All the black swallows leave us
at the short horizon of the quarter.
We cut off the wings
of the wild doves:
with cautious love caught on our roofs.

Ora che Domina Luglio

As yet no faith arouses me:
so that the light comes to me
and I dont feel it's morning
and I know my day's caught
in a meaningless whirl.
If I were sod!

A spade would have shaken me,
I'd give grass and fruit
to this highflying season.
But I'm a dry spring
the flocks keep away from
now that July rules.

Andare a vedere una giovane
for a dead girl —

In a moment you forgot us,
your hand falls from your breast
and straightens your new dress out.
The countryfolk came
and uncovered before you.
They recognized you then.
They took handfuls of grain
that belonged to you on your wedding day.

Viaggio di ritorno

My mother walks
from beds to fireplace,
goes under and over
the ploughman on the hill.

Mother, I'll raise the walls of the house,
the chimney cock will sing on the tiles,
and you will have gone already.

Spent water
the worn-out Italian papers
nothing else now to say.
I'm going back to my bare land.

Between country and town bare land,
the silence of the bell
and a voice how much further away.

Il Garibaldino novantenne

Of all the things that I recall
(as a beast who has the power
the puddle of piss and fountain:
I too am a young mule, picked at the fairs
who has already had three masters)
what I remember most of all
and vividly is a bit of an alley
near my house. It had and it has
always a white cover of sun
that comes with midday: the houses
in front are squat and go down to the valley.
Here they carry on a throne the ninety-year-old
Garibaldian.

A ninety-year-old Garibaldian was
that old bull that caught the sun
at Fuori Porta Monte.
I moved around him as I would a monument;
he had the huge body of a snowman
and coals for eyes.
Once or twice
— as even is done
with an animal
to show he is understood
I set before him the support
and the portrait of the General
whom he never actually saw.

A niece would come and feed him
hot bread with a spoon,
to open the stiff bronze lips.
And I'd hide, playing blindman's buff,
under his heavy mantle of wool:
warmer was he than a bull in the stall,
colder was he than a snowman.
When the sun came down, four men
would carry him down into the house.

La mia bella patria

I am a blade of grass
a blade of grass that trembles.
And my Country is where the grass trembles.
A breath can transplant
my seed far away.

La felicità

Make me happy henceforth with your eyes.
In the sky's depth my own eye gets lost:
nor are the dead any poorer than we are
who have stretched ourselves out in
                                            the grass.

Notte in campagna

Lie down under the elm,
the sky has fewer stars for the wind.
The Pleiades are burnt out,
the Bear is unhinged
on the brightened horizon.

I want you, not jugs of strong wine
nor origanum and salt on the bread.
You remain stretched out
hurt by someone who's
                played with you fatefully.

ROBERTO SANESI

Ora e qui

Yes, I have to confess it, for years now
reality, wearing its ridiculous
cocked hat much like a

character out of Brecht, has nervously
winked at me from corners, but seldom
spoken my language, and assured me
it was not exactly myself.
And now I wonder, observing
photographs and landscapes, clouds and bits
of colored paper, trees, women,
geodes round and red as angry fists
rotating in my eyes, how far this
experience of things whether total and false
—not whether true and partial—goes and I take
refuge
in evoking the shades of history
as if they were all (and no one renounces
first person singular) not already the projection
of my conditioned will, but the sum
of what is dead, out of some prophecy.
So,
amid the varying moments of time, in every pause,
where my poetry runs out of breath,
is a ruined threshold, an empty temple
where the wind keeps signalling something.

Dai padiglioni del vento

Is a wheel of flame, a bird, a song or an orchard
of apples the world, and you recognize it, with
words wide
heard in the ear when the sky slides
into its ditch of exile.
But when
winter calls you, it's too late then to affirm, too
late to refute truth, to destroy traces, to deny
the exhausting act of being a man, with his
intelligent power of muscles and memories.
At the intuitive hour
when the moon rises from mirrors and white is slain
and all saints and heroes grope in the sewers and
a butterfly's body
scribbles on windows letters of love, all the lives
that you havent lived

237

condense mute and possible in shadowy transit. Burnt.
From the four
pavilions of wind issues one voice, and it's always
yours.

Dialogo aperto

We are
two amid blue celandine, and sometime
shadows (but who falls on your face, who
in my thoughts pursues you if you do not run,
a memory?) of repentance, of pain, in this sky
corroded by twilight, a memory,
for how much hasnt been, and now you seek me
with a voice that is not your own, Answer,
not a tablet where the wind nestles
the spider's retreats, unknown envy, our
impossible love, not this, but with gestures of anger
the shadow leans over my figure, and a figure
the shadow touching me with a cold sound. Answer,
isnt this perhaps why your flame kindles
the celandine? And I look at my hand. We are
two amid the silence of the mind and the silent
troubled darkness of what's not been, two shadows
hesitant at the garden wall. Answer, dont you hear
the reverberation of geranium, the mole's bite, a cry
of earth stirred in its thoughts, when the blackbird shakes
remembrance and the branch with a tough beak? Why
wont you ever answer? We would have time and world
if you did not exist.

THEODORE ENSLIN

New Sharon's Prospect
for Ray, and Sonny, and Josie

A few years after the Pilgrims had founded Plymouth Plantation,
and the Puritans had settled Boston and Salem, there were a number
of books written about this "new" England, usually by men in the
employ of English merchants, to attract settlers to a land soon to be

exploited. One of the best of these books was William Wood's *New England's Prospect*, a handbook in prose and verse, describing the natural resources, as well as the life to be expected there among the native Indians. Now, three hundred years later, the backwoods sections, particularly those of north New England, have gradually "gone back." In some ways, so have the people who still live there. Seeing it in the hard, but close-knit life of one family, I have tried to find out "where they are" in relation to a world that rarely guesses how close to the bone, how careless of what many think "the great concerns" some men still live. In that sense it is a
prospect.

> Blaze from a pair of trees.
> I see how these are blazing—
> walk that way—
> away—
> and when I've walked away
> from them
> the blaze is there.
> A little fire warms my back,
> stays on this sidehill
> in another's dooryard.

October 2. To New Sharon. A family here as biblical as the name of their town. T's father, bent, heavy, but with air of a real patriarch—sire of thirty-two children, living a life we read about, but rarely see. T and I sit in the kitchen with another brother, and the Old Man. The three heads bend at the same angle, impossible for an outsider to duplicate. A common purpose in it—a solidarity there. Archaic it may be, but it is indicative of a life that works—for them. Slow speech, not too much of it, while in the next room the women, mother, daughters, and daughters-in-law sit sewing and chattering.

Father and Sons

> Heavy,
> slow-muscled,
> bent,
> he sits near these young men
> who swing tough:
> An old tree
> with saplings at the foot.

September 10. Talking with T, my best woodchopper, today. Something almost ferretlike in his look, which is wholly of the woods. He looks down when he talks—a habit with many solitary men. His wife comes up with him on good days, and marks the logs for him to cut. Pregnant, she'll be with him until she has to go to have her child. They have two. A third died a year ago of pneumonia—probably in an illheated shack somewhere. Both of them feel this keenly. He says, "It was awful quiet, and I knew it shouldn't be. She was always raisin' hell, you know, kid fashion. And I looked over to her highchair, and she was dead."

The Wife

"All loused up"
the world. Yes,
all loused up.
   But, would you say so,
seeing her come up over the hill,
eight months pregnant, and heavy,
to bring him a sandwich
                 when he had to work so late?

October 17. T Speaking of his boyhood: "We never had much time for school. The Old Man always had a load of wood to get out, and we had to make up so much time when we went back that we kinda lost courage. One time the truant officer come down to the house, and told the Old Man we'd have to go to school. Dad says, "All right, I'll send 'em, but you might just as well start sendin' down food orders the day I do." He never got bothered again. Sister and I used to cut birch with a bucksaw. We could saw five cords a day, on the yard. Then chainsaws come out, and the Old Man bought one. Bet us a dollar one day he'd beat us with it. I filed that bucksaw blade like a bobcat's teeth, and we went to sawing. We sawed like hell, but we beat the Old Man three to one. Warn't he mad!"

New Sharon Dooryard

If you dig there
scraps of generations
                 broken
will be thrown up.

A hard chance.
                    The dead pine
          drops more branches
                         each windy night.

November 3. T's father sits next to the kitchen stove, eyes closed, deceptively drowsy, hat with three toothpicks in the band, pushed back. He rules his clan from here. He raises his right hand: "Madeleine, put a stick of wood in that stove." "No wood in the house, Dad, and there's none split." "There's an axe out there. You know what it's for. Josie, feed the horses. The mare'll take four quarts. Hm, can't hear the saw. Stub'll be havin' trouble. I'll see to it. Old Lady, how many wreathes you made?" "Twenty-three." "Make two more, and we'll eat." He gets up, leisurely and assured, and heads for his woodlot.

The Old Man Strikes Fire

The eyes washed by sorrow
and the hard life —
by the sun,
or snow in April heats.
Blue in them,
blue north horizon
cold on windy evenings.
His light goes out.
He turns back
to momentary affairs.

October 5. The Old Man makes me welcome with a sly peep across his glasses. A prodigal son drives in to the dooryard, but dares come no farther. His mother goes out to talk to him, but the Old Man refuses, even though I can tell it's nothing but his fierce pride that keeps him in his chair. He comments, "Well, if he thinks I've changed since he told me I was a damned old thief, I hain't!"
          November 17. A crosscurrent of feuds and blood enmity here, but one which no outsider may enter, I would not wisely contradict, or even agree with one who spoke of Old Man T: "He'd get up at two in the mornin' and yard five sticks three miles, if he thought he could steal it." T, talking to the Old Man of a comparable exploit. "How come you twitched that wood so far, Dad?" "Well, the horse was standin' there doin' nothin', and the girls didn't have anythin' to do, so I thought they might just as well haul it down."

November 25. The Old Man's House was given him by the town—apparently to keep him at a distance. Even here, such a self-sufficient tribe is considered a danger. Not able to divide their solidarity, the townspeople attempted to isolate it. But the best of the bargain went to the clan. Even in its despairing old age, it is a patriarch's house, with its ancient pegged beams and square rooms—the central entry, low pitched roof under the dead pine. To the three hickories, and the hopvine that covers one end of the gable—planted undoubtedly by an early settler who loved them—this is a ruler's
homestead.

> As if it wouldn't stand another winter,
> the hopvine dragging at one side,
> moss an inch thick on the roof,
> sills gone into ground.
> > Outside of the cup.

The Pull

> Gently, gently,
> all must change
> from what was not
> to this that is /
> is not again.
> Strains as the yoke is drawn—
> one long and level pull.
> Ah, gently, gently,
> whips and curses
> break the spell,
> and nothing is
> as nothing is.

December 7. T and his father have a deep affection for horses. They aren't always kind or indulgent toward them, but they "look out" for their welfare as they would for one of the family. In summers, they follow the fairs, entering as many of the pulling contests as possible. They do this quite as much to show their pride, as for the "first" or "second money" they usually win. Now the Old Man has a team of chestnuts which he rarely works, but exercises daily. Fair time will come again. T reminiscing: "The Old Man used to drink a lot—home brew we made. Got so he'd have eight quarts a day—two before breakfast two more at dinner, two for supper, and two after chores. But he was disbarred from the pullin' down to Rome one year. Feller said he was too drunk. He hain't had a drink since. He don't care 'bout us usin' the stuff, but that cured him."

New Sharon, Now

Old bones,
hair combings,
bent matches,
tinfoil,
leavings
all heaped in with ashes.
Kitchen stove crusted
      over.
Have this
      and know:
Untidiness is the essence of despair

The Youngest

The last of his long line,
she runs slim-legged:
    As a colt.
An old man's child,
but with some of his young fires
breathing.
    She's happy to be alive.
I doubt if she knows this.

Ede's Brook

Seems to have called a halt.
Steaming kettle hole.
The girls with pails,
pick their way carefully.
Half the water will be frozen
by the time
they get back to the house.

December 12. There is a magnificent well in the New Sharon

Dooryard. Near forty feet deep, the keyed stones hold their position in a perfect circle, as they have for over a hundred years. A flat slab, at least ten feet across, caps it, from which the center was cut out round so that a bucket could be lowered. Admiring it one day, I asked the Old Man about the water. "No good. We lost two from diphtheria—have to haul water from the brook." Probably generations of dead cats, or sheer neglect, poisoned it.

The Well

To have that water
stoned in by master hands,
the flat top cut for generations
to throw down their buckets,
and still not wholesome,
(mound of horseshit
smoking at one side)
is cursed.
The women walk by,
talking about other things.
Some times they must think about the well,
        festering.

December 30. T went for a load of hay today—for all the family horses, but to be stored at the Old Man's under a sagging roof that passes for a haybarn. A cold day, and we were glad enough to get the truck loaded with the coarse, homemade bales. Once arrived at New Sharon, however, the men vanished, and the two youngest girls were left to unload and stack. I could hear a few snickers as the masters rounded the corner of the house—presumably because I chose to stay and help. Probably they look upon me as the Indians did the "squawmen." But it was pleasant to pitch the bales, steady them for Josie, the youngest, who certainly shouldn't be carrying eighty-pound loads, laughing at the scratches and sudden skirls of hay and fine snow in the sharp wind. Red, and out of breath, we finished it. Not for nothing all those nostalgic tales of haying. Going in to the fire, I couldn't help feeling that the others, toasting their shins and hands, had missed something.

After the Hay Load

The men left me alone
with the girls
—probably laughing
when I chose to stay with them.
After all, it's woman's work
to pile the bales neatly
in clutter and disorder.
But we stuck at it,
covered with beggar ticks
and straw, from the coarse
fields
            untended.
Laughing a little when a string sagged
enough to collapse a whole bundle,
our faces and hands were red
from the cold and the thistles
and
perhaps the close work
                        too—
At a steadying chore.

December 5. All of T's family will be working in my woods now. Very casually the Old Man asked me if I had much ash to sell. After I'd answered that I did, the talk drifted to other things—a coon hunt, the possibility of more snow. Finally, as he was leaving, the Old Man remarked, "We'll be there in the morning." They will. T went directly home, asking me if I'd come to help him. He wanted to polish the harnesses for his horses. "I'll be working with the Old Man!"

The Christmas Fern

A dark morning.
We followed the horses
at a rein's distance
over the new snow
in the twitch trail.
The others were concerned
about the chance of another storm,
but, for the moment,
I was glad that the team

stepped over
a green frond
that had worked free to the winter air.

January 5. The fear of loneliness, even when we are not physically alone. It is most evident in the women here. They don't have the opportunity to get out—even to the store to talk with neighbors whose "next doors" are often miles away. They pine, these women, turn yellow from loneliness quite as much as from spending the long winters in dark kitchens. They turn "queer"—alcoholic and suicidal—much more easily than their men. I see it, even in the close society that the Old Lady and her daughters have at New Sharon. Perhaps it explains their continuing interest in me—someone "who's been to the outside."

The Old Lady with Her Girls

Sometimes it must be
lonely to the point of a scream
they have in silence—
sitting—talking aimlessly—
sewing—
or just trying to keep warm
by little fires
the men haven't time to tend.

Baldwin's Mill

was burned last summer.
The roof had bowed:
Slight curve, but unsafe.
Looking at the charred trees there
and the cracked chimney
smothered now in snow,
I asked him about it:
"Baldwin come from New Hampshire.
Sawed hard wood there
until it warn't no use."

January 8. There is an abandoned mill, now a charred millsite, just outside of the village. Nostalgically, I'm sad to see its swayback "shake" roof gone, after its owner decided that it was no longer safe. (Wasn't it there that I found the little giltframed mirror which I keep in the kitchen?) Asking about it, I had the same answer that I have nearly everywhere here: A case of lost courage. Baldwin, the man who built and ran it seventy-five years ago, "gave up." So much energy, so much *of* men, physical and dream, that lies abandoned in these lean woods. Against that, there must be an integral pitting of forces, sometimes crafty and underhanded, as in the Old Man's tribal strength.

November 22. The Old Man looks out over these hills with the air of a proprietor, and I'm sure he can't think of himself as anywhere else on earth. But the affection he feels for his country is a calculating one, not much given to sentiment, or even curiosity, beyond the living it can afford him. Several times he's asked me the name of Potato Hill, which is my closest neighbor, and when I asked him the name of some of the peaks that one sees spread out to the north of New Sharon Crossroads, he didn't know. Probably he never cut wood there.

The Dooryard's View

When he stands his ground,
he's planted,
not without reason.
(Oh
    don't disturb the root.)
But if the breeze touches or stirs him,
he knows it's *here*:
Won't question.
    Won't look up.

November 19. Strange mixture of old New England with contemporary U.S. T lives in a pioneer cabin with his animals around him, but with the latest model chainsaw in his dooryard. He wouldn't start a new job on a Friday and he hauls his water from the stream. But he can take the engine out of a truck, and replace it as well as any garage mechanic.

A Crossroads

He sees strange fortunes in a winter sky
(a dragon's shadow in his stream)
off color by the moon in clouds.

He says, "Blood."
Then looks at the paper,
sees:
TRACTOR FOR SALE
chuckles, and fires up,
      "I'll have me that!"

November 1. Shoemakers' children! Often, I go down to T's camp to bucksaw firewood for his wife, while he cuts saleable wood on my east ridge. It seems almost on principle that he never cuts more than a day's supply. Nor is he different in this from most of the woodsmen here.

Within the Bounds

"All I know"—
It works, in woods he knows as nothing else.
Works on him.
      He looks up as if to ask a question,
then reaches for his file.
Sure, quick strokes along the sawblade.

The Peddler

"I can tell you, these're good ones—
none of your store boughten apples.
Well yes, a little more'n what they ask,
but look what you're gettin'.
I guess prob'ly.

     ———

"I heard about that.
      Say he went off,
left her flat.
No firewood, no nothin'.
      I tell *you*, Mr. Man!"

January 19. This is still the country of the itinerant peddler— The housewife's friend who will sell her anything: a pair of shoes, a bushel of apples—sometimes at prices below those of the stores, often above the going rate Sometimes he's a cheat and a quack, but he is trusted and respected. He carries the news, the undercurrent gossip from house to house, and that's worth a few extra pennies, even where they're hard come by. Mary Dalrymple talks about peddling herbs and ferns when she was young, but her old cousin, Johnny Grant, still hawks his wares—even to Mary who's been an adept.

The Expedition

That day, they were blind to everything
but the distance.
     That made it good.
(When they went for water,
the girls fished out a few cones
from the home brook,
same shape and color as the ones up country.)

November 29. The life is so hard, so impossible at times, that I think these people complicate even the simplest things, fearing that they might be too easy, and so doomed to failure. Old Doris (the Old Lady), several daughters and sons, the Old Man, inevitably, with the small "spotting" axe that he always carries—his sceptre—set out to get pine cones today for their Christmas wreath industry. But not to their woodlot, nor to mine, where plenty of pines grow, but eighty miles to the north, where they filled two small shopping bags.

The Last Load Out

We hadn't much time before the mill closed,
and I knew he was afraid of snow.
The leisure in the way he talked.
put knee to a log,
        swung it up
into the tier, was without waste.
He didn't say what he was thinking,
but we all knew he was racing
against the wind.
A few snowbirds huddled in the bare elm tree.
He shook his head as he tightened the last chain.

249

A Case

They call me that we have a case at the hospital. It is a fine night, not late, only a little after eleven. When I arrive, they tell me, "Mr. H—is going to operate. The patient is in the first bed on the left in the men's ward." I go in.

It is dark but some light comes from a wall fixture above the bed. He is a man in early life. I begin to ask the usual questions. I explain that I will give the anaesthetic for the operation. He says, "My name is Pisgah." I nod and go on with my questions and examination. He appears tired and in some distress. The exact nature of his condition is still in doubt.

It is true, when he tells me his name, I have a momentary surprise, which I suppress. The name is that of the mountain mentioned in the Bible from which Moses is said to have viewed the Promised Land. As a child, the name had intrigued me. It also occurs in a hymn, as if it were a man's name: Pisgah's Mount. I had often thought, singing the verse: who was Pisgah? I had used the name later, rather at random, for a person who existed in a story I was writing.

It was a story upon which I had exerted myself and then, in one sense, abandoned. Pisgah, in fact, was the person in that story with whom I was most concerned. I had written two extended versions, and others more fragmentary without being able to bring them to any satisfaction.

That I had not finished those pieces did not mean that I had abandoned the work. To abandon a piece of writing is one thing. To abandon a work, is another. A particular piece of writing is a means, for a writer, which may not always finally serve the work. Thus, I write this, which also serves, for the moment.

I give the anaesthetic while my friend Mr. H—does the surgery. The details of the case are of no consequence. It goes well. Towards the end, when my attention is not too pressed with technical details, I have the chance to look more closely at Pisgah's face.

It is the face of a man asleep. As he sleeps, he is remote, both from himself and from us. Yet he sleeps by my will. I check his pulse, his blood pressure, his colour, his muscle tone, and gently assist each breath.

In the story I had often had the experience that Pisgah was difficult to lay hold upon. His character seemed to change. Even the details of what he did or said. I had wanted to discover who exactly he was. So that I could, in some way, come to terms with him, to finish the story. Now, suddenly, I felt him alive against my hand. And that life dependent upon my attention. If my attention should fail, I might lose him forever.

I speak occasionally with Mr. H—. Sometimes about the details of what he is doing. Sometimes about other things entirely. Neither of us speaks of the man with whom, in our several ways, we are involved.

Later, before leaving the hospital, I make a last routine visit to Pisgah's bed. He is now partly awake and responds to a touch on the face or a simple question. I look again into that face, somewhat firmer now, and occasionally tightened by the first twinges of pain from the incision.

"Who are you?" I ask. He smiles faintly, out of his half-sleep, as if amused that after all this time I should not know.

CID CORMAN

A Child Performs Shimai

he dances
for his dog
in the garden

he cries look
dog watch dog
and the earth turns

the dog leaps
mountains rise
the sky quiet

potatoes
everything
becomes his fan

The Religion

dark morning
over the hills
cold flooding down
through the pines

my hands clap
invoking warmth
beating time to
a slow snow

The Offerings

Too many things on the altar.

A petal would do.

Or the ant that stops for a moment
at it.

The Contingency

Fell from the ceiling
black. I struck it with
the nearest object. It

coiled; another blow
flattened to a stain.
The vicious centipede.

The House

It's quiet, almost too quiet,
I'm alone in it. That's
part of it. I dont know

where the old people have gone to.
Probably visiting
children. It's none of my

business. It's a good time to write.
The cries of the birds are
so small. It's as though I

were listening through the wrong end
of my ears. It is the
not being here that sings,

trying to find its way back. How
difficult it is to
follow its vanishings.

The Counter

talking, the
two of us only,
over soup

Mischa, it's
his place, raises
the question of

water, how
some guy comes in
for coffee in-

sists on a
glass of water, 3
glasses full

as if he hadnt
enough, alone,
to do

borrows a
toothpick and—
and asks for the key

to the john, that's
an awful lot
for a dime

"in this" he nods,
"I know
I am right." I say

nothing It's good
to be wrong too
sometimes. But

never argue with
one who
has to be right.

Mister Young

Not grace, Lord knows, but
a fury.
To bury meat
rather than

give it to people,
those at least
who were given
to mocking

him. Dignity is
like that. Mean
and silly, but
anyhow

marvellous. There is
in most men
equal malice,
ignorance

and innocence. He,
for instance,
cares enough for
his mink and

chinchilla out in
Idyho
to inter their
pelts for no

other reason than
sentiment.
Poor critter, man,
who often

does worst by his own
brethren. He,
who caught bare in
a fire with

only a shirt on,
said that he'd
just as soon throw
that back in.

"Five miles either way
from the two
nearest towns" is
near enough.

The Touch

The sprinkler
blocked by the
thick trunk of
an old pine

sprays the far
end of the
bench, but the
emergent

flourish falls
short, only
to touch me
more. Magic.

The Declarations

We had said all
that we had to say

saying long ago
nothing. And trusted,

rightly I feel,
what we felt, we knew.

Silence is sometimes
less inarticulate

than the artful
confusion of words. We

lived in one house:
that in itself was to feel

much. And this bare house
I have come to now,

like all houses,
houses all we may know

knowing the fieldmouse
and the scorpion.

Asters burst gold
against white stucco

and rust-barred windows.
Bare chestnuts hold

glazed wicks to the sun,
candelabra.

I'm not there and
you're not here and yet

everywhere
we move together.

Who's away, who's come,
and who's to stay.

Questions reveal
us answerers

Visiting or visited
we need not

certainly be
strangers to each other.

I am your son, father.
Father. Is

that a statement
or a profound prayer?

CID CORMAN

The Obbligato

This hill is far
enough.
It's true. Either
you are here

or you're not. And
if you
are, this is the
place to stand

and take the earth
to task,
to give it all
you've got and

not ask back but
of it,
as grace, its food,
its flower,

to be like those
who brought
you here, who per-
sisted, who

bore you, nursed you,
taught you,
who saw through nights
sang to you,

because they felt
they must,
because they loved
even this.

EUGENIO MONTALE

A Mia Madre

Now that the chorus of Greek partridges
blandishes you in eternal sleep, broken-up
happy troop scattered towards the wine-rich
slopes of the Mesco, now that the struggle
of the living gathers fury, if you yield
like a shadow its remains
                    (and isn't a shadow,
O gentle one, isn't that what you
                                believe)

who will protect you? The cleared street
is not a way, only two hands, a face,
those hands, *that* face, the act of one
life that is none other than itself,
only this places you in the elysium
teeming with spirits and voices in which
                    you live;

and the question that you leave is itself
an act of yours, in the shadow of the
                    crosses.

Dal Treno

The bright-red turtledoves
are at Sesto Calende for the first
time in living memory. So the papers
advertise. Face glued to the window,
in vain have I sought them. A collar of yours,
but of another hue, yes, a bulrush bowed
its head and was husked. For me only
did it flash, fall in a pool. And its
fiery flight blinded me to the other.

L'Anguilla

The eel, the siren
of the cold seas that leaves the Baltic
to reach our seas,
our estuaries and rivers
that travels upstream deep, under the spate
                    opposing,
from branch to branch and then
from hair to hair, attenuated,
always more within, always more in the heart
of flint, filtering
through gullies of slime until one day
a light struck off chestnuts
ignites its flicker in pools of standing water,
in the channels that go down
from the terraces of the Apennine to the
                    Romagna;
the eel, torch, lash,
arrow of Eros in earth
that only our gulches or dessicate
Pyrenean streams lead back
to paradises of fecundation;
the green spirit that seeks
life there where only
heat and desolation gnaw,
the spark that says
everything begins when everything seems
burnt out black, buried stump;
the brief iris, twin
of her whom your eyes enchase
and you make shine intact amidst the sons
of man, immersed in your mud, can you
not believe her a sister?

Piccolo Testamento

This that at night keeps flashing
in the calotte of my mind,
mother-of-pearl trace of the snail
or emery of brayed glass,

is neither light of church or factory
that may sustain
clerical red, or black.
Only this iris can I
leave you as testimony
of a faith that was much disputed,
of a hope that burned more slowly
than a hard log in the fireplace.
Conserve its powder in your compact
when every lamplight spent
the sardana becomes infernal
and a shadowy Lucifer descends on a prow
of the Thames or Hudson or Seine
thrashing bituminous wings half-
shorn from the effort, to tell you: it's time.
There's no inheritance, no goodluck charm
that can ward off the monsoons' impact
on the gossamer of memory,
but a history endures in ashes alone
and persistence is only extinction.
Just was the sign: he who has realized it
cannot fail to find you again.
Everyone recognizes his own: pride
was not flight, humility was not
vile, the tenuous glitter.polished up
down there was not that of a match.

ROBERT DUNCAN

From The Day Book
—excerpts from an extended study of H.D.'s poetry

March 10, Friday

Naming the stars out of the seas of heaven, men drew a .net-work. The knots were suns, were burning. What the poets who bound the dragon of their confusion spun were lines of association [where figures of light appeared, giving direction.]* All life is oriented to the light from which life comes. The bees in their dances are oriented to the sun and, if it is dark, will dance in relation to a candle flame. Men found at night a new orientation in the stars, found a heaven, a spreading fish-net of lights, that became a projected screen of where and when they were as they danced, an image of another net that in memory we throw out over moment and place that are suns in time, the net of our selves. The bees dance to tell where the honey is.

They memorized as they realized. In turn, now, the surfaces and involvements of the brain were an imprint of the seas above, the sky-dome above was the image of another configuration in the skull-dome below. So, a net-work there too bound the dragon of a confusion in constellations of living cells that made up a body or series of imaginary bodies a man was, is, would be.

It was a map. It was a great design of where they were and then of when. Night after night, in the country these nights, I am learning my stars. The wavering cold of a mixed winter and spring, as if those distant lights were within the aroma, the fragrance from mingled March blossomings—lemon, lilac, grasses—within the pervading aroma, takes part. These earth-sparks seem just to have flown up into those real points of the ancient ways in which the book of when-where sparkles and glows. As we come home from an evening with neighbors, Orion is in the high heaven.

❋

The figure of the giant hunter in the sky brings with it, as often, the creative presence of Charles Olson. [Since the appearance of *Origin*

* *Note.* Brackets [] represent overlays, redevelopments and expansion of the original text, where the author wishes to indicate these strata as part of the structure as process.

I a decade ago, my own vision of what poetry is has been transformed, reorganized around a figure that emerges from his work. This man, himself a "giant"—six foot seven or so—, has been an outrider for me, my own Orion. But another factor enters here to orchestrate the music of images that plays between the stars and events in life. It was this same time of year, in 1955, when Olson read aloud to us the beginnings of a new sequence, *O'Ryan*. The scene in the bare room at Black Mountain comes with its cold night and the blazing winter sky at the window.] The fugitive hero of that sequence had a likeness in another contemporary—Robert Creeley. [In Olson's *O'Ryan* the ancient hunter of the skies, the poet in Olson reflected in the poet in Creeley, the rueful figure any of us is as men we are—"who

> told you your flesh is
>
> as rosy as your
> baby's as rosy as
>
> Rosy, as, your
> moth-er's, as who got you up

—appear drawn on the cover of the White Rabbit edition by Jess, a new O'Ryan-Orion. "Overall, mover of the unnumbered." Olson names him.] The sky reminds me.

✿

Radical! Our roots are in the sky. The Milky Way appears, cross-section of our galaxy. In the earliest news out of heaven, what they said, the *mythos*, was that it was the slain body of the dragon, it was the flow of everlasting mothering milk, it was light, it was rhetoric, river, fluid. A stream of suns.

✿

Otherwise, other *ways* (as Charles Olson gave me the instruction in his *Against Wisdom As Such* that our wise is our ways), if there are not these roots in the sky, this when-where map or gestalt of what we are, otherwise poetry is a litter. "Litterature," Lewis Carroll called his collection of bits and starts out of which he put together *Sylvie and Bruno*. "The reader will overlook my spelling," he wrote.

✿

In our time, Joyce, gathering up his mountain of litter, sorting and resorting, accruing scraps upon scraps, took a patron in that "Dodgeson." He too made out of the mound of twenty-five years labor a pun upon literature [and wrote a crawling language that must enter here, if only to play adversary, for I have taken thought in this ground too.] Like Milton, Joyce was blind. *Finnegans Wake* has its roots among letters and in the body as if it were not moved by the stars. The work has intestinal fortitude, true to an internal chemistry. Its seasons are rounds of digestion. He had lost sight of the heavens.

❋

In a man's guts there are no gods. There is agony, there is pleasure. Pain that binds down the spirit to its own when-where. Pleasure that may be taken as we may take thought.

In the flight of the imagination, in the reading of the stars, in taking thought, we go out of our selves—flame out of the wet wood—out of literature then, out of matters of pain and pleasure.

❋

The consciousness bent down to a literature lives on its wits in a sulfurous burning. And if we come under literary dictates, all is voluptuous or all agony, is a matter of what we like and do not like, of literary taste, of good-and-bad, is hell.

As the other consciousness we see in the light spread out in the heavens. Gods there; and in the darkness, daemonic stars.

❋

In the map of stars we began to map our selves. Our projection of what we are was also a first poetry. A first making of a thing or image that projected a spiritual form. Well...there must have been another projected spiritual form, not only this but also this, where the adam named their things and kinds of the earth, another network of sticks and stones and names that never hurt one. In our "literary" listings and groupings, we are doing all of that, nothing more. We make constellations of the works of poetry that are, if they be anything linked by gender, works of our selves, drawings of our spiritual kinship, of when and where what we are is happening.

When we first come into the attraction of words in poetry, it is, often, the craft of the net, the novelty and ingenuity of how the language is turned, that strikes us. We mistake the effect for the art. The "flippancy," the uptodateness or regularguy voice of Williams—the risk of those knots, the daring recovery of the loss—appears interesting in itself, a performance, an advantage one might take in the language. To be original. To challenge the communal thing. Will he make it?

To tie fancy knots and to contrive a greater show of abilities. But all these original knottings are mistaken, are "hey-ding-ding" [as H. D. objected to Williams's mannerisms in 1916], lead to nowhere, if they are all novelty, things of 1916, not lasting forces. [Williams was right, in turn, to insist that they "filled a gap" and that the important thing was that he had seen in them the necessity of improvisations.] The knots that are flames are not originalities but origins.

"I think you have the *spark*," H. D. wrote Williams in that 1916 letter about his *Postludes*, "and when you speak *direct* are a poet." The spark lies in, is, the word wherever it is spoken direct, directs what we are then, for we involve our selves in saying. In poetry we make things real by working with every word as *directive*, as the immediate condition of or presence of the poem itself. [We cannot afford to "fill a gap." As we learn what the force of a poem is, we learn that gaps must be acknowledged where they are, if the music hold. In this concept there is no mere effect but what may appear as effect must prove to be a locus, a necessity, of the structure.]

For the knots of the net are actual suns—are, in poetry as in dreams, directions in the imagination between actual events and man's self and their realization in the art—governors, are terms of the real, are when-wheres that co-existing in the word and the world make actual events real.

March 12, Sunday

Neither Pound nor William Carlos Williams nor Eliot subscribes, as H. D. does, wholly to the psychological universe. We must go to the work of an art historian, to Malraux's *Psychology of Art* which began to appear in those early issues of *Verve* in the late 1930s, to find the eye that sees not values (the painting as a culture-commodity or the poem as an item of education), not aesthetic qualities (the painting or poem as a paradigm of the Beautiful), but primarily the means of human experience, and more, the ground only an art makes for experience to become communal and actual. Our own lives, like our dreams, are fleeting and insubstantial, unless they cease to be our own and are shared, created in the medium of images or words, delivered over into the commons of man's life and dreams. In works of art, what otherwise had been a passing fancy becomes operative fantasy—the *Phantasmagoria*, as Goethe called his *Helen*, or the "Dream, Vision" of H. D.'s Trilogy— to become our history, for our inner history to become a ground of reality, for the gods to flourish, "stepped out from Velasquez." The images and utterances that Jung attributes to a Collective Unconscious were all gathered by him, not from the unconscious but from the ground of man's adventures in consciousness, from the works of art (for the telling of a dream belongs, like the telling of a story or the working of an image from stone, to these orders), and are creations of man's conscious life in the community of language.

In this spirit, in this sense of the meaning of art, Malraux spoke in those early fragments that I read in 1938, preparing my mind for following as I did the inspiration of H. D. ten years later when *The Walls Do Not Fall* appeared. These passages were germs of a new involvement in life, of a conversion from aesthetic to psychic and operational concerns in art, or else they are waste, where Malraux pictured our work here as "the metabolism of destiny into consciousness," "across particular modes of expression, a plane of communion amongst men," or again: "That Jonah in the belly of the whale and Joseph in the pit prefigure Christ in the tomb, that the visit of the Queen of Sheba foreshadows the coming of the Magi—such beliefs quickened in the sculptors an emotion that, in due time, infused their representations of Jonah, Joseph and the Queen of Sheba with the very breath of life."

March 13, Monday

We know that an idea, a novel or a poem, may begin at some point or germ, grow, finding its being and necessary form, rhythm and life as the germ evolves in relation to its environment of language and experience in life. This is an art that rises from a deep belief in the universe as a medium of forms, in man's quest as a spiritual evolution.

In contrast, conventional art, with its conviction that form means adherence to an imposed order where metric and rime are means of conformation, rises from a belief that man by artifice must win his forms (as models, reproductions or paradigms) against his nature, areas of control in a universe that is a matter of chaos.

❋

Schrödinger, contrasting organic and inorganic forms in nature, writes: "Starting from such a small solid germ, there seem to be two different ways of building up larger and larger associations. One is the comparatively dull way of repeating the same structure in three directions again and again. That is the way followed in a growing crystal. Once the periodicity is established, there is no definite limit to the size of the aggregate.

"The other way is that of building up a more and more extended aggregate without the dull device of repetition. That is the case of the more complicated organic molecule in which every atom, and every group of atoms, plays an individual role, not entirely equivalent to that of many others (as in the case of a periodic structure). We might quite properly call that an aperiodic crystal or solid and express our hypothesis by saying: We believe a gene—or perhaps the whole chromosome fibre—to be an aperiodic solid."

*

Genetic thought along these lines is akin to poetic thought that sought an organic structure. Free verse, later projective verse as expounded by Charles Olson, developed a new sense of metric and rime towards an aperiodic form. Each individual articulation of the poem plays its role in figuring and shadowing the life of the whole. Here, structure is not given but emerges from the cooperation of many events in syllable, in word, in phrase, to be satisfied only as their complex interrelations are fulfilled.

*

Marianne Moore is a master of a poetry that is periodic in its concept, which has its counterpart in her concern with social conformities, in her admiration for rigor, for the survival of vitality where character-structure resists experience. "He 'Digesteth Harde Yron'" is not "comparatively dull," any more than a crystal is, unless, like Schrödinger, we are concerned with its structure. Her zest for language as a vitality in itself contends thruout with the use of metric to make a conforming pattern; but once the form is set, as it is in the stanza, there is no form, no further experience, realized in its extension. The poem presents examples of itself, a series that may be complete at any point, because, otherwise, it is extendible *ad infinitum*. The form of the whole in conventional verse does not rest in the fulfillment or growth of its parts but in the convention it keeps. Even departures conform. Between its appearance in *What Are Years* (1941) and its appearance in *Collected Poems* (1951), Marianne Moore eliminated three lines of stanza six of "He 'Digesteth Harde Yron'," all of stanzas seven and eight, without altering the "form" of the whole. We see stanza six not as a new entity in itself but as an amputated stanza.

The uncertainty she has often shown about the total form of a poem is a corollary of a periodic or imitative structure where, as Schrödinger observes of mineral crystals: "there are no definite limits to the size of the whole." There is no plot, no process of the poem towards fulfillment. The history of the poem, for Marianne Moore, consists of instances, as her natural history consists of examples. In her technical brilliance (as late as the poem "Style,") she is the peer of Williams or H. D. or Pound, her contemporaries. But in her poetics, in her thought and feeling then, she is a poet of a different kind.

✣

It is not their exemplary character-structure but their fullness of life, their ripeness in what they are, that moves us in H. D., Pound and and Williams as poets. They move in their work thru phases of growth towards a poetry that spreads in scope as an aged tree spreads its roots and foliage. The late Cantos, *Journey to Love*, or *Helen in Egypt* have their art in the language to convey scars and informations of age as a man may gather in his face and form accumulations of what he is in cooperation with the universe about him.

✣

March 14, Tuesday
[Men believe in money and in war as they believe in elves and gods, to make real their lives. Swords, spades, drawings on the walls, poems keeping their time too, are conditions of the real, of What Is, man-made. All makers are at work between thought and the actual, feeling their way. It is what we call Poetry or The Making that articulates the feeling in language towards the fullness of experience.] "The 'larger universe,' here," William James writes, "which helps us to believe both in the dream and in the waking reality which is its immediate reductive, is the *total* universe, of Nature *plus* the Supernatural."

✣

In a letter to Williams in 1908, Pound writes: "Here is a list of facts on which I and 9,000,000 other poets have spieled endlessly:" There follows a list of themes—Spring, Love ("a delightsome tickling. Indefinable."), Trees, Winds ("Flop thru and over 'em"). The tone is not only vernacular, it is sophisticated. It protests its superiority to some shame incurred in poetic themes. "Delightsome tickling" covers with male bravado the word "love" lest the poet be caught in. some "unmanly" emotion.

*

Compare Dante in *De Vulgari Eloquentia* speaking to his peers concerning the themes of poetry: "These we call the *worthiest* of those subjects which can be handled; and now let us hunt out what they are. And, in order to make this clear, it must be observed that, as man has been endowed with a threefold life, namely, vegetable, animal, and rational, he journeys along a threefold road"—finally concluding: "Wherefore these three things, namely, safety, love, and virtue, appear to be those capital matters which ought to be treated supremely, I mean the things which are most important in respect of them, as prowess of arms, the fire of love, and the direction of the will."

*

The direction of the will is disturbed. Pound's "translations" become more and more disparate in voices. In his version of *The Women of Trachis* Heracles cries out: *"Splendor. It all coheres."*—a full agony in a structure that shakes between the sublime poetry of the choruses and the ridiculous verse of the Cockney maid. There is the Nessus shirt that is the shirt of consciousness too, where Heracles is heroic as Pound is by his strength of character in adverse fate. For both the tragic fate arises from the heroic refusal of some area of our human complicity.

*

"We are alone," Freud sensed in writing *The Dream-Work* in the last year of the nineteenth century, "in taking something else into account."

*

"We have introduced a new class of psychical material between the manifest content of dreams and the conclusions of our enquiry." It is this area between the manifest and the conclusions of his enquiry that Pound cannot face as a conscious artist. The poetic genius "rescues" the content. This is the authenticity of the Cantos.

Because the poem-work is like the dream-work, in the Cantos we too read, as Freud saw the dream was to be read, "as it were a picto-graphic script, the characters of which have to be transposed individually

270

into the language of the dream-thoughts."

Where intelligence is awareness, Pound is a marred intelligence. But since intelligence is something larger and operates whether we are conscious in intelligence or not, the Cantos have their full poetic powers.

❋

We may see here the deeper significance of the role translation has had for Pound as a poetic task. "The dream-thoughts," Freud writes, "and the dream-content are presented to us like two versions of the same subject matter in two different languages."

❋

As, too, we see the importance of the ideogram for Pound, for it is his route towards that "as it were a pictographic script"—the *condensare* of the dream or poem.

Poems are for me only occasions of Poetry, of coming into his consciousness of things as potentials for making a universe real—celebrating, is it? or evoking? Of singing and dancing What Is.

❋

[Dante was a citizen—of Florence, and in the image of Florence, citizen of an idea, the City of God—and the safety he speaks of is a civic order, his prowess of arms, the defense of that order. But his idea is colored too by the prowess of arms in which Christianity won its place, by the dreams of conquest and subjection upon which the order of Christendom—threatened as long as any other religion existed—was based. This City of God was an armed fortress in defense against the City of Allah, the City of Buddha—in armed defense within against the insurrection of uncivil heresy.

Yet for those of us too who would be members of mankind, in all the variety and complexity of what man has been, there emerges another order that we would keep. Safety, and prowess of arms, come to have a new meaning.]

❋

James in his *Principles of Psychology* and Freud in *Interpretation of Dreams* are concerned too with just those three themes that Dante names. For James and Freud work, with a conviction in the necessity, to extend the meaning of, to "charge to the utmost" as Pound writes

271

the duty of the poet in the language must be : "prowess in arms, the fire of love, and the direction of the will."

*

[James and Freud in the nineties studied out hallucination, hysteria and neurosis, where man's safety, love and virtue were threatened and even lost.

James saw that man must cope with a more and more complicated picture of the real, if he desired. fullness. His pluralistic philosophy imaged a manhood where ideal, practice, fiction and even aberration had each its individual role to play in the composition of realities. Freud saw that the unconscious activity of man, whatever he had not faced in himself, where arts, wars, rituals of flower worship and death orgy, forbidden sexual cravings and the highest ideals were mixed, must be part of his conscious engagement in life, his responsibility, or else the old hubris threatened.

Our safety lay in our imagination of what man was, not in the defense but in the opening of our minds. Our prowess must lie now not in defeating the enemy but in the more problematic, the longer effort to understand our common humanity with him.]

*

There is some battle the two men—Ezra Pound and William Carlos Williams—had to fight that made for the jargon of their letters where felt realities contend. Not contrast but contradiction appears, a gap between ideals and practical ends, so that cynicism and embarrassment gathered about the words Spring, Love, Trees, Wind. Pound and Williams are often embarrassed before their inspiration. And then, as if to disavow their manliness, their sincerity, in writing to each other they cultivate this other Male-Talk. It had its counterpart in the girlish-idiotic manner cultivated by some women. Was it an American dis-ease? We do not find this voice in Lawrence's letters or essays. A displacement of affect, a male hysteria. It was the crux of H. D.'s objection in that letter Williams quotes in the Prologue to *Kora in Hell:* "It is as if you were *ashamed* of your Spirit, ashamed of your inspiration!—as if you mocked at your own song."

*

In Williams's reply we see that back of the challenged "hey-ding-ding touch" that Williams, defending, said: "filled a gap that I did not know how better to fill at the time," lay something else, a felt need of the man in his struggle for individual feeling against the popularly debased meanings. "The true value," he goes on to say, "is that peculiarity which gives an object a character by itself. The associational or sentimental value is the false."

[The secret of the poetic art lies in the keeping of time, to keep time, discovering the line of melodic coherence. "Here," "there," what once was, what is now — this return in a new structure is the essence of rime — the return. . . of a vowel tone, of a consonant formation, of a theme, of a contour, where rime is meaningful, corresponding to the poet's intuition of the real. "The heart of Nature being everywhere music," Carlyle has written in "The Hero as Poet," "if you can only reach it." H. D. in her work with Freud followed, she tells us, "my own intense, dynamic interest in the unfolding of the unconscious or the subconscious pattern."] There is something in the unfolding of the poem that corresponds to the unfolding of the psyche. The poet, like the scientist, works to feel or know the inner order of things. The form in process of the poem, the form in process of the psyche, correspond in turn to the form in process of What Is, "There world ever was, and is, and shall be, Heraklitus says, "a Fire, kindled in measure, quenched in measure."

March 21, Tuesday

I had gleaned from some reference to a dictionary that the word *verse*, our verse in poetry, like our *prose* in poetry, was a term of ploughing. *Prose*, forward in the row or line; then "turning to begin another line" (as now I find it in the O. E. D.) *versus*.

As men plough forward and back did they once write turning
.enil eht fo dne eht ta

But in verse now, we *re*turn to begin another line. We do not reach the end or margin.

❀

It is fanciful philology. To demonstrate that, once words cease to be conventional, customary or taken-for-granted in their meaning, all things begin to move, are set into motion. In the figure of ploughing we see that prose and verse are two necessary movements in one operation of writing. That here what we call the ploughing of the field we also call poetry or our own operation in poetry. Writing that knows in every phase what it is doing.

❀

Forward and back, prose and verse, the shuttle flies in the loom.

THEODORE ENSLIN

"This Do, in Remembrance"

I may never
    see your room again,
and this
        is difficult
  to realize.
I cannot place you elsewhere,
although
        we will meet
in various places
      nervously
acknowledging
    that we know each other.
    It would spoil
    the things we had together
to remake promises.
    I know that.
You were wiser
           from the start
than I was.
But I make apologies
where I mean none.
We deserve
      more kindness
than we give ourselves.
To each other
  we were gentle.

EUGENIO MONTALE

The Man in Pajamas

I was out in the corridor, in slippers and pajamas, clambering now and again over a pile of dirty laundry. My hotel was regarded as first-class because of its two elevators and hoist (almost always out-of-order), but provided no closet for sheets, pillow-cases and towels in temporary disuse and the maids had to heap them up in whatever convenient corner. After hours I'd generally arrive at these far corners, and found myself no favorite of the maids for doing so. However, after offering an adequate tip, I'd receive tacit permission to amble about wherever I pleased. It was after midnight. A telephone rang softly. Was it my room? I headed quietly back but then heard someone answering; it was room 22, the room next to mine. As I was near the answering voice, a woman's voice, said: —Don't come yet, Attilio; there's a man in pajamas in the corridor, wandering about. And he might see you.

I heard from the other end a confused cackling. Mah?—she replied—I don't know who he is. Some poor dope who's always doing it. Don't come, please. Until I let you know.—She hung up with a bang, I heard steps in the room. I made a hasty retreat gliding away as if on skates. At the end of the hallway was a sofa, another pile of laundry and a wall. I heard the door of room 22 open; from a crack the woman observed me. I couldn't just stay there; I started slowly back. I had about ten seconds before passing 22. In a flash I went over the various possible hypotheses. 1) return to my room and lock myself in; 2) idem with variation, namely to inform the woman that I'd heard everything and that I intended to do right by her and retire; 3) to ask her if she was really going to have Attilio over or if I was simply a pretext she had adopted in order to avoid an unpleasant nocturnal bullfight; 4) to ignore the telephone conversation and go on with my strolling; 5) to ask the lady if she meant eventually to substitute me for the man on the telephone to the tune of number (3); 6) to seek an explanation for the term "some poor dope" by which I believe she designated me; 7)…the seventh was aborning in my brain. But now I was in front of the slight opening. Two dark eyes, a red night-jacket over a silken blouse, a head of hair cropped short but rather curly. It was only an instant, the edge closed suddenly. My heart hammered. I went into my room and heard the phone ring again in number 22. The woman whispered, I couldn't make out what she was saying. I returned to the corridor stealthily and then could hear a little: It's impossible, Attilio, I tell you it's impossible…Then the click of the receiver and the sound of her steps towards the door. With a bound I leapt for pile number two of dirty linen, mulling over hypotheses 2, 3 and 5. The crack of light appeared again. Obviously it was impossible for me to stay there. I wondered: am I a poor dope, but how would she know? And if my wandering about saved her from Attilio? Or saved Attilio from her? I wasn't made to judge such matters, least of all the lives of others. I turned back, dragging a pillowcase on my slipper. Then I said aloud in a voice that rather reverberated in the corridor: — I've finished my stroll, madam. But how do you know I'm a poor dope?

—We all are—she said and closed the door abruptly. The phone started ringing again inside.

The Butterfly of Dinard

The tiny saffron-colored butterfly that came every day to find me at the café, on the Place de Dinard, and brought me (or so it seemed) word of you, will it come again, once you have gone, again to this gusty chill sort of square? It was unlikely that a cool Breton summer would arouse from stiff kitchen gardens so many sparks and all similar, all of the same color. Perhaps I had met not butterflies but *the* butterfly of Dinard and the crux of the matter was whether the morning visitor came just for me, whether it deliberately skirted the other cafés because in mine (chez Cournouailles) there was me, or whether that particular corner was merely inscribed in its routine daily itinerary. Morning work, in short, or secret message? To resolve all doubt, on the eve of my going back, I decided to leave a good *pourboire* for the waitress, and with it my address in Italy. She would write me a yes or a no: if the visitor gravitated towards life still after my departure or if it were no longer to be seen. I waited then for my little friend to settle on a vase of flowers and pulling out a hundred-franc note, a scrap of paper and a drawing pencil, I called the girl over. In a French more hesitant than usual, stammering, I explained the matter, not all of it, but a part. I was an amateur entomologist, I wanted to know if the butterfly would still come back, as long as it could endure to in the face of the cold. Then I stopped, in a sweat and terrified.

—Un papillon? Un papillon jaune—said the pretty Phyllis with a pair of wide-open eyes à la Greuze.—On that vase? But I don't see anything. Look closer. Merci bien, Monsieur.

She pocketed the hundred-franc note and went off bearing a cafe philtré. I lowered my head and when I raised it again I saw that on the vase of dahlias there was no butterfly any longer.

ZEAMI

The mind must go ten tenths, the body seven.
First be heard, then seen.
If the dance does not proceed from the song, there can be no
e-motion in it.
Eyes out mind back.
A sense of the right moment. And the moment makes the day.

The opening *jo* should be basic in style, direct in theme, without
excessive minutiae, votive, a tone at once engaging and flowing.
The development *ha* should turn to detail. The opening
had impulsiveness about it, but the development means to vary the
form richly, to render it more explicit, allow each element scope:
here mimicry is more in order. Here quietness and forcefulness
both find shape.
The close *kyu* is to resolve all detail, to discover conclusion, to
arrive at repose, emptiness through fullness, which requires a
strenuous effort brought to pitch released. The development was
aimed at exhausting all the resources that the opening provided, as
the close is intended to resolve everything brought into play.

Within each phase the phases occur also, as in each line, so that
the structure, sounded, danced, left alone, is an exfoliating from within
at every point, the flower from the flower.

FRANCIS PONGE

The Murmur

The Artist's Condition and Destiny

Science, education, culture are certainly benefits to the man whom
they elevate to a level of higher life: it would be, for a twentieth century
Frenchman, only exceedingly disgraceful (as well as a little ridiculous)
to deny it.
However our experience also proves that they create many needs,
and more undoubtedly than they can, at their own level, satisfy.
(Business interests enter here. Everything is soon nothing but a
bazaar.)

In addition there's a part of man that is always quick to escape them. An animal part perhaps...or divine, I mean rather...Important anyhow. An instinctive and wild part which cannot be repudiated. It's just this that preserves a deep desire for leisure; for stripping down; for their resources; and for natural consolation.

Summed up, science-education-culture: all would tend to end up with an inextinguishable thirst for repose, for sleep, for night, even for savagery and death, if there didn't intervene, proportionately, some antidote of the same order, which enraptures and suddenly overwhelms man altogether, troubles him and composes him in his natural milieu, makes him hungry and feeds him, and properly speaking recreates him.

If I have spoken of an antidote of the same sort, that's because there are actually others. "Long live death, down with Intelligence!" or "When I hear Culture mentioned, I take out my revolver": we have heard such statements, havent we? And when I say that it all tends to end up... Well we've recently been pretty close to the end.

But it can all also very well end up with who knows what fanaticism of reason, what infatuation with intelligence, at which we would see the same brutality, and the revolver would be pulled out this time in the name of culture...or shears, for emasculation.

Here we are perhaps approached suddenly for an objective justification and definition of the Fine Arts (Literature and Music and Theatre, etc., all together).

But let's get at things now from another angle.

Whatever the reader of these lines may be, life, since he can obviously read, leaves him some leisure. And not only his life, but his thought too, since it entrusts this leisure to another man's thought. (Reader, in parentheses, you're welcome then to my thought...)

But if that's my only thought now: to preserve your leisure for you, to engage you more deeply in it—and if I manage to... Then perhaps I am an artist.

Note that, brief as it may be, this leisure you could employ in contemplating nature, one of your "semblables" or even your own thoughts. You could occupy it even with singing or whistling some air of your own invention of the moment, or with dancing, running, playing with your body. Indeed it's all legitimate and you do go in for these at times, and many others do. But none of them would be enough to distinguish you from animals.

But it happens that some men are capable—God knows why—of producing—God knows how—such objects as can be chosen by you so that their contemplation or their study deeply occupies your spare time, satisfies, suffices it and engages you in nothing else.

278

Here one of these strange objects falls under our eyes... Yes, very clearly the work of one of our fellows... Made from a material and parts that nature never furnishes except separated or in a very different raw state. Now, this object appears to us at once interesting, pretty, beautiful or sublime. It seems to serve no practical purpose at all, but its consideration or contemplation provokes in us—first by some instinctive response, as if upon meeting some organic inner accord called us—then by many deep or elevated feelings—and we desire to appropriate it, or at least to preserve its service for our eternal pleasure. This pleasure is in fact accorded us through service. The desire, however, comes to us from showing it to those we love, to have them share our interest. On some of them it produces a similar effect. They assure us, as well, that such is its destined purpose, if not perforce perhaps its author's intention.

Such an object is a work of art. One who has produced it is an artist. And it seems that such objects, as also the interest and love they inspire, are met with only amongst men.

Should you think now that we're going a little too fast, we will advance as soon as—mirrors at once and treasures—they meet there as always.

And let them not scoff at us here for seeming to hand us back to History...to one of its principal commonplaces. That would really be a misunderstanding. We believe precisely only in what we can see of it. We see old masterworks. And what should we say of them then but: here's what's clearest in History, and sometimes all that there is of it...?

Foolish indeed would be the societies which, taking no account of a secular observation, would chase from its midst its artists. They would surely break down, for having not recognized what is primary in man: not opinions—nor even needs—but tastes.

And must one recall still that quiet works have more power to change man than conquerors' boots?

More power finally, I may add, speaking of the first artist to appear, than all the sermons together of all his contemporaries, which can have only a wearying effect by their monotony...

It's on this last point, it seems to me, that it is useful to insist now. For the dominant tendency (I don't mean only of a particular camp) seems to be very much that of misjudging artists, to the extent of not considering them—isn't that the word in play now—except as another *intellectual* category.

On the importance of their role and the power of their blessing, our purpose—otherwise understood—is to rate them a more serious and just consideration.

Not that opposing, according to the current antithesis, for example intuition to intellect and to conviction charm, we would wish for them only the consideration and condition of charmers... No: to charm and convince are, from our point of view, much too near them both to be opposed other than as poles of the most fastidious of wiles.

No doubt, we can easily see: from sponsor to directed art, from the state of the clown to that of engineer of the spirit, from the jesting poet to the thoughtful one, from towers of ivory to soap-box meetings, from the true to the beautiful, to the good and from the attractive to the useful—the condition of artists for centuries has been set down between these paired terms.

But all these pairs together imply on man's part only one idea of himself, from which no matter how old and strong it may be, and in our time more imposing than ever, our wish has been precisely to help in disengaging ourselves.

What idea? OK! that precisely according to which man would be above all a spirit to convince, a heart or a sensibility to charm.

That's the idea, frankly rather humiliating, which for centuries has borne not only all the poetic arts—that wouldn't be too serious—but all philosophies and all religions—in appearance contradictory—and finally all systems of education and government which have come down to us till now, in Western society at least, and in the name of which people, more or less fanatically, it must be said, evangelize, subjugate and throw themselves one upon the other.

How has such an idea anchored so firmly in man's mind? No doubt because it derives from an antecedent idea, one very glorious in truth, that man seems to have gradually forged for himself in the vicinity of Jerusalem, Athens, and Rome in turn, according to which his person would be the place, quasi divine, where Ideas and Feelings would be born, the only things worthy consideration in this world; and he above all a mind and a heart.

It's explained, after all, that man may have thought this idea not only glorious but also advantageous, so far as he could keep the illusion of progress, thanks to it, in the knowledge of the universe and in his power over it, as in the organization of his own society...

It seems, however, by some signs, that he would be quite willing now to change...

Perhaps, as I have previously mentioned, sermons and oaths—and certain obligations that follow from them—have decidedly begun to weary him. But even more undoubtedly the punishments, of which recent times have not been niggardly with...

So, many would like to change... But let's realize that this may be hard. How renounce, in fact, being a mind and a heart? There are many even yet who imagine some explanation—more or less original—which may permit them to stick to them. I won't waste your time with these recent theories, you know them as well as I. For instance, that the world is absurd; it's only a question of adapting oneself to it. It would be only despite it, and we would get out unhurt, minds, hearts, on condition only of a little disillusionment. No hangmen, no, nor victims: only judges, in the abstract: rather sad, but proud anyhow and lord quite capable still of some sentences each day.

No doubt it will need some more sensational "current events" (as they say) yet, so that the intelligence or soul as such may finally lower the flag (was it black). And so that man finally may start to worry: these ideas, these feelings of which he is so proud that they emanate from him, wouldn't they go out of him as the threads of certain puppets, that some skillful men manipulate... What am I saying, some skillful men? It is man himself, become his own dupe, who abusively decides his fate, according to the ideas that he develops. He finds himself thus, as in a constant state of intellectual drunkenness, led somewhere beyond the world, on some scaffolding... But why say scaffolding? Scaffold painted better than it is!

Yes, some hecatombs yet... Ah! let some at least morally be exempted, so as to be allowed to try to remedy only this.

Never, indeed, since the world became (I mean the sensible world, as we are given it each day), no, never, whatever mythology be current, never has the world, even for a second, suspended its mysterious functioning. Never, however, in the mind of man—and no doubt precisely since man no longer considers the world as his field of action, the place or occasion of his power—never has the world in the mind of man so little and so poorly functioned.

It no longer functions at all but for some artists. If it still functions, it is only through them.

Yet, it is just at this point that the artist must reappear, and the consideration due him become evident for all.

Let us suppose in fact that man, sick of being considered as a mind (to be convinced) or as a heart (to shake), is conceived one fine day for what he is: something after all more material and more opaque, more complex, denser, better bound to the world and harder to displace (more difficult to mobilize); finally no longer so much the place where Ideas and Feelings are born, than one—much less easily (even by himself) violable—where feelings are confused and ideas destroy one another... No more would be needed to change everything, and for man's reconciliation with the world to be born of this new pretension.

At the same crack then would the continuing power over man of the work of art be explained, and his eternal love for the artist: the work of art being the object of human origin in which ideas are destroyed; the artist, man himself insofar as he has made proof (through work) of his anteriority and posteriority to ideas.

The function of the artist is thus very clear: he has to open an atelier, and take the world to repair it, as it comes to him, in fragments. Not so much as a wise man, but as a watchmaker. An attentive repairer of the lobster or lemon, of the jar or jug, is what the modern artist most is. His role is modest, obviously. But there's no way to get away from it.

But where does he get his power from, and what are the conditions required for him to operate? OK! he gets it chiefly, I'm sure, from a sensitivity to the way the world functions and from a violent need to keep it whole, but then—and this condition is the sine qua non—from a particular aptitude in himself for managing a determinate medium. For the work of art takes all its virtue at once from its resemblance to and its difference from natural objects. Where does the resemblance come from? From the fact that it is also material. And its difference?— From being an expressive material, or rendered so by the occasion. Expressive, means what? That it lights the intelligence (but must also at the same time extinguish it). But what are expressive materials? Those which already contain some meaning: languages. It's only a question of bringing their meaning to BEAR.

So, to take an example from Belles-Lettres, the non-meaning of the world may well be the despair of those who, believing (paradoxically) still in ideas, are obliged to deduce from it a philosophy or an ethics. It cannot make poets despair, because they do not work from ideas, but use words grossly. Hence, no consequences. Except for a profound reconciliation: creation and recreation. So it is that for them in the end, whether or not a thing signifies, the world functions. And this is really after all what we ask of them (in works as in the world); life.

But still one has to allow *it* to them. Which means, for artists, work. Which means at first to do nothing, to bury themselves in their fruitful leisure.

And I'm not saying that you have to, as it were, maintain them. No, we know better: even in the worst conditions, as they say, of existence, the artist feels so much more existent than anyone that he will produce whatever he must...

Only, not to beset him with reproof and reprimand, not to try to kill in him his pretension, not to persuade him of his non-justification.

And finally, if one can, to accept his lesson.

Humanity's destiny will in the end be the same as its artists'.

The only thing (for both men and their works) that allows life is a resolute insubordination to ideas.

Man is not the king of creation. No. But its persecutor. Its persecuted persecutor.

One more animal? I think so. But one of the best endowed? Maybe. Certainly one of the most insensate.

Insofar as, by his efforts to dominate it,—he risks alienating the world, he must at each moment, and that is his function as artist, through *works* of his indolence be reconciled to it.

The Lute of Gassir

Four times did Wagadu appear miraculously in the light of day; four times was she lost, so that men did not see her: once for vanity, once for infidelity, once for greed and once for dissidence. Four times did Wagadu change her name. First she was called Dierra, then Agada, then Ganna, then Silla. Four times did Wagadu turn her face. Once she looked to the north, once to the west, once to the east, once to the south. For each time Wagadu stood upon the earth, in the eyes of men, she had four gates: one to the north, one to the west, one to the east, one to the south. These are the directions from which the power of Wagadu comes and towards which it goes, no matter if Wagadu be made of earth or stone, or lives only as a shadow in the mind and memory of her sons. For Wagadu herself is neither stone, nor wood, nor earth. Wagadu is the power that lives in the hearts of men, recognized when eyes allow her recognition, heard when ears hear the blades clash and their sounds upon the shields, and now unseen because exhausted and hard-pressed by the indomitability of men, when she falls asleep. But sleep overtook Wagadu once for vanity, secondly for infidelity, thirdly for greed, and the fourth time for dissidence. But when Wagadu recovers for the fourth time, then will she live so powerful in the mind of man as never again to be lost, and neither vanity, nor infidelity, nor greed, nor dissidence, will be able to harm her.

Hooh! Dierra, Agada, Ganna, Silla! —Hooh! Fasa!

Each time that Wagadu was lost for the fault of men, she acquired a new beauty, so that at each turn her magnificence increased. With vanity came the song of the Bardi [Diare], which was repeated by every people and which soon won their praise. With infidelity was the golden rain brought to man and the rock-pearl. Greed brought writing, which still the Burdama employ and which to Wagadu was the craft of women. But dissidence will give to the fifth Wagadu the capacity of enduring the rain from the south and the rocks of the Sahara, for each man will keep Wagadu in his heart and every woman a Wagadu in her lap.

Hooh! Dierra, Agada, Ganna, Silla! —Hooh! Fasa!

The first time was Wagadu lost for vanity. In those days did Wagadu look to the north and was known as Dierra. Its last king was called Nganamba Fasa. The Fasa were strong. They turned old. Every day the Fasa fought with the Burdama and with the Boroma. They fought every day and every month. But the struggle ended. Through battle the power of the Fasa grew. All the men of Nganamba were heroes [Gana]. All the women were beautiful and proud of the power and heroism of the men of Wagadu.

All the Fasa were getting old, those who didn't die fighting the Burdama. Nganamba was very old. Nganamba had a son who was called Gassir, and he too was rather old for he had eight grown-up sons, who had in turn sons of their own. All of them lived at the same time, and Nganamba reigned in his family and was the first among the Fasa and among those dogs of a Boroma. Nganamba became so old that Wagadu was lost and the Boroma again became thieves and slaves [Dion] of the Burdama, who have assumed the law of the blade. If Nganamba were dead already, would Wagadu be lost for the first time?

Hooh! Dierra, Agada, Ganna, Silla! —Hooh! Fasa!

Nganamba did not die. A jackal gnawed at Gassir's heart. Gassir said each day to his heart: "When will Nganamba die? Gassir, when will he become king?" Gassir anxiously awaited his father's death as a lover awaits the rising of the evening star. When by day Gassir fought like a hero against the Burdama and with the reins of his horse whipped the unfaithful Boroma, then did he think only of the struggle, of the blade, of the shield and the horse. But when Gassir came at nightfall back into his village and sat in a ring with the other men and with his sons, then he heard how the heroes extolled his deeds; but his heart was not with them; his heart was listening to the breath of Nganamba; his heart was full of aching and longing.

The heart of Gassir was full of burning desire for the shield of his father which he could only carry when his father was dead, and for the blade too which could only be his when he was king. The anger and longing of Gassir grew and grew each day. Gassir was avoided by sleep. Gassir lay down, but at his heart a jackal gnawed. Gassir felt the aching rise to his throat. One night Gassir arose, left his hut and went to a wise old man [Kiekorro], who knew more than anyone else. He went in and said: "Kiekorro! When is my father going to die, Nganamba? When will he leave me the blade and the shield?   The old man said: "Ah! Gassir, Nganamba will die; but he will not leave you the blade and the shield. You will carry a lute. Others will inherit the blade and the shield. But for your lute will Wagadu be lost! Ah Gassir." Gassir said: "Kiekorro, you lie. I see, you are not wise. How can Wagadu be lost when her heroes win every day? Kiekorro, you're a fool!" The wise old man said: "Ah, Gassir, you cannot believe me. But your way will bring you to the peacocks. You will understand their cry, and this will then be your way, and that of Wagadu."

Hooh! Dierra, Agada, Ganna, Silla! —Hooh! Fasa!

The next day Gassir betook himself with the others to fight the Burdama. Gassir was enraged. Gassir said to the heroes: "Stay here. Today I shall fight the Burdama alone." And the heroes stayed behind. Gassir rode out alone to meet the Burdama. Gassir cast his javelins. Gassir rode headlong into the Burdama. Gassir brandished his blade. Gassir struck a Burdama to the right. Gassir struck a Burdama to the left. The blade of Gassir was like a sickle amidst the grain. The Burdama were terrified. The Burdama cried out in terror: "This is not a Fasa, this is not a Gana, this is a Damo [a being unknown even to the narrator]." The Burdama turned their horses. The Burdama dropped their two javelins and fled.

Gassir called the Gana. Gassir said: "Get their javelins!" The Gana went out. The Gana collected the javelins. The Gana sang: "The Fasa are heroes. Gassir was always the first hero amongst the Fasa. Gassir has always done feats of prowess. But today Gassir was greater than Gassir." Gassir rode into the village. The heroes rode behind him. The heroes sang: "Never as today has Wagadu won so many javelins."

Gassir let himself be washed by the women. The men gathered from round about. Gassir did not sit with them. Gassir left and went out into the fields. Gassir heard the peacocks. Gassir went up to them. A peacock sat on a bush, Its young sat in the grass. The peacock was singing of its struggle with the serpent. The peacock sang: "Every creature must die. King and heroes die, are buried and rot. I too shall die, be buried and rot. But the Dausi, the song of my struggles, will not die. It will be sung and will live more than any king and hero. Hooh! who can accomplish such a thing! Hooh! Who can sing the Dausi! Wagadu will be lost. But the Dausi will survive and live on!"

Hooh! Dierra, Agada, Ganna, Silla! —Hooh! Fasa!

Gassir went to the wise old man. Gassir said: "Kiekorro! I have been to the fields. I have understood the peacocks. The peacock claimed that the song of his deeds will live longer than Wagadu. The peacock was singing the Dausi. Tell me if the Dausi is known also amongst men, and if the Dausi will survive life and death." The wise old man said: "Ah, you are running up against death. No one can stop you. Since you cannot become a Diare. Ah, Gassir! When the kings of the Fasa still lived by the sea, were there also great heroes and they fought with men who possessed lutes and sang the Dausi. Often the Fasa were terrified hearing the Dausi of the foe. They were themselves always great heroes. They had never sung the Dausi to them, for they were Horro, that is the first, and the Dausi was sung only by the second, that is by the Diare. But those others no longer fought like heroes, for the light of day, but like men thirsting for the glory of the night. But you Gassir, seeing that you cannot be the second amongst the first, will now be first amongst the second. For this will Wagadu be lost." Gassir said: "Then let Wagadu be lost!"

Hooh! Dierra, Agada, Ganna, Silla!—Hooh! Fasa!

Gassir went to a craftsman, Gassir said: "Prepare me a lute!" The craftsman said: "It shall be done. But the lute will not sing." Gassir said: "Craftsman, do your work, the rest is up to me." The craftsman made the lute. The craftsman brought the lute to Gassir. Gassir took the lute. Gassir struck the lute. The lute did not sing. Gassir said to the craftsman: "What is this? The lute doesn't sing!" The craftsman said: "That is what I had predicted!" Gassir said: "Make the lute sing." The craftsman said: "For this there is nothing more I can do. The rest is up to you." Gassir said: "What can I do?" The craftsman said: "This is a piece of wood. It cannot sing if it has no heart. You must give heart to it. The wood must be on your back when you fight. The wood must sound to the blows of the blade. The wood must absorb the blood that flows, blood of your blood, breath of your breath. Your ache must be its ache, your glory its glory. The wood must no longer be wood of the tree from which it is cut, but must enter into your Diamu [stock]. For it is not to live only with you, but also with your sons. Then the sound that comes from your heart will echo in the ear of your son and will live in the people, and the blood that gushes from its heart will flow over your body and will live in this wood. But for this will Wagadu be lost!" Gassir said: "Then let it be lost!"

Hooh! Dierra, Agada, Ganna, Silla!—Hooh! Fasa!

Gassir called his eight sons to him. Gassir said: "My sons, today we shall go and fight. But the sound of the blows of our blades must not be lost any longer in the Sahel. They must resound for all time. You and I, my sons, wish to live before all the heroes in the Dausi. My eldest, today you and I want to be the first in battle!"

Gassir rode out with his eldest son and the heroes, as leaders, in the struggle. Gassir had the lute set on his back. The Burdama approached.

Gassir and his eldest son rode up to them. Gassir and his eldest son fought as leaders. Gassir and his eldest son left the others far behind. Gassir did not fight like a man; he fought like a Damo. His eldest son did not fight like a man; he fought like a Damo. Gassir found himself up against eight Burdama. The eight Burdama had him dangerously hemmed in. The eldest son came on. He slew four Burdama. One of the Burdama struck him with a javelin in the heart. The eldest son fell dead from his horse. Gassir was infuriated. Gassir cried. The Burdama fled. Gassir dismounted. He lifted his son's body and placed it upon his shoulders. So did he ride back with the other heroes. The blood of his eldest son's heart dripped upon the lute which was fastened to his back. So Gassir, at the head of the heroes, rode back into Dierra.

Hooh! Dierra, Agada, Ganna, Silla!—Hooh! Fasa!

The eldest son of Gassir was buried. Dierra mourned. The urn of the dead was red with blood. At nightfall Gassir took the lute and struck it. The lute did not sing. Gassir was all in a rage. Gassir called his sons to him. Gassir said to his sons: "My sons, tomorrow we will ride out against the Burdama."

For seven days Gassir rode with the heroes to battle. Each day a son rode with him as leader against the Burdama. And each one of the seven days Gassir bore the body of one of his sons on his shoulders and on the lute back to the village. So every evening the blood of one of his sons entered the lute. After these seven days of battle, great was the mourning that reigned in Dierra. All the heroes and all the women were clad in white and red. Everywhere the blood of the Boroma flowed. All the women lamented. All the men grew angry. Even before the eighth day of the battle arrived, all the men of Dierra assembled and said to Gassir: "Gassir, this must come to an end. We are ready to fight when it serves. But you, in your great craving for battle, are without judgment and without limit. Take yourself far from Dierra! Some will follow you. Take also your Boroma and your beasts. We others prefer life to glory. Certainly we do not want to live without glory, but neither do we wish to die for glory!"

The wise old man said: "Ah Gassir! So today is Wagadu lost for the first time."

Hoooh! Dierra, Agada, Ganna, Silla!—Hoooh! Fasa!

Gassir, the last of his sons, the youngest, his wives, his friends, his Boroma, went into the desert. They rode through the Sahel. Many were the heroes who escorted him to the gates of the town. Many turned back. Some accompanied Gassir and his youngest son into the Sahara.

They rode far: day and night. They arrived where there was nothing. In that solitude they lay down and rested. All the Gana and all the women and all the Boroma slept. The youngest son of Gassir slept. Gassir alone stayed up. Gassir sat by the fire, Gassir did not sleep. Gassir arose. Gassir listened. Gassir felt near him a voice. It sounded as if it came from within him. Gassir listened. Gassir began to tremble. He heard the lute sing. The lute sang the Dausi.

When the lute had sung the Dausi for the first time, in the village of Dierra king Nganamba died; when the lute had sung the Dausi for the first time, the anger of Gassir was gone; Gassir wept. When the lute had sung the Dausi for the first time, Wagadu for the first time was gone.

Hoooh! Dierra, Agada, Ganna, Silla! —Hoooh! Fasa!

Four times did Wagadu appear miraculously in the light of day; four times was she lost, so that men did not see her: once for vanity, once for infidelity, once for greed and once for dissidence. Four times did Wagadu change her name. First she was called Dierra, then Agada, then Ganna, then Silla. Four times did Wagadu turn her face. Once she looked to the west, once to the east, once to the north, once to the south. For each time that Wagadu stood upon the earth, in the eyes of men, she had four gates, one to the north, one to the west, one to the east, one to the south. These are the four directions from which the power of Wagadu comes and towards which it goes, no matter if Wagadu is made of stone and earth, or if she lives only as a shadow in the mind and memory of her sons. For Wagadu herself is not of stone, not of wood, nor of earth. Wagadu is the power that lives in the hearts of men, now recognized by the eyes that allow her recognition, by the ears that hear the blows of the blade and the sounds on the shields, and now unseen because exhausted and hard-pressed by the indomitability of men, she lies fast asleep. But the sleep of Wagadu came once for vanity, the second time for infidelity, the third for greed, the fourth time for dissidence. But when Wagadu recovers for the fourth time, then will she live so powerful in the mind of man as never again to be lost, and neither vanity, not infidelity, not greed, nor dissidence, will be able to harm her.

Hoooh! Dierra, Agada, Ganna, Silla! —Hoooh! Fasa!

Each time that Wagadu was lost for the fault of men, she acquired a new beauty that at each turn increased her magnificence. With vanity came the song of the Bardi, which was repeated by every people and which soon won their praise. With infidelity was the golden rain brought to man and the rock-pearl. Greed brought writing, which still the Burdama employ and which to Wagadu was the craft of women. But dissidence will give to the fifth Wagadu the capacity of enduring the rain from the south and the rocks of the Sahara, for each man will keep Wagadu in his heart and every woman a Wagadu in her lap.

Hoooh! Dierra, Agada, Ganna, Silla! —Hoooh! Fasa!

This song I heard first in 1909 in Togo from a Bardo of the Djerma whom one of my comrades had met in northern Togo and had sent to me. The Djerma are a small people who live along the western reaches of the Niger and border the Haussa. Of them we know that for centuries they were driven from the eastern regions of the Niger. Since amongst the eastern peoples the art of the epic has long since vanished, this song is considered very old. —Leo Frobenius

(Translated from the version in Italian of Siegfried Walter de Rachewiltz, translated from the German of Frobenius, translated presumably from the original African dialect)

CÉSAR VALLEJO

from the Poemas Humanos

In sum, to express my life I have only my death. And after
everything that's happened, at the end of scaled nature and of
the massed sparrow, I fall asleep hand to hand with my shadow.

And on descending from the venerable act and from the other
groan, I repose thinking about the intrepid march of time.

Why the rope, then, if air's so simple? What's the chain for,
if iron exists by itself?

César Vallejo, the accent with which you love, the word with
which you write, the little wind with which you hear, only know
of you by your throat.

César Vallejo, prostrate youself for that, with indistinct pride,
with a nuptial couch of ornamental asps and hexagonal echoes.

Give yourself back to the corporeal honeycomb, to Beauty;
aroma the flowered corks, shut both grots to the enraged anthropoid;
in short, mend your disagreeable stag; grieve for yourself.

For there's nothing denser than hate in the passive voice, no
stingier udder than love!

For I can't walk any longer except in two harps!

For you no longer know me, for instrumental, long-windedly,
I hound you!

For I no longer bear worms, I bear closed vowels!

For now I implicate you so much you nearly whet to nothing!

For now I carry not only timid but ferocious vegetables! Thus the
love that ruptures during the night in my bronchia, secret deans
brought during the day and, if I wake pale, it's because of my work;
and if I sunset red, because of my worker. This explains equally
these fatigues and this refuse, my famed uncles. This explains, in
short, this tear I toast for the happiness of men.
César Vallejo, it's simply
incredible that your relatives linger like this,
knowing that I go chained,
knowing that you rest freed!
Fit to kill luck of a dog!
César Vallejo, I hate you with tenderness!

Exists a man mutilated not from combat but from an embrace,
not from war but from peace. He lost his face in love and not in hate.
Lost it in the normal course of events and not in an accident. Lost it

290

in the order of nature and not in the disorder of men. Colonel Piccot, President of "Les gueules cassées," wears his mouth eaten away by the gunpowder of 1914. This cripple I know wears his face eaten away by the immortal and immemorial air.

Face dead on the living trunk. Face stiff and hammered with nails to the living trunk. This face turns out to be the dorsum of the skull, skull of the skull. I once saw a tree turr its back on me and another time I saw a road turn its back on me. A back-turned road only grows in places where nothing was born or no one died. A back-turned road only advances through places where there've been all deaths and no birth. The man mutilated from peace and from love, from embrace and from order and who wears his dead face on his living trunk was born in the shadow of a back-turned tree and his existence elapses along a back-turned road.

As his face is stiff and defunct, all psychic life, all animal expression of this man, in order to move itself out, takes refuge in the hairy skull, in the thorax and in the extremities. The impulses of his profound being, on going out, back away from his face and his breathing, his sense of smell, his sight, his hearing, his speech, the human radiance of his being function and are expressed through his chest, through his shoulders, through his hair, through his ribs, through his arms and his legs and his feet.

Face cut up, face clogged, face bolted, this man nevertheless is whole, he wants nothing. He has no eyes and he sees and cries. He has no nostrils and he smells and breathes. He has no ears and he hears. No mouth and he talks and smiles. No forehead and he thinks and withdraws into himself. No chin and he desires and subsists. Jesus knew the man whose functions were mutilated, who had eyes and couldn't see and ears and couldn't hear. I know the man whose organs are mutilated, who sees without eyes and hears without ears.

I Am Going to Speak of Hope

I don't suffer this pain as César Vallejo. I don't ache now as an artist, as a man or even as a simple living being. I don't suffer this pain as a Catholic, as a Mohammedan or as an atheist. Today I just suffer. If I were not called César Vallejo, I'd still suffer this same pain. If I were not an artist, I'd still suffer it. If I were not a man or even a living being, I'd still suffer it. Today I suffer from the depths. Today I simply suffer.

291

I ache now without any excuses. My pain is so deep it had no cause nor does it lack cause. What could be its cause? Where is that thing so important that its cause could cease to be its cause? Nothing is its cause; nothing has been able to stop being its cause. Why has this pain been born—for itself? My pain comes from the north wind, from the south wind, like those neuter eggs some rare birds lay in the wind. If my bride were dead my pain would be the same. If they cut my throat out by its roots my pain would be the same. If life were finally of a different order, my pain would be the same. Today I suffer from the heights. Today I simply suffer.

I look at the starving man's misery and see his hunger is so distant from my suffering, that if I were to fast unto death, a blade of grass would always sprout from my tomb at least. The same thing happens to the lover! How engendered his blood is compared to mine, my blood without spring or drinker!

I believed until now that all the things of the universe were inevitably fathers or sons. But behold, my pain today is neither father nor son. It lacks a back to darken, just as it has too much chest to dawn, and if they put it in the dark dwelling place it could not give light and if they put it in a lighted dwelling place it would cast no shadow. Today I suffer no matter what happens. Today I simply suffer.

Discovery of Life

Gentlemen! Today is the first time that I realize the presence of life! Gentlemen! I beg you leave me alone for a moment so I can savor this marvelous, spontaneous, new-life emotion, that today for the first time enraptures me and makes me so happy I'm crying.

My joy comes from what is unpublished of my emotion. My exultation comes from not feeling before the presence of life. I've never felt it. He lies who says I've felt it. He lies, and his lie probes me so deep that it would make me miserable. My joy comes from my faith in this personal discovery of life, and no one can oppose this faith. No matter who he was, his tongue would fall out, his bones would fall out, and he'd risk picking up others, not his own, to keep himself up before my eyes.

Never, until now, has life been. Never, until now, have people walked by. Never, until now, have there been houses and avenues, air and horizon. If my friend Peyriet came over right now, I'd tell him I don't know him, that we must begin anew. When in fact have I known my friend Peyriet? Today would be the first time we became acquainted. I'd tell him to go away and come back, to drop in on me, as if he didn't know me, that is, for the first time.

Now I know no one, nothing. I observe myself in a foreign country where everything appears in birth relief, light of unfading epiphany. No, sir. Don't even speak to that gentleman. You don't know him and such careless chatter would surprise him. Don't put your foot on that little stone; maybe it's not a stone and you'll plunge into the void. Be cautious; we're in a totally unknown world.

How short I've lived! My birth is so recent there's no unit of measure to tell my age. Why I've just been born! Why I've not lived yet! Gentlemen: I'm so tiny the day hardly fits in me.

Never, until now, did I hear the carts' clatter carrying rock for the broad Haussmann Boulevard. Never, until now, did I advance parallel with the spring, addressing it: "If death had only been something else . . . ." Never, until now, did I see the aureate light of the sun on the cupolas of Sacré-Coeur. Never, until now, did a child approach me and look so deeply into me with his mouth. Never, until now, did I know a door existed, another door and the cordial song of the distances.

Let me alone! Life has struck me today square in my death!

Common Sense

—There is, mother, a place in the world called Paris. A very big place and far off and once again big.

My mother turns up my overcoat collar, not because it is beginning to snow, but so it may.

My father's wife is in love with me, coming and advancing backward toward my birth and breastward toward my death. For I'm hers twice: by the goodbye and by the return. I close her on returning. That's why her eyes gave so much to me, just with me, in flagrante with me, happening by terminated works, by consummated pacts.

293

My mother is confessed by me, pointed at because of me? How come she doesn't give an equal part to my other brothers? To Victor, for example, the eldest, who is so old now people say: He looks like his father's younger brother! It must be because I've traveled much! Because I've lived more!

My mother grants a map of coloring principle to my stories of return. Facing my life of returning, remembering that I traveled two hearts along her womb, she blushes and stays mortally livid when I say in the treatise of the soul: That night I was happy. But more she becomes sad; more would she become sad.

—You look so old, my son!

And steps along the yellow color to weep, for she finds me aged in the sword blade, in the mouth of my face. Weeps for me, becomes sad for me. How can she miss my youth if I'm always to be her son? Why does a mother ache finding her sons aged, if their ages never reach hers? And why, when the sons the nearer the end they come, the nearer their parents? My mother weeps because I am old in my time and because never will I age in hers!

My goodbye started from a point in her being, more external than the point in her being to which I return. I am, because of the excessive deadline of my shift, more man in my mother's eyes than son. There resides the pure whiteness that today sheds light upon us with three flames. I say to her, then, until I hush:

—There is, mother, in the world a place called Paris. A very big place and far off and once again big.

My father's wife, hearing me, eats her lunch and her mortal eyes lower softly by my arms.

Violence of the Hours

All are dead.

Died Doña Antonia, the wheezer, who made cheap bread in the village.

Died the priest Santiago, who liked to be greeted by the young men and country girls, acknowledging everybody indiscriminately: "Buenos días, José! Buenos días, María!"

294

Died that fair-haired Carlota, leaving a child of three months, who up and died also, eight days after her.

Died my Aunt Albina, who used to sing about the old days in the sierra while she sewed in the hallways for Isadora, the hired maid, that honorable honorable woman.

Died an old one-eye, whose name I don't remember, but who slept in the morning sun, seated in front of the tinsmith's door.

Died Rayo, dog big as me, shot by lord-knows-who.

Died Lucas, my brother-in-law in the peace of the waists, whom I'm reminded of when it rains and there's no one in my experience.

Died in my revolver my mother, in my fist my sister and my brother in my bloody viscera, the three of them tied together by a sad gender of sadness, in the month of August of successive years.

Died the musician Méndez, tall and very drunk, who practiced melancholy toccatas on his clarinet, at whose series of proofs the hens in my ward used to doze off, long before the sun went down.

Died my eternity and I am waking it.

The windows have been shaken, elaborating a metaphysic of the universe. Glass has fallen. A sick man launches his cry: half through his tongued and surplus mouth, and completely intact through the anus of his back.

It's the hurricane. A chestnut tree in the Tuileries' garden must have been toppled in the 60-mile-an-hour wind. Capitals in the old quarters must have fallen, splitting, killing.

From what point do I interrogate, hearing both shores of the oceans, from what point comes this hurricane, so worthy of credit, so honorable in debt, straight at the hospital windows? Ay the immutable directions that oscillate between the hurricane and this direct effort to cough or defecate. Ay the immutable directions that thus graft death into the innards of the hospitals and wake clandestine cells, so poorly timed, in the cadavers.

What would the sick man, the one asleep right over there, think of himself had he perceived the hurricane? The poor guy sleeps, face up, at the head of his morphine, at the foot of all his sanity. A dram more or less in the dose and they will cart him off to be buried, belly ripped open, face up, deaf to the hurricane, deaf to his ripped belly, over which the doctors are accustomed to debate and ponder at great lengths only to finally pronounce their simple words of men.

The family surrounds the sick man clustering at his regressive defenseless sweaty temples. A sense of home no longer exists save around the sick relative's night table, where his vacant shoes, his spare crosses, his opium pills impatiently mount guard. The family surrounds the little table for the space of a high dividend. A woman puts back, at the edge of the table, the cup which had almost fallen.

I don't know who this woman is to this sick man, for she kisses him and can't heal him with her kiss, she looks at him and can't heal him with her eyes, she talks to him and can't heal him with her words. Is she his mother? Well then, why can't she heal him? Is she his belovéd? Then why can't she heal him? Is she his sister? Then why can't she heal him? Is she simply a woman? Then why can't she heal him? For this woman has kissed him and has watched over him and has talked to him, even has real carefully covered his neck for him and, the truly astonishing fact is, *she's not healed him!*

The patient contemplates his vacant shoes and socks. They bring cheese. They carry earth. Death lies down at the foot of the bed to sleep in his tranquil waters and does sleep. Then the freed feet of the sick man, without trifles or unnecessary detail, jerk in circumflex accent and pull away, in an extension of two lovers' bodies, from his heart.

The surgeon auscultates the sick for hours on end. When his hands quit working and start playing, he allows them to drift blindly, grazing the patients' skin, while his scientific eyebrows vibrate, played upon by the uncultured and human frailty of love. And I have seen these sick die precisely from the surgeon's spread-open love, from the lengthy diagnoses, from the exact doses, from the rigorous analysis of urine and excrement. Suddenly a bed is encircled with a folding screen. Doctors and orderlies were crossing in front of the absent one, sad and close blackboard that a child had filled with numbers in a great monism of chalky thousands. They kept on crossing, looking at the others as if it were more irreparable to die from appendicitis or pneumonia than to die aslant the path of men.

Serving religion's cause this fly sails successfully all around the sickroom. During the surgeons' visiting hours her buzzings undoubtedly absolve our chests, but then increasing to a roar they take over the air to salute in the spirit of change those who are about to die. Some of the sick hear this fly even in their pain and on them depends, and for that reason, the lineage of the gunshot in the dreadful nights.

How long has this named-by-man anesthesia lasted? Science of God, Theodicy, if I'm forced to live under such conditions, totally anesthetized, my sensibility turned toward the inside! Ah doctors of the salts, men of the essences, neighbors of the bases! I'm begging you to leave me with my tumor of consciousness, with my raw sensitive leprosy, no matter what happens, even though I may die! Let me rack myself if you wish, but leave me awake in my dream with all the universe embedded, even though I go through hell, in my dusty temperature.

In the world of perfect health, the perspective on which I suffer will be mocked, but, on the same plane and cutting the deck for the game, another laugh percusses here in counterpoint.

In the house of pain, the cry assaults held notes of the great composer, bottlenecks of character, which give us real chills, arduous atrocious chills, and, fulfilling what is prophesied, freeze us in terrifying uncertainty.

In the house of pain, the cry uproots excessive frontier. The cry itself of happiness in ecstasy, when love and the flesh are exempt from the goshawk and when after union there is enough discord for dialogue, cannot be recognized in this cry of pain.

Then where is the other flank of this cry of pain if, to estimate it as a whole, it breaks now from the bed of a man?

From the house of pain cries break so gagged and ineffable and so brimming and overflowing with so much fullness that to weep for them would be ridiculous and would really be smiling.

Blood in the thermometer rises in arms.

It is not pleasant to die, lord, if nothing is left in life and in death nothing is possible except on the basis of what is left in life.
It is not pleasant to die, lord, if nothing is left in life and in death nothing is possible except on the basis of what is left in life.
It is not pleasant to die, lord, if nothing is left in life and in death nothing is possible except on the basis of what one could have left in life.

CID CORMAN

Out of the snow
beginning to
fall I feel these

eyes also give
way. Come and come,
go and go, snow.

As much as there is
there there is little

here snowflake or ash
already too much.

"Do you hear . . . ?" "I should like to
breathe in to you all my life."
"I am not old, I should not

be dying." Ah if only
they knew the stars, the stars, are . . .
like ghosts struggling from the night.

LOUIS ZUKOFSKY
   "A"-16

An

   inequality

   wind flower

Third Series (1966~1971)

CID CORMAN

Poetry as Bond

Perhaps the most quoted, though belated, and unanthologized, lines of Dr. Williams are:

> . . . It is ridiculous
> what airs we put on
> to seem profound
> while our hearts
> gasp dying
> for want of love . . .

I recall still how—in 1954, shortly before I left America for the first time for Europe, thinking that I might never see him again alive (though, in fact, I did—miraculously enough)—at his instance I read to him and Floss the Coda, just completed, of that same poem and was moved, as who would not have been, to read to them his words remembering their wedding

> . . . At the altar
> so intent was I
> before my vows,
> so moved by your presence
> a girl so pale
> and ready to faint
> that I pitied
> and wanted to protect you . . .

I mention these points because there is scarcely any other poetry of our time, by Dr. Williams or anyone else, that stands less in need of explication. That is its grace and its power; its appeal is direct, it is honest, and it is fully joined to insight and feeling a lifetime found out. And it sings with a peculiar and a general voice. It is the mark of a poetry that exceeds judgment; it lives its love in us.

Here and there I find lines in other poets of our time carrying similar "sense"—lines that elude the critics for the lines do not need *them*.

So simple an utterance, at summer's end or fall's country end, dreaming towards an idea of the incarnate God, found by Wallace Stevens:

> This man loved earth, not heaven, enough to die.

And in his strongest poems, or phrases, comes back each time the hauntedness of a solitude a man must find in feeling night reduce him to a heart and a hammer at that heart, each altering breath.

> . . . The leaves cry. It is not a cry of divine attention,
> Nor the smoke-drift of puffed-out heroes, nor human cry.
> It is the cry of leaves that do not transcend themselves,
>
> In the absence of fantasia, without meaning more
> Than they are in the final finding of the air, in the thing
> Itself, until, at last, the cry concerns no one at all.

As simple and reached as Pound's *dakruon* at Pisa that gave him a crystal ball by which to read a grasshopper's fortune, one day's dew.

What am I driving at? How rare poetry is. And how immediate it must be. As rare as something seen and at once loved — not even for any "what it is," but for the sudden access of realization that *each* one is possibly together "more" than *any* one:

> For you I have emptied the meaning
> Leaving the song . . .

I look at paintings and prints on my walls, works of friends, living and dead, who will live on other walls, in other eyes, to the depth of other hearts, longer, to help life sing itself alive.

Such work as keeps us at the edge — not wrapping us in dream and hiding us away — but such as more reveals, more discovers us where we are, how we are, what we are, and the love called for from us for it is our only use.

> What is the use of talking, and there is
> no end of talking,
> There is no end of things in the heart.

Words: such as return to me, from within me now, and weigh what I have yet to give.

If I have nothing to offer you in the
face of death, the ache behind every ache, the instant man
knows, I have no claim as.poet. My song must sing into you a
little moment, stay in you what presence can muster—of sense
more than meaning, of love more than sense, of giving the life
given one with the same fullness that brought each forth, each
to each, each from each, nothing left but the life that is going
on.

A Grace for the Meal Coming

Thanks to the sun, the earth and the earthworm,
thanks to the worker in the field and hearts
through whom this food comes to this table, we
receive, as for the dead, these preparations.

The Garden

The garden is littered, after the gale,
with torn greens and stiff cicadas.
The sarcophagi of Egyptian kings—

as I have written a friend—could not be
finer in workmanship or more
compact than this insect's carapace and

wings. The things we see, the things we are, sing—
or suddenly appear crouched like
a frog wondering where my foot will fall.

Leuca

If at Nar-
dò you could
see Christ carved

of olive,
knees buckling
nail-strained, you

might also
feel the tree
reaching leaf-

green-silver
sun and go
on to gaze

upon the
middle sea,
rest on the

dividing
together
splendor. A

moment all
measure and
no measure

is Santa
Maria
di Leuca.

Here at the
fountain of
"ifs" to drink

and vanish.
Here painted
wax flares at

heart's altar.
Man, shadow,
massed to catch

the silent
word, word of
no hope, haste.

Who was the
threadbare white-
haired woman

at Patù
stopped the wrist
beyond the

chapel at
the charred pre-
historic

home you were
about to
enter, to

ask you where
you'd come from?
And what's to

come but the
extended
breakdown back

towards Greece,
flocks, tufa,
trulli, souls

trolling the
mirror for
their keep? Here

the edge is
all edge down
and sheer—but

farmed in the
face of it.
And the sea

at this point
clear, all the
alls of wet

weighing the
sky, bringing
each man his

horizon,
the breath to
know: *When you*

have gone as
far as you
can, you must

go further
and further
until—like

a roof that
fails to end
but goes on

upward in-
to stairs, stars—
you offer

completely
what you there
are: more heart

open to
the verge of
nothingness.

ANDRE DU BOUCHET

Nine Poems

The Uninhabited

We'll halt,
for height, in wind that doesn't dry distances,
on the gravel bed standing.

Our support gusty. Sky
abrim, opening more.

Solidity

From the road, further down, thrown back to
wrists, when it receives us.

Rocks.

I'm interrupted, like daylight arising.

Before blue asphalt
sinks through my knees. As, in a few days, the
glaciers of heaven,
on the summit levelled.

To forget, at the site of the sun, already, day
blazing
returning.

No More to Await

Mountain after mountain,
as they assemble at my back, may distances
diminish!

Linked to light,
                    morning-glory. Like blue to its haft.

Ploughshare

                    Cold's felloe
air before us fashions—and beyond return, like
lightning.
          It.

The Night

                    Where earth, today,
                              under this charge,
submerges the sun, all, surrounding it, as grass in
mows where meadow abrupts,
                              I saw it.

Solstice

                              Since we halted, under
the wind where, after the sun, you weren't expecting
it, I've leapt, summer, like a mass exploded, the
mountain,
              bound both
                    suns.

Heat soon.

Forgotten, here . . .

                    Forgotten, here, what cuts.
Sky. As, from the other side, by soil turned up.

     Sky I'd never seen rest on earth a-spiral.
Or dazzling.

                    After the cold rising, towards
the other day. I strike day burning among
vanished walls.

                              Outside, to what's left, and
which a face, as you halfturn, reaps again.

Murgers [✻]

                              Mountains in shackles (tarnished
face of glaciers) where she for tomorrow
scorches.
        Even the house under my feet.

The Earth . . .

                                        Earth,
and on ahead, as blind as sun after a new downfall.

        To meet you again I return.

✻(*Murgers* "is simply a local country word referring to the stones which peasants collect
out of tilled fields and pile up on the margin."—A du B.)

ANDRÉ DU BOUCHET

The White Motor

I

I've stripped away
this kind of arbitrary bandage

found myself again
free
and hopeless

like a bundle of sticks
or a stone

radiate

with the heat of a stone

like cold
against the field's body

but I know heat and cold

the fire's limits

the fire

whose head
I see

whose white limbs.

II

The fire pierces at several points the blind
side of the sky, the side I'd never seen.

The sky that hoists itself just above the
earth. Black brow. I don't know if I'm here
or there,
          in air or in a rut. These are
pieces of air that I tread on like lumps.

My life stops with the wall or starts to
go just where the wall stops, at the burst
sky. I don't cease.

III

    My report will be the black branch that
elbows into sky.

IV

Here, it opens its white mouth. There, it
defends itself all along the line, with
these retrenched trees, these black beings.
There too, it takes the heavy hot form of
fatigue, like limbs of earth flayed by a
plow.

I stop at my breath's edge, as at a door,
to listen to its cry.

Here, outside, there is upon us a hand, a
heavy cold ocean, as if the stones found
accompaniment.

V

I go out
into the room

as if I were outside

amidst
motionless furnishings

in the heat trembling

by itself

beyond its fire

is only
nothing

wind.

VI

I move, reunited with fire, in the vague paper
confused with air, unprimed earth. I offer
my arm to the wind.

I go no farther than my paper. Far far
ahead of me, it fills a gully. A little
further off in the field, we are almost
equal. Knee-deep in the stones.

Aside, one speaks of a wound, one speaks
of a tree. I recognize myself. So as not
to be mad. So that my eyes do not become
as weak as the earth.

VII

I am in the field
like a drop of water
on redhot iron

itself eclipsed

stones open

like a pile of plates
held
in one's arms

when evening breathes

I stay
with the cold white plates

as if I were holding earth
herself

in my arms.

VIII

Already spiders scurry over me, over dismembered
earth. I stand up straight above the tilth,
over the short dry waves,
                    of a field fulfilled
become blue, wherein I move without ease.

IX

Nothing's enough for me. Nor I enough for anything. The fire that blows will be that day's
fruit, on the road being fused, which succeeds
in turning white to the stricken eyes of stones.

X

I slow down to look at the empty field, the sky
above the wall. Between air and stone I enter
a field that has no wall. I feel the skin of
air, and yet we dwell apart.

   Outside us is no fire.

XI

A great white page pulsing in the
devastated light lasts until we have come
up to it.

XII

Leaving the hot door, iron handle, I find
myself before a noise that has no end, a
tractor. I touch the bottom of a rugged
bed, I don't begin. I've always lived. I
see more clearly the stones, especially
the shadow that insets, the red shadow of
earth when fragile on my fingers, under
its pall, and when heat has not hidden us.

XIII

This fire, like a wall, smoother in its vertical
prolongation of the other and violently struck
at its peak blinding us, like a wall I won't
let petrify.

Earth again raises its harsh head.

This fire like an open hand to which I refuse
to give a name. If reality has come between
us like a wedge and kept us apart, it's
because I was too near this heat, this fire.

XIV

So, you have seen these splinters of wind,
these great discs of broken bread, in the
brown country, like a hammer outside its
gangue swimming against the unwrinkled
current whose rugged bed, whose route,
alone is seen.

These fine splinters, these great blades
laid down by the wind.

The stones erect, the grass kneeling. And
what I don't know of profile and back, once
it is quiet: you, like the night.

You move off.

This unharnessed fire, this unexhausted
kindling us fire, like a tree, the length
of the slope.

XV

What remains after the fire are discredited
stones, cold stones, the small change of ashes
in the field.

There's still the coachwork of the foam that
clicks away as if it gushed back from the tree

anchored in earth by broken fingernails, this
head emerging and setting itself straight, and
silence reclaiming us like a great field.

Extinction

The knot of breath rejoining,

                      higher, bound air,
     and lost.

This bed dispersed with the torrent,
                    higher, by this
       breath.

To dream ourselves torrent, or invite the cold,
through all inhabited locality.

From the mountain, this breath, perhaps, at the
start of day.

The air lost bedazzles me, closing upon my step.

Far from Breath

Having clashed, unwittingly, with air,
I know, now, how to descend towards day.

Like a voice, which, on its own lips,
would wring the light dry.

The pincers of this expanse,
                    lost for us,
     but only this far.

I accede to this soil that doesn't reach our
mouth, soil that grasps the dew.

What I tread is not displaced,
                  the expanse increases.

Cession

The wind,
           in the waterless lands of summer,
     leaves us on a blade,
                  all that remains
       of the sky.

In several crackings, earth grows keen. Earth
stays stable in the breath that strips us bare.

Here, in the motionless blue world, I've almost
attained this wall. Day's depth is still before
us. Depth aglow with earth. Depth and surface
of the brow,
           flattened by the same breath,
this cold.

I recompose myself at the foot of the façade
like the blue air where the plow puts down.

       Nothing quenches my step.

RENÉ CHAR

The Brittle Age

*To Dr. Jean-Louis Lévy in memory of his daughters
Françoise and Madeleine.*

i

I was born like rock, with my faults.
Uncured of my superstitious youth,
no longer of limpid firmness, I entered the
brittle age.

ii

The way the world now is, we stretch a candle
of unsullied blood above the real and sleep
beyond sleep.

iii

What everywhere dominates unnoticed: alchemies
and their will o' the wisps.

iv

The creator is pessimistic, his creation
ambitious, ergo optimistic. The rotation
of the creature conforms to their adverse
prescriptions.

v

Faithfully we learn never to be consoled.

vi

Without the shore's backing, don't trust
in the sea, but in the wind.

vii

I have from birth aggressive respiration.

viii

You must greet shadow with eyes half closed.
It leaves the orchard without plucking there.

ix

To suffer from the ill of intuition.

x

Night rushes upon poetry, awakening breaks,
when one is so exalted as to express it.
However long the leash we allow it, poetry is
hurt by us, and we by its escapes.

xi

It may happen that our heart be, as it
were, driven from our body. And our body
is, as it were, dead.

xii

The impossible we never quite attain, but
it serves as our lantern. We will avoid
the bee and the serpent, we will disdain
the venom and the honey.

xiii

The hawthorn blossoming was my first
alphabet.

xiv

Comfort is a crime, the source told me
in its rock.

xv

Be consoled. In dying, you restore all
that has been lent you, your love, your
friends. Even this fresh cold so many
times garnered.

xvi

Death's great ally, the one wherein she best conceals
her gadflies: memory.
Even while the persecutress of our
odyssey, which lasts one waking night until
the pink tomorrow.

xvii

Man: the air he breathes, one day breathes
him; earth takes the remains.

xviii

Words, words, too apathetic, or so loosely
hung together! Knucklebones hurrying in
the hand of the seemly cheat, I denounce
you.

xix

Killing has ungirded me forever. You are
my ungirding forever. Which to heed?

xx

Who would dare to say that what we have
destroyed was worth a hundred times more
than what we had dreamt and transformed
without respite while murmuring among
the ruins?

xxi

No man, unless he is of the living dead,
can feel himself at anchor in this life.

xxii

The history of men is the long succession
of synonyms of one selfsame vocable. To
contradict it is a duty.

xxiii

What was is no more. What isnt must become.
At the labyrinth's two entrances leap up
two hands full of eagerness. Without some
spirit, what is it that inspires the
livid, the atrocious, or the blushing
lady distributor?

xxiv

How would the end justify the means? There is
no end, only perpetual means, always more
machined.

xxv

Remove the breath from work, its dynasty in-
conceivable; get rid of the liberal arts, that they
stop reflecting all, that's the charnel house.

xxvi

The incalculable meanness of man *under*
man, through fatality and disposition, can
it be melted by a durable heart? Some,
indefinitely, congeal or ruin themselves
over this hereditary work-in-hand.

xxvii

Whatever I may sketch out or undertake, it is
not bounded by death or by any hazardous
halfhearted liberty which plunges headlong
into it for which I feel co-responsible,
but for the harvests and mirrors of our
burning world.

xxviii

To the end he had a genius for escaping;
but he escaped through suffering.

xxix

To suppress absence kills. The gods die
only from being with us.

xxx

To lick one's wounds. The demonic ball
opens to the sole musician.

xxxi

At once to live, to be deceived by life,
to wish to live better and be able to, is
hell.

xxxii

There was in this man all the impatience
and grimace of the universe, and also
quite the contrary. That diminished his
bitterness, gave a treacherous tang to
his hope which, thus alienated,
did not evade us.

xxxiii

Misfortune is often rewarded with an even
greater affliction.

xxxiv

"I revolt and so branch out." This
is what men should say at the stake that
raises their rebellion.

xxxv

When the sun commands, do little.

xxxvi

Like nature, when it proceeds to the
mending of a mountain after our
damages.

xxxvii

*Venasque**

The frosts in a rout summon you,
Men more burning than the bush;
Long winter winds will hang you.
The stone roof is the scaffold
Of a church congealed standing.

xxxviii

Distant inclemency is fluent and
fixed. So, a proud look sees it.

xxxix

If you don't accept what you are offered,
you will one day be beggars. Beggars
for greater refusals.

xl

True clarity is discovered only at the
bottom of the stairs, at the blast of the door.

xli

Kindly clothe me in soft snow,
O heavens, obliging me to drink your tears.

xlii

Sorrow is the last fruit,
the immortal, of youth.

xliii

To start on one's way on one's own two
feet and, until nightfall, to keep
going on it, recognizing it, and dealing
well with it—this way—for, despite
its hated stages, it shows us the straws
of fulfilled wishes and the earth crossed
by birds.

*Author's note. A village in Vaucluse (France), high up near Mt. Ventoux. The church
is Romanesque and the site Celtic.

324

Old Japanese Songs
(based on pre-Manyōshū tradition)

That old liar
Crow
Said only
Together together
Went on alone.

Pearl
In profundity
Who am I to give
Myself
To someone else.

Cock crow
Dawn known
Bells of
The temples telling
Dawn dawn, night is done.

At wind rise
Clouds tent
Tatsutayama
Bursting
Morning glories.

KUSANO SHIMPEI

Rock

in rain wet by it.
by itself.
rock is.
is millions of years.
in vague.
mist.

Annual Ring

moonlight.
sunlight.

straight up to the Bear the spirit of the tree.
and straight down into magma.
that alone in common and the trees free of
    day and night. time will sometime
    gusty sough and seep through trees.
not that.
in trees the time born.
is one with outer time silently precise.

wind. rain. lightning. sleet. snow. blizzard.
    quietness.
and in the long dry season's night they want
    to stretch straight up and reach.
confusedly vaguely.
the blows and caresses each precisely recorded
    within.
in images. in their own cores.
history solidly condensed.
whole woods ineluctably sink.

moonlight.
sunlight.

in darkness.
light never discovers.

wind. rain. lightning. sleet. snow. blizzard.
    quietness.
reflecting knotted bark whirlpools of annual
    ring warp and physics too,
even dead just as they were.
annals of a trillion vortices
history in these beautiful flowing points remains.

moonlight.
sunlight.

viva the trees viva!

326

Forest

trees trees.
trees.
full moon.

> roots of towering firs tunneling through
>   gravel grip rock circle it reach straight
>   on down.
> crawling all over them the huge roots of
>   beeches.
> the rugged roots of oaks grappling with
>   those of the beeches right through
>   fossil shells.
> luxuriant low striped bamboo all over the
>   place excrement and urine seep into.
> roots of the Judas tree and oak intricate
>   only to separate out.
> rootlets antennae.
> absorbing watery nutriment up and up to
>   extend all directions out.
> nutriment rootlets of the Judas trees
> absorb's passed on and on to oak roots
> and half of what the oaks suck up
> rises to Judas trees and half
> remains in their own fat roots.

humus. clay. gravel. rock. gravel.
each in lateral bands.
each a special color but all together black.
thousands of roots crawling through black
  surviving each other going on.

> thousands of roots. and no sign of motion.

under full moon.
trees trees.
trees.

Minami Akitsu

in rice fields dew drops.
a thousand million suns glistening.
Minami Akitsu.
gorgeous morning for a walk.
Gen   (our Kai dog)
Kuro   (N's blackie)
Kennedy   (O's collie)
Liz   (K's crossbred setter)
already used to it raring to get out with me.
two months. only two months I've been here.
Gen!   Kuro!   not the wheatfield hey!
the rascals at my bidding running wild kicking up
                    dirt and light.
by the field bare elms and snowbells.
dangling snake-gourds.   and on gourd vermilion
                    morningshine.
(as little like yesterday.   as yesterday sky's
                    layout)
each morning differently fresh.
but every freshness classic.
meaning trees and earth.
whistle.
and out of scrub a hundred yards away.
come flying.
first Gen.   second Kuro.   third Liz.   and a poor
                    fourth forlornly Kennedy
                    with his bum paw.
(not the fields!   not the wheatfields!)

plantain at the rice fields withered edge.   speedwell.
                    parsley.   wild rocambole.   dead-
                    nettles. and so on.
the beautiful blossoms in winter.
from the start set against summer's heavy greens.
a weight.
wild rocambole and parsley.   dead-nettles.
even in December.
flourishing.
where's the weasel.
as yet unseen.

something weighing at center.
prickly black ball of devil's-tongue root.
my stomach.
sometimes.
no one knowing of the two bleedings since
                    coming to Akitsu.
but my old friend (terribly old friend)
                    weighs and stays.
prickly devil's-tongue root.

on the narrow patch through snowbell woods the
                    dogs lined up.
for a moment.
then off into pampas grass.
if that's what you want—go.
I'll go myself
tea fields.
Dososhin.
around the farmhouses high *keyaki* and oak and
                    bamboo thickets.   chestnut
                    and maple too.
roof on roof of leaves.
a shrike shrieks.
at a bend in the path a home-made red mailbox.
in the shopping bag lugged along.
put there by a clerk peanuts eggs toiletpaper
                    two cans of mackerel.
(feed for the rainbow trout and Gen)
hey! not that way! this!
not to the Nakamura Bakery sign today.
by the Primary School down by the rough slope.

        (something weighing at center!)

fragrance of tea blossoms.
radish and spinach rows.
Dososhin.
and.   like a haircurdling cock-crow.
whistle.
all the names at once impossible.
whistle.
four tongues come creeping out of the bushes.
ok let's go home.

same way as day before yesterday now.
hills woods fields and ricefields December.
the sky's beauty also blossoms in winter.

    (oy! the prickly devil's-tongue root weighing
                       at center)

Minami Akitsu.
end of the walk premium.
beyond the thickets.
Fuji.

Skylarks and Fuji

soil between balls of thumb and forefinger crumbled
        falls.
on cottonweed velvet falls.
and falling returns to the ricefield path. soil that
        will be Fuji.
crumbled between balls of two fingers ordinary tiny
        grains thought of as the source of Fuji
        listening all ears to skylarks singing
        February 15th 9 a.m.
winter solstice past and even with midwinter winds
        warm. three eager larks flying off to
        three quarters of heaven singing.
beyond bare *keyaki* and oak. a little higher than
        keyaki much lower than the larks.
Fuji blows snow.
(light and wind and scattered snow-dust.)
from the ricefields of Akitsu to the land's end
        adjacent.
gust out of gust.
snow-swept.

soil of a history of a thousand million years crumbled
        between two fingers. and that selfsame
        soil's.
mutation.
mass.
tremendous volume.
Fuji.

the larks now heaven's.
piccolo.

at this immensest moment.
shines alone.
a tiny.
diamond.

diamond Fuji.

the soil that fell from between two fingers the same
        that fellows.
the heavy mass.
in these ricefields better finally not to try to think
        but hear February 15th's piccolo.
far see white Sung ware.
life again fresh alive.

(time to go home.)

Half a Sun

after Fuji's.
left side sun coming in.
from top north.
flowing steep down perhaps no cloud.
quick black snow smoke.
shaking sinking sliding away. moment.
jumps.
crimson pudding.
o half a sun now.
mightiest member of the universe.
blind my two upstanding eyes with a whack of light.

Untitled

Fuji.
in the West set.

                a full moon.

in the East floats.
lifts.

Translated by Susumu Kamaike and Cid Corman

WILLIAM BRONK
Colloquy on a Bed

Listen, the celestial motions, though they make
an order of sorts and this is an order, in part,
accessible to the mind, it is not to be thought
that this is a rational order. Not to our minds.
How should the scale, alone, make any sense?

There is evidence to be seen in addition to this
that, like it or not, this place, this universe,
in any rational sense, is hopelessly
insane. Hopelessly: the saving word.
How should it otherwise be meaningful?

No, I do not love you, though the small hairs
around your eyes can make me tremble, stop
me talking, thinking even. You can go.
But you remind me passion does exist
as hopeless and as meaningful as the universe is.

The Difference

I can no more imagine the image of man
than as to say I had never seen him, than if he
were the creature inferred in a postulate of a world
without us, unvisited ever, projected but not
observed. Not the same, surely, as we think
ourselves to be, some way diverse from us:
if we should say he had clawed toes,
a hairless skin, it is only a way to say
a difference, not that we know what it is,
but to say it were there, as we know, of ourselves, it is there:
that of man observed as well as of man unseen,
we know only the **difference** is there, that man is not
his clothes (or his nakedness), those assertions of drab

or fancy, nor what he does, his pretensions of role,
his obediences. We are frightened of much unknown
and make up tales to tell us, the way we explain
noises at night, domesticating fright.
Not any explanation touches man.
Keep me from craziness; I have no belief
in reason, but let me be, if I can, without.
I wait for belief the way the Millerites
expected a Coming. Mornings chasten me;
I come down from the hill and put my robe away.

Some of the things we think and say of the world
are reasonable, but none of them is true.

The Smile on the Face of a Kouros

This boy, of course was dead, whatever that
might mean.   And nobly dead. I think we should feel
he was nobly dead. He fell in battle, perhaps,
and this carved stone remembers him
not as he may have looked, but as if to define
the naked virtue the stone describes as his.
One foot is forward, the eyes look out, the arms
drop downward past the narrow waist to hands
hanging in burdenless fullness by the heavy flanks.
The boy was dead and the stone smiles in his death
lightening the lips with the pleasure of something achieved:
an end. To come to an end. To come to death
as an end. And coming, bring there intact the full
weight of his strength and virtue, the prize with which
his empty hands are full. None of it lost,
safe home, and smile at the end achieved.

Now death, of which nothing as yet—or ever—is known,
leaves us alone to think as we want of it,
and accepts our choice, shaping the life to the death.
Do we want an end? It gives us; and takes what we give
and keeps it; and has, this way, in life itself,
a kind of treasure house of comely form
achieved and left with death to stay and be
forever beautiful and whole, as if

to want too much the perfect, unbroken form
were the same as wanting death, as choosing death
for an end. There are other ways; we know the way
to make the other choice for death: unformed
or broken, less than whole, puzzled, we live
in a formless world. Endless, we hope for no end.

I tell you, death, expect no smile of pride
from me. I bring you nothing in my empty hands.

CID CORMAN

"Not the least lash lost"—
ah, but if one is!

My mother, way back,
would cup it in hand

gingerly and quick
say, blowing it off,

Wish for something good!
But what could I have

wished better than her
doing what she did?

The Portrait

The shadow behind
recurs like the mind
showing me again

as the light goes on
flooding it herself
the way she was young

to see to love what
being here she cant
any more become.

———————

Men die and know it.
What more warrants
art than this?

Water see sky—
or simply
face the belovèd.

SEYMOUR FAUST

Fragment

As real
    the boat contains the gods
It moves
underneath the belly of the sky
    and ferrys the sun over
The wind drives the rain this evening
a cold night in April
    I try to integrate
hypotheses
the lines on which I prolong
    my days beneath the sky

Small Favors

She represented the group
in Albany
a slim woman
getting older now
nicknamed for a flower

    and spoke once to the staff
in a hostile environment were she nearly lied
to avoid a damaging admission
    a useful person

adroit
intelligent
self-possessed
her feelings disturb her equanimity
like undercurrents the sparkling plains of summer
the water touched in areas by the wind
or which
transparent unexpectedly
    uncovers the bright roundworm
or stiff pike

Now You See It, Now You Don't

1

After a stretch of time I couldn't foresee
and prior to a blank
                         I try a poem
as if it is important
real
or I can do it
                         Look up
the craft across the sky
                         a 727
look down
                         its gone

2

Rangers cameras on
        as if a fir or other spiky tree
        should open a bank of eyes at its cone
and look down
The landscape peering through

3

The C-47 search plane
        crosses the white range
and bobs forward in silence like a float or buoy
        over a manless spread of lakes and snow
Hardly a detail counts there
It is all alike

4

The three-part diesel lunges
        from the underpass
        a flat expanse of trees and a parking lot
engine units bobbing
        and a long horn from the exhausts
a diminishing perspective down the tracks
Black lanes of traffic east and west
blue fumes
        the dressed-up girls
taking up your mind

Look over the rail
4 silent sets of parallels
go north
and then the train.

5

Lifeless on sunday
the projecι area
full of skeletal structures
blazes in the sun
     Between 10 and 2 pm
the contrasts are sharpest
the perspectives through the planes are least intense

Cranes hang
a third again as high
a high immobile angle over them

upright oblongs
sun angling through on every floor

LORINE NIEDECKER

My life
    by water—
        Hear

spring's
    first frog
        or board

out on the cold
    ground
        giving

Muskrats
    gnawing
        doors

to wild green
    arts and letters
        Rabbits

raided
 my lettuce
  One boat

two—
 pointed toward
  my shore

thru birdstart
 wingdrip
  weed-drift

of the soft
 and serious
  Water

I walked
on New Year's Day

beside the trees
my father now gone planted

evenly following
the road

Each spoke:
Peace

CID CORMAN

Shadow

gong

shadow.

What you are
I am. As if
to admit

the look in the
mirror of
the mirror. Not

nature to
be upheld—but
seen for what

it is: unseen
unless as
an edifice.

The path through the temple
never takes me to it—
but never to be there

is always to be here
under the bending pines
bringing shadow shadow.

Not myself
and not you
alone, but

each within
the other
moving out:

the tides of
earth and sky
shaping from

horizon
horizon,
orison.

SEYMOUR FAUST

Waterfront Winter

1

Alkes
Hovsul
Havtjeld
Savannah
   in Brooklyn ports
by empty yards
on Sundays
   hour by hour going by
the sun traveling the ecliptic
and the zodiac beyond the brilliant blue
   Freight cars
standing on the tracks
with stencilled facts on them
   Property of Chase Manhattan Bank
Metropolitan Life Insurance Company
painted mint green or brick red
doors pinned
concave wheels on tapered axles
   cobra brake shoes
Yesterday the yard engine moved them
   cargo swung
cables running through the blocks
Yesterday pastrami sandwiches
   and pea soup with croutons
Christmas creches
"Vote Coalition" on the walls and "Tony Pro"
   Tank cars lined against corrosion
   on the double track
      shells for fatty acids
In a chalk scrawl on a freight car's side
"TWU" it says
   "Back to Work"

2

ARINE SULFU
on lettered boards
picked up in the surf of southern beaches
a liquid sulfur carrier
goes down without survivors in the gulf
    I'm 36 I hear myself repeating
like the broken spoken words from Thresher
cut-off voice transmission

3

Over the wooded hills the deer
in the environment where the migrants separate
from which the migrants gather
swifts and swallows in an aerial whirl
    above the marsh
terns over the hollows in the dunes
tidal pools the yellowlegs invade
in summers inlets
        scaups and canvasback in winter

Bio 1

funny
I'm hearing something
something is getting audible
something is crossing a level of sensitivity in the inner ear
something is getting through

    •

it is a voice
in a receiver of limited range
the topography makes it erratic
it comes & goes
there is silence
or a message from distance

    •

we wanted someone
speaking for us
a mirror for us
a huge lens
a mirror of enormous radius of curvature
say of fifty feet
so if you looked at it   edge on
you'd say there was no curve
something that would reach
        way way out
to an island universe
and reflect ourselves

        •

there was something to be learned
        something groping for
hands on the inner wall of ancient caves
something being overlooked
M 81 the pearly spiral
        that was it
or
in the clear expanded field
the liquid limpid circle under the ocular and objective
of highest powers
        that was it
in silence
        or in sound

        •

now he reminds you of the sun
no one dips a toe to test it ever
the huge loops touch it by the rims
in them
nothing twice the same
        it was worth hearing
we wanted to be reminded
we didnt mind hearing by indirection about god
or hearing by silence all about him
or seeing him in the huge circles
        projected by the moon in ice-crystal cirrus
or in the roundworm undulating down

through elodea
emerald clouds of spirogyra
infusoria
gradual opacity of water
till it is opaque

•

or plants
from fungus up
or from euglena up
past hydra, volvox, red and blue-green algae
or animals
from euglena up
something of that too
we looked into it in detail
we told each other of it
told children to look
we were sure they could take it
they would think about it
they would know
I was they
so were you
how did we forget
isnt it
what you wanted now

•

I know we dont care about the moon
the close-up shots moving into impact
and the coincidences of timing
how the missile moved towards collision with a circle
50 miles across
a planet off
        or when it did
and those clear pictures
        or the solar barge at the foot
of Khufu's pyramid
absorbing
irrelevant
but it is

RENÉ DAUMAL
The Poet's Last Words

From fruit left to rot on earth can still spring up a new tree. From this tree, new fruit by the hundreds.

But if the poem is a fruit, the poet is not a tree. He asks you to take his words and eat them immediately. For he cannot, by himself alone, produce his fruit. There must be two to make a poem. The one who speaks is the father, the one who listens is the mother, the poem is their child. The poem which has not been listened to is lost seed. Or again: the one who speaks is the mother, the poem is the egg and the one who listens is the fertilizer of the egg. The poem that is not listened to becomes a rotten egg.

•

It's this that, in his cell, a poet condemned to death was thinking of. It was in a small country just invaded by the armies of a conqueror. They had arrested the poet because in one of the songs he used to sing on the roads he had compared the sadness that had gnawed the flesh of his body to the bone with the murderous fumes that had burnt the soil of his village even to its rock.

Tomorrow at dawn he will be hanged. But they have allowed him this grace, that before dying he may recite before the people a last poem.

•

He was saying to himself in his dungeon: Up to now I only made songs for amusement. This will be my first and my last poem. I shall tell them:

—Take these words, let not a single seed be lost!
Brood upon my words, make them grow, make them
    speak!
But what shall I say to them then?
I have only one word to say, a word as simple as the thunderbolt.
One word which swells my heart, one word which rises to my throat,
    one word which revolves in my head like a lion in a cage.
It is not a word of peace. It is not a word easy to understand.

But it should lead to peace, but it should make everything easy to understand, provided that it is taken as the earth receives seed and nourishes it even in destroying it.

When I am rotten, in a few days, may a tree of words spring from my rottenness. Not with words of peace, not with words easy to understand, but with words of truth.

•

But still, what shall I say to them?

I have only one word to say, one word as real as the rope which will hang me.

One word which itches me, one word which devours me, one word that even the hangman will understand.

I shall open my mouth—I shall say the word—I shall shut my mouth— and that will be all.

As soon as I have opened my mouth, you will see go back into the earth the spectres and the vampires and all the thieves of speech, the cheats in the game of life, the speculators in death:

Those who make tables turn,

those who balance clocks,

those who seek in the stars reasons for doing nothing.

The daydreamers, the suicides,

the maniacs of mystery,

the maniacs of pleasure,

the imaginary voyagers, the mapmakers of thought,

the maniacs of the fine arts who don't know why they sing,

dance, paint or build.

The maniacs of the beyond

who don't know how to be here.

The maniacs of the past, the maniacs of the future,

conjurors of eternity.

You shall see them return to the earth as soon as I have opened my mouth.

As soon as I have pronounced the word, the eyes of the survivors will return to their sockets and each of these men and each of these women will look in the face the depth of his fate.

Abyss of light! Harrowing darkness!

As soon as I have shut my mouth, their eyes will return to the world, charged with the central light, and they shall see that outside is the image of inside. They shall be kings, they shall be queens, they shall see each other, each all alone as the sun is alone, but all lit

348

up by the fire of a unique solitude within, as without by the fire of a unique sun.

•

But I dream and I surrender to a much too easy hope.
And they shall certainly say:
    —This fool, it is time he was hanged. This useless mouth, it is time it was shut.
Or perhaps again they shall say:
    —His words are not words of peace, these are not words easy to understand. They are demonic words. It is time, indeed, for him to be hanged.
And regardless I shall be hanged. Well then, I shall say to them:
    —You havent much longer to live than I do.
I die today, you the week after.
And our misery is the same and our grandeur is the same.
But they will think that these are words of hate. These wretches are so sure of being immortal! And regardless I shall be hanged.
What shall I say to them? I should really say to them:
    Wake up!—but I wouldnt know how to tell them how and they would say:—But we are not asleep. Hang, hang this impostor and may his tongue fall from his mouth!
And I shall be, regardless, hanged.

•

And the poet, in his cell, banged his head against the walls. The stifled drum-beat, the funeral tom-tom of his head against the wall was his penultimate song.

All night long he tried to root up out of his heart the unutterable word. But the word grew large in his breast and choked him and rose in his throat and kept revolving in his head like a lion in a cage.

He repeated:

Regardless I shall be hanged at dawn.

And he began again the dull tom-tom of his head against the wall. Then he tried again:

There would be only one word to say. But it would be too simple. They would say:
    —We know already. Hang, hang this dotard.

Or else they would say:

> —He wants to snatch from us the peace in our hearts, our sole refuge in these evil times. He wants to put into our heads rending doubt, while the invader's whip is already rending our flesh.
>
> These are not words of peace, these are not words easy to understand.
>
> Hang, hang this malefactor!

And regardless I shall be hanged.

What shall I say to them?

•

The sun arose with the sound of boots. He was led, teeth clenched, to the gallows. Before him his brothers, behind him his executioners. He said to himself:

Here then is my first and my last poem. One word to say, simple as opening one's eyes. But this word gnaws me from belly to head, I want to open myself from belly to head and show them the word that I hold within. But if it must be made to pass through my mouth, how will it clear the narrow orifice, this word that fills me?

Then he was silent for once: his mouth kept still. And again he was silent: his whole body became like a silent rock.

(He was like a white rock, like the statue of a ram before a flock of sleeping sheep; and behind him the wolves were laughing already.)

•

The sounds of bayonets and spurs were heard. The time allowed was over. Upon his neck the poet felt the tickling of the hemp and in the pit of his stomach the talons of death. And then, at the last moment, the word burst from his mouth, shouting:

Get your weapons! Your pitchforks, your knives,
Your stones, your hammers,
you are thousands, you are strong,
free yourselves, free me!
I want to live, live with me!
strike with the scythe, strike with the rock!
Act that I may live and I, I shall bring the word back to you!

But this was his first and his last poem.
The people had already been much too terrorized.
And for having swung too much during his life,
the poet swings still after his death.

Under his feet the tiny eaters of rottenness lie in wait for the carrion that ripens on the branch. Over his head revolves his last cry, which has no one to rest upon.

(For it is often the fate—or the fault—of poets to speak too late or too soon.)

1936

WILLIAM BRONK

Copan: Historicity Gone

The stelas stand in a large grass plaza, blazed in the full sun. One feels a festivity, a real party, though no one is there. Jim, who flew us in and who comes here in various weathers, says he likes it better in the rainy season, misty, mysterious. It has more than one expression, no doubt; but here in the assertive brightness of the light which is somehow joyful and triumphant, it is hard to think for long of any different expression.

And it is not what we expected either, though how should we say what we expected or how we formed our expectation? People were there before and pictured it and wrote about it. We took the wrong idea or failed to take the right one though it may have been there. What is transmissible? Most of the photographs are clear. Catherwood was skilled and patient with his drawings. He and Stephens discarded the first wood engravings made from the drawings and had them done again on steel in order to have truer pictures for their book. But one can sense in Stephens's account a resigned dissatisfaction with even that result. It wasn't quite as he saw it though he said it was the best to be had. And now if we look for what the pictures have shown us, what we find in addition to recognition each time is a start of surprise at how different things are from what we thought we were shown. And indeed, what is this to the rubbled and tree-grown mounds which were there before such restoration as has been done, or the restorations to the constructions they mean to suggest? What are we looking at or for? At the foot of the great stairways the structure we look out towards is the ball-court, no doubt, or a part of what stood there once and served as one. But underneath this court is another which this one overlies, and under that one, another. We are looking at what we see, which no description gave us, which never existed. What we see is new and if we mean to see it we must look at it as something new. What we see is not what is there, though surely something is there and we seem to see it.

Across the city, on the river side, a section shows where the river veered and cut away the hill which made the acropolis. Earth had been brought and built on, the structures covered and built again at a higher level, a succession which ended in those buildings whose ruins now still stand at the top. We fly by in the plane and see the levels of stratification, the past exposed, so that it ceases, in a sense, to be the past and becomes again a present, a continuing present, contemporaneous with the structures at the top, within its own various levels, and with us, so that it is our present which enlarges, and we see ourselves as we are: more than we were. Students of the past trace and analyze strata to characterize the sequence of cultures; but, more than history, don't we look to find ourselves there, though history is the guise we give ourselves as if we meant not to speak directly of our subject, and history served as that Mayan mask, complexly devised of plumes and false faces, to cover our nakedness. For it is we who are naked here, exposed in layers by the river's cutting away of those successive domestic and ceremonial disguises in which we sought to hide ourselves. It is our absence, indeed, which is our presence: the disguises are there still and we are not there, we are nowhere; we are as we were. What we call the past is an aspect of our present.

How should we say, consequently, who these figures may be, carved on the stelas, half-covered, chubby, epicene, vaguely-faced, though their faces once may have been more special-featured? Their feet, in elaborate boxings and lacings of sandals, turn outward almost all the way; and their hands, held across the breast, are backside-under and half-closed, the fingers turned in, as though to conceal the emptiness they hold. It is said they hold scepters, and perhaps they do, but the convention of the hand position seems an unnatural convention to us. We see something of the forearms, a little of the leg above and below the knee, and the face. The rest of the figure and the space around it are encrusted and overlaid with armband, girdle, kilt and headdress so elaborate that only because they are carved in the same stone mass, does the figure seem able to carry them. It is by its accoutrements that the figure asserts itself; and that we see it at all is as if, in an illustration, it were indicated as underneath by a dotted line. Take the regalia away, is there anyone there? There seems to have been no concern for such a question and no concern is, in effect, a negative answer. These figures—

were they priests or kings, perhaps, or gods?—were anything at all only by the force of their iconography invénted to distinguish them, and this is forgotten and not discovered again. In the mass of their stone, their anonymity frightens us, and it would hardly help to know what names they bore, as though the names themselves were again another bangle. It was their nothingness which was not faced, or faced rather, was thought to be concealable under a heavy overlay. There are a few carved heads to be found in the ruins which have little or no adornment. Death's heads are very numerous and these are unadorned. Those notably alive were rich in ornament; death was a stripping away. They were often reminded; they did, of course, their own reminding and felt a need to.

At the top of the acropolis, there is a structure with a richly adorned doorway carved with glyphs and figures and the leaves and tendrils of stylized plants. At the base on either side, as finial to the sill or plinth to the side pilasters, is a kind of death's head which seems less a skull than a skinned decapitation. We don't know what it may be which is depicted here. One figure is almost naturalistic; others are only partly anthropomorphic. Does it say that the idea of death underlay whatever was thought to be in the carving above it, that death was basic? Can we read that human experience is expressible in symbols, that one aspect of it is in relation to other aspects, and that this relationship is one of support and generation? Visually diverse elements are brought together in this carving. Even though we don't know what these elements represent as part by part, their existence as a related structure is an affirmation that our experience is structural and is discernible as structure. We can see this much without knowing what definition they gave the elements, though they must have known. This combination of elements, some natural, some other than natural, has seemed to some observers to represent a cosmology and man in the cosmology occupying his space. We do make cosmologies and we treat them on various levels of belief. It doesn't seem urgent that we understand the one here; its statement, if we could read it, seems unlikely to support us. Perhaps it is only in that sense that we take cosmologies seriously if we do at all. And what prevents us from taking them seriously if we do not is a sense that we are not capable of devising a cosmology which is effective in supporting us, a sense that however much we may desire it or however ingeniously we may pursue it, it is not to be devised. Our interest in knowing how to interpret this inscription as cosmology is an interest in knowing how someone else failed as we do too.

There were two panels in Temple 11 covered with hieroglyphs. We would be gratified to read them. And yet we are completely certain there is no great news they could tell us. They know no more than we and their reference is their own. This is not to disparage them but to recognize our own limitations and to say that they were human like us. And behind Temple 11 is the long stairway which leads to another temple and is known as the Hieroglyphic Stairway because its whole vertical surface is an inscription. Scholars can read some dates here as, of course, elsewhere on the various monuments. Their time was another reckoning from ours and we take satisfaction in finding the correlations of the two so as to state one in terms of the other. One duration in terms of another duration would seem to be the nature of time and to make such a statement was a satisfaction of the Mayans as well. It was apparently at Copan that some of the Mayan time statements were sharpened. A heavy, rectangular slab, called Altar Q, carved with glyphs on its surface and human figures on its edges, seems to have commemorated some more precise astronomical reading by which time was reckoned, with the result that their calendar was made to correspond more closely with the movements of heavenly bodies. We recognize here our own uncanny desire to measure ourselves against the sun and stars, counting revolutions, unrolling the concentric circles which surround us, to make them linear and historical. At Copan, the line of history broke a short generation after the dating of the Hieroglyphic Stairway and Altar Q. No monument discovered has a date later than the year we number 800 A.D. They may have continued the reckoning of time after this without recording it in monuments. Perhaps they deserted the city; perhaps they stayed nearby. Life can continue without a reckoning of time. It has a kind of latitude and time is one way to speak of that latitude. But when time comes to a stop as it seems to have come to a stop around Copan, the latitude remains. Perhaps the people went away. More probably they stayed and not too far from there. They stopped making monuments and may have no longer reckoned the calendar or thought consciously of the temples and sacred precincts, but remained as much or as little as they were before. The whole set of our minds is splinted so in time and history, our thinking structure fails to stand without them, and we are reluctant and uneasy, thinking of timeless man, of man without history. When we come back now to Copan, we feel at home there because, however remote or alien its terminology, we sense through all our ignorance that time and history have been here once. It seems entirely natural, too, the only human reaction, to feel regret and melancholy and bewildered protest that all these structures are empty and fallen, that something stopped here a thousand years ago. We assume of time and history that they are continuous and progressive and always were. The insistent questions that confront us here and characterize us are, "Where did these people come from?" and "Where did they go to?" We are brought to face the discontinuity of time and history, the continuance nevertheless of man, and the equivalence as answers to these questions of *nowhere* and *here*. We assume that we, too, came from somewhere, go someplace; but of ourselves also we would have to answer *nowhere* and *here*, and know that one answer said the same as the other. And, together, the answers say, insofar as we can be characterized, we are they and they are we, timeless and unhistorical. It is true that we have on either occasion invented times and histories for ourselves and, by an act of will, imposed them as long as strength lasted. We invented these the way we invented speech and buildings and costumes and the changes of modes in these; but, whatever we are, we are without them and apart from the changes in them. These things in themselves can be said to have times and histories; but they have little or nothing to do with us. We lean on inventions, though, to give us standing. We dress ourselves in inventions and house ourselves there. We give ourselves mythic identity, find something we ought to do and project rewards. We are never what our pretensions claim, though at times we seem to be when our pretensions succeed for awhile, when will and self-denial and force mold us into some image we impose upon ourselves and on those around us, so that common consent gives us the role we claim for ourselves. To say we make something of ourselves is a form of praise for a person or a culture.

There is a large mask on a stairway in the East Court, a wide-eyed human face with symbols beside it that show it to mean the planet Venus. It is something to say of Venus, and what else should we say? But without the label we should never have found it out. The Mayan culture and this whole site as exemplar are mask and metaphor. So are we.

One of the strongest impressions that we have is that under the mask and metaphor something is there, though it is not perhaps man that is there. There is something which is. Nothing else matters. Copan is a liberation. It is all gone, emptied away. To see it is to see ourselves gone, to see us freed from the weight of our own world and its limitations. One aspect of the roles we assume is taken as something more than whimsical self-indulgence. It is the assumption of the responsibility for our own natures and environment. It is to say that both can be bettered and that we know the direction of betterment and can work that way, and that given time enough and good will and energy, we can evolve a world subject to our reason and wisdom, which are sufficient for that, and that this then will be the world, the world that is. One supposes that whoever may have lived at Copan may have thought this way and that the development of this city may have been directed toward that end; one supposes that whoever may have lived here is we. That the idea is historically absurd is only in part our own absurdity: it is the absurdity of our historicity. Whatever we are, we are not historical. The world we make and ourselves, so far as we make ourselves, ourselves in the particularities of time and place, as cultural man—all this can be destroyed and make no matter. We are happy at Copan to witness our own destruction and how we survive it. If something may be said to happen, what happens to us is not what happens. The evident destruction of Copan is witness to this as we, in our own lives, are witness to the same things. We are delivered from our continuous failures and frustrations. Perhaps more importantly, we are delivered from our self-limited successes, the awful banalities of the good life.

Joy and desire surround us without our doing, without our understanding.

The world or what we term the world, that medium in which we find ourselves, and indeed whatever of it we set apart and term selves, is not related to what we make of it and not dependent on what we make of it or make of ourselves. It is not in the least altered, nor is our basic nature altered, by any cosmology or culture or individual character we may devise, or by the failure or destruction of any of these, as all of them fail. If they seem for a time to succeed, they blind us as though they were real; and it is by our most drastic failures that we may perhaps catch glimpses of something real, of something which is. It merits our whole mind. The good society and the good life are more than we could imagine. To devise them or to assert and defend their devising is not the point.

COPAN: Unwillingness, the Unwilled

What do we want? Say everyone were healthy and beautiful, were rich and together and would never die: well, hardly. But that or something like it had seemed to be what we want. Just the same any increase in personal favor, relief from some particular ailment, or to live if only a little longer,—these partial benefits seem good. But, in either case, it is the imminent certainty of deprivation, whether whole or fractional, we stand on. How should we seem to want these things without that certainty?

So; what *do* we want? Sometimes, to go, in other ways also, counter to the truth, to mark ourselves off from what there is around us, and make that subject to our will: to be masters of some sort, of the political-military sort that leaders and conquerors are, or of the intellectual sort that devises a rationality strong enough that it seems to impose that rationality on what there is. But what there is continues outside and beyond any rationality imposed on it, and political-military mastery is brief and apparent. The notion that man's condition can be stated in such a way that there is, for one thing, we and, for another, our environment, which we master or fail to master, is in itself a wrong idea. It might be said that we are everything, that the only reality is internal, there is nothing outside of us. Or, it might be said that we are nothing, have no real being, that there is only something else whose existence ignores us, and asks us for nothing. The two statements seem to be opposed but may not be. They are equivalent, at least, in denying the duality. Whatever there is, if there is something, we, if we are, are part of it. There are not two realities: man and his medium, of which one is the subject and one the object. It is only by a willful act in the face of the truth that we become an entity separate from what there is around us; and how much the more willful it is to presume to master what we have marked ourselves off from.

There is something which is and we are not separable from it. Then, if we want something, it is something wanted through us; we are the instrumentality of a desire which it would not be quite accurate to call external, because we are part of the wanting, but neither is it right to think it personal. If something is wanted, we feel the want but we are not apart in wanting it. It is always tempting though to transmute the something wanting into personal terms, to look for, or even to find, our own satisfactions as though that were what was wanted, as it proves not to be. At any rate, our personal satisfactions, once had, often seem nothing; whatever it was that was wanted, it wasn't that, and we are puzzled by trophies that seem to have been won by someone we don't even remember. Not always though.

The attempt to put personal desires in place of the general want which we feel, is a simplification, and makes the problem of desire appear to be something we could hope to solve. Isn't it, at bottom, a trial to be something of our own, a separate part with its own desire? It is interesting that our separation is rarely a branching and gradual departure, nor is it a process of development by which inherent and hardly perceptible tendencies express and realize themselves. It is a removal to an existent position as though it were transferable, as though we were molten and gave ourselves into some mold that we saw in order to borrow the form of that mold. We might make much of the implications of external labels which are neither natural nor inherent—of name and place and time and function. It is the somewhat removed mold, often, that seems to attract us, though sometimes the removal is only the distance from actuality to pretension. It may be that the attraction of hypocrisy is only the unnaturalness of the position which it offers, a position which is well-defined because of its falsity. We are uncertain where something real begins or ends, or of its nature; the false can be sharply defined however hollow it is or however little it means. The human situation seems less a come-as-you-are party than a party to which we are bidden to come as our favorite character and, though we are sometimes cheap or shy, we do fairly well. We put on the costume and badges, the mental attitudes, the facial and vocal expressions of *something*, of *someone*. Such an action gives shape and clarity to our desires, gives them poles and simplicity; it sets us up as some sort of marked-off existent. It is of course evasive. It is hard to face how insanely evasive until we have watched the fatal despair with which we fight off the loss of an assumed identity. An assumed identity is made from appearances and lets us be nothing and yet appear to be something. We don't so much want to be something as we want to be allowed to look like something, to be granted general recognition—even acclaim—as what we pretend to be, to win the prize for Best Costume. A declared identity is an assertion of independence, often an aggressive and defiant assertion as though our separate person were a prime value; and it is an avoidance at the same time of any person we might have inside lest it look like the nothing it fears to be. Avoidance, removal, displacement: these seem to be the center of our wanting to be something, our assumption of an identity on our own, as though in order to be something it were necessary to move away, to break some existing connection, whatever we sense it to be. But it may be the other way: that we want to be something in order to justify our real desire, which is to move aside. There are societies where it is recognized as essential to have an assumed name under which to function and to conduct a mature life, suppressing a real name such as it might be. In certain ways, our own society admits the same need.

We may well be nothing or if not, are tenuous and frail. Resoluteness of being which seems to make us something acts to block our emptiness into which something which is might flow. If we start playing a role and let our energies and devisings embellish and serve that role, we are reflecting however in error, the flow into our emptiness of energies and intentions from what seems outside, but which finds some sort of reception in us. Something enjoys being. Our imitation in our own right, of being, may pass for pious homage or a satisfaction at least, of those self-generated desires. We envy actors who have a role into which their passions can be directed, or else we envy the dead, that melted flesh no longer faced with the question.

If something wants through us, if we are the instrumentality of a desire whose source is not internal, then to interpose our own will or personal desires is an avoidance of reality, and the wants which our willfulness includes are irrelevant wants and may be dimissed as not important, as not what we want, no more than we want, as we seem to, an endless life, endless wealth and fairness and company. Order and security, to be caressed and honored and to caress and honor in turn—we seem to want these things, but in order to make us a separate enclave, a refuge apart from what may be wanted through us. If we are not to falsify life, but to have it for what it is, we must leave ourselves open to it and undefended, observant of what may happen, since our private will is not relevant and we are not capable of apprehending or assisting any other will, and what we observe and feel·is perhaps less will than being and the nature of being. We have made up complicated frameworks of activity and attitude on the foundation that somehow we grasp what may be wanted from us, some challenge or imperative. The challenges and imperatives may not be anything like each other in any respect except in this: that they assume our receiving them. But in experience (and on the contrary) nothing is revealed to us of what our nature may be, or of what we must do. Nor, though we spy on it most diligently, do we learn things of consequence about whatever else there may be besides ourselves. We have no inkling of its wants or purposes or whether it has any. There may be some divine or historical or biological or evolutionary determinism and we may be wholly subject to it—it may want something of us—but it is without our consciousness, and we cannot bring our wills to consonance with it, not knowing what it is. I think we are totally unable to effect it: that any action of ours which is contrary is null by its contrariety, and any consonant action is an action not by us but through us, not by our will or any necessity. We have supposed that there are wants and purposes, but it seems likely that none exists.

How empty all those schemes are, and they are very many, which propose our necessity or which propose that we need to do this or that in order to assert or maintain our own existence, or to realize what may have been intended for us. Noting that we do devise as a convenience a kind of machinery of social and political and economic organization, we project that a more searching and more diligent devising would make use of what there is and organize reality into the mechanism. Noting that we do personify ourselves, that we devise a characterization by means of, say, the superego, or historical imperative, or evolutionary vectors, moral precept, or what we will, we project that our courage and intelligence have the means to produce in our own person the fulfilled and realized man who has dared to embody reality in himself, not flee from it, and so has permitted reality to have real being. But what there is—we are part of what there is—is what it is regardless of us. It has real being without our help. We are whatever we are, squirm or resolve what we will to avoid it. We can make as though to run away and leave only a token of ourselves behind, but the token we leave behind is what there is. Anything else is pretense and subterfuge. We need not want anything; nothing needs us to want.

There are things which we feel, certain angers, rejoicings, fears. These feelings astonish us. Set beside our expectation of a real world, they seem not to have the habit of reality. They seem unrelated, and there is a lapse of time before we take them as real in the absence of a more expected reality. We learn at last, and accept the learning at last, that these feelings come to us without our willing or acceding or inventing. They come from beyond our skin like approaches to us, like messages; and we respond, trembling and shaking, or vibrating in tune as though we were instruments a music were played on and we arch and turn to have the contact closer. Our responses are presences that tower around us, seemingly solid as stone.

WILLIAM BRONK

Conjectural Reading

I read it wrong. It wouldn't help to say
I didn't invent the reading, that all I did
was read it the way that anyone else would read,
the way that tradition established, the only way
so far as any one knew. I read it so wrong
that—Is there tradition?—the idea seems dubious.
Who is the *everyone else* that reads, and who,
indeed, is the *I* to be wrong? It might be said
—Lew used to say it—I wasn't even wrong.

Oh, it was *rational* as the term says,
meaning: I am; the world is;
there are other people; and they are; we begin
and end; there is a middle somewhere between;
in the middle something happens and this is the point;
we are measured by that and add our measure to all.

The trouble with rational is, it seems to make sense,
in the end it doesn't make any sense at all.

Conjectural reading and reason reading from that.
We read the language wrong. These words are not
the words; syntax misses. May I hear it again?
There has to be some way to read so it says:
it is unmeasurable; the whole is here;
there is nothing to come; it neither was nor will be.

Of the Natural World

Of the natural world, nothing is possible
but praise if we speak at all. We can be still.

The steadiest speakers are quiet after a time.

I could be quiet now and not wait for the time
when the quiet comes except that so little sound
is hardly to be heard in the loud joy of the world
and I get impatient and practice the world's sound.

The Abnegation

I want to be that Tantalus, unfed
forever, that my want's agony declare
that such as we want has nothing to say to the world;
if the world wants, it nothing wants for us.
Let me be unsatisfied. Hearing me scream,
spare me compassion, look instead at man,
how he takes handouts, makeshifts, sops
for creature comfort. I refuse. I will not
be less than I am to be more human, or less
than human may be to seem to be more than I am.
I want as the world wants. I am the world.

ACHILLES FANG

An Apology

G. W. F. Hegel, whose *reductio ad absolutum* tolled the bell for
speculative philosophy and rang in Logical Positivism, and whose hop-
skip-&-jump dialectics acted as a spiral wheel (a definite improvement
on the mesmerizing back-&-forth pendulum of Chinese non-philosophy)
to set in perpetual motion the austere law of historical materialism
(to the delight of Chinese Marxists), made the irreverently profound
statement about Confucius (551-479):

> Confucius is a pragmatic sage who has nothing whatsoever to do with
> speculative philosophy,—but merely good and even excellent moral
> precepts, from which there is nothing special for us to learn. Compare
> Cicero's *De Officiis*,—we certainly have more and better books of
> moral preachings than all the books of Confucius. On the basis of his
> own works we may rightly say that it would have been better for his
> reputation if they had never been translated.
>
> (*Lectures on the History of Philosophy*

We may or may not agree that Cicero *et al.* are better than the twenty
books of the *Analects*, but the man with the greatest comic gift amongst

362

all the philosophers (according to Bertolt Brecht, who adds that Socrates is Hegel's equal) did not go too far astray when he rejected Confucius, who "has the most conical hodpiece of confusianist heronim and that chuchuffuous [曲阜 ch'u-fu, Confucius' native place in the kingdom of Lu鲁, where Mt. Taishan is] chinchin [請請 ch'ing-ch'ing] is like a footsey [夫子 fu-tzu] kumgoloo [孔…] around Taishantyland" (*Finnegans Wake*, p. 131) and "who was Chung Ni 仲尼 " (E. P., *Cantos* 76 & 53).

Brecht may not have had in mind the *Tao-te ching* of Confucius' senior contemporary when he wrote:

> I would be glad to be wise.
> The old books tell us what wisdom is:
> Avoid the world's contention,
> Live out your little time,
> Fearing no one,
> Using no violence,
> Returning good for evil —
> Not fulfilment of desire but forgetfulness
> Passes for wisdom.
> But none of this can I do:
> Dark indeed are the times I live in.

This "wisdom" has very much the ring of Chapter 80, say, or chapters 65, 68, 8, 7, 50, 55, 42, 63, 64, of the book attributed to Lao-tzu ("Forgetfulness," an important theme in *Chuang-tzu*, is not emphasized in the *Tao-te ching*). Is Lao-tzu's pragmatic wisdom, then, any more acceptable than that of Master (fu-tzu) K'ung?

The truth of the matter is that the *Analects* is a book for slaves and the *Tao-te ching* for sovereigns; the former is a sort of Castiglione's *Il Cortegiano* and the latter Machiavelli's *Il Principe*. Neither has anything to do with philosophy, speculative or otherwise. Sanctified and even deified as the two men are, they offer us nothing remotely resembling philosophy; to be sure, the *Tao-te ching* does seem to contain snatches of the speculative, but they sound sublime only because writers of hagiography have misinterpreted such passages and the tribes of sinologists and asinologists have mistranslated them. In short, the terms "Confucianism" and "Taoism" have no philosophical significance.

If the *Analects* with its twenty books consisting of about four hundred ninety chapters is too fragmentary, the eighty-one short chapters, mostly rhymed, of the *Tao-te ching* are scarcely more sustained, for they contain many repetitions and are often badly written. In fact, some iconoclastic vernacular scholars who date Lao-tzu's book from the second century B.C. are not too wide of the mark. Contrary to the uncritical belief that Chuang-tzu was inspired by Lao-tzu, the case is quite the opposite.

We know little of Lao-tzu and no more of Chuang-tzu, a junior contemporary of Mencius (372–289), beyond what we hear of him throughout the book attributed to him. Of the thirty-three chapters of the book a large number were written by followers or forged by semiliterate scribes, especially those chapters and passages that are lucid and that appeal to our lower instincts. There is, however, little doubt that the greater part of the first seven chapters are Chuang-tzu's own contribution. Whether Chapter 17 was actually written by him is a moot point; we cannot doubt, however, that it projects the spirit of the first seven chapters and clarifies certain ambiguities and obscurities in them. The language of Chapter 17 is sustained and powerful. Whether the following translation does justice to the wonderful writer, who has been *the* source of inspiration for all Chinese writers of standing, the translator cannot claim; it is hoped that it is no worse than other versions. The only claim would be that it is meant to be more accurate.

Editor's apology to translator & readers. Accompanying this text were careful and complete textual annotations, explaining various possible readings and elaborating certain passages as well as relating them to other sections of *Chuang-tzu* and the Chinese canon. These notes merit eventual publication, but their presence would dog the reader, I feel, and detract in the end from attending to the text itself, which must bear its difficulties even as the original does.

CHUANG – TZU
Chapter 17
Autumn Flood (Ch'iu-Shui)

1

1.

Autumn flood in season came: all hundred
tributaries poured into the Yellow River,
its rampageous flow so extended neither
ox nor horse could be seen on the River's
other side or on the banks of any islet
in it. There and then the Liege Lord of
the River, riding high, congratulated himself
upon having assumed complete possession
of all the bounty of the world. Going down
stream he went East until he reached the

North Sea. Then gazing Eastward
strained to look upon the water's end, but in vain.

2.

There and then was the Liege Lord of
the River confounded and crestfallen,
and he turned to the Overlord of the
North Sea with heavy sigh saying: "The
commonplace—'Having hearkened unto
Tao a hundred times, he thought himself
incomparable'—describes me only too
well. I hardly used to believe my ears
when I'ld hear someone belittling
Chung-ni's great wisdom or disparaging
Po-i's high principles. But now that
I have seen your immensity, it would
have been pathetic if I had not come
to your gate: I would have remained
forever a figure of ridicule to
the intelligent."

3.

The Overlord of the North Sea said: "A frog
living in a well cannot be told of the
ocean, for its habitat limits it; nor can
an insect flourishing in summer be told
of winter's ice, for the season sways it;
an opinionated fool cannot be told of Tao,
for he is bound by one doctrine or another.
Now that you have moved beyond the shores
and reaches of the River to be graced with
sight of the Great Sea and are abashed,
you *can* be told of the Great Verities.

4.

"Of all the waters of the world none greater
are there than the Seas. Ten thousand rivers
flow into them incessantly, yet they never
run over; the Wei-lü drains them continually,
yet they never go dry. Their volume remains

365

unchanged regardless of spring or fall, stays
unaffected by flood and drought. Immeasurable
their superiority to trickles like the Great
River or the Yellow River. But I have never
gloried in this for I, whose form is moulded
by Heaven and Earth and whose life-breath is
endowed by Yin and Yang, am poised between
Heaven and Earth as a pebble or shrub is
on a great mountain. Compelled to see
how open I am to ridicule, how can I
then glory in it?

5.

"Wouldnt you agree that the Four Seas
lying between Heaven and Earth are like
eddies in a vast backwater and the Middle
Kingdom set within the Seas like a kernel
in the royal granaries? The world has ten
thousands of things and man is merely one
of the host and he lives only in that part
of the Nine Provinces where grains are
grown and boats and carts can go, isnt man
as one of the ten thousands like the tip
of the hair of a horse? What the Five
Legendary Emperors put their minds to,
what the founders of the Three Dynasties
labored for, what men of profound feeling
were concerned about and what men in
high position sought, was limited to
themselves alone. Po-i was reputed
honorable and Chung-ni reckoned
most learned: instances of those who
enjoyed great reputation. Is this
any different from your former
self-congratulation?"

6.

The Liege Lord of the River asked:
"Should I then regard Heaven and Earth
as great and the tip of the hair of
a horse as trivial?"

7.

The Overlord of the North Sea replied:
"No, not at all. Things are such
that their precise capacity is immeasurable,
their particular occurrence indivisible,
their peculiar portion inexplicable, and
their especial Coming-into-being and
Passing-away indeterminable. Thus,
a man of much knowledge, having
considered the far and the near, does
not scorn the smallness of one thing
nor glory in the largeness of another,
for he knows that precise capacity is
immeasurable; having studied past and present,
he does not fret about the indeterminability
of any length of time or eat his heart out
over anything's transiency, for he knows
that any particular occurrence is indivisible;
having examined the principle of
fulness and emptiness, he does not
rejoice in success or grieve over
disappointment, for he knows indeed
how inexplicable is any one's portion;
having arrived at a clear view of
the Open Road, he neither exults in life
nor desponds over death, for he knows
indeed that one's especial Coming-into-being
and Passing-away is indeterminable.

8.

"But, then, the aggregate of man's knowledge
is far less than his ignorance and the
length of his life shorter than the
period before his birth. He, however,
in his extreme littleness attempts to
explore the realm of the greatest
magnitude. No wonder he is confused
and confounded, bogged and bewildered.
From this point of view, who can be sure
that Heaven and Earth delimit the realm
of the greatest magnitude or that the

tip of a hair defines the most
minute?"

9.

The Liege Lord of the River said: "Most
would have it that what is finest is
formless and what is greatest is
beyond encompassing.
Is this true?"

10.

The Overlord of the North Sea replied:
"One who is small can never see a
large object in its entirety; one
who is large can never see a small object
in all its detail. A speck, smallest of
all small things, and the wall of the
city, largest of all large things, each
requires a scale of its own; this is
only natural. The terms 'fine' and
'coarse' may be applied to any thing;
but it is impossible to count what
has no form or limit what cannot be
encompassed. What is coarse can be
captured in words and what is fine
comprehended by intelligence; where
'fine' or 'coarse' cannot be said of
something, then it is indefinable
and beyond the mind's reach.

11.

"So the Great Man in his daily conduct
will not resort to hurting others, but
not pride himself either on being
humane and decent; what he does he
does not do for profit, but he does not
despise profiteers; he does not strive
for wealth, but does not think himself
virtuous for yielding the field to
others; in managing his affairs, he

tries not to use others, but he does
not boast of being independent; (he
steers clear of avarice and fraud),
but he does not despise those who are
insatiable and corrupt; if his daily
conduct varies from the conventional,
he does not pride himself on being
eccentric; if he finds himself with
and meets the multitude, he does not
look down on the time-servers and
sycophants amongst them; no status
or bonus will induce him to change
his mind, nor will death or disgrace
bring him to entertain dishonor. He
knows full well, indeed, that right
or wrong can never be determined
and small or large never finally
discriminated. There is, you know,
the saying: 'The Man of Tao no one
hears of, the Man of True Worth
no one gazes at; the Great Man has
no self of his own.' Such is the
utmost statement of distinction."

12.

The Liege Lord of the River asked: "How,
then, are the intrinsic value and
precise magnitude of the ten
thousands of things, to say nothing
of all that transcends this world,
to be determined?"

13.

The Overlord of the North Sea replied:
"From the point of view of Tao, things
have no high or low value; each from
its own standpoint believes itself
high and others proportionately lower;
in daily life the value put upon one
is not determined by oneself but by
others. Differentiation amongst the

ten thousands of things as to large
and small depends upon each thing's
own scale of regard; if Heaven and Earth,
say, are thought of as kernels of corn
and the tip of a hair as a mountain top,
the real differences between things become
apparent. As to utility, each of
the ten thousands of things has or
hasnt it to the extent that it believes
itself having or not having it; if we
recognize that East and West, although
they are set one against the other,
cannot negate each other, the true
utility of each becomes distinct. As to
character, each of the ten thousands of
things is right or wrong, insofar as it
so regards itself; if we realize that
Yao and Chieh were what they were
because they couldnt help it and that
one cannot be criticized by the other's
standards, the actual character of
each thing becomes clear. In bygone days
Yao and Shun humbly refused the throne
but became emperors nevertheless, Chih
and K'uai humbly declined it too and
their lines were broken; T'ang and Wu
contended for kingship and became kings,
Po-kung also contended for it and was
destroyed. This is to show that acts of
humble refusal or contention, and the deeds
of a Yao or a Chieh, may be of either high
or low value, depending upon occasion;
there is no rule in this.

14.

"A roof-beam may shatter a city wall, but
not plug up a hole; as a tool it has limited
application. A Bucephalus or Pegasus may
cover a thousand li a day, but arent up
to a wild cat in catching rats; their skills
are incommensurable. At night an owl can
snap up a flea or detect the tip of a hair,

in broad daylight it gapes at a mountain
blindly; its own powers are incommensurable.
So the question arises: Why should anyone
praise right and attack wrong? Why should
anyone praise peace and order, and attack
disorder? Such a person is ignorant of
the principle governing Heaven and Earth
and of the true nature of the ten thousands
of things. It is like praising Heaven and
attacking Earth, like praising Yang and
attacking Yin; it is clear that this
wont do. A person who, nevertheless, will
speak of the one only without recognizing
the other is either a fool or a knave.
Fact is that the Emperors and Sovereigns
did not have one and the same procedure
for nominating successors to their thrones,
nor the Three Dynasties one and the same
procedure for choosing heirs; those whose
actions did not conform to the practices
of their times were called usurpers,
while those who found themselves conforming
to the current practice were called
legitimate. Best be still, my Lord of
the River. How can you distinguish
between the gate that opens upon high value
and that upon low, between the house of
the small and that of the great?"

15.

The Liege Lord of the River asked:
"What am I to do then? Or what am I
not to do? What stand should I end up
taking in regard to rejecting or
accepting, advancing or turning
back?"

16.

The Overlord of the North Sea said: "From
the standpoint of Tao, how can anything be
regarded as having low or high value at all?
Confusion is the rule in this world. So

dont order your thoughts too nicely or
you'll find yourself at odds with Tao.
Again, how can anything be regarded
as meagre or abundant? Imbrication
is the rule in this world. Dont try,
then, to be too consistent in your behavior
or you'll find yourself contradicting
Tao.

17.

"Magisterial as the sovereign of a state,
it has no private virtue; eternal as
the altar whereon rites of sacrifice
are performed, it has no private
sanctity; vast as the immensity of
horizon at all four quarters, it has no
line by which to be defined; as it encompasses
and embraces the ten thousands of
things, what is there to assist or
support it? This is what is known as
the 'Uncharted.' All the ten thousands
of things being of one and the same measure,
how can one be regarded as inferior and
another superior?

18.

"Tao—being beyond beginning or ending—:
the Coming-into-being and the Passing-away
of things are brought about by it, but
neither their waxing nor waning controlled
by it. The year cannot be retarded,
nor the four seasons halted. Increase
decrease, wax wane: anything that ends
must have begun. Thus may we discourse
of the mystery of the great truth and
the principle governing the ten thousands
of things. The ten thousands of things
live their lives 'on the go' like
horses; on no occasion do they stay
unchanged, at no time do they remain
undriven. What are you to do? What are

you not to do? Let things
take their course."

19.

The Liege Lord of the River asked:
"If so, of what value is Tao?"

20.

The Overlord of the North Sea said:
"One who knows of Tao is certain to be
aware of the Principle, one who is
aware of the Principle is certain
to be conversant with Contingency,
and one conversant with Contingency
does not destroy himself for the sake
of things that lie beyond him.

21.

"The Man of utmost attainment is neither
scathed by fire nor drowned by water,
he does not suffer from heat or cold,
nor is he prey for birds and beasts.
This does not mean that he is always
on the look-out for trouble; it simply
means that he has looked into the issue
of risk and security and no longer concerned
over good or bad luck, is leery of running
ahead or turning back, so nothing can
ever hurt him. Hence the saying: 'Heaven
within, Man out; attainment depends on
Heaven.' One who knows the difference
between the conduct of Heaven and
that of Man will base himself
on Heaven and take his stand
on attainment, bends or unbends with
due deliberation and discussion of
the Limits of the Principle by
reverting to the Essential.'"

22.

(The Liege Lord of the River) asked:
"What is Heaven and what is Man?"

23.

The Overlord of the North Sea replied:
"An ox or horse with four legs is Heaven,
harnessing the horse's head or piercing
the ox's nose is Man. Hence the saying:
'Dont destroy Heaven for the sake of
Man, dont destroy your life for the
sake of your intellect, dont martyr
yourself for the sake of glory.
Abide by this undeviating and you will
revert to the True.'"

2

1.

Unipede admires Centipede which admires
Snake which admires Wind which admires
Eye which admires Mind.

2.

Unipede says to Centipede: "With my one
leg I manage by hopping along. What else
can I do? You, sir, have so many feet
to run on. How come?" Centipede
replies: "It's not what you think. You've
seen a man sneeze, havent you? Out of
the spray he lets loose there are big
drops that look pearls and small
drops more like mist; the variety
of drops falling is infinite. I
simply go as I find myself; I
dont know why it is."

3.

Centipede says to Snake: "I crawl on
many feet, yet am not near as slick as
you are who are footless. Tell me
how and why this is. Snake replies:
"When you see the nature given you,
where's there space for choice or
change? Do I need feet?"

4.

Snake says to Wind: "I creep by wriggling
my spine and ribs. And so seem to have
a most unusual shape. You, sir, however,
rise from the North Sea in a swirling
mass and sweep on in to the South Sea,
seem to have no shape at all. Tell me
how and why this is?" Wind replies:
"That's true: I do rise up in a
swirling mass from the North Sea and
sweep in to the South Sea. Anyone,
by laying a finger or setting a foot
on me can pin me down. But when it
comes to snapping a trunk of a great tree
or lifting the roof from a house,
I cant be beat.

       Point is that whatever
is lost to the least thing great victory
may still accrue; but only the wise man
gains it."

3

When Confucius was at K'uang, some
Sung troops encircled him and his
entourage. But he went right on
singing the Odes and strumming his lute.
Tzu-lu came over to him exclaiming: "Sir,
you seem to be enjoying yourself!"
Confucius said: "Listen. For a long time now
I've been trying to avoid Adversity, but

find no way to; that's Destiny. For
a long time now I've been trying to
gain Success, but to no avail; that's
Chance. Under the reign of Yao and Shun
no man in the kingdom had to face
Adversity, nor was it because of
any wisdom; under that of Chieh and Chou
no man in the kingdom enjoyed Success,
nor was it for lack of wisdom. Time
and circumstance made all the difference.
As a fisherman has courage enough to
brave crocodiles and dragons when he
plunges into the depths, as a hunter to
brave rhinoceroses and tigers when he
stalks through the jungle, and as a
hero will face death as if he were
merely on his way home when flashing blades
cross before his eyes, so your wise man
has courage enough, because he knows
Adversity is ruled by Destiny and Success
dispensed by Occasion, not to flinch
when confronted by the direst possibility.
Yu (Tzu-lu), dont worry, I'm one who lives
at Destiny's behest." Shortly thereafter,
the officer in charge, in full regalia,
came over and explained: "We thought you
were Yang Hu, and so this encirclement. But
now we are sure that you are not. Goodbye,
sir; we shall be going on now."

4

Kung-sun Lung made inquiry of Prince Mou of
Wei: "As a youngster I studied the Way of
the ancient emperors and as an adult I became
well-versed in the conduct called humane and
just, I succeeded in breaking down the seeming
differences between things and splitting up
the hardness and whiteness of rock, I affirmed
the unaffirmable and asserted the unassertable,
I dismayed the wits of the hundred and one
sophists and confuted the neat arguments of

all the polemicists; I was proud of being the
most accomplished. But now, after having
heard Chuang-tzu, I am shaken up and confused.
I wonder if my eloquence is inadequate or my
intelligence little. At any rate, I dare not
open my mouth in his presence. Why is this?"

Prince Mou, leaning on an arm-rest, first gave
a great sigh, turned his eyes to Heaven, smiling,
then said: "Havent you heard of the Frog of the
dilapidated well? He was telling a Turtle of
the Eastern Sea: 'Am I enjoying it here! I hop
about on top of the well-curb, leap in, loll
on a chunk of broken brick; I float at times
on the surface, arms paddling away, cheeks
bobbing aloft, and at times touch mud bottom,
feet sinking into it, toes buried there. I
despise your red-worm and crab and tadpole,
none of them my equal. Indeed I live and
am absolute lord of this water hole, alone
enjoy the dilapidated well; what more could
anyone ask for? Sir, come along, if you like,
and see for yourself.'

"The Turtle of the Eastern Sea had no sooner
put his left foot into the well when his
right knee was embedded; he managed to drag
himself out of it at length with difficulty.
And this misadventure soon afterwards he
related to the Liege Lord of the Eastern Sea
remarking: 'A breadth of a thousand li is
not the limit of space, nor a depth of a
thousand ells that of profundity. Nine years
out of ten were there floods in the days of
Yü, yet the water increased not in volume;
there were droughts seven out of eight years
in the time of the T'ang, yet the coasts did
not diminish. Your domain does not change or
move with time, nor does it expand or dwindle
in scope: this is the felicity of the Eastern
Sea.'

"When he heard this, the Frog of the dilapidated well was so distraught and dejected that he could do no more than blink. Knowing full well that you are ignorant of the most fundamental matters, you still dared challenge Chuang-tzu to debate; it is like asking a mosquito to bear a mountain on its back or a worm to race the Yellow River—it's too much. Also, knowing full well that you are incapable of treating of the most profound and abstruse of subjects, you were in a rush to score points; werent you like the Frog of the dilapidated well?

"And please note that Chuang-tzu is on the verge of treading the Yellow Spring and soaring to the Nine Heavens. Not limited to South or North he scours the four quarters free and unhampered, and plunges into the unfathomable; not limited to East or West, he rises from the original depths and returns to the great thorofare. And all you do is blink, trying to roust him out with your cleverness and corner him with your glibness. This is no better than hoping to spy the grandeur of Heaven through a bamboo tube or to probe the depth of Earth with a pick: how ridiculous you are. Leave me, go away. But wait, one other thing: Havent you ever heard about the boy of Shou-ling trying to ape the stride of one of Han-tan? Before he could acquire the coveted power, he had lost even his own former capacity to walk; all he could do was crawl home. If you dont leave off soon, you will forget your former ways and become estranged from your chosen profession."

Kung-sun Lung, mouth-open and tongue-tied, fled.

5

Chuang-tzu was angling along the bank of
the P'u. The king of Ch'u had despatched
a pair of courtiers to him with the
message: "It would please me if you were
to concern yourself with the administration
of my kingdom." Rod in hand, Chuang-tzu
did not even turn his head in answering:
"I am told that in Ch'u there is an exalted
tortoise, dead some three thousand years
now, which the king keeps in the Ancestral
Shrine, laid out in a bamboo receptacle
swathed in gorgeous silks. Now, tell me,
do you think this tortoise would have preferred
being the honored cadaver it is, or
being alive dragging its tail through the
mud?" Both courtiers replied: "It would
have preferred being alive and dragging
its tail through the mud." Chuang-tzu
said: "You may go, gentlemen. I shall go
on dragging my tail through the mud."

6

While Hui-tzu was Chief Minister of the
kingdom of Liang, Chuang-tzu decided to
go visit him. Someone, thereupon,
reported to Hui-tzu: "Chuang-tzu is coming
to replace you as Chief Minister." That
shook Hui-tzu and for three days and three
nights he had the kingdom scoured for the
man. Eventually Chuang-tzu turned up and
said: "Down South there is a bird known
as the Phoenix. Have you heard of it?
Well, this Phoenix sets out from the South
Sea and heads for the North Sea; it rests
only on wu-t'ung trees, it feeds only on
bamboo seeds, it drinks only of pure spring
water. Now, there was an Owl who was the
proud possessor of a stinking Mouse. While
the Phoenix was flying by, the Owl spotted

379

it and squawked 'Shoo!' Are you trying to
shoo me out of the kingdom of Liang?"

7

Chuang-tzu and Hui-tzu were walking across
the sluice-way over the Hao when Chuang-tzu
remarked: "The trout swim about with such
ease and grace; they must be enjoying themselves."
Hui-tzu retorted: "You're not a fish,
how can you know that they're enjoying
themselves?" Chuang-tzu answered: "You're
not me, how can you know that I dont know
they're enjoying themselves?" Hui-tzu
replied: "I grant that, not being you I
cant know what you do. But, you are not
the fish either and so it is quite indisputable
that you cannot know if the fish are enjoying
themselves." Chuang-tzu said: "Let's start
from the start again. When you asked me,
'How can you know that the fish are enjoying
themselves?' you did so because you felt you
knew—though you are not me—what I might
or might not know about the fish. And I
knew about the fish—without being one,
of course—through walking across the
sluice-way over the Hao."

CID CORMAN

In the hills
for a few days—
couldnt write

Gone further found
less—maybe
you know the place.

_____

380

The cry
is the
breath

So vast
cannot
wait.

WILLIAM BRONK
Writing You

What I should do is phone; the circuitry
is there and we're both somewhere in the circuitry.
I need to talk. What should I find to say?
You know how it is: it rings; you answer; no click;
no dial tone. Hello? Hello? No word.
Not even goodbye,—I couldn't give you that.

Listen to this: to write you requires a scheme,
subtends an apparatus, such that here
be an I, you be he there, space
discerns the entities, depicts them such
as the scheme requires. Are you lost? I am.
I want to be not lost. I write even so.

Tell me what to do. I want to show.
Schemelessness. Undress. To speak from that.
I want the secrecy; I want it said.
To speak from wordlessness. There are certain things
that happen and we don't know: proteins meet
and shape each other. We are the husk of this.

Whatever happens happens in some such wise,
under attention. I hate all huskiness.
Let me be where it happens, let me be the hidden cells
and silent if silence is all there is to say.
I want to talk though. I want to talk to you.
I despair of what to say. Goodnight. Goodnight.

I Thought It Was Harry

Excuse me. I thought for a moment you were
    someone I know.

It happens to me. One time at The Circle
        in the Square
when it *was* still in the Square, I turned my head
when the lights went up and saw me there with a girl
and another couple. Out in the lobby, I looked
right at him and he looked away. It was no
        one he knew.
Well, it takes two, as they say, and I don't know what
it would prove anyway. Do we know who we are
do you think? Kids seem to know. One time I asked
a little girl. She said she'd been sick. She said
she'd looked different and felt different. I said,
"Maybe it wasn't you. How do you know?"
"Oh, I was me," she said, "I know I was."
That part doesn't bother me any more,
or not the way it did. I'm nobody else
and nobody anyway. It's all the rest
I don't know. I don't know anything.
It hit me. I thought it was Harry when I saw you
and thought, "I'll ask Harry." I don't suppose
he knows, though. It's not that I get confused.
I don't mean that. If someone appeared and said,
"Ask me questions," I wouldn't know where to start.
I don't have questions even. It's the way I fade
as though I were someone's snapshot left in the light.
And the background fades, the way it might if we woke
in the wrong twilight and things got dim and grey
while we waited for them to sharpen. Less and less
is real. No fixed point. Questions fix
a point, as answers do. Things move again
and the only place to move is away. It was wrong:
questions and answers are what to be without
and all we learn is how sound our ignorance is
That's what I wanted to talk to Harry about.
You looked like him. Thank you anyway.

Something Like Tepees

Glances and recollections, letters of sorts
is what we get from each other. Rose called.

I had forgotten. Well, no I hadn't. I'd stopped
expecting. We learn. Not much. Not finally.

We learn. That we aren't, as we thought we were, alone.
There are others here. All right. It isn't much.

Remember once. There was a time we meant
to make something like tepees, I out of you,

you from me, and live there, make it home
as though to make a house were what we meant.

Journeys do not end in lovers meeting.
Nor end. Sometimes we touch and touch again.

DENIS GOACHER

Ab Origine

Deep there between
darling deep where
I lay as I wake
as it seems in between
death and light is it
life but I've seen
was it me were you
there was such
in dreams or they told
what we knew never had
we believed when young
nothing new for we saw
what was old all past
that a few seconds' light
if a child is sure
for we hang then so
and depend on dreams
to repeat what we knew
never found but were told
many lies of the form
it would take and we said
when young not true

we depend on our lives
to decide we'll find
once known never lost
that we'd have when we should
and the child proved right
as we knew when we saw
that the other was you
and time is the right
that we take that we look
till we find what we knew
that we said we would wait
for we'd seen only once
but enough that before
we ever knew
we were young only now
we have seen when we saw
that the other we'd known
that we'd seen when sure
that the other was always you

premature spring

scratter of birds
some preep some yawl
engines eat up the hills
with a delicate blush sky spumes
foundries overtiming
chrysalids now sticky
men sure they once were highwaymen
rain swells the western air
bulls their roaring loins

ponies thunder the forests
long hair torn by trees
and Irish green floods
dark towns with magic
new paint caresses caravans
fish outload the dories
then
the gull stands on his sky
parting like too soon spring

means
time not love is slow
to end

If Rilke Was Right

. . . Sind wir vielleicht hier, um zu sagen: Haus,
Brücke, Brunnen, Tor, Krug, Obstbaum, Fenster, —
höchstens: Säule, Turm . . . aber zu sagen, verstehs,
oh zu sagen so, wie selber die Dinge niemals
innig meinten zu sein . . . .

—Die Neunte Elegie

If Rilke was right, here to praise
"House, Jug, Fountain, Bridge,
Window — possibly Tower."
how many houses, paths leading
leave before will shall die?
When did I first know "house"
distinct from corridor, stair?
Young, never lived in a house
but stairs knew well and doors
of home and neighbours' lodging,
so probably thought —
"My house? — third floor right
east end of the bridge" —
made to praise then
would've glorified bridge not house.

But I found it in the same half-town
left by a sea captain uncle:
that garden stuffed with nasturtium, briar rose,
grew devotion
to standards of blood and sun
carefree there as dancing imagined
through eglantine.
Inappropriate name: "The Anchorage."

Having no house I broke a jug.
Noon. A room by the river.
This only time I ever caught a fish
I ran for help seeing blood

unnerved broke my mother's new jug
slopped water to wash that mouth
too inept to unhook and give him his river.

But, who has not learnt passionately
soon enormity of windows?
High above a snow-wrapped square,
waiting for proof afternoon
had declined, we knew, to evening—
snow, glass, watch, ever—
then climb years till it shrinks
till panes in darkening air
are beads on your sweetheart's throat,
after, keyholes to lives we long to know.

Toll gates I knew; itinerant parents.
Rivers; boats at their moorings,
rocked under tunnels
flicking gleams with a silver knife—
how bridges alter when we're over
sometimes in three strides
rise-descend
like dreams of flight, slow.

Saw her, once, in a scarlet hat,
whose trail among lions and silent fountains
drew many pictures on Nelson's square
one bitter Sabbath March afternoon.

Towers now
loom lost in literature:
great Henry James his Ivory
Yeats' symbolic "half dead at the top"
dental domain of Giant Decay
Rainer Rilke's, a Swiss anachronism . . .
So come to praise the sound went thin
in Fountains Abbey.

When Rilke was right is not hard to decide.
Mankind bears the sight of horses in a lorry.

Rising

It is to do with children, with singing,
Don't waste eternity in you

All day loving as though your last
Don't waste eternity in you

Warm our blanket greener than garden
Pray dawn rising

Long pterodactyl ghosts
Envy an airplane's roar

Pray dawn rising

Death not decent, no descent,
Love each day, it is your last

Tallest tree has raised our sky
Don't waste eternity in you

Shall I speak now of youth or heaven
My left arm the river of death

When blackbird's one with wet earth bank
Beak's quick light

Don't waste eternity in you

Where shone aureolas of dandelions
They tried garlands for size

Pray dawn rising,
It is to do with children, with singing

JEAN DAIVE

décimale blanche
(white decimal)

at the edge of

———————————

I drifted
between refusal and insistence
looking at everywhere

snow
the name unmaking form
origin/avalanche
               remaking absence

———————————

separate
   for ever   apparent   discovered

cleared

porous

in silence
in sickness

     and possessing the gift of breath
               the gift of healing

while I skirted time
                    to reattain the attribute

———————————————

(the initiate
in the separation
reconsiders all knowing

the dead
is embedded in annihilation
in the circle of all attitudes
and seeks to escape
the state of unfulfilment

———————————————

only my body
and what is outside
the physical motion of my fall

  parcels of emptiness
dividing visits hearths globes

    the labyrinth
of an unfulfilled attitude
is the clew of all labyrinths

            its transfiguration
            within death)

———————————————

peaceful as embrace

            the voice the pivot

———————————————

where one of shadow is declared C.

now
time effaces the mortal fable

———————————

the old woman tossed my voice away

unearth she says
unearth

      it snows
           below the bowl
           snow body of the summit

the old woman is four times

———————————

the race awaited one of shadow
and wanted to call him C.

one of one appeared
and C. was his name

———————————

I was at once this fire before her
      the race already
      beyond the cinder
      kneeling in the cold

———————————

I walk to get going

lit from below through death
was I   ever   whiteness

———————————

I heard weeping in the race adjacent
                    hear
unearth unearth

hear man
in his isolation
bemuse himself with dragon stories

———————————

she says
white is not the division of four grays by
zero but the division of their decimals by zero

———————————

                time lours
and I quiver through the flame

the bowl is empty
where she drank with the race

———————————

it is said that transparency comes from above
hers came from the salt

  appeared
in the light of the four decimals of the name

  seen   called   despite

then
the blue the blue and the descent in the
                    spiral of the name
by the cry's counterweight

———————————

I have called I have called C.
oh the alternation of blue and white in time

then

---

upon leaving absence
like a burst of laughter denying embrace
the old woman

          who is two times C. and once
              me once

---

          mother

          ma ma and me

---

sole
nul in himself
closed

he was the instant
he was who sees himself pass

white insect set within death

---

and the instant/water surprised between
          sluicegate and soffit

---

distances/embraces

        only the bowl
and anew

           immense
                  the snow
above the thirst opening upon myth

---

        in the beginning
        I was four times

        then I buried my sex
        to live in crystal

---

she disappeared
under cover of snow
to take place at depth in the void

who incarnates her name becomes decimal
she says

---

she says
I have sought the name whose spoken chain
ordains the world
animates forces/silences/speech
and possesses the whitness
of refusal and insistence

I've heard her weep within her race

---

no one knows to what she yields
when she follows and exceeds

no more does it matter that the sea is green
for the blue no longer makes us sick
she says

(she is the blue bluer than the sea)

———————————

she is the winter
    white
    the black point of the storm
    on the low horizon

(yet the snow did not make her white)

she is at the heart of the eternal
              instant whiteness

———————————

avert o vault
what dark science of the alert
detain that of the astonished
in the path of a line

what place loses her
what point finds her again

———————————

o line
what divergence knows its angle
what cry makes abyss in the voice

she calls and she calls and she rests

now that the cry has dispensed the
           voice the word

———————————

she passes far up in the sky
and reveals to me its edges its blue its stain

she is what seems never to end

blue her face
but passing way way behind
the water of her eyes

she speaks she lies she is simplified

---

divergence of no direction
image of no figure
she enters into silence
covers the polygon of death

---

she ages in the attitude of the line
and the wrinkle is the visit of her face

---

power of the first division

of the lump of earth
announcing the initiate's entry into death

formula of presences
physical formula of beginnings

the initial
opens the book the pursuit of the labyrinth
the torture
of gestures of words of attitudes
denouncing the transforming proportion

of the shadow in its shadow

the red matter of its space

---

waves of transparent earth
crepuscular
heights
that underground negations
reduplicate
        and the eye that remains in
            the dust

past
inexhaustibly
at the edge of the visible

white
of a light
without hearth without object

---

the breath succeeding memory of differences
space becomes mental
        bandage
on its horizon
torn
within
the gulf within the abyss

and I leave my look on its look
behind its face
after this world

        the void
the void
the abstract void precedes me into death

---

near possible
some thing a sign
like a statement
a very white saliva

appearance simple
            despite the matter of the name
upon leaving silence
                cold

---

lost in contemplation of its end
negation is detached from itself

and beginning in the beginning
the water that dreams of it
and disposes of it in the maze of the
                      invisible
seeks the slick perfection of the sea

on the soils (the visits)
that a dark device floods
slides a slip of water
that metamorphoses knowing
into elemental rag

---

at the base of the staircase
where the spiral lasts a moment
hesitates
staggers the step

it is the terrifying
instant whiteness

which time never resumes

---

time describes a circle in space

and space inside begins
other circles larger
other times longer

———————————

no resemblance goes back to oneself or god
no image
no silence

only the last instructs the spheres
and contains all beginning

———————————

he substitutes space for furniture
which contains all the light
he opens its infinite drawers
inhabits them
shuts them
and climbs climbs
to the closed room
where the sky seeks its stars
and the moon its tides

———————————

he looks at
the yoke lost in the lands
prolonging snow
the furrows
the black rays of the sun

things/beings hastening to one same white
point

———————————

he looks at
the universe immobilizing a phrase
(the phrase its algebra he its letters)
that silence spells/simplifies
that the voice denounces/repeats

---

repeats
for the simple sums give the surface
and the double sums the motion

---

four is the attribute of C.

---

other times
when laughter bore embrace
when blue devastated slate and sea

---

he climbed the hill again
again climbed the avalanche
where summits mingle

with this insect voice
and his face wide open

gesture unlimited
scarf knotted

---

the comb is the last degree of gesture
and I am what falls
what is added and is added no more
place of visit and place of knowing

---

named
and at once despite me
realized

in the counter-light of death

I rise from the depth of my resemblance
at the enigma's limit

night after night
I've disappeared been disappearing

it is dazzled
it falls in the tissue of cold

---

at times the return
(is it haste)
comforts the delayed

who tarries amidst
himself
the word
to take the place of absence

---

the clew
while it divulges the fable of life

amid the imaginary web

the other reveals
the eternal weaver

———————————————

    arc immense over the sea
    when the back bends
    or when gesture lifts avalanche
    when shoulder yields

———————————————

she read something about the quantum leap
she read
        without knowing
she fulfils what the lamp and the window
                begin

———————————————

amid the three glimmers

            pure lamp of no book

———————————————

far
like seeming

the white voice
what line constrained pensive
allusive to what's no longer roof/corridor

so pure

tree effaces water and there begins again

———————————

      I enter and leave
      and seek what opens and closes itself
                again

———————————

I saw vanish under the wind
the last glimmer the last night
in the lengthening of the light

then the wing was more slow
and the angle more wide

across the sky
the stain unfolded tree/water

on the other side
no leaf

———————————

dreaming the slow geometry
of flagstone and slate

what a theorem
in the discovery of what is roof/corridor

———————————

she speaks/she renews her precipices

———————————

she says
absent
she was the one of the three glimmers
remaining despite the cold
withdrawn from window and lamp

———————————————

she says
she haunted what absence no longer contains
the glimmer
that embraced it before her
she felt for a moment its unknown pain
in declaring the lamp and window innocent

JOHN TAGGART
Egg

1

Egg in a box.
Egg in a space.

The egg is in an aluminum
box
    in a room with
orange curtains
in the light

of winter without trees.

The light encloses.
The room flowers.
The egg remains.

2

    You can imagine the space
as empty.   Take away the walls
and horizon of the aluminum

room. Remove
the smooth hand from
Barcelona drawing a

four-toed horse
upon the egg.

Move the world away; put
its light in brackets.   What
remains is

the thumping of blood
vessels around your
skull, hissing

nostrils as you breathe . . .

3

                        and paler
than this paper, more brittle
than your wife's teeth upon
the glass as she drinks

water in the early morning, this

weight, this so cool
weight holding down the
skull in the box.

Winter, Radio Poem

  waiting

for friends

to

come, in-

to my right

eye, I

pump

the gas

pedal to

the radio, a song, &

like the girl

says: I

don't

know

clouds anymore.

Position

    The parade deposits

no bodies; I

walk in praise

of all metals, the

aluminum cube in

the desert

Not "for no good

reason, the fact

only," but

the hum, the

shifting

absence.

The Drum Thing
for John Coltrane

Egypt smothered.

They, bent together, a night group,
plains which fuzzed
white by hotting themselves

without an hunger whipping itself to hump
the woman died hard within herself.
The plains conceal themselves
for the desire, for the poacher their tied-down blimps
    held by
a cable, in being enormous fruit, brown pears
with an equation for the heated changes:

she dies, herself being
dead, stiffly in the old manner.

Drums.

In the morning stumbles her ghost,
the skin off the muscles,
and in moving has the skull and horns of a deer.

From the suburbs out of an old Ford others
come with her, animal shapes in walking.

A fly-covered horse hangs from
a tree in the sun, heaved
there from a swing chain, its belly ripped out, wind now.

The grey tongue of the horse has only flies.

Four day-blue shadows
themselves roll over, keep low
and in time
with the column,
with the dead moving on the plains,
stiffly, with bells, in the old manner.

The K Variations

1

The leper and his wife.

The way her behind—she
is lying

.in bed on her belly—
erupts

with purple ulcers (like
the lady ape) again

and again, although
a guest is present.

The way her husband
keeps shouting

at
her, Keep covered!

2

To
be pulled,
in, through
the ground-floor
window
of a
house
by a
rope, to
be yanked,
up, through
ceilings, the
furniture, &
attic without
consideration,
by a person
who

pays
no attention, until
the rope
breaks
through
the
roof.

3

He
walks
down the street
crosses
it
is
snowing he
has
a suit-
case a
bag in the
other hand

he
walks
the light
fades

he
walks
down it
is
a dog
rushes
at him
kicks
it in
despair the
delay.

410

JONATHAN GREENE

Where Are the Fine Lines

Where are the fine lines?
We can't lay it down so.
Let the figure have some reign
& he destroys the well-knit page,
spills over the carefully drawn borders
into another land: strange to himself
to wander there.

            Lost in a wood.
This is a fiction we imagine.   Death
in the movies, on television, in the
imagination of a dying man.   These borders
are no longer tangible.   That is fiction we imagine
is real, that a man dying alone in a wood might
experience it less.   Levels & layers removed from
what they were, a forsaken simplicity.

                        I *am* lost.
This is literal & exact.   The woods are traditional,
optional, no longer to the point.

The Author

It is his last book.
We see this end
and say *no*.   But we know
it is *yes* . . . try to spoil
a line, re-arrange pages.

    Language
without a voice MEAN
you write striving
upwards in bed.   Or later,
think to strive or speak

lost lines we cannot hear.
(You think we hear and

go on sputtering breath.)
We remember the book.
We say "at least" to his last breath.

A Small Puddle

A small puddle of phlegm or sperm in all this
sun light, a corruption in all this mindless
passivity.   Signet of an untold narrative.

Artaud studied the faceless, unformed flesh.
I too. *Eat my heart out*, living among (st),
unrecognized.

A poem full of lies, can you believe the intent
that does not rise to surface: to be a huckster
selling that pool to the backyards of America.

A Short Visit

Walking in & out of lives.
I thought the chronology always moved forward,
those places left, frozen in their place,
not the actual in front of the eyes—but I hold back
from the return, hold back the knowledge of no return,
touch the Beloved of a former life & ask her
her meaning. *Are you still waiting.*
The thought (naturally) occurred
as the could-have-been can always occur.
We choose other, choose the chronology . . .

But I wanted
a way back, wanted to feel my way
along those roads known by heart,
the ones that "could be driven blindfolded"
& were, in that life.

Touch that life.
Hold it a sweet minute & hightail it out of there,
the roads left behind for our own purposes labelled
necessary miles not *good* or *bad.*

What are the ways in.
Facts are hopeless.
I could waste night with stories
the measured distances do not know.
Do the words tell (add them up)
      what tale,
            tell me.

SEYMOUR FAUST

From the Myth of Telepinus

1

The weather changes
the cold front passes through
with winds of 40 miles an hour
    the window panes shaking in the frames
clouds move by quickly
    the rising sun
lights the sky beyond them
penetrates the higher clouds
and backlights the strata underneath
    the room is quiet
the turbulence outside

2

Now the room is empty
the foyer dark and quiet
the outer door is closed
no one loiters on the porch
only the wind and light
in the cubic courtyard
the cornice blazes at the planar blue
its floral motif
    the gate is shut

footprints mark the dust
of the pathway east

3

Let them not interfere
let them stay out of my way
he disappeared
    he went off somewhere
he was so angry
    he put his right shoe on his left foot
his left shoe on his right
he hid himself in the east
    the water vanished from the ditches
        the grain shriveled in the fields
    the cattle died
the sun dispatched his eagle
find him search him out
    outstretched
he coasted over valley
his wingtip pointed at the mountain
the streams gave back a tiny image
he didnt find him
    she sent storm to look
he hammered on his door
and no one answered
no one
in an empty house
    send the bee she said
I sent the eagle
    what good is the bee
She sent the bee
spelled his orders out
    find him
    sting him
    smear his eyes with honey
sting his feet his hands
    smear them with wax and honey
he found him in the east
he found him sleeping off his journey
he was angry waking
from those many years

O you worm
your father was a worm
you clump of nerves
blind automaton
right on the thumb
right where god touched jacob
I'll stomp your damn town into mud
no I wont
how impersonal
how nature cares for its little ones
pinhead idiot
your brains are in your ass
stupid stupid stupid
and so forth
the bee cant bring him back
the sun dispatched a man
    let him take this spring
        let him bathe him in it
    strike him
        with the eagles wing
    get him on his feet
        make him move
he took the spring
he took the eagles wing
he found him in the meadow in the grove
there where the bee had found him
    he struck him with the spring
bathed him
    in the eagles wing
You ape he cried
your father was an ape
where do you get your rights
he raged
and people died
I was asleep he said
why must I talk he said
sheep and cattle died
he bottled up the streams
    they overflowed
he caused an earthquake
6 on the Richter scale
shattered windows
shattered the houses like a pot
    and so forth

415

4

Lake Tears birds
its warblers and finches
spend bits of their fractions of time
in balsam fir
    dwarf dogwood covers its plateau
marsh plants follow underwater
its shallow slope
    in the short sharp arched
    blue needles clustering
    in the close symmetrical cone
    of branchlets
    which are the whole tree
    in the single vertical prong
    that leads its growing
    round the blue ovoid cones
    tangent and upright and apart
    the tips of the bracts its built of
    pointed with a tiny spine
    exuding a clear sperm
        the wind finds a constant incarnation
the rounded boulders cluster
Feldspar Creek its outlet stream
adds itself by the steep ravine
to Opalescent Creek
by a right angle
    by rapids and defiles it fills
Avalanche Lake
    Over the boards of a spillway
Lake Colden
    by a right angle
by rapids and defiles
    descends
from the flowed lands there
becomes a torrent
filled with its giant stones

DENIS GOACHER

Cauchemar Espagnol

Because of the bells I left.
Loud, swift and insolent
As bitter women of middle years
Chagrin and yellowing breasts
Accusing finger and eye
Chickens in rout with clanging tongues.

I flew up into the hills
Certain it should not be Sunday:
The wine was prickly, bread a day old,
But plums like young Arab girls:
The sea-sound was more than a prayer
And dried salt served for oblation.

Past noon on a half-shade terrace
Grew round me the tomb of black sleep:
A stallion of burning copper
Raced, cased in silent screams
Down the evil Roman road
Mane tossed high, the maize waved,

Green whorls cracked by drum beats
Sky a single sun
The air spins with fucking flies
The mad straight road flees from me
My hooves fight, fight for sound,
To drown the tolling in swollen ears—

The almond trees! The Almond trees!
Their blossoms hideous bells
The hard green cases burst
By the clappers of pounding bells
And my brazen stallion shrieks
And my hooves can make no sound.

When I woke sea-song was calm
Calm as the stones, the sheep,
The tower and time-deserted farm;

My ruined mind mute in the skull,
I tasted salt and prayed for fruit,
Cold green fruit from the underworld.

Log Book

If not love what grinds our week?
Trees blaze, fire-flies glowing,
a sense of nature's yearning
to explode—that love I speak
of's anger, real pride:
we must
sling out anguish, ennui, slide
to dimensions known—
fervid life in a fir cone,
see brightness magpies see,
walk those halls down an owl's eyes,
initiate of crows' valley,
all pre-dawn's hermetic cries—
is it not of love I speak?-
So we'll live another week?

Black Redstart

Firetail
linney nor shippon has
bed for
under their constellations

Wrecked about sky
some lovers!
That synod of poets'll
filch sweet note
the first falters—
they like you sing
orchard or ruin
soon—save self!
Bryony guards her berry

Starfinch
this wall old enough?
nest in my heart
know stone

though apple dying
grass water trees consort

Come redstart here!
find wall and
nest your heart
my wall
heart

WILLIAM BRONK

The Mask the Wearer of the Mask Wears

Yes, look at me; I am the mask it wears,
as much am that which is within the mask.
Nothing not mask but that.   That every mask.

The mask will fall away and nothing lost.
There is only the mask-wearer, the self-aware,
the only aware, aware of only the self.

Awake, it dreams: is every character;
is always more; is never only that.
It contemplates; tries any mask of shape.

Any is nothing. Any is not what is.
But that it should be.   That it should seem to be.
That it be no more than that, and yet should be.

And that it turn to look, look favorably,
look lovingly, look long, on what there is.

419

CID CORMAN

In Answer

The point is
not ourselves,
not me—nor—

as it turns
out—you. Then—
we ask—Who?

No who, no
what, no known,
and nothing

to be known.
No point. And
none in this.

And never-
theless, this.
Speak to man.

DAPHNE MARLATT

Letter to Cid Corman

3577 W. 31st Ave.
Vancouver 8, B.C.
November 3/68

dear Cid,

Sunday, & the fire in grate burning above a mass of cinders the
kitten is staring into. Friday, Saturday sunny & chill, most of the
leaves fallen now, or those still hanging almost transparent in
their yellow—had never thought before of that kind of leaf also
"yellowed with age" (or to be *read* as such). Sunny days are cause
for celebration here: one learns to drop schedules & rush into the
outdoors. Walked a few feet from the sea today. Both of us had
almost forgotten that clarity of water (high tide stared into from
embankment) & that familiar odour of salt-rotted logs, the beaches
were habitually filled with driftwood from the booms...

Also want to enclose some recent poems. Haven't been writing
much since we arrived, partly because what little energy I have right
now is going into the teaching. I get much too involved with just
one course, & have to teach myself to reserve something. Have been
learning that I can go in "unprepared" & have a good discussion about
a story, better perhaps than otherwise since I've no place in mind
that I feel we "ought" to get to. The exciting thing of course is the
mutual discovering—& best of all as the class dwindles, those who
are staying really do want to talk.

Yes, what you say about play, children playing, makes sense to me.
& what you say about freedom, most importantly, the capacity to
move with joy as you put it despite conditions. In & despite. In,
because children really do use whatever is at hand. ok,
improvisation. There is something in play that is joyous & totally
absorbing & refreshing to the player, that is, unlike work, play
restores or recycles energy) in that it stems from the self without
strain, without reflection (self-consciousness): a total response of the
being, or something like it. From something larger than the parts

we know of ourselves. Especially the parts that subject themselves
to obligation, whether put on us or made up by us.

And so, from that, knowing? as realization (recognition)—language.
What it is we do, or feel or think etc. What it is. i.e. it is. & not the
"like," which I was wrong to use—that is where language flounders.
Your "away from" or "out of" bringing me back to what you said of
fire: utterance, "the going forth of substance." Which is something
deep in us: they spoke in tongues, tongues of flame, the fire sings.

Why conflagration is a terrible roaring, lunatic,
raving—where language is lost from meeting ground.

love to you both
Daphne

How was the bread? Blessings.

Readings

rain ge
rainiums
dried out

shrouds

fog's dis
embody stalks

if trees, dilute
solutions of them
selves salvage

limits of
a ten
        sion

can eye
appraise what
fog says

only now

Postcard frm a Distance

wd the kookaburra, some
exotic, crest, all
zebra feathered, beak
too curved for

        humming bird's
        thought "honey birds"

in the well of some
profuse
bruise

masquerade?

no answers white
distance lies
its long neck tokens

        "not well"
        not much more than
        nots
            thunderbird or
        woodpecker wd
        peck

dry blood?
rust?
nevertheless

its black eye speaks
too proud for words.

Moon Moon

eyes at the
page, hand

wobbles its
shadow, it's

cast
     (broke
spells

who's eyes to
see by?

Grin

yr eyes' grey
     green eyes
10 stories up
frm false creek haze

(sun february spring?
promise

"all gravy" grey
distance only
imaginary

       up
       false creek mist/

frm here on in
i'll call yr eyes'
haze heat's
early green.

Green

cap
    tivates
small wings' yellow
baring

beard
      (cloud behind
accumulates day
wings on what

she tears out of eye
shot shoots or
rapidly fractures

    ox y
    genate
    each
    cell

her breath moves
toward, bedding
chlorophyll restores

suspiration, his, in
ternal grow
            (she does
wings toward

    read,

day's downpour

Letter to Cid Corman

                                 June 2/69
dear Cid,
       no spate of poems about the baby yet. He *is* a poem.
You're right abt the dance, we go thru at every nursing, a number of
alternatives all response, to his sleepiness or gas (comical grimace
of refusal) or need to be changed. Learning what things to do in the
face of his not being able to tell me, yet. Tho in the last 2 weeks
he's widening his range of vocalizations: now includes PLEASURE
sounds, burbles. Best of all in terms of person keys, the long
shuddering sniffs after a crying jag: to comfort himself? That comfort
so much there, a bodily oneness we lose being able to think of our
bodies.

I'm enclosing something begun in Napa, worked here. Mokelumne
Hill is a small one-street town on 49, in the gold hills, typical historic
flavour. Centre a hotel goes back decades, we stayed at. Montage:
trying more & more to get at that reality we live in several
referential planes at any one moment.

425

...Re basic babyishness: finally getting over emotional regression—
blues after original high in wch I last wrote.   Came to the point I
cdn't listen to him cry without crying too, such patent misery.   Joy
& sadness at a very surface level, began to cry when the dr. suggested
he'd keep me in the hosp.   another day!   Felt no distance frm
anything, certainly not frm Christopher, in wch to objectify, think
abt what was happening—feeling response immediate &
overwhelming. In some ways a renewal of energies, no drain in
speculation.   Hmm, in words like fountain, or pouring out, realized
must be connected with the milk coming in...

love

Daphne

Mokelumne Hill

Of orange trees (angelica) see green: as what the eye needs
morning when oil glazes skin. heat. (of the day's not to be
yet) this freshness, freshet, water—lifting the glass to lips
—comes on a sweet taste

        after sour? Night. Night's
mouth sour—grapes at not being able to . . . Repeat: they
had got up first. Our entrance frm hall must (frm the
dark) have struck them as blind, day begun some hours
already. We see them small with table between, engaged
in some kind of close . . . "Let's' move out to the verandah"
...morning. Hits the face. Or does he see them close?
(Or even notice) Our choosing of seats conservative
(stumble): each woman between two men or the reverse.
Corners. Each to his own place.

        Their faces filled with sun
raise distance (blank wall ahead): A turning towards me
(not) cd watch trees, past D's head to the building's end;
C opposite has that surge in full vision; D also turning
towards—green heaves—a green eye juggles with

        this
HEAT: skin exposed glance made no comment on: Heat's
small sweat beads over the forehead upper lip. Of orange
angelica see green: water we last night swam in, A & me, in

silence shine. Two women down there with kids undress
voices rise (splash) nonsensical (what to do in this heat)
their children calling, see me see me . . .
                                    to preserve
(angelica) moment of falling.

. . . up some hours already. (what have YOU done with yr
dawn?) Can be clarity at this hour, here only, white, siding
behind C's head (or tipsy leaning?), 4, geometric on 4 legs
rickety each on flooring (at the mouth of minehead
                                        on
pickaxes: some a little drunk their grins or tipsy leaning,
lean over, falling. she. Was stung by insult or. bore him
heavily to the point: In the photograph small. stands
solemnly contained, one man's arm hung easily round her
neck . . .
        Yesterday dusty as what lies in the town museum
after (night's excitement). Little boots. Even axes look
small. Or a revolver, fits in the palm almost miniature.

                        Surely it's the aftertaste in mouth
that wakes us, gone sour.

. . . climbed the hill looking for coffee. no place open even
(sounds of the street: a bell) dog only solitary (tolls, heat
takes its toll) a morning kitchen help might sleep. Angelus.
Some inevitable pacing of the day here (their plates of ham
lookt good)

            slam: screen door air wisp hair, tired face, or
tired of sundays' sameness: ham coffee juice eggs.
                                            . . . had
sd, any chance of coffee? oh past her he recognized some
place her leisurely walk. Banters, redhead? No, one with
the tight ass . . . scene frm somewhere: that quiet glimpse
of someone's kitchen, still-hung pots depend. Hadn't even
noticed. Does A?

            She sez even before that (evening, she
went to bed first. 3 of us sitting in chairs under the orange
tree, 2 of us, some close) sun woke him, or anyway never
sleeps in, read, every page of the sunday paper. Needs
patent (walls between) all that activity light thru
newsprint . . .

the only woman hanged. in this part of. the country.

Look, mama, look. Mama! (breakfast comes. her hand.
blue plates of ham grease won't jell on.) Look at me. I'm
looking. No, LOOK at me. look at me JUMP. (coffee
cuts. the strawberry taste of jam good with ham.)
                                                    D must
be now on his 4th or 5th cup, wiping drops frm moustache,
hears what (eyes down) she comments: thinks the whole
town shd wake when he does (all that silence out there),
don't you love? Unanswered. Mouth makes its gesture rue
some bitter pip (old-time. old town. This town a movie
set we sit in, picturing ourselves. For whose benefit?

                                                    I sd,
Yellow — the afternoon haze enthusiasm plays, tricks of
the eye, A, will you take a picture of the street? (climb thru
window to verandah's edge?) In view of the drop, grange
or masonic hall's impossible stone furthering windows,
eyes . . . for evidence. He sd take it frm the street. A long
way down.
                A long time. WHEN're you coming to bed?
I'll be up in a few minutes — or so he thought. Or so
he sd.
           . . . as sleep infects the day yr breath swells (unripe
oranges last night slit by his knife, green, hardly sections
yet, or sectioned like some minute flower-pattern, unflesht)
The stink of yr mouth at breakfast...A deep slap somewhere? If it hurts she only smiles.

                              Coffee increases sweat,
or secretes violence. Her hand level as any man's to shoot
him down.

With its saloon last night set in theatrical light of window
piece, by piece, 1895, no not a date he sd. A number men
remember. O the tiffany there you wd not believe, liqueurs,
preserved sweets. Riches their swell tits muffle — largesse
or, pianissimo — They laugh together...

Will she see us when she comes down? one. shot in the
dark. two shots mid rows of bottles oh her small face

428

appear, collar up, out to see, solemnity of, unmoved clang
of the bar (boys) nightlight . . .

                                     A's voice makes furred
toward her. Presence at the table cuts. Not pathos,
pathetica, heart-shape face. Something dates her...angel-
lique? As of liqueur that was popular then. Speaking of
men, midway between the angels &. It is that slight tension
walks, she does, a line to maintain it against any jumping-
off place.
                   Speaking of dates, I sd: they are into machines
that play violin & piano combined. They are into milk
bottles & gaslight & little boots . . . I sd, how old do you
think that trunk is? Wch sits a yard behind me in this bar
in wch we . . .

A's voice light with the last 5 minutes, the "last" scotch,
the "last" cut, in a medley that lights & colours his passing,
coins changed, whirr of memory searches for, goes on,
continues on down . . .

I will leave them/him to look at the trunk. Get up alone
in the space of it. Time. Was the trunk inviting hands,
eyes. Whose lid lifts heavy & round to imitate a chest
(coffin), must of paper space to rest in . . . A good idea.
San Francisco no date, what? D: a good idea.

                               Walls to
travel, not even newsprint casts some light on. Whose
needs an abandoned piece of luggage. Set in the museum
after.

Drain the last bit of orange frm the glass: tipt up, throat
exposed to morning throbs continuous life line of want.
& tho the verandah slopes we sit on, into that space heat
poses . . . orange tree vertical. Its relief of green.

                            Will that
be all now? (last drop) Who so stands, pencil poised,
waiting for the smallest nod to add us up, slap by A's plate
("thank you" upside down), no smile even . . . to collect the
plates.

Unripe oranges & a morning walk. Was last night, only
audible scene. Hurried steps outside shutters 2 feet away.
Heels. click click. Angry. click. or hurried (don't know
what to think) . . . Oh come on. (firmer footsteps after)
Don't you touch me! Let's go / Let go! (off the deep end)
& his "wait" urgent now: was she going to jump?

As silence prior to, silence maintained in the museum after,
space, for wants to contract in. So we move into the must
of hall in single file mount the stairs. The windows of our
room are open, shutters open, cool frm the as yet unsunned
street comes up. To pack up. To A: You missed the
balcony scene. What? Coming to bed so late. (can't
resist.) He comes thru: what scene? She didn't jump or
shoot. Blind anger. As I cd see (so late, so isolate). You
shoot me & I'll shoot you! (was it a wrong move?) for his
gun, for arms, his, to surround.

Back in the car, luggage stowed, up out of the dead end
street, into highway sun streams in the pines high up, hair
tied . . . D with his arm round C who eyes what streams by
in the splash of window frame, sez: Good idea that firewood in the trunk. Did you see it? See? An arm of pine
on a hot day creak out.

STEPHEN WIEST

Poems from the Other Side

poem 1

crowd/dreams recede

a dust of dark. birds
from stalks in the north field
rises,   their signal curse
weighting the glistening balance

winging,   as from mirrors

after whistle of first blood
wild grapevine strews the wall
knotted season, advent of sour fruit

bones, stalks, the flesh and flower
                a knife-angled sun
assumes, and then, in January, night

bell notes (days grow) may clear
        but.
                last night's concert is diminished

rings of motion suffice

systems move however elliptical
as in an alpine idyll
hollowing voices charge

        the same
                the

poem 2 (anniversary for G.S.)

note on the heart's triangle

youth absorbed in a scar

two busy the base
of a star

explosive oak, fog traces,

limbs proliferate desire

in stellar imagination
a single line creates
constant radiance

poem 3 (nebula)

facets swirl . foam of light
fog traces land roll/nerve shards
        suckle a next lust

wings embrace the scream
scalding in the dream

        o the flesh in all this tradition
stargazer .   in light
as the light was born, the mother search
cast beyond the spindle, oratorio of thought

we approach
        as lovers the approach of spring
the jelling fluid of the eye

the motion
        in which

        there is no appeal

poem 4

1.

rhythm of the heart
        as snow is shaped
                stars

        from the long journey
        where the head turns
        to kiss the scarred hand

present themselves to the myriad whiteness

of the field   all then
is light from darkness
  light
       and
           cold

       for instants of heat
           you would give yourself
       for the yellow lights
          on an empty road

       marking a space you know
       to a town you know
       that fear is manageable
       you have done that before

               exposing

      o

    finally a face

(each has been the dancer with spotlight flesh
o pure smile and friendly with the drummer of
course (you slouched foot-tapping in the audience
too) reasons resistance the terrible stars now
that we know etc) etc

2

you, you — the poetic I
translation of reality
mutation to a wall
for a little heat.

it is a cold walk to the woods
even with a tune
how absolute beyond the galaxy
no flag there

there is so much light

"communicate. with their spirits."
They told me nothing. "child."
Did their silence not make me love?

Am I not calm as winter
now, spared that, that hopes.

snow touches the flesh

stars light it

poem 5

1.

air sharp, the last wood film, held
this room; cyclical oaks,
where surrounds of bones
grew brooding on their glad comforts—
o you think one thing, it is not true:
fire inhales itself, could do no less
to stir the rhythm of that day
words sprawled on the tidal field
as sky detached more true
from this kiss, frail atmosphere,

there
fire objects, its containing·   .
aureoles burn on
no imposition too precise
to guide two eyes across its grist

and nine o'clock chancing
near enough this dayiced window
mirrors its fury within orion's points

2.

birds erupt
at a flame sting
on the drained walls
wingbreaking on brightness

    fly death
           /the train carries its own shudder

within the hour a land retains exertion

3.

the glass distorts the table
lips and fingers
oil of the wine
dried points
red

international glass
memory glass
oil of the lips

4.

what was mastery becomes undone
clear and motionless
an uncurtained window
graphing the brown violence

winter brought it home
I stand beyond my words

poem 6

the shadow cast   as a prayer for the dead
across   a venetian sunday

             black   on white buildings
in snow

those   some red roofs/arc of fir   colors
made something of wind

rushing water   a long long train through night

          black birds swirled graphing
               a wave

there was silence
                    dotted with motion

                 poem 7

     the aeons that gave this evening light
     illumine me I watch the snow reflect
     the meridian of the universe
     from within my porous
          radius/returning then returned

     beyond analogy   . conscious

     simplicity

                         .mystery lies in wind
     and a cold field

               .light. beyond the wind/all goes cold
                         in the copper laugh

               . . . .

falling in snow
          snow loses its radiance

     burns   points in my eyes/that meant so much

won in springs/mounted in lust
I watch the snow reflect

poem 8

lighter than "air"   star, heavy in the void

to be,   shot   /into your   .in the absence.
                          brilliant depth

from here still
the red mythic
paling of the universe

to count your returns
to cultivate advantage

DENIS GOACHER

Estuary

Living, then, eye-far—
tide stranded
coracles wand masted
and
the sand barge
those men die
when 35.
Graves guard playground
mites may care to use

Something left though
sundown
western breeze
till red eye

yield—
water light—
each boat at least
one star—
Appledore
Instow
those who can
over the bar

The Invaders

"Freedom not a poetic theme"—
no lover, woman,
flower, quick hunting dog
bothers to be free—
Think, that island, Lundy

Bluebells in your wood my friend
purple orchid lilac clover
oboe bell the columbine
scatter of cows fall hill
rhododendron's cutting leaves
bird's eye forget-me-not
there my campion simple ragwort
yellow poppy concubine
buttercup and clover maze
to smugglers' path to
watch tower then sea
half widow silken shawl our eye
spiral green-red cliff
stone   shale   some slate   greet invader

Linger, friend, time
as one small fishing boat
resisting current, sunlessness—
Nature, what is crime?

Answer to Goethe
for h. r. h.

He thought the "naturel" in woman
so near to art—
but sentimental nannygoats
picking their flowers.
Hard, inexact

Have you seen cows
long-lean from milk weight
when time sway home?
There's all your food
for work
as art

More a side of wood
up chimney flame
proclaiming female
hearth love then
wild orchid and shepherd smock
open a window
yes, but yes, they reign

PHILIPPE JACCOTTET

The Perpetual Loss

I would have so much wished to recapture
something of that world I still saw, despite
everything; although it seemed to me at times
so remote, or so ragged. I would have wished
it because I had found in it my deepest
satisfaction, and because I continued to
have no glimpse of any other. It was not a
divided pleasure, it included all the others
or rather created them, when it was there,
as one might say that in divine love are all
the kinds of love imaginable gathered up,
tremendously condensed. But to attain it
again required, in my great weakness, an
enormous effort, i.e., to close myself to
all sorts of reasons for discouragement, for
dumbness: the thoughts of others, innumerable,
divergent, incoherent, but sometimes so strong,
the sadness that drags at the bottom of all
life, the horror that sullies some of them,
the threats of the future, the impinging cares,
the least disturbances, to which I had become
more and more sensitive, being more uncertain.
I had first to proceed to a work of groundclearing —
which became for me always more difficult — without
which speaking had no sense. Yes, speaking was
justified in my eyes only if it was truly I who
spoke; over which I hesitated, for I would have
liked to speak as good as the best, and as I
saw that I could speak only rather poorly and
naively if it was I who spoke. This was one of
the worst obstacles: to come to accept without
excuses one's limits, one's lack of brilliance,
one's uncertainty, to manage not to feign genius,
breadth, originality; truly to speak as I could
speak — and in addition as I knew sometimes, even

if rarely, was given to me to do. But it was
necessary constantly to start again, and strangely
enough each time it was more difficult: instead
of being able to profit from certain acquired
advantages, like a rhythm or movement or a unity
of color or tone, not a thing to do! All was
lost, as if someone else, and not me, had written
these pages, or read them now. Quite the opposite,
the truth of these pages already written—a truth
I recognized with simplicity—troubled me by pre-
venting me from rediscovering any other; their
presence almost accomplished—accomplished in
relation to that moment—paralyzed me; nevertheless,
wasnt I obligated to assure a continuity to my
"writings"? I saw that the answer was no, that it
was a naive wish, quite external and a mistake. It
was on the contrary necessary to forget everything
and only to listen to something within, even though
saying so seemed to many of our contemporaries
more and more old-fashioned, but nevermind. This
was what happened to me, how deny it, or avoid it?
I had no other law than a sort of breath from away
off that seemed to me had to be grasped, or modelled,
or illuminated. Nothing but speaking of it appeased
me, could make me, for a while, smile

    I hear, it is nine o'clock, the tired voices of
my neighbors, questions and answers whose sense I
cannot follow; and the sound of a vessel being put
away, of a pan set to dry in the asphalt courtyard,
that a dog brings tumbling down. Then, shortly
after, the door will be closed, the light put out,
only the dogs will roam about still for some time
in their corner, barking at the passing of some
late walker, or of a cat on the top of the ruined
wall at the foot of which they rest.
    Some words, running water and further off,
mingling with it, scraps of songs on the radio and
the croaking of frogs which seems to be excavating
the night, making it again as vast as it was in
childhood, or at the first moments of love. And
suddenly you would think that several birds started
up at the same time and cried out: some whistling a

long sweet whistle that seemed to prolong the extent
of a wing's beat, others clattering like rattles.
Others yet begin a true song: would this already be
the nightingales? These are notes quite clear that
succeed one another at the same pitch, but ready, it
would seem, to risk variations; and indeed they try,
rising suddenly to a higher level, but always in uniform groups, with a rhythm quite as uniform. The
sound that the frogs make, which dominates the others
because it is uninterrupted rather than by its intensity, to the point that it seems deafening,
recalls the sound that children make in rubbing elastic
bands stretched across the bottom of a matchbox: a
resonant scratching, a grating vibration—as if on
strings of water: patient labor, indefatigable,
monotonous, colorless music, which as vaguely evokes
instruments of a Balinese orchestra. Voices or chatter
of mossy, guttural waterskins from grottoes, word credited
to the stagnant humidity, to darkened ditches.

Almost no one walks in the streets. Nine o'clock
however has hardly passed. The bell of a pan. The
afflictions, the fears of night. But if you didn't have
this rest . . . Suddenly it seems like everything has become
larger, lighter, more breathable. "The soul reascending
to its castle." Now the weak one returns to life, finds
shape again. Beautiful dreams of nightwatchmen, of
guardians, of those under the night's influence. Their
thoughts are clearer than those of captains.

(Gratitude to the growing thunder of these years:
it relieves us definitively of the need to speak aloud
what compels us to strain our voice, to falsify it. It
keeps us from thinking ourselves effective or important.)

One last sentence apropos of the rain "which will
not be for this night," the bike you bring in, the
big door you bolt, another door further on that bangs,
an engine humming hardly louder than a bee. The last
outbursts of day, of the cares of day. And the voice
of moist assemblies becomes more insistent, and one
would say more numerous: as if the whole night were
croaking around the building.
We shouldnt be silent, and so let everything slip

442

away like lost, vain, dead things: we get discouraged
too quickly. What does it matter if no one listens
to these words? If we love the world, we owe it to
ourselves to honor it without more ado; to put upon
all things the crown of words, this glittering array,
"vain adornments," vain diadem . . . A crown upon braided
waters, on the brow of rocks.

Why are we weary? We are really far too weak, and
concerned about the other, about his words. There is no
confirmation to be sought but in what the world once
praised returns to us, and which is nothing else than
life itself. The silence that we gain is also death.

I should like to send news of confidence to my
friends whom silence taints and destroys. That is all
I would like; whereupon I could bring to an end any
additional task whatsoever, provided that it was not
vile or in contradiction to that news, but I do not
know where to again find it, where to find the words for it
I'd like them to be so simple and so clear that I'm
overcome by timidity at the idea. What I dream is
perhaps too ambitious, and my sense of it also is
too vague or too remote. Does speaking of it
bring it closer to me? There is no way to be sure.

I hear the sound of a constantly running water,
and yet it can only be the wind. I close my eyes,
I close myself altogether, I dont want to know what
it is that ruins me, I want only the sounds of this
night, the bearable freshness of the air, the mira-
culous repose of the inhabitants who are stretched
out like the water, in the bed of night.

May such a night as this opening around me
Rejoin you amidst your frightened wakefulness
And bear you the diadem of its waters.

To your frightened wakefulness
I send news of the night
Of its end at least on the heights:
Spires so bright that they flame
Impatient to light the dawn
Multiplied in the lower air.

A sound here, another further off: space, breathing.
The hunting cry of the screech-owl is bite, rip, derisive
laughter. A talon's slash in the silence, the night's
silk gashed. From this ball of feathers so soft and so
warm issues the bent, sharp, crooked cry. I know that
tomorrow doubts will return, but this will have been
said anyhow, and this ground gone over again. Honor
to be saved perpetually. May there rise only these
fragments of songs, this tenacious murmur.

Murmur of a patience
Smoke at night's end
Lamp out at the shops

Words bound to things nearby
Like flame to the faggot

A trace hardly noticed
A little opening in the rain

With spring, suddenly plunging waters.

End of Winter

Little, nothing to chase
the fear of losing space
is left the wandering soul

But perhaps, lighter,
uncertain of enduring,
is the one who sings
with voice most pure
the distances of earth

Trees

I

From world confused, opaque
with skeletons and seeds
they patiently break free

so as to each year be
more sifted by air

II

From ilex to ilex if eye wanders
it is conducted through trembling mazes
through swarms of sparks and shadows

to a grotto scarcely more profound

Perhaps now that there is no stele
there's no longer absence or oblivion

III

Trees, tenacious laborers
gradually lighting earth

And so the longsuffering heart
perhaps, purifies

from Sunrise

Is this the true light
with these blazing veins
these savage teeth?

Is this the just light
that bites as it blinds?

And can it be eternal
so clad in tears
and sighs?

What eyes will we need
and what patience,
or what quite sudden blindness
to see day?

Wishes

I

Long have I desired dawn
but cant bear to see sores

When will I grow up?

I've seen mother-of-pearl:
did I have to close my eyes?

If I am lost
lead me now
hours laden with dust

Perhaps in mingling slowly
pain with light
I'll go on apace?

(In the unknown school
to find the path that passes
through the longest and the worst)

II

What then is song?
Only a sort of glimpse

If it could still inhabit house
like a bird
that would nest even in ashes
and which flies through tears!

If it could at least keep us
until we are confounded
with the blind beasts!

III

Evening come
gathering all things
in the enclosure

To milk, to feed
To clean out the trough
for the stars

To set the near in order
spreads in the expanse
like the sound of a bell
around itself

WILLIAM BRONK

In Praise of Love

Unless to you, to whom should I praise love?
It is a throwaway, a breath on the air,
gratuitous, as if not elicited.

And how should I feel the absence, the emptiness,
the failure to be there except as someone not?
It was you, that one, the one not there.

The Use-Unuse of Us

At Charlie Carleton's farm which several more
have claimed since it was his, and Charlie dead
for years. He must have been.
                                    Look at it there:
The group the buildings make. Only the house
used now, and that not much.
The barns idle. Their sides. Sag a little.
But there it is. The group. Only its shape
as if its shape were all it meant to be.
Nothing ever besides.

                    Did Charlie build
the place? He put it to use. Use it must
have meant to him. And, of course, *it* using him.
What uses who? Who what?

                        As if
something were said—we dont catch what.

We are used or not used; and Charlie, I think
it doesn't matter. Anyway, nobody asks
us, Charlie. No use to. We ask ourselves.

JONATHAN GREENE

Going Through It

Tired of "being strong"
you want me to take over.
There is equity.
You throw off a burden,
another takes its place.
Just compensation for
pain incurred.   Credits &
debits in an other-
worldly account.
Never exactly balanced.

The face in the mirror.
The empty bed.
Tired of ambivalence,
tired of always
"being there."
Empty spaces in
between in-
frequent visits
past midnight.

*

And the perspective.
The open parenthesis.
The lost family
in the heart, a
forsaken enclosure.
"Saving oneself"
for god-knows-what.
Figures of expression.
Literal meanings.

*

How retrace steps down a
forked path back to
its joining. What does
History say about
"repeats"?
The stories recur
in sleep.

*

Holding back & letting go.
The hand a fist.
The hand opening in
invitation.
I face the humiliation
of mistaken invitations.
I reach the clear air.
I fall back.

Part of the story
goes like this:
Knowledge & Experience
were out-of-joint,
running an awkward race
as if one danced
while the other ran
full-steam.
Then the roles
switched.

O, the horses
of instruction
made hard bargains.
Each pulling a
separate direction.
And I wanting
every one of them.

The Pronouncements

The pronouncements of fortune
have left me out of breath
                                                                    &
I want her to go over them again
slowly so I can understand
                              in time
with my slow understanding which
dwells for months on the same
                                      small perception
turning it over & over in my mind.
till the poem is written

                                  & when
it is written I relax & go to sleep
only to wake to pronouncements
                                  of the future
she has to tell me now
& can't wait & *you will have*
                                  time enough
later for sleep & thus through the
emptiness there are many
                                  movements
to hide the emptiness —
but finally I lie awake without
                                  understanding
& want to know & cry out from the cold
why the years have subtracted
                                  knowledge
& left me to face this end
without knowing if this is
                                  the methodology
of a slow dying

MARIO LUZI
The Judge
from *Nel Magma*

"Do you think you're really in love? Look
deep down in your own past" he insists,
darting well within
his queer bantering presbyopic glance.
And waits. While I look far out
and nothing else comes to mind
but the steady sea under the gulls flying
just at the fringe of the island rocks,
where naked earth becomes darkened
by its humps or another place prepared for seed
is darkened by its clods and a few stalks.
"Yes, I may have sinned a lot"
I end up answering, clinging to something,
if only to my guilts, in that heathery light.
"Weep, weep you must over your mistaken love"
his voice comes on again like a squall
whistling high above that sandy waste.
I listen and don't even wonder
why it is him, not me, this side of the bench
busy judging the ills of the world.
"Perhaps" I reply while my mind's already elsewhere,
while the way is lit up step by step
and here in the bar the day still full
flashes in the eyes of a young girl unbosoming herself
during her free hours and the man who has given her
                the change
wears a white jacket and comes
towards us with two glasses brimming
cold, putting one here and one there on our table.

Between Night & Day

"Where are we?" mumbles my half-slumbering companion
shaken by the jerk
of the train stopped in midjourney.
"Near Pisa" I reply

peering out into the gray depths at the ashen
violet of hills fading into color of iris.
A halt in the long to and fro
between home and beyond, between lair and field,
I can't help thinking of him
who has often spoken of our life
as the travail of a strange animal between ant and mole.

And it must also be a thought
not unlike this
that shapes to a guilty
smile his
lips with his head thrown back against the seat this dawn.
Die or submit to the yoke
of the species' humbleness, I read
in that servile gluttonous face,
confident of the good fate
of the soul and, why not, of the inexorable revolution
          at the gates.
"Even you are in the game,
even you carry rubble
stolen from the ruins
for the walls of the edifice" I think;
and I think of a love greater than mine
that overcomes this repugnance
and along with a more perfect wisdom takes the good
and for good closes an eye upon the corrupt and rotten.

Fly, flare of swallow
arrowed from the rain,
above the cry of the railroad man
fading away saying ok
to the train slowed down in the thick grass.

"You must grow in love
and in wisdom" intimates to me that face
defeated sweating in this light of uncertain day.

The One & the Other

"To stay faithful, to bind to others one's destiny,
this does count for something" he insists
twisting his face with doubt, the face of a man
    in the wrong.
"It does count for something" she replies
lost in thought and staring out at the wind working
from one to the other end of the valley left as pasture.
"Just to think so is already much.
Virtue, nowadays, taken for a rag and
    made fun of . . ."
he continues, lifting his hand solemnly between wheel
    and gearshift.
"True" she begins while watching
the mountains come up from way back
and lock upon the straight line of asphalt.
"Yes" and from between lips escapes a sound
partly moan and partly rattle of dentures.

A moment of silence follows, longer
for me than for them, while I think
of which of the elements is missing, fire
or air, in this dead cell.
And meanwhile I see them such as they are,
unlike, but equal in their uselessly cautious actions,
keeping distance between themselves and their true
    scope and grief.
"It's love, love that's missing
if you'd realized it
or had the courage to state it so"
I say to myself thinking of them, and the time, the
    place, loses definition
and I am creeping up upon a shadow or the tail of
    a possum.

In Two

"Help me" and she covers with her hands a face
drawn, eaten by a senile jealousy,
which moves not to pity as she would like but

to bewilderment and horror.
"Only you can do it" insist from behind that screen
her lips hard
and parched, pressed by her palms, blubbering.
I find no answer, look at her
distressed by my coldness quiver a little
from elbows propped on her knees to pale nape.
"Unnatural love, love unfaithful to its cause"
I reflect, and summon my mental powers
to a single point between desire and remembrance
and think not of her
but of the journey with her between heaven and earth
by an upland road that cuts through
the covering of grass browsed by few flocks.
"See, at bottom you can't find one word"
moan those tormented lips
crushed against her teeth, while I am silent
and search over her head the fiery vaulting of the hills.
She waits and meanwhile it doesn't escape her antennae
how far I am from her at this moment
when she is revealing to me her scars and I want her
            and think of her
as she was at other times, on other slopes.
"Why preserve a love distorted by its end,
when there's no more growth
or happy multiplication of every good,
but possessive restraint and that's all" I'd like to ask
but not of her who now behind her hands weeps
            convulsively,
of myself perhaps indulging in deceit through meanness
            or convenience.
"Even this is love, once you learn to recognize it
in this humble form,
in this dejected guise" they answer me, and I'm a
            little fearful of them
and a little ashamed, those bony hands
extended from which a tear descends dropping from
            finger to finger.

JOHN TAGGART

Death-Bean Agent
for Jim Hanlon

How it
is come
to this
is
not clear,
but I
am
the death-bean agent.

The 4″ green velvet
bean
hung
alone in the air

the day a fat man
died.

The bean's
smell
was
the smell of that occasion.

I
tried to paint
it: floated
in permanent green light.

The smell
would not stay
in any
one color; I

kept painting.
Children
called
me
bean-man: "Bean-man, you
stink!

and so does
your wife and kid!"

I
said
nothing; my wife said
nothing, and watches me in my sleep.

What can I say, say
to any of you, except:

leave
the little bean-
elegy man
alone. He

may have
a
secret
you
might need,
could
put to use
someday — and
I
am
the agent.

FRANK SAMPERI

Morning and Evening

A man going away to sorrow.
The furnished room: a bed a chair an end
table and a lamp on it. Lo giorno se
n'andava . . . : he lay dying.
        Morning and no sun — nevertheless wandering
under a hill, a man looking toward rocks
and so much farther down a wood.
        Architectural pomposity: reflections of
cars and pedestrians in the shop windows in
the skyscrapers of maximum glass.
        Sitting under light as if it were a tree,
no shadow anywhere around him, a man who no
longer remembers, seeing the whole world
among branches.
        With star and from star and from one's
gathering of the significance of each, a
transformation whose flowering's a new heaven
and a new earth.
        From a hill, a man down from a hill, weary
of solitude and the cold night, sees the waves
against the sunrise and the gulls under the
cliff.
        To gather a spirit up out of its own con-
sciousness: He stood at the foot of a hill
and the flowers and animals around him gave
off odors suggesting the perfection of
fragrance beyond the hill. Walking slowly,
passing by the stream to the left of a grove,
the grass everywhere perfect in the morning
light, some birds swift under branches,
some lighting some hovering, he came to a
place of roses and lilacs to the right of a
grotto, and then past a willow climbed the
fullness of path.
        Continuing: If he was capable of seeing

the phenomenality behind any impossibility
of extrication, then to be in the dark and
at peace was more of the nature of a forth-
coming transfiguration.

One would have it illusion another fault
and either may take offence at the other's
sense of former and latter.

Concerning two lines opposite each other
whose point in common (and equalizer) is
a perpendicular: the point in common (and
equalizer) if infinitely removed would still
remain the point in common (and equalizer).

Foreknowledge's fault: neigher light nor
darkness, and then light and darkness and
the inclusion completing the one dispelling
the other.

He wandered into an area of shops and bars:
people hung about the corners—streetlights
and neons dominated—no inkling of hope in
the signs—if there were stars no reason to
look up: a man could determine his direction
by relation to mechanical light.

He walked along a shore and then up a
path to a hill—dawn at the edge of grass.

Awake! and the hills remain. Sleep! and
the awakening that is a dream sees the land
sleeping in the folds of the horizon.—More
snow on the ground—however, not so bad—
the wind's died down.

He walked along the shops under the El—
a few blocks down, the ocean.

At the foot of a slope, a man in the light
from branches, sees clusters of birds in
the glare above the hills.

Concerning an angel dying by a river and
a man sorrowing in a street and the nature
of the prefiguration of the one or the other
depending upon whether one's by a river or
in a street:

An angel came down a hill and moved among
the flowers along the river-bank to a place
where river and grass twisted toward deepest
wood; then following more to the right than

the line of the river he saw a white flower
and a path. Sorrowing along the path,
imagining flowering trees on a hillside and
birds in the shadows of a grove, he moved
as if downward, taking his sense from his
movement down the hill, and came to a brook
reflecting animals fleeing to woods and at
the same time revealing as if under glass
birds dying in a withered tree. Then going
on, he passed under overhanging rocks to a
meadow past vines. He kept close to shadow
and a little ways down turned in on grass
leading toward what seemed sea. In memory
he saw a land exempt from the misery that
placed the hill under the deepening of
shadow. When he reached the roses at the
foot of the slope what seemed sea was instead
ice; then he took the path beyond the lilies:
along the way, off behind the rocks in the
weeds, a stirring of animals. After crossing
a stream and climbing a hillock, he moved
down into a valley. He felt as if he were at
the edge of a field next to a forest in
moonlight under sky sloping toward stars. Then
he came to a path leading upward past mountain
ledges looking down on land revealing to
each level its horizon. Continuing along the
path, seeing eagles swooping down on prey,
remembering the grass gradually fading as he
approached declivity, he moved into a grove
where leaf and songbird trembled under faint-
est wind, and then down above branches
growing out of cracks in rocks to a field in
snow. Then he turned to the left and some
ways up beyond the trees under the hill
came to forsythia in bloom on a slope.

If a work is primarily addressed to God,
then it follows that the audience isn't
essential—in fact, a period that places
the movement in the audience whose referential is the standard that impedes draws to
itself a principle whose point is finally
to exclude totally: therefore, it is right

to say that no identifications can be
telically intended when a work is so primarily addressed.

The other movement: We moved to another
place—and what seemed to be direction of
another sort was, in truth, only a second
period devoid of a wake but nevertheless
profound enough to transform memory.

"Do you think a writer needs a room of
deepest darkness?"—"Yes!"—"Does deepest
quiet mean darkness?"—"No!"—"Then why
use the word deepest. . . ."

"Is it possible to write amidst noise?"—
"No doubt—a truism even speaks of a part
inwardly contained."—"Yes! but if one
contains himself even amidst noise, can the
word be anything but dynamically scanned?
that is, each to each discontinuously
rooted?"—"To project no argument as answer
would place the meaning in an implication
whose release would be to draw to itself a
view no longer implicative."

Conversations with oneself: they've a way
of going on even in book shops where one goes
only to browse—and then after satiety, one
finds himself in a street ostentatiously
structured toward the intellective that gathers
in only for the sake of the river-god who
demands that the flow continue—and the shops
along the way are not an afterthought. From
this it becomes valid to say that what is
commonly called direct vision is, in truth,
just that and no more, that is, the integument
is the reflection; therefore, if you walk a
street and come out with a presupposition that
is a plain whose perspective is homeric, then
you are as they say in the world but not of
it.

Given a beginning, it is true to say that
by the second or third day a man's words falter—
he falls away from that confrontation that
makes him secure even tho each step shows him
to others a man to be shunned.

461

There are those who are so sure of a place
in letters that smugness is the upshot to the
idiom nothing can displace them—this comes
from a contemporaneity moving them to conceive of themselves as the originators of a
movement whose touchstone is in proportion
to the audience's relation to the referential
wholly civil.

One can go on writing like this for a
lifetime and still not be false to a movement
opposed to a work in progress.

From Leibniz' "Car (quelque paradoxe que
cela paraisse) il est impossible à nous d'avoir
la connaissance des individus et de trouver
le moyen de déterminer exactement l'individualité
d'aucune chose, à moins de la garder elle-même;
car toutes les circonstances peuvent revenir;
les plus petites différences nous sont insensibles;
le lieu ou le temps, bien loin de déterminer
d'eux-mêmes, ont besoin eux-mêmes d'être déterminés
par les choses qu'ils contiennent" the clearest
insight is: state as unity as space and civil right
as time; therefore, seen this way the differential
calculus is progressive.

Deeper thought reveals a yes and no in the
statement: propositions de fait propositions
de raison.

Mind discouraged again—long walks as
curative—hope this place causes me to
move about differently each day.

There's a sorrow that arises from a contemplation unable to come to grips with a work
that needs to complete itself and say: it's
a new period and the time of fulfillment
closer.

"Should a writer feel guilty that he makes
no money from his work?"—"No!"—"Even if he
makes no money another way?"—"If his work
brings in no money, then he's in the same
position as any other unemployed worker;
however, since it is granted that the audience
substantiates his position as artist, it
leaves him little hope of help from 'welfare'—

therefore, he must let go of the one and take
on the other, that is, poverty and not feel
guilty."

Since civilization is not for the poor,
there isn't much to it—by the poor one means
the world before God; therefore, one obviates
the condescending tone "does not include."

". . . quod ideo est quia scientia habetur de
rebus secundum quod sunt in sciente, voluntas autem
comparatur ad res secundum quod sunt in seipsis.
Quia igitur omnia alia habent necessarium esse
secundum quod sunt in Deo, non autem secundum
quod sunt in seipsis, habent necessitatem absolutam,
ita quod sint per seipsa necessaria; propter hoc
Deus quaecumque scit ex necessitate; non autem
quaecumque vult ex necessitate vult." When natural
theology appropriates the above, we get an image
of God as "mechanical wizard": that is, the State
has succeeded in drawing its variables unto itself.

"Can you honestly say that modern literature
is beyond these traps that are societally
'formalized'?"—"It would seem that the most
argute state propaganda is to imply the
contrary in its use of its most intransigent
subjects: that is, 'free society' conducive
toward free literature, which is to say,
each author is left more or less alone to
satisfy the audience occupying a mean
reflective position, which the 'lone author'
conceives as his to mould by astonishment,
taking his sense to act from 'free society'
granting him this illusion to discover,
thereby giving ample praise to a progressive-
ness whose Unitary Field Theory is discontinuous, therefore, circular, and whose
image is shoreline to sea. . . ."—"Can you
tell us anything about merit?"—"Yes! it
doesn't work here."

"Unde perfectio naturae angelicae requirit
multiplicationem specierum, non autem
multiplicationem individuarum in una specie."

Modern criticism views let us say a
16th century poet and proceeds to divest him of

an 18th century critic's view, never owning
up to it—else why criticism at all—that the
next century stands to rid him of his slant.
There's something ad infinitum about this.

It seems that I haven't said what I've
wanted to say, that is, when confronted by
such a tradition—and yet the idea is not
opposed to tradition—no reason to write seems
to be the honest action, that is, of course,
if we accept audience as end, but since God
is the reason we write, then it follows that
the perspective that is historical is pointless.

Little relation to the civil: does this make
me uncivil?

"Isn't it a pity that in the end an artist
becomes just another example of grandiose
state propaganda!"—"Yes! but even more
piteous is the image of his youth."

It is better not to know what I've written
yesterday—not that one writes to discard, but
when there's a sense that I'm not right today,
then the next day leaves me in the position
of a viewer of things under the hill; therefore, it is fair to say: I have no world.

Everything down here just teems with the
give and take that is exploitative.

To take up what was said above: if one continued to write as if the right hand were
unaware of the left, then at the completion of
such a work he could only be as much surprised
as any possible reader. But the sorrow that
arises from such a writing can only be compared
to a journey unaware of every step along the
way but the end in mind fully presupposed and,
of course, the reason for moving. This end
in mind should be solace, but somehow, because
of the steps along the way, it leaves the sorrowing man ever in a state of renewal or better
vigilant enough to know that if tense then
bowed, if relaxed, that is, suggestive of flesh
bespeaking least or more truly no bone, then
blessed, full of the peace that gets you thru,

that is, least or again more truly no trace
of the other world, that is, circle, passed
thru.

One wishes to write honestly: therefore,
is it honesty to be concerned primarily
with the rhythm of language? isn't the triumph
in the very vanquishing of language?—Don't
be misled: language is your better part, and
the flow is life.—If language is the better
part, then since you call the flow life, it
follows that language is to matter as the flow
is to soul, which is to say, if so, then
the flow is a consequence of the matter
language. . . .—Logic is circular: is the angelic
nature circular?

Again: light and darkness—if evil is a
privation of the good, then evil is not an
opposite; does this make the good tautologic?

"When you pose a statement in the form of
a question, have you already answered it?"—
"Yes! but it seeks to enlist another—this
establishes it as an argument, altho the
calm to be revealed makes it ever singular."

"There's always so much more going on—a
writer could draw completely only haphazardly—
you it seems place yourself—it's criticism;
I do it not to hurt, but to make you, eventually, of course, realize yourself more in the
way that is cultural—in a position too
inward; therefore, you force the reader to
bow his head—this kind of art is at least
from the historical view immature and
altogether misleading: it uses simple words
and expects us to come up with an even greater
simplicity and yet at the same time gives also
indirectly the involvements that are of greatest
complexity—you cannot expect a people inured
to surface to accept your depth."

No one, of course, speaks to me in the words
of the above; therefore, why not give myself
over to such words! they place me in direct
relation to my daily walks—people move I move—
rapidly: is the street the river? the sidewalks

its banks? buildings a wood's tallest trees?
is a man insane to see distortion of this sort?
or is it really the builder who in the with-
drawal from "the natural whose presupposition
is creation" impedes the will only to make it
take stock, that is, unlearn the learning,
come finally to the glory that laid no traps?
     Should mention that the words meant as
criticism ended up in praise of...: can such
a writing be valid?
     The gloom reaches down—a valley a prey to
deepest shadow: what's above?
     Lovely birds my birds singing in the
backyards of stone and rubble—
     So many windows from the ground floor to the
5th facing the row of tenements opposite, and
each to each immutable except for the snap
of shade the fall of light and the abysmal
yawning gap the backyard.
     window sill in light

     blind

     branch bird
     shadow

     radio
     Light altering things—angelic nature
in time and not time that is planetary, but
rather time that measures virtually—what
kind of time is that? is it cosmic time?
out of a man's reach?—Read of angelic
power! its movement that can be either
continuous or discontinuous—is the discontinuous its better movements? and yet
either movement in no way to be compared to
"things corporeal in movement"—does it
leave you guessing? science distorting an
ancient definition—taking unto itself for
the sake of the more intense or better
world-wide slavery—should a man damn science?
or rather see it rightly, that is, that
which is for the sole consideration of truth—

466

is truth outside? more complex than in head?
therefore, why consideration of motion? and
the other aspect of science, that is, the
more prudential whose impediment is use-value
as substance (and this not to say that the
other side's any better—in fact, in a way
even worse—feigning a system conducive toward
free movements). . . . You've again written
indirectly—and yet you've been direct in the
way that abstracts from here and now: thus
another inverse ratio.

A man in deep darkness hears birds and
imagines flowers.

Let there be words to express a child's
gaze at moon: in father's arms, she points
at the moon and says: bird! not knowing the
moon's name—then hearing its name, she delights
in it—says it over and over—they pass the
shops, the avenue busy as ever; and then at
a corner father sees the moon just a little to
the side of an apartment building—he reminds;
child says again over and over: moon moon . . . :
sleep my child heavenly under moon!

What constitutes a true definition of
sentimentalism? a risk involving a man in a
past whose ambience is sensible? should an
angel look down upon a man? God forbid!

"You must not let them get you down—whatever
they say, it's beside the point: that is, their
ultimate interest is how much is in it for
them; therefore, to subsidize you would be
false to an age checking every gift to see how
much is risk how much is to their advantage
(that is, 'the force behind,' which leads
upward to munificent capitalist, who in
turn draws us completely to participate in
the choral praise of the Material Ideal,
the State)."—"When you use the word choral,
are you thinking of it anteriorly? I mean,
the dance?"—It is now late afternoon:
hear paraphrastic words: How do I know?
the Father has told me.

Writing of misery and in the long run

isolated from the world, a man can only
move along streets as if no relation were
possible. Yesterday, for instance, everything
went wrong, and so he thought of streets,
but once out and amidst the flow things fell
away or began to topple—so he was left
alone in a plain—of course, he knew that
this was illusion; but again, he thought
what is the cause of this illusion: "The
only cure for your malaise is manual labor—
you should stop your wandering, feeling as
if the world were in distance—your logic
is leading you astray; therefore, work hard—
forget the inwardness—the great thing about
our century is just this: we've succeeded
in getting everybody into the hard labor
market—and it's good—it keeps the inward
ones from going off on pilgrimages. You
must not see this as an error, rather you
should—using all your strength—come to
its feast—it doesn't exclude; in fact, it
wants you and your children. I repeat: give
yourself to physical labor—what you do is
not labor—it can't be measured." There's
movement in air but it isn't light.

I've returned from another long walk—
the day so depressing, but, of course, it
isn't the day, it's the sorrow so deeply
inward—and maybe to use depth is still to
be in perspective—a reason why there's
something frustrating about that direction,
too.

One involved in a way foreign
to anterior and posterior must consider it true
that work done "isn't looked back to"
for a different reason.

Angelic knowledge despite "species
connatural" is still a confrontation.

There can be no audience when a
work's vision is total.

Since the final pleasure is the whole work
in mind, then "in the end" implying only
"some statements" does not hold.

The park was crowded today—no reason to
stay away—but always why parks built within
city rather than cities within park—not
right to pose this even as a question let
alone become sorrowful over it—but nevertheless
you find yourself being drawn to them—yes!
to take a breather—and the best reason for
being there is the child.

Then there is the movement away from the
park: along the streets is the direction,
and the sense is supposedly straight—this
illusion adds to the sentiment "my city."
No man can escape this trap—for by
extension the suburbs and deserts are but
the city in extension. So you continue to
walk, and every relation comes to you
insincerely.

Now you think of various religions and
sciences—and when seen from the standpoint
of the city, an image of the world belabor-
ing an issue never to be at rest, and the
stress is just that, that is, the encomium
to commotional world, and the city the
better for it, teaching the citizens no
life only burden of death, reduces the mind
to stoical severity as its only triumph
over quotidian movement.

You have your work—no amount of impediment
can hold you back—you must if need be think
that each word is in praise of the Word—
it comes to that! give yourself up to Him
and then place is yours or better is of no
account for just that reason of love.

The world has its own, therefore, it seeks
to establish the Christ-Phenomenon as the
outcome of the Graeco-Roman Hebraic clash—
this makes it cultural; therefore, those
who labor for a new culture are justified in
their desire to exculpate themselves from
any action that deracinates: that is, they
wish the crime to be enacted by the masses.
Antichrist cannot triumph, for the life has
nothing to do with progress as such, that is,

the conservative and liberal dependent upon
the so-called infinite straight line—nor
is tradition of any concern, nor does this
mean that restatement is necessary.

You must come to grips again with the
principle of individuation: the difference
is formal the singular material—the
singular cannot be known in itself because
intelligence is spiritual, therefore, it is
by way of abstraction that the singular is
known simpler than it is; however, species
intellectus angeli, quae sunt quaedam
derivativae similitudines a divina essentia,
sunt similitudines rerum, non solum quantum
ad formam, sed etiam quantum ad materiam.

It now seems valid to see man's relation
to the Gift, that is, the image of a man at
the foot of a hill, revealing the angels
similarly disposed—the signification of this
revelation shows up the fault of pantheism.

When it is said that the angels behold God's
wisdom, the meaning is: dwelling in His City;
but when it is said that they do not comprehend it, then the heart obviates: are they
at rest in it? establishing a kind of trust
holding even them in check—God's wisdom
completely informs them, holds back nothing
that is theirs; therefore, no tragic ache
can subsist in them.—"How do you explain
the Fall?"—"How do you explain Salvation?"

It might be mentioned here: if a man in
stressing the angels' inability to comprehend the Divine Wisdom states nevertheless
it isn't necessary to know everything in it,
then he says in effect the same that was said
above.

The morning and evening knowledge of the
angels is a refinement of the principle of
individuation: that is, to know things in
God and things in themselves is to know
angelically. (It should be mentioned again:
the principle of individuation does away
with any knowledge of things in themselves.)

When it was said above that "the singular
cannot be known in itself because intelligence
is spiritual", it was done more to state the
implication, intelligence, rather than that
"the singular cannot be known in itself
because of the matter."
  Aquinas has treated Aristotle and Plato
justly by quelling all talk concerning tabula
rasa and innate ideas.
  A good morning walk! cloudy at first,
therefore, streets almost deserted—then
after a pause at a book store, started again
to walk—this time to a park—sun out, therefore, streets becoming crowded—in the park,
the various kinds of people, more various
because of the outfits rather than "the head
structure, the skin"—therefore, words come
to mind: why then argument running out *race
race!*—sitting down, letting the child play—
two girls playing catch in the distance—
coming closer to move the child to join them—
child responds immediately! before that:
lady walking dog responds to child because
child shows no fear of dog—lady moves away—
girls take unto themselves the whole movement—
beyond: the fountain and around it the various
kinds—ball remains in a puddle—child moves
away—girls who remain also as fixed as ball
nevertheless fall away—then the walk continues
along streets lined with paintings—child
sees the ones representing birds various
animals—there is the clash between the bright
ones and the somber ones: the sun shines forth!
finally out of it—now only shops to see—
just before turning up a street heading toward
home, a playground: groups gathered here and
there along its fence: sun now noon!
  To a man whose shoes are falling apart a
movement toward a park is a movement toward
unearthly existence.
  He came to a park and then after some
searching for a place to sit to a bench as if that
time were without reference to another time

far back or up ahead. . . .

Neither to sow nor to reap—

It is important that you let go none of
your principles—

Songs tonight may get you thru the night
better than drink—

But the angels are being reduced to the
clever atomic theory—

Fly up and then out unto areas of transformation—

Let the mind awaken in the way a man opens
a door to a hallway of darkness and feculence
and still senses the odor of lilacs—

To be in the way implies no end because
the beginning is no longer implicative—

None of this will get you anywhere, altho
you can go on indefinitely—

A drunk all bloody upsets the balance of
commercial movement—no one cares—if he were
to drop dead in an alley, they'd leave him
and say the better place, but the law requires
that a truck come to cart him off to immemorial ground—"life goes on"; no man can
stop to give thought to a drunk all bloody.

"Give us another form rather than that old
reform, and you'd see no Skid Row—"

"You'd see fields and no notion of surplus
could arise from them—"

See the drunks sitting at the windows above
the restaurant—

See the drunks unable to get up—

Legless men selling shoe laces—

But they have nothing to sell—they're simply
unable to get up off the street—

Wounded animals! the pedestrians see no more
than images of animals—

Sorrowful animals! bloody animals! dragging
their broken, dispirited bodies thru forests—

No traffic has concern for them—

No charitable organization is truthful
enough—

No longer face to face charity—rather
relegation to institution bent on screening

applicants—
    Traffic continues—
    Shop owners stand outside shops—
    They pose—
    Cigar their sign of success—
    Policemen stand at corners—
    Shop owners and policemen greet each other—
    Legless drunk finally drags himself into an
alley—
    Traffic triumphs—
    To stress even this aspect of city is to say
it incorrectly, that is, the others use similar
tactics—if you're against a race then the best
way to write against it is: raise scatologic
news up front! that is, single out and let
mob carry out sentence universally.
    My beloved's lost in Babylon—
    My beloved nevertheless sings of the waters
of Babylon—
    My son, the beloved, is a shepherd to none
of the people because none know my son,
the beloved—
    My beloved son gather up my lost people—
    My son, the beloved, is a shepherd to all
of the people because all know my son,
the beloved—
    And then there is the East—which one comes
off best?—pit them against one another—
see both as outcomes of clashes, therefore,
of little importance except as Types
    None of this makes sense! East as Beginning
West as End—East and West opposites
    Not to the Sun!
    A man awakens early to go down to the
freight yards—
    A man awakens from *that* awakening to know
that the level is street—
    A man falls down in the street—
    Rain—
    Litany is invalid too because it presupposes
an audience equally interested in the same
object of adoration as the speaker.
    Walk downtown—go to areas of renovation—

think upon the meaning of a structure built
with a look toward the horizon.—But what
about the meaning of tall buildings con-
fronting you with a closeness that is almost
natural?— See it as lie!—Yes! every lie
misleads you. What is right architecture?—
One thing is sure: it is not nature presupposed
by motion.

Every statement that you make if it releases
you from a notion that is dialogic alters
the ostensible dialog in a movement ultimately
concerned with the Light that Is and the light
that is by participation.

"To write as if every substantive were not
valid unless first adjectivally qualified—
this presupposition's behind even the most
austere work: therefore, do you mean to imply
that your work is not so founded?"—"Yes!"—
"Then you must be saying something other than
what the work conveys."—"You seem to be
criticizing yourself—not me."

Children in a garden—

Waiting to catch a train, a man thinks back,
oblivious to the empty station and the hills
behind it—

Children in a street—

A man walks the whole city without a cent
in his pocket—

Cents in this city are dollars in another—

What next: children up from a wood come
down a hill—

Like what?—

Like shadow—

Birds fly up as children run down—

You'll have to go for blocks before you
see a tree in this city—

. . . then you walk along warehouses till
you come to the tallest building—you turn
right and some two or three blocks up you'll
find a park. . . .

"The nature of city speech: to keep you
moving: up and down."—"I don't think you're
using the word nature correctly."—"I get

your meaning—birth is different from purpose.'

An experiment: go to a park—sit on a
bench and listen—then go home and try to
write the variety of voices: you can't do it—
no man can—you're always trying to make it
simpler than it is: that's the reason why
no man is capable of banning works of art.

Necessary question: then how is it possible
that city structure impedes the will?

What is the nature of grief?—To see a man
who belongs to no city is to see grief;
however, to be in the world but not of it
is his way to Life.

If you spent your whole day trying to find
reasons why you should love God and man,
then you'd be in the very predicament that
is against nature.

It seems that images of poverty can be used
only for the sake of propaganda, that is,
the end involved is the State paternally
concerned for its whole household: so the
wonder is: how can the State act paternally?

Again the contradiction is: seeing the city
from the top floor of the highest building,
and then later on, seeing a drunk dying in a
doorway.

Passing by a home for the aged, you see
the old people grouped under beach umbrellas,
and the flowers and grass seem immobile.

You've reached a depth of despair from
which no gathering up is possible: to wander
is to have little voice to interest others—
in a place of depth, the cry to a world above
reaches never so high but only returns back
revealing you even deeper than before—but
there's an end to this depth, this you repeat
to yourself as you go down even lower than
the depth occurring from the cry returning.

Given a notion of blessedness, how much
more salutary is the grace whereby blessedness
is merited.But once blessedness is attained
no notion of merit is compatible with it—
charity completes itself, seeing fully.

Nothing that is natural shall be done away
with, but the perfection that comes from
blessedness shall but say: fulfillment implies
no opposite.

But what about a world principle that would
do away with "specific difference"? wouldn't
one be right in seeing such clearing away as
"spiritual democracy", that is, for the sake
of imposing on a world order incapable of
right movements the notion of "numerical
difference"?

If there's longing for confraternity with
the angels, then every movement a man makes
to establish such is a movement toward
specific difference.

The differential world is the glorified
body.

The world is prison—
I'm allowed to walk about—
No one knows me—
Or better they're told to shun me—
I gather flowers—
I reach out to birds—

From the standpoint of the world's own,
there's no better way to "welfare" than the
one that engenders a feeling of repugnance
toward nature.

Following again the way downward, you come
to an impasse that shows you to yourself as
the maker of your own obstacles—but once
clear of the impasse, which presupposes that
the way out is thru the realization that
accuses oneself, an image of deeper clarity
comes thru: you as victim.

Why again the dread? is it true that the
exclusion will take place shortly? You know
that they can't harm you—if you order yourself properly, no circumstance that tends
to bow can truly overcome—remember, the
city has no intrinsic power, I mean, it can't
act upon you unless you place yourself in a
position of passivity— do you mean to say
that the city's in the same position?—yes!

its principle of movement seems to be general
consent, that is, given an extreme populus
honorabilis apparent virtual interiority
must follow—but what about the general
consent: how did it come about?—the answer
is obvious: to turn away from God is to turn
toward self—yes! and the city's founded on
self-reliance; from this it's safe to say:
the State, the Material Ideal, is the Self
magnified blown up a thousand times—now
that you know this you can walk anywhere and
feel no oppression—but the impossibility of
relations that brings a man to the realization
that each man moves toward specific difference,
turns the movement upon itself, leaving him
groveling in darkness, gathering to himself
a justification that is metaphorical: that is,
the darkness that releases one from heat—but
you know that this is impediment; therefore,
release yourself from feelings of oppression.

No identification is possible when a man
says: see the child standing by the window
looking out at the rain.

What good is it to see the drunks sprawled
out on the sidewalks, if your seeing can't
go beyond, that is, to gather them up and feed
them—does it do you any good to go away
sorrowfully—the injustice writhes at the
root; therefore, do your work of transformation.

To use *you* is to imply *I*—
Every time?—
Yes—
Then why the distinction?—
Call it a circle—
Persons in dance—
Motion is its first principle?—
It depends—
Go to a wood—
Find a pool—
Look into it—
There's no more wood—
There's heaven—

Totally light—
Do you mean it's buoyant?—
You see pun—*I* don't—
But to see heaven in a pool is not to see
heaven—
The moment you looked into a pool to see
heaven was the moment you in heaven saw a
man looking into a pool to see heaven—
"I've seen you walk along the markets by
the waterfront—you don't buy—I hardly ever
see you walk the neat streets."—"You don't
always see me—but it's true! I prefer the
streets that look like time."—"That's a
strange simile: aren't all streets involved
in time?"—"Yes!"—"And wouldn't one be right
to say: old street— anteriorly contemplative;
new street—posteriorly active? and also
respectively: back; front?"—"Yes!"—"Then
give up the old streets—go over to the new
streets."
"Time is always old—new time is 'here one
moment gone the next'—future time is similar,
that is, the only difference is: it's just
a little ways up the river; therefore, time
can't be anything but old, that is, circular."
"You were wrong from the start—no man can
be serious in this society—yesterday, for
instance, I heard an illiterate in front of
an office building ranting about the injustice
of the people in 'high places'—he said to be
phoney is their motto and they want their
workers to follow suit."—"The illiterates
make sense—once I heard a drunk amidst
fashionable street say: I'm right everybody
else's wrong!"
"Ornament is beside the point: is the world
ornamental?"—"No!"—"Then how can you say
that the world is prison?"—"I meant in so far
as it is 'strapped in.' " —"Then society is
ornamental?"—"Yes! however, I prefer the word.
State."—"Do you mean that the State is society's
stance?"
Remember that the Occident takes its force

from the fall.

To say "total light, therefore, total
vision" is to say more than any proposition,
because one *knows* wherein the *place* is
angelic.

You hear: is the converse true if to use
you implies *I*? and if so, does it alter the
stuff that follows? to tell yourself that
it is true and that the stuff that follows
does remain constant is to hear: a yes or no
tips the scale. . . .

Beware of the moon mirrored—in water?
what about the back black fender of a parked
car?

A drifting out toward open sea—
Open window—
Angel—
Beloved—
Words gathering around a word—
Cliffs under moon—
Birds lighting—
Sun under tree—
Downward the journey—
Upward the bird—
Blazing forth the journey's downward under
tree—
Beyond open window sea—
Between open window and sea angel—
Beloved's the word that gathers the world
to himself and then upward fulfills—

Awaken to see neither open window nor
open sea—
See the stars from the burnt hill—
Awaken the city—
Sing the stars—
Cry out to the angels above the city—
Sing the stars the angels the angels
the stars—

When you find yourself looking out of a
window—the last light of the day metaphorically
in the position of a shepherd leading sheep
toward the darkness that is no more than a step—
then every ache that is memorial comes before

you, and, because of the possibility of a future
intending breakdown, you sorrow as if renewal
were but deceptive action, that is, a mask
revealing a reality everywhere unresolution.

"Why pay any attention to a future no where
in your power— that is, if you know that time
is old, therefore, circular, then you're already
in a position that has nothing to do with it—
therefore, walk in the light knowing that there
is no impediment."—"But today I see only
death."—"Then I can only say: you are blind!"

It is the intensity of activity that impedes
contemplation; therefore, any system that
pretends to release even tho enslaved is one
that seeks to get the most out of you without
incurring the loss of profit that comes from
revolt.

Poverty seems to be the only action capable
of reducing an intensity of activity.

"Are you seeking future things?"—"An intel-
ligible metaphor for in the world but not of it is:
if one finally contains place, then to be in it
is tautologic."

---

on
  a
bridge

behind
  branches
an

angel—
  a
memory

of
  sea
  a

longing
 for
home

scattered
 by
the

dance

---

no
grass
no
trees

a
block
of
homes

cars
speeding
by
in

rain

Behold the hill
And beyond
Against a wood
The birds above

The burning grass

lie
   down
angel
   broken

at
  the
wing—
   the

river
   flower
below
   you

withers
 by
the
   wood

_____

so
close
the trees
birds

and
grass
along the
river

ending
below
this hill
my

home

_____

482

                    there are

    the children linked arm in arm on
    the circle of green
                        and in the midst:
    a tree

    _____

    a beginning of snow
    and in a garden
    in moonlight
    an angel

    inwardly radiating

    _____

    under
      the
    branches
      above

    the
      water
    from
      the

    hill
      beyond
    the
      wood

    a
      flower
    in
      sleep

    _____

    shaking
    the
    dust

483

the

feet

and

yet

smiling

———————————

the

angel

passed

thru

the

city

———————————

and

moved

up

———————————

484

and

down

trusting

in

the

path

———————————

    Night longer
than usual
vision plainly
lost
music
evidently
best
under streetlight
little else
to communicate
sound draws them in
the circle
the fire
the rose
back from walk
remembering the reading
nepenthe
coming in after 9
a long table simulates
committee room
room again
furnished room
sorrow futile
to move
city
seeks to
bow

485

or balance in a way
indifferent to either
extreme
sit amid the ashes
cry out
stars listen
woods give back

    Words
hills
woods anciently
sung
overheard
from under a wall
reveal
a depth
 the voice
another man
given up to himself
pondering
reflecting
you

    Reflecting
traffic
a window
of the corner house
shaded by the only tree
on the block
fails to reveal
the tugs
going toward
the opposite
shore

        Almost for three weeks
the same walk
theaters
markets
warehouses
coat old
lining torn
returning
facing the wind
the water to the right
memory

        Cast
into
darkness
words
meaning little
people wandering about
no flower
no hill

        Then over to waterfront
ships
and beyond
hills
and everywhere
falling
snow

Thomas Jefferson

1

My wife is ill!
And I sit
            waiting
for a quorum

2

Fast ride
his horse collapsed
Now *he* saddled walked

Borrowed a farmer's
unbroken colt
To Richmond

Richmond How stop—
Arnold's redcoats
there

3

Elk Hill destroyed—
Cornwallis
carried off 30 slaves

Jefferson:
Were it to give them freedom
he'd have done right

4

Latin and Greek
my tools
to understand
humanity

I rode horse
away from a monarch
to an enchanting
philosophy

5

The South of France

Roman temple
"simple and sublime"

Maria Cosway
        harpist
on his mind

white column
and arch

6

To daughter Patsy: Read—
read Livy

No person full of work
was ever hysterical

Know music, history
dancing

(I calculate 14 to 1
in marriage

she will draw
a blockhead)

Science also
Patsy

7

Agreed with Adams:
send spermaceti oil to Portugal
for their church candles

(light enough to banish mysteries?:
three are one and one is three
and yet the one not three
and the three not one)

and send salt fish
U.S. salt fish preferred
above all other

8

Jefferson of Patrick Henry
backwoods fiddler statesman:

"He spoke as Homer wrote"
Henry eyed our minister at Paris—

the Bill of Rights hassle—
"he remembers . . .

in splendor and dissipation
he thinks yet of bills of rights"

9

True, French frills and lace
for Jefferson, sword and belt

but follow the Court to Fontainebleau
he could not—

house rent would have left him
nothing to eat

• • •

He bowed to everyone he met
and talked with arms folded

He could be trimmed
by a two-month migraine

and yet
        stand up

10

Dear Polly:
I said No—no frost

in Virginia—the strawberries
were safe

I'd have heard—I'm in that kind
of correspondence

with a young daughter—
if they were not

Now I must retract
I shrink from it

11

Political honors
        "splendid torments"
"If one could establish
        an absolute power
of silence over oneself"

When I set out for Monticello
    (my grandchildren
        will they know me?)
How are my young
        chestnut trees—

12

Hamilton and the bankers
would make my country Carthage

I am abandoning the rich—
their dinner parties—

I shall eat my simlins
with the class of science

or not at all
Next year the last of labors

among conflicting parties
Then my family

we shall sow our cabbages
together

13

Delicious flower
of the acacia

or rather

Mimosa Nilotica
from Mr. Lomax

14

Polly Jefferson, 8, had crossed
to father and sister in Paris

by way of London—Abigail
embraced her—Adams said

"in all my life I never saw
more charming child"

Death of Polly, 25,
Monticello

15

My harpsichord
my alabaster vase
and bridle bit
bound for Alexandria
Virginia

The good sea weather
of retirement
The drift and suck
and die-down of life
but there is land

16

These were my passions:
Monticello and the villa-temples
I passed on to carpenters
bricklayers what I knew

and to an Italian sculptor
how to turn a volute
on a pillar

You may approach the campus rotunda
from lower to upper terrace
Cicero had levels

17

John Adams' eyes
        dimming
Tom Jefferson's rheumatism
                cantering

18

Ah soon must Monticello be lost
                    to debts
and Jefferson himself
                              to death

19

Mind leaving, let body leave
Let dome live, spherical dome
and colonnade

Martha (Patsy) stay
"The Committee of Safety
must be warned"

Stay youth—Anne and Ellen
all my books, the bantams
and the seeds of the senega root

CHARLES OLSON
Letter to Cid Corman

sat may 30

CC:

very damn happy to have news of souster,
jimmay (? is that james boyer m? who took some
earlier exception? and what is TRACE?) and yrself
there Belgique (and mel!

paul b did write, but
didn't spell it out, having (in a go of a para
before the book got into his hands) offered as
interesting an analysis of the method as i cld
imagine (was delighted to hear what he thot of
the going-about things, the off-play (the offbeat? down-beat? how does—or is there—an
analogy to (as i'd gather any of us do) to jazz?

and think yr remark that WCW puzzles most
by his likes, exact

(i'm sure, now that it's up to me, that i'll
not get ich to LC, ither! just the sort of impossible
i am able at—packages!

(tho i am managing the enclosed, to you, with *all*
thanx: imagine, Cid, it's
out there! just what you
damn well sd, you wanted!

and handsome, it still
strikes me, altogether
an ideal page: the way
they set!

glad, also, to hear ur news of a long one (&
that MN did help to shoot you forward). For, judg-

ing by yr dramatic monologue in Artisan, i'd hazard
that some such space is more proper to you

    (the maxies are now up to 25 (or 26, tho 26,
done yesterday, has me altogether fucked up today:
came out like that asymptotes (which i don't think
i like—jazz-verse, or piston-pushing, i'd call em

And am hung, just at the moment, between the way of
25 (almost formal) and such as 26 (jumps)

    but the pleasure of the serial form is, just
                             (over − + so thruout)

---

such a keyboard, to play on
                It's going to be a devil to
accomplish the publishing of. Not so much the 1st decade
(what Williams has). That's close to Gloucester, and
stays inside a homogeneity because of the content. But
right off—bang—with 11 (with John Hawkins), the book
starts its range.
        I figure, tho, that all i have to do
is keep answering my own lead—to toe in. And that the
bending back to G ought always, actually, to give any
reader a "shape"
              For I have the hunch that a long form
is a shape question—that form, in the sense in which
we (who are staying out in the open) seek it, is still
to be achieved inside each unit—that none of us are
yet able to be sure what a form, over, say, a poem of
such length as Dante's Comedy—or better, for my
choice, the Odyssey—can be
              In fact my desire, in
these "Letters", is to try to reach some form to sustain
just such invention as I have taken it a poem is (you
may recall my argument, in my first letter to Cree,
that each poem is in search of its own language, that
there is a language fit to each unit of expression

Now what I find out
(making one such unit hook on to another, and so make
a continuum) is that one is flying in the face of an
understandable necessity on that part of any reader to
have some thread or cloth to the language which makes it
possible for him to go along from one piece to the next.
And—like I say—it's the devil to give him that, without losing the composition of each piece (according to
the light of the day it's done!)
                    And what you find yrself
doing, is establishing yr own self as the rail. Which ex-
acts something no single poem can: one is suddenly required to be "right" in the fiercest of ways; one is
suddenly up against one's own limits, in the most rigorous
(and moral!) imperatives. Suddenly, *all* of life is
under levy—all the vectors, not just of force, but of
conduct! And judgement sits (perhaps why I mention, for
the first time, Dante!)
                    For if one won't (as I can't!)
proceed by "story" (in the Homeric, and Shakespearean

---

size; and one can't (as I won't—don't) buy EP's
"history-plus-ego", the morality of, the "Good State"
(the Confucian "process"), or WCW's false-organism,
a "City" (the false-relativism to either
of the above absolutes: the "story," or "society")
                                        —then,
one is in trouble!
                    (Maybe all my ancient catholicism
is, without my knowing it, working from below. Maybe
I shld, for the first time, read that damned "Comedy,"
to see how Dante was working out a combo of self,
a sort of narrative progress (from one to the other to
the third of the "states" of the soul), plus a working
"authority" such as heaven & damnation allow

                                        That is,
just such relativism as the principle that is form is never
more than the extension of the content (when the "form"
is seeking itself in a content now running, say, to the

497

length of 125 pages!), invokes problems which are identical with those of, say, the Serial Universe

               And no man is a poet who is
a relativist. At the smallest point he is—as he is at
the furthest—an absolutist. Because the content is no
objective thing. It is, hisself, hisown experience.

               Now I do believe, of course, that we
have already won a clarity & a penetration of this false
duality. And won it just where we ought: by the poem.
I refer to, the poem as both a particular and an intensity—as an object from a subject, the poet. But when
Bill talks abt the "inevitable," I despair. For, unless
I am doomed (by my own earnestness!), this is "naturism"
(the flower, etc—"perfect"—the "primrose" or "Paterson"). And doesn't even have the intimidation that
Christianity's "perfection" holds in itself (what made
Dante powerful, I'd guess)
               (Narrative, anyway, is the
true "argument" for any particularism—is the way it
achieves an absolute (to be defined as "relevance to
anyone, not just to be poor human maker of same"

               and why Melville & Homer &
Shakespeare have been my masters (however much so many
think Pound is)

               And narrative, (for me in these Max letters), is,

----

I believe, *the authority* which the case (of the form as
of 125—or 250 pages—) must rest on:
                              the building-up,
over the space & shape of it, of individuals & events
so crucial
               (they need not be, I take it, "significant"
people or happenings, or "intelligent," or necessarily
"natural" (common, or whatever is WCW's guide to
choice)—
               it is not the fall of a prince who is proud,
or of a dope who gets tangled (American naturalism), or

the peacocks of history (either of my own, or of any chosen
time—like the Quattrocento, say)

                                    it is any of them,
whom, in my "wisdom," I come to know. And use. (And
it is just here, like I say, that the burden of being
"right" is suddenly "fell" upon one! One then is an
edge (a butter-knife) of life so sharp (has to find
out how to be so sharp), that it is hell to pay, to
pay oneself out at such intensity—to achieve such
inevitability!

    Just now it seems to be mostly the narrative
problem. It is too late, in writing-history, to my
mind, to drop back to the straight-on "plot" (though
Cree, in his short stories, taught me one lot about
what prose, at least, can still do—and keep that
rail). But in verse's context, the jumps our reality
imposes on us will cut off (will lead one to cut off
any chronological tale) very damn sharply. In fact,
what it does is *enable* one to do a person or in inci-
dent, up fast. One presents the thing wholly differently, from the moment it enters the mind. That is why
(and where, I'd argue) significance does come in:
that it is how the person or tale is used, is how
it gets the like intensity to an image or a rhythym
(into my mind pops Ep's Tale of Jim X—which seems
to me, allegory tho it is, to be the finest single
sign of narrative's possibility in long verse
we have
((Cree wld allow in, here, i guess, my own
tale of the guy & the birds in the Kingfishers))

    Anyhow: the experience is teaching me much abt
how little use our own personal powers are,

---

until they are exercised in bending a form out of
a content which is, by its very quantity, a universe. Then the morality of particularism is up
against itself, for sure. For it ill becomes it

to appropriate any of the old absolutes. Confucius,
or Christ, or Thomas Jefferson or, on the distaff
side, Moses, or Lincoln, any of the "mothers" of the
perfect) won't sit, aren't good enough (or are
too good!) to be at the gateway (or even to be the backside,
of the presentation
                    Or Aristotle (who is, actually,
the chief god of materialism, of the present honorless
society—of the "poems" of Korsybski, the Intro gang,
or—the comic of the lot—Buckminster Fuller!

        I claim narrative (Melville's, most, but
Homer's Odysseus, certainly; and am back, just now,
reading Shakespeare—Cymbeline) just because i take
it the morality any of us is led by the nose to
(if we refuse to eat any other bale of hay—
if we finally resist being Balaam's ass
                                    (((this is the
        hardest choice of all, for us particularists!)))

        ((((psychology, & sociology, are equally that
            parable, even the Jungian, which looks so
            decisive, but is, i find out, only a hidden
            Swiss mt-climbing Parsifal—the Holy Grail
            school of materialism!))))

the morality any of us is led to, if we stick it, is

*by tales, to reveal anew, the humanism that art is the mora-
lity of

*And that it is only to be discovered in the medley of
one's own event by driving that content toward a form
unknown even to the maker in the making

        In other words I don't know what I am up to!
And must stay in that state in order to accomplish
what I have to do. Which is the weather, I guess, which
makes this fierceness I speak of

            ❋❋❋❋❋❋❋❋❋❋❋❋❋❋❋❋❋❋❋❋❋❋❋❋❋❋❋❋❋❋

((OK
One thing I have meant to ask you: do you have an

---

address for M..Jean Riboud? and does his listing there,
as contributor, mean that a copy of ICH has gone off to
him?
   (He is a most intimate friend, and I want to get
   in touch with him, at least to send him a note
   saying the ICH he has is inscribed fr, Mr O!)

And please tell Shoolman the same, fr me, please?))

** ——

(More). It's crazy, how I did force Melville out of his
Protestant Christian frame—how I did insist he didn't
get his context fr, Puritanism (or, for that matter, fr
Transcendentalism—Platonism). And surely The Confidence
Man proves that I wasn't whacky abt Moby-Dick (as Clarel
also does, fantastically, in the midst of both its Judaism
and its Catholicism

   And Shakespeare, likewise. Though how to see that
man's commons (over the plays, at least after the histories, and through Cym, WT, and Tempest) is one big labor.

At the moment, I'd fix them both on sex, actually: that
WS so suffered from woman that he raised up T & C, Hamlet,
& Lear fr the suffering, A & C fr the dream, and settled,
in the last three plays, for a chasteness of father &
daughter, father & son;
                        and that Melville is as queer as
he is (notably, in MD; frenetically, in CM; and hermaphrodite, in Clarel) just by opposite cause: that he forsook
sex, harshly, lost it, in the amortization of it in the
U.S.
   Thus Homer still comes out my chosen one, that,
there—he, too, it seems to me, resting his humanism in
the flesh (refusing all residence of spirit elsewhere

(((i can't, for the life of
me, see that WS's putative universality rests on anything
else but the pain of persons, the torture of desire in
himself)))

   that Homer is the coolest—and could build a
universe as cool (in either poem)—just because the flesh,
& desire, were, for him, solids he knew his way in and
around and about, with neither the despair nor dream which
M and S both had over it
                         —which comes to this: that woman

———————————————————

was known, was completely experienced, to him (an
accomplishment, than which . . . . and of such import,
that I don't think of another (writer) who has it
as Homer does

not that i don't think the world is always made up of
any number of men who do. But they don't write.) Like

Cree had it, in a note in yesterday:
                         "Mason would
rather fuck I guess. I can't say as I blame him. But
haven't seen a poem born yet."

        well. well. well, mister

        olson! ////////////

This has turned out to be a memorial letter! Call it,

the Corman Letter! To celebrate, the publication of:

ich (I, in english, and in Amurrican, Hey, Bud!

                yrs, o

PS: why i guess i have always been death on Billy
(Bud) Christ's, Blossom, is: that after the Tempest
(and Mr H. Melville cld read), the snowy-white

belonged to fairy tales

        (not to tales of, "fairies"!)

that Clarel is a different matter (a big poem) becoz
the homesexuality there is left in the context of
the man's own blundering (is not given J. Christ,
for elevation   (suddenly!)
        (((crazy, to realize, that
          it is exactly an erection that M
          is coy abt, when Billy is strung up
          fr the yard-arm!!!! that old biz that
          at death, the male....

(what does woman have, as a physiological accompaniment
? ? ? ? ? ? ? ? ?

    In fact, Clarel, I begin to surmise, is, content-
wise, probably the most open M ever allowed himself to
be, from his own flesh
        (tho MD rides, just because there
his skin and his flesh—and so his mind, and prose—
are in a full-play. But it is the f-p of the poet (who
lets go, shrewdly), not at all the downed realist who
is working out Clarel

    What marks WS is, how engaged he stayed, from
Venus & Adonis (and the sonnets) right to the end (even
in the histories, ex., Rich II, it is, though steadied,
and folded into the characterization—into the plot,
rather (the egg white left with the yolk, as, in the
stuff from 1600 on, it is yolk, yolk, yolk

    ((yak yak yak, somebody will call this Letter!))

Homer is the *royal* one: disposes of it (like kingdoms!

    I am led to believe (by this long PS) that what
I am doing is trying narrative (what i have argued is
still the source of any inevitability a long poem can
have, even tho such narrative is broken up (as lines

are, images, rythyms)
                    that I tie narrative & this sex
thing ("flesh thing," better) together, simply, that
is where the honor is—that flesh is the tragedy
(& so the beauty) of man's life, however much
Homer, Shk, HM—or anyone of us—use other things
(as well)
                ((((DHL kept most single of all))))

to jabber about

        OK. I'll Stop. And let you go abt yr.
several businesses.)) Let me hear fr you on yr jaunt. And
do keep coming at me what fate ICH hath. And give my
regards to all & sundry: Souster, or whoever (I'm pleased
S is giving it a ride, simply, that, why i don't know,
but, I like his crazy sheet—and intended, before Cree
took it for his broadsheet, to let S have a new go on
verse (a sort of 2nd PV—and inscribed to WCW) for
Contact.

        OK. Best. And this, a way of telling you,
how very damned much. Etc.   O
                            Charles   . . . .

Editor's note: As a memorial to Charles Olson this verbatim printing of one letter of his still in my possession—relating chiefly to *In Cold Hell, in Thicket* (ICH) and the Maximus poems. I believe the year is 1953 (ICH had appeared in April). Belgique refers to my essay on and poems by *Origin* poets first translated into French by Philippe Jones in *Le Journal des poètes,* December 1953 (the original English printed in *Serif,* September 1969). Mel refers to a former student of his, young lady, at Black Mountain College (whom I had recently met in NYC). LC=Library of Congress. MN= "Morning News" (CO poem: #10, first series, *Origin*). Artisan=little mag in England, edited by Robert Cooper. Shoolman is the lady who first provided funds for *Origin* and suggested it to me. Contact = Souster's little mag in Toronto. *Intro* was a shortlived little mag run by some articulate young teacher-followers of Korzybski in the Long Island area. The original letter is typed with a few corrections/insertions by ink and a few emphases indicated by marginal stars. The spelling is unchanged. Both sides of small white letter paper—the size of this page— were used. Four sheets in all. Pages are indicated by line breaks and the original line-to-line breaks are kept exact. The letter came with an inscribed copy of ICH.

GARY SNYDER
Meeting the Mountains

He crawls to the edge of the foaming creek
He backs up the slab ledge
He puts a finger in the water
He turns to a trapped pool
Puts both hands in the water
Puts one foot in the pool
Drops pebbles in the pool
He slaps the surface water with both hands
He cries out, rises up and stands
Facing toward the torrent and the mountain
Raises up both hands and shouts three times!

with Kai at Sawmill Lake northern Sierra 20. VI. 40069
writ for Philip.

PHILIP WHALEN
For Kai Snyder

7:V:60 (an interesting *lapsus calami,* in view
of what I'm about to write)
A few minutes ago I tried to perform a somersault
And found I couldn't—
I was afraid and I couldn't remember how.
I tried and fell over on one shoulder,
Rolled about and could nearly go over backwards,
But I couldn't go head over heels over head.
Finally I hurt my chest. Then I walked up and down
What kind of psychomotor malebolge had I got into
"This is old age, &c."

After thinking it all over and imagining how
It might be done
I performed three forward somersaults, 7:V:70
Age 46 years 6 months 37 days.

WILLIAM BRONK

Morning Greetings Exchanged

A bird, as I went by the bare vine
on Thompson's wall, made cheeps of the world, at me,
to itself, however they do, whatever they mean:
I think they don't mean anything.

Sorry if they do, because I suppose that they're wrong,
but if right, who hears them—other birds?
This makes them equivalent creatures, like us.
"Welcome, bird," I say with presumptive stance

as if I were here first as *this* I,
this bird, I suppose I probably was;
but birds, maybe this kind, are older than me,

older than man, and birds are bird, men
are man, anonymous. Neither makes
event or history. We say we do. Cheep.

Beatific Effigies

Etruscan smiles and smiles from Vera Cruz:
didn't they know? They knew what we know
—that it couldn't go on, and of course it didn't go on.

Not bravery. I despise the bravado whose open eyes
are shut to what it sees, that gallantry
that smiles at whatever, refusing what comes.

Taking thought, they could no more escape
than we escape that hopelessness thought has
for a subject, that set in the way it works.
There isn't a reason discernible to smile.

We smile, though, in a world we can neither invent
nor imagine, a world beyond thought, no thinkable world.
Thought is what we think and then shed;
we turn and look back on thought, lamenting it.

To be

Man. A man
on the stage
gazing out —
lights blazing

into his
eyes — at the
audience
in the dark

wondering
as he stands —
if he should
provide the

platitude
provided
him. Stands there
and wavers

and the dark
begins to
murmur, close
round the man

for whom they
came — saying
nothing — to
let them know.

———————————

For what we lack
We laugh, for what we have are sorry; still
Are children in some kind. Let us be thankful
For that which is, and with you leave dispute,
That are above our question. — Let's go off,
And bear us like the time.

Appendices

Appendix I

Authors Published in *Origin*, 1951-1971, in order of appearance

First Series (1951-1957)

* Charles Olson
* Samuel French Morse
  Paul Verrier
  Vincent Ferrini
  Catullus / Cid Corman
* William Bronk
* William Carlos Williams
  Katherine Hoskins
  Richard Wirtz Emerson
  Constance Hatson
* Robert Creeley
* Cid Corman
  Richard Eberhart

* Paul Blackburn
* Denise Levertov
  Stuart Z. Perkoff

  Richard Wilbur
  Dick Boyce / graphics
  Harry Smith

* Rainer Maria Gerhardt
  Nemi D'Agostino
  Klaus Bremer
  Philippe Thoby-Marcelin
  James Merrill

* Wallace Stevens

* Robert Duncan

* Theodore Enslin
  Kathleen Raine

  Rene Laubies
* Gottfried Benn
  Edgar Lohner

  Harold Dicker
  Leonard Casper
* John Hay
  Seymour Gresser
* Larry Eigner

* Gael Turnbull
  Erhard Manfred Gaul
  George Forestier
  Albert Arnold Scholl
  Hans Egon Holthusen

  Claude Vigée
* Antonin Artaud
  Rene de Obaldia
  Francois Cariés
  Julien Alvard
  Philippe Jones
* Irving Layton
* Paul Carroll

* David Galler
  Thomas F. Williams
  Edward Dorn
  Elijah Jordan
* Wade Donahoe
  Sanford Edelstein
* Eugenio Montale
  Donald Finkel
  Thomas Brackley
  Edith Reveley

Tokonoma authors are not identified, for they are to live in their anonymity.

The authors starred were featured.

All the uncredited translations are by the editor.

John Logan

Joel Oppenheimer

Fernao Mendes Pinto

Jacques Rivière
* Henri Michaux
* René Char
Federico García Lorca / Paul
Blackburn
Van Haardt
Giuseppe Ungaretti
* Astrid Claes

* Chuang-tzu/Corman

Guillaume Apollinaire / Cid
Corman
F. R. Scott
Pierre Trottier
Giles Henault
Louis Dudek
Raymond Souster
Robert Beum
Frederick Eckman
Roland Giguère
Eli W. Mandel
Phyllis Webb
Fred Cogswell
Jay Macpherson
Daryl Hine
Jonathan Williams

* Troubadour poetry / Paul
Blackburn

Patrick Fetherston
Robert Cooper
Alan Brownjohn
Roy Fisher
Martin Seymour-Smith
John Manson
* Margaret Avison
André Breton

Second Series (1961-1964)

* Louis Zukofsky
* E.C. (Edwina Curtis)

Gary Snyder
Steve Jonas
Roberto Sanesi
* Lorine Niedecker

* Zeami/Will Petersen and
Cid Corman

* Frank Samperi
Carol Berge
Philip Whalen
* Robert Kelly
* Catullus/Louis and Celia
Zukofsky

* Ian Hamilton Finlay
Thomas McNicholas
Barbara Moraff
Michael McClure
Mary Ellen Solt

* Rocco Scotellaro
Giacomo Leopardi / Cid
Corman
T'ao Ch'ien / Cid Corman
* Kusano Shimpei
* Akutagawa Ryunosuke / Cid
Corman and
Kamaike Susumu

Cesare Pavese
Pier Paolo Pasolini
Emilio Tadini
Enzo Fabiani
Margherita Guidacci
Giuliano Gramigna
Nelo Risi
Alberico Sala
Luciano Erba
Paolo Volponi

* Saint-John Perse
* Jean-Paul de Dadelsen
* Francis Ponge
Su Tung-p'o / Cid Corman

Pablo Picasso / Giovanni Papini
Donald L. Philippi
C. H. (Claire Howell)
Mel Strawn

512

Clayton Eshleman
* Seymour Faust
Eric Sackheim
Bill Burnett

Will Petersen
Herbert Read
* César Vallejo / Clayton Eshleman

* Bashō / Cid Corman and
    Kamaike Susumu

Third Series (1966-1971)

* The Blues/Eric Sackheim
Maurice Merleau-Ponty

Mary Barnard
* André du Bouchet

Umberto Saba

Pre-Manyoshu songs/Cid
    Corman

* Douglas Woolf

* Josef Albers
John Dewey
Rainer Maria Rilke

Paul Valery
Martin Buber
Anni Albers
Gerard Manley Hopkins

* René Daumaˡ
* Daphne Marlatt

Achilles Fang

* Denis Goacher

* Jean Daive

* John Taggart
* Jonathan Greene
Michael Howden
George Johnston

Arthur Rimbaud / Denis Goacher
* Paul Celan

Stephen Wiest

* Philippe Jaccottet

* Mario Luzi

* Hitomaro / Cid Corman and
    Kamaike Susumu
Brian McInerney
John Perlman

Appendix II

Major Works not Utilized

So that readers may realize some riches of the three series of ORIGIN that space has precluded, I append here a mere listing of the items chronologically and by issue. All of them, in one form or another, are now available or will be shortly elsewhere, with a couple of exceptions.

First Series

I : First "Maximus" poem, "The Story of an Olson," and "Adamo Me," by Charles Olson

II : "In the Summer" and "Mr. Blue" (short stories) by Robert Creeley, "A Po-sy, a Po-sy," by Charles Olson

IV : "Brief an Creeley und Olson" (translation) by Rainer Maria Gerhardt; poems (in Haitian French) by Philippe Thoby-Marcelin, "Human Universe" (essay) and "To Gerhardt, There, among Europe's Things" by Charles Olson

V : "The Motive for Metaphor" (the first extended essay by anyone on Wallace Stevens) by Samuel French Morse

VI : "Apollonius of Tyana" by Charles Olson

VII : "Three Old Men" (dialogue essay) by Gottfried Benn, "The Party" (short story) by Robert Creeley

VIII : "In Cold Hell, in Thicket" (entire issue selected poems by Charles Olson)

IX : "Work in Progress" (a large prose fragment) by Harold Dicker

X : "The Problem" (an uncollected poem) by William Carlos Williams

XI : A large selection from *The Theatre and Its Double* (translated by McRichards) by Antonin Artaud (first presentation of this now well-known work)

XII : "On Measure" (essay) by William Carlos Williams, poetry by Paul Carroll

XIII : Poems (from his Black Mountain period) by Ed Dorn, poems by David Galler and Donald Finkel; "Pictures" (story) by Thomas F. Williams

XIV : Poems (amongst his earliest) by Joel Oppenheimer

XV : "Notes towards an Oral Poetry" (first essay on the subject) by Cid Corman, a large body of early poems by Paul Blackburn, and most of the existent poetry of Wade Donahoe

XVI : "The Death of Europe," Charles Olson; the Artaud-Rivière correspondence

XVII : "Mrs. Polinov" (short story) by Irving Layton, "Themes and Variations from Chuang-tse" by Cid Corman

XVIII : A large selection of Canadian poetry, including French-Canadian work

XIX : Poetry and prose of Astrid Claes

XX : First poems of Roy Fisher, "The Agnes Cleves Papers" by Margaret Avison

515

Appendix III

Notes on the Contributors

Margaret AVISON. Born in 1918 in Galt, Ontario. Has lived mostly in Toronto. Her two major collections so far have been *Winter Sun* (University of Toronto Press, 1960) and *The Dumbfounding* (W. W. Norton & Co., 1966).

Paul BLACKBURN. Born in 1926 in St. Albans, Vermont. Death, by cancer, in 1970, New York. He lived largely in New York City, but his work on Provencal poetry took him several times to France. His mother Frances Frost, was a well-known newspaper poet. There have been many small books, but the most comprehensive are *The Cities* (Grove Press, 1967), and *In. on. or about the Premises* (Cape Goliard /Grossman, 1968). Teaching at Cortland State University at the end.

William BRONK. Born in 1918, Hudson Falls, New York, where he still lives. The bulk of his work has appeared in *Origin*. *The World, the Worldless* (New Directions, 1964) was the first collection widely available. And in recent years Elizabeth Press (New Rochelle, New York) has been doing his books: *The Empty Hands* (1969), *That Tantalus* (1971), *To Praise the Music* (1972). His essays and early poems will appear in the near future under the same imprint.

Paul CARROLL. Born in 1927 in Chicago, where he has lived mostly. His editorship of *The Big Table* during the early sixties, though brief, is well-known. There is one volume of poems, *The Poem in Its Skin*.

Réne CHAR. Born in 1907 in the Vaucluse, at L'Isle-sur-Sorgue, where he still lives. One of the early surrealists and a good friend of Eluard and Camus. His work as a leader in the French Resistance is realized most powerfully in his famed *Feuillets d'Hypnos* (written during the war): There have been many collections since and he has been a major influence on poets of the succeeding generation. His work is most readily available in English in *Hypnos Waking* (ed. by Jackson Mathews, Random House, 1956) and in a version of the *Feuillets d'Hypnos* done by the editor with the author's assistance (Mushinsha/Grossman 1973).

Cid CORMAN. Born in 1924 in Boston. In 1954 he left America for the first time and has subsequently lived mostly in Europe and in Kyoto, Japan, visiting America several times in the interval. Of his fifty books the most readily available are *Livingdying* and *Sun Rock Man* (both New Directions, 1970), volumes of translations of Bashō,

Kusano Shimpei, and Francis Ponge (Mushinsha/Grossman 1968, 1969, 1973), and, most recently, *Plight* and *Out & Out* (Elizabeth Press, 1970 and 1972) and *0/1*(1974).

Robert CREELEY. Born in 1926 near Boston. Well-known for his editorship of the *Divers Press* and *Black Mountain Review*. Has taught widely throughout America and has lived in Europe. Many titles, mostly now by Black Sparrow (in limited editions) and Scribner's (in regular and paperback editions), the most recent being *Pieces* (1969), *A Day Book* (1972), and a radioplay *Listen* (1972). He has edited a number of anthologies.

Jean DAIVE. Born in 1941 in France. The work of his presented here is his major work to date. There is also, more recently, *Le Palais de quatre heures* (Brunidar, 1971). He is editing a new small review, *Fragment*, in Paris, where he resides.

René DAUMAL. Born in 1908 in the Ardennes. Died in 1944. Perhaps the most precocious poet France has had since Rimbaud. The unfinished parable *Mont Analogue*, perhaps his best-known work (Gallimard, 1952), has given him a curious reputation. His satirical first book, *La grande beuverie* (Gallimard, 1938), is still largely unknown, as is, in English, his poetry, *Poésie Noire, poésie blanche* (Gallimard, 1954). Gallimard has gradually been issuing all his works, his studies in Sanskrit writings, essays, and letters.

André DU BOUCHET. Born in 1924 in France. Lives in Paris. One of the editors of the recent literary review published by Galerie Maeght, *L'Ephémere*. Author of a number of books, including one on Giacometti. Most of his best early work is collected in *Dans la chaleur vacante* (Mercure de France, 1961), which is translated in entirety in *Origin*. *Ou le soleil* by the same publishers offers the more recent work. He is also a fine translator from English and German.

Robert DUNCAN. Born in Oakland, California, in 1919. A voluminous writer. His big book on H.D., long in the making, is anticipated shortly. Perhaps the most available volumes are *Roots & Branches* (Scribner's, 1964), *Bending the Bow* (New Directions, 1968), and *The Opening of the Field* (Grove Press, 1960). Many small press publications. One of the constants of the San Francisco literary scene.

Larry EIGNER. Born in Swampscott, Massachusetts, in 1927, where he still lives. Palsy has made him a typewriter poet. The largest collections of his work are *Another Time in Fragments* (London: Fulcrum Press, 1967) and *Selected Poems* (Berkeley: Oyez, 1972).

Theodore ENSLIN. Born in 1925 in Chester, Pennsylvania. More familiar for his adult life on Cape Cod and in the past decade at Temple, Maine. A large and growing body of work. Most readily available now are *The Country of Our Consciousness* (Berkeley: Sand Dollar, 1971) and *Forms* (I: 1970; II:1971; III: 1972; IV:1973), *The Poems* (1970), and *Etudes* (1972), all published by Elizabeth Press.

Achilles FANG. Born in China during the T'ang Dynasty, according to some reports. Has lived near Harvard University since the mid-forties. Now teaching mainly Taoist thought/poetry there. Known for his scattered essays on Chinese studies and Ezra Pound.

Seymour FAUST. Born in Philadelphia. Pennsylvania, in 1930. Has lived largely in New York City. One small book done too long ago by the Hawk's Well Press of Kelly & Rothenberg.

Ian Hamilton FINLAY. Born in 1925 in Scotland. Has lived as much out of the cities as health and income have permitted. Migrant Press (Ventura, California) did a pamphlet of his early poems called *The Dancers Inherit the Party* in 1961. His work has moved through the style of his poems in *Origin* into concrete poetry/art, the form in which it has become best known. Two of his short plays are available in the Penguin drama series, and there are many small press items and re-presentations in most anthologies that include recent Scottish poetry/prose.

Denis GOACHER. Born in 1925 in England. Has lived largely in London and now in North Devon, though he has traveled much on the continent as well. Known for his magnificent reading voice on BBC's "Third Program" for many years. And as an actor also. His belated first solo collection, *Logbook* (Grosseteste Review Books, England) appeared in 1972. A second collection, *Transversions*, was published in 1973.

Jonathan GREENE. Born in 1943 in New York City. Lives in Lexington, Kentucky. Some small press publications, most recently *The Lapidary* (Black Sparrow, 1969) and *A Seventeenth-Century Garner* (Buttonwood, 1969). A book

designer "by trade," he has himself published titles as the Gnomon Press.

Philippe JACCOTTET. Born in 1925 in Moudon (Switzerland). Has lived in Paris, but for some years now in the foothills of the French Alps in Grignan (Drôme). Many books and important translations especially from German and Italian (Hölderlin, Rilke, Musil, and Ungaretti). Most convenient current presentation of his poetry in *Poésie* 1946-1967 (Gallimard, 1971) and his poetic journals; *La Semaison* 1954-1967 (Gallimard, 1971).

Robert KELLY. Born in 1935 in Brooklyn New York. Has done much editing. Well known for his teaching at Bard College, and elsewhere. Voluminous writer with many small press books, most of the recent work published by the Black Sparrow Press (Los Angeles) *Flesh: Dream: Book* (Black Sparrow, 1971) and *Kali Yuga* (Cape Goliard/Grossman, 1970) may be the most accessible.

KUSANO Shimpei. Born in Nagano Prefecture, Japan, in 1903, has lived mostly in Tokyo in recent years. He has lived and traveled in China as well as widely elsewhere. He is the guiding spirit of the *Rekitei* poetry group and the most beloved of living Japanese poets. Many books of poetry and essays. Available in English is *Frogs & Others* (Mushisha/Grossman, 1969). His name is presented in Japanese style.

Irving LAYTON. Born in 1912 in Rumania, but has lived virtually all his life in Montreal, where he has done much teaching, now in Toronto. Perhaps the most useful of his many titles remain *The Swinging Flesh* (McClelland & Stewart, Ltd.,

1961), his collected stories, and *A Red Carpet for the Sun* (same publisher, 1959). There are, of course, more recent collections of newer work. Any anthology of modern Canadian poetry includes his work.

Denise LEVERTOV. Born in Essex, England, in 1923. Since marrying Mitch Goodman in 1948, she has lived mostly in the United States and is now generally regarded as an American poet. Her books, mentioning only recent work, include *The Jacob's Ladder* (1962), *O Taste and See* (1964), *Sorrow Dance* (1967), and *Footprints* (1972), all published by New Directions. She has taught in a variety of schools in recent years and is known for her anti-war activities.

Mario LUZI. Born in Florence in 1914, where he still lives. He has helped edit a number of magazines and published a number of volumes of poetry and essays, as well as translations from English and French. His three key volumes of poetry are *Il Giusto Della Vita* (1960), a collection of all his poems up to *that* time. *Nel Magma* (Garzanti, 1963) and *Dal Fondo Delle Campagne* (1965). The most recent is *Su Fondamenti Invisibili* (Rizzoli, 1971).

Daphne MARLATT (neé Buckle). Born in 1942 in Melbourne, Australia, though she is inevitably associated with Vancouver, where she now resides. There are three key collections so far: *Frames* (Ryerson, 1968), *Leaf/Leaf/S* (Black Sparrow, 1969), and more recently the cycle of prose poems of her pregnancy/delivery *Rings* (mimeo).

Henri MICHAUX Born in Belgium in 1899. Almost as well known now as a painter. He has written some fine prose works, the most recent of which is a series of studies on the effects of drugs. There are many volumes of poetry under the Gallimard imprint. New Directions did a volume of his selected poems in the fifties.

Eugenio MONTALE. Born in Genoa in 1896. He has lived mostly in Turin, Florence (during the Second World War), and Milan. His books of poetry published by Mondadori, are *Ossi di Seppia* (1925), *Le Occasioni* (1939), and *La Bufera e Altro* (1956). *Satura* (1962) and *Xenia* (1964-66) are pamphlets. His essays are collected, and his prose sketches have been published under the title *La Farfalla di Dinard*. New Directions brought out a selection of his poetry some years ago, and there is a selection also in the Penguin Modern European Poets series.

Lorine NIEDECKER. Born in Fort Atkinson, Wisconsin, in 1903 and died there in 1970. The most convenient collection of her work, though it doesn't have her final poems (some of which are represented in this anthology), is her *Collected Poems 1936-1968* (London: Fulcrum Press, 1970).

Charles OLSON. Born in Worcester, Massachusetts, in 1910—though most of his early life was spent in Gloucester, Massachusetts. He died in New York City in 1970. He was the key figure in the late history of Black Mountain College (North Carolina). His most representative books, many of them small press items, are *Call Me Ishmael* (Reynal & Hitchwork, 1947, and also in many reprints), *Selected Writings,* including *Mayan Letters* and *Apol-*

519

lonius of Tyana (New Directions, 1966), *The Distances* (Grove Press, 1961, *The Maximus Poems* (I—III) (Jargon/Corinth, 1960), *The Maximus Poems* (IV—VI) (Cape Goliard/Grossman, 1968), and *Letters for Origin* (Cape Goliard/ Grossman, 1970).

Francis PONGE. Born in Montpellier, France, in 1899. Many books, virtually all now available from Gallimard. In English there are *Soap* (Jonathan Cape, Grossman, 1969) and *Things* (Mushinsha/ Grossman, 1971). He lives now in Bar-sur-Loup (Alpes Maritimes).

Frank SAMPERI. Born in Brooklyn in 1933. Lives in New York City. The first and second volumes of his poetic trilogy, *The Prefiguration* and *Quadrifarium* (Mushinsha/ Grossman, 1971, 1973), are available. The final volume, *Lumen Gloriae*, is also now available.

Roberto SANESI. Born in 1930 in Milan. Has edited and translated a good deal. His volumes of poetry include *Oberon in Catene* (Schwarz, 1962) and the *Rapporto Informativo* (long poem, some years later), and there is more recent work not as yet definitively collected. He has traveled widely in the West, but resides still in Milan.

Rocco SCOTELLARO. Born in Tricarico (province of Matera, in southern Italy) in 1923 and died in 1953, a painful loss to his community (of which he was the political leader and an unusually beloved one). His poetry is collected in *E Fatto Giorno* (Mondadori, 1954), his prose in *Contadini del Sud* and *Uva Putanella* (Laterza, 1954). The prose-work was the springboard for the better-known work of Danilo Dolci.

Gary SNYDER. Born in San Francisco in 1930. Has traveled widely and lived many years in Japan. Dwelling now near Nevada City, California. The most convenient collections of his work are the three volumes published by New Directions: *The Back Country* (1968), *Earth House Hold* (essays, 1969) and *Regarding Wave* (1970).

Raymond SOUSTER. Born in Toronto in 1921 and still lives there. There are many volumes of poetry and a recently published novel of his RCAF war experience. The most convenient collection of his work is the recent *Selected Poems* (Toronto: Oberon Press, 1972).

Wallace STEVENS. Born in Pennsylvania in 1879 and died in Hartford, Connecticut—where he lived most of his life—in 1955. All his work has been published by Alfred A. Knopf. The largest units are *The Collected Poems* (1954), *Opus Posthumous* (ed. by Samuel French Morse, 1957), *The Necessary Angel* (essays, 1951), and *Selected Letters* (ed. Holly Stevens, 1966).˙ His *Notebooks* are now being edited by Holly Stevens.

John TAGGART. Born in 1942 in Guthrie Center, Iowa. Lives in Shippensburg, Pennsylvania, and teaches at Shippensburg State College. His only book to date is *To Construct a Clock* (Elizabeth Press, 1971).

Gael TURNBULL. Born in England in 1928, but has lived extensively in Canada and the United States—so that though he is now generally regarded, as anthologies more and more reveal, as an English poet, it is a relatively recent recognition. There are many small press books (a number under his own Migrant Press mark), but the most readily available sizable collection is *A Trampoline: poems 1952-1964* (Cape Goliard, 1968).

César VALLEJO. Born in 1892 in northern Peru. Died in Paris in 1938. The poetry and plays are not yet fully available. The largest collection is the *Poemas Humanos* (1939), available in a bilingual edition with English translation by Clayton Eshleman (Grove Press, 1968), and the earlier *Trilce* are published by Mushinsha/Grossman (1973).

Philip WHALEN. Born in Oregon in 1923. Has lived for extended periods in Kyoto, but now resides in San Francisco. The key books, apart from two novels, are the large volume of collected peoms *On Bear's Head* (Harcourt, Brace & World, Inc./Coyote, 1969), *Severance Pay* (San Francisco: Four Seasons, 1970), and *Scenes of Life at The Capital* (Bolinas: Grey Fox Press, 1971).

Stephen WIEST. Born in 1941 in Baltimore, Mayland. Teaches at Johns Hopkins and lives in Aspers, Pennsylvania. A large body of work, as yet unpublished.

William Carlos WILLIAMS. Born and lived most of his life in Rutherford, New Jersey, where he was a practicing physician, as well as a prolific writer (1883-1963). Most of his work is available under the New Directions imprint. "The Desert Music" marks the turn into the later poetry.

Celia/Louis ZUKOFSKY. Celia (Thaew) is best known and celebrated in her husband's work— whether throughout "A" or in *BOTTOM: on Shakespeare* (Ark Press, Texas: 1963)—to which she has provided a musical setting of Shakespeare's *Pericles*—or in the short story *It Was* (Origin Press, 1961, reprinted in *Ferdinand*, Jonathan Cape, (1968). The Zukofskys now live in Port Jefferson, Long Island, New York. Louis Zukofsky's "A" 1-12, first printed by *Origin Press* in 1959, has been reprinted by Doubleday in the U.S.A. and Jonathan Cape in England. "A" 13-21 was published by Cape in 1969. The shorter poems are gathered under the title of *All* (W/W. Norton, 1971). *Prepositions* is a collection of critical essays (London: Rapp & Carroll, 1967). *A Test of Poetry* (The Objectivist Press, 1948, with a later reprint). There are other prose works and collections under the Grossman mark, the most important being the recent "A" 24 (1972). Louis Zukofsky was born in 1904.

Acknowledgments

(continued from page iv)

Acts of the Apostles," "A Vase of Various Flowers," "The Bach Trombones," "Her Singing," "The Arts and Death," "My Young Nephew Sends Me His Picture," "'In Our Image, after Our Likeness,'" "At Tikal." All reprinted by permission of the author.

Paul Carroll: "Las Tentaciones de San Antonio."

Cid Corman: "Mister Young," "The Counter" from *Livingdying*. Copyright © 1970 by Cid Corman. Reprinted by permission of New Directions Publishing Corporation. "A Child Performs Shimai," "The Religion," "The Offerings," "The Declarations," "The Obbligato," "Leuca," and "The Portrait," from *Words for Each Other*, Rapp & Carroll, London, 1967,. © Cid Corman. "In Answer," from *Out & Out*, Elizabeth Press, Copyright 1972. "A Note on Dylan Thomas," "Wallace Stevens," "The Contingency," "The House," "The Touch," "Out of the snow," "As much as there is," "'Do you hear...?'" "Poetry as Bond," "A Grace," "The Garden," "Not the least lash lost," "Men die," "Shadow," "What you are," "The path," "Not myself," "In the hills," "The cry," "To Be." Translations of "The Lute of Gassir," "Old Japanese Songs," and "The mind must go" by Zeami. All reprinted by permission of the author.

René Char: "The Brittle Age."

Robert Creeley: "Le Fou," "A Song," "The Innocence," "A Marriage," and "The Crow" from *For Love* by Robert Creeley. Copyright © 1962 Robert Creeley. "Three Fate Tales" and "The Grace" from *The Gold Diggers and Other Stories* by Robert Creeley, Copyright © 1965 by Robert Creeley. Reprinted by permission of Charles Scribner's Sons. "Notes for a New Prose," "The Letters of Hart Crane," and "D. H. Lawrence's 'Studies in Classic American Literature'" from *A Quick Graph* by Robert Creeley, published by Four Seasons Foundation, Bolinas, California, Copyright © 1970 by Robert Creeley. Reprinted by permission of Four Seasons Foundation. "Letter to Cid Corman." Reprinted by permission of the author.

Jean Daive: "Décimale blanche." Reprinted by permission of Mercure de France.

René Daumal: "The Poet's Last Words." Reprinted by permission of the author.

André Du Bouchet: "Nine Poems," "The White Motor," "Extinction," "Far from Breath," and "Cession." Reprinted by permission of the author.

Robert Duncan: "The Second Night in the Week," "Processional of the Dead," "Love Poem," "Friedl," "Songs for the Jews," "A Dream of the End of the World," and "From *The Day Book*." Reprinted by permission of the author.

Larry Eigner: "I Have Felt It," "Clearings," "Act," "Environs," and "A Gone." Reprinted by permission of the author.

Theodore Enslin: "Pasturage," "In the Rain," "Village Gossip," "A Sunday Interval," "A Theory of Time," "The Song of One Lost," "March—Temple, Maine," "Landscape with Figures," from *The Place Where I Am Standing*, Elizabeth Press, © Theodore Enslin 1964, "New Sharon's Prospect," from *New Sharon's Prospect and Journals*, ©, Theodore Enslin 1967, "This Do, in Remembrance," Ediciones El Corno Emplumado, © 1966 Theodore Enslin. Reprinted by permission of the author.

Achilles Fang: "An Apology." Reprinted by permission of the author.

524

ologist of Morning. Reprinted by permission of Grossman Publishers.

Francis Ponge: "The Murmur" from *Le Grand Recueil-Méthodes* © Editions Gallimard 1950. Reprinted by permission of Georges Borchardt, Inc.

Frank Samperi: "Morning and Evening." Copyright in Japan, 1971 by Frank Samperi. Reprinted by permission of the author.

Roberto Sanesi: "La Cosa," "Ora e qui," "Dai padiglioni del vento," and "Dialogo aperto." Reprinted by permission of the author.

Rocco Scotellaro: "Suonano mattutino," "Monelli," "Ora che Domina Luglio," "Andara a vedere una giovane," "Viaggio di ritorno," "Il Garibaldino novantenne," "La mia bella patria," "La felicità," and "Notte in campagna." From *E'Fatto Giorno,* © 1954 by Arnoldo Mondadori Editore. Reprinted by permission of Arnoldo Mondadori Editore.

Gary Snyder: "Meeting the Mountains" from *Regarding Wave.* Copyright © 1970 by Gary Snyder. Reprinted by permission of New Directions Publishing Corp. "Night Highway Ninety-Nine," "Bubbs Creek Haircut." Reprinted by permission of the author.

Raymond Souster: "The Flight of the Roller-Coaster" from *The Colour of the Times.* Reprinted by permission of McGraw-Hill Ryerson Limited. "The Toy Ladder" from *The Years.* Reprinted by permission of Oberon Press.

Wallace Stevens: "Long and Sluggish Lines" from *The Collected Poems of Wallace Stevens.* Copyright 1954 by Wallace Stevens. Reprinted by permission of Alfred A. Knopf, Inc.

John Taggart: "Egg," "Position," "The Drum Thing," Copyright 1971 by John

Taggart. "Winter, Radio Poem," "The K Variations," and "Death-Bean Agent." Reprinted by permission of the author.

Gael Turnbull: "An Irish Monk, on Lindisfarne," "Homage to Jean Follain," and "A Case," from *A Trampoline: Poems 1952-1964,* © Gael Turnbull 1968. Reprinted by permission of Jonathan Cape Ltd.

César Vallejo: Poems Nos. 84, 86, 87, 88, 89, 90 from *Poemas Humanos/Human Poems,* translated by Clayton Eshleman. Copyright © 1968 by Grove Press, Inc. Reprinted by permission of Grove Press, Inc.

Philip Whalen: "Address to a Younger Generation," and "For Kai Snyder," Copyright © 1970 by Philip Whalen. Reprinted by permission of the author.

Stephen Wiest: "Poems from the Other Side." Copyright January 1970 Stephen Wiest. Reprinted by permission of the author.

William Carlos Williams: "The Desert Music" from *Pictures From Brueghel and Other Poems.* Copyright 1954 by William Carlos Williams. Reprinted by permission of New Directions Publishing Corporation.

Louis and Celia Zukofsky: "Catullus/IV Phasellus ille," "Catullus/XI Furi et Aureli, comites Catulli," "Catullus/ XXXI Paene insularum, Sirmio," and "Catullus/XXXVII Salax Taberna, Copyright © by Celia and Louis Zukofsky 1969. Reprinted by permission of Grossman Publishers. "A"-16 and "A"-13 reprinted by permission of Jonathan Cape Ltd. "From: *Bottom: On Shakespeare.*" Copyright © 1963 by Celia and Louis Zukofsky. Reprinted by permission of the Ark Press. "Two Letters to Cid Corman." Reprinted by permission of the author.